The Social Dimension of Sex

Roy F. Baumeister

Case Western Reserve University

Dianne M. Tice

Case Western Reserve University

D1411584

Allyn and Bacon

Boston ■ London ■ Toronto ■ Sydney ■ Tokyo ■ Singapore

Senior Editor: *Rebecca Pascal*
Editor-in-Chief, Social Sciences: *Karen Hanson*
Editorial Assistant: *Whitney Brown*
Marketing Manager: *Caroline Croley*
Production Administrator: *Deborah Brown*
Editorial-Production Service: *P. M. Gordon Associates*
Cover Administrator: *Jenny Hart*
Composition Buyer: *Linda Cox*
Manufacturing Buyer: *Megan Cochran*

Copyright © 2001 by Allyn & Bacon
A Pearson Education Company
160 Gould Street
Needham Heights, MA 02494-2310

Internet: www.abacon.com

Library of Congress Cataloging-in-Publication Data

Baumeister, Roy F.
   The social dimension of sex / Roy F. Baumeister, Dianne M. Tice.
     p. cm.
   Includes bibliographical references and index.
   ISBN 0-205-32442-8 (pbk.)
   1. Sex. 2. Sex customs. 3. Sex (Psychology) I. Tice, Dianne M. II. Title.

HQ21.B36 2001
306.7—dc21

                                        00-026645

Printed in the United States of America

10 9 8 7 6 5 4 3 2 1   05 04 03 02 01 00

Dedicated to the memory of Warren (1989–99)

CONTENTS

1 What This Book Is About

Sex.

The fascination. The grand adventure. The threshold of adulthood. The supreme act of love, or just playing "hide the salami." The ultimate and perfect communion of souls and bodies, or an animal craving that blocks spiritual progress. An overrated dalliance, or the world's greatest natural high. Five minutes of grunting and heavy breathing, once or twice a week. Trying to make a baby, or trying not to make a baby. The fulfillment of endless longing. Something to do when the movie is over. The beast with two backs. Shame, guilt, pride. A conquest, an ego trip. An exercise in communication, or a colossal misunderstanding. Feeling completed, or feeling used. An exchange of bodily fluids. Sin, sin, sin. Fifty dollars for ten minutes. Dirty jokes. Censorship. Fear of being raped. Groupies. Phone sex. Was it good for you too? If that's the best you can do, I'm going to put my panties back on. Did you come? The biggest mistake I ever made. You'll go blind if you don't stop. What did it really mean?

President John F. Kennedy had to wear a stiff back brace because he tore a muscle in his back during a sex orgy at the White House (Hersh, 1997). The seemingly rigid, upright posture that can be seen in many photos and films of Kennedy's public appearances was a result of that brace. When Lee Harvey Oswald's first bullet struck Kennedy during the Dallas motorcade, the back brace prevented the president from bending and ducking to avoid the later shots, which killed him. In a sense, then, his sexual escapades led indirectly to his death.

Presidential candidate Jimmy Carter subscribed to the Christian virtues of marital fidelity and sexual propriety, but one time, at the end of a long interview, he dropped an offhand comment that he had occasionally "lusted in his heart." That one remark made headlines and caused his lead in the election polls to drop by 20 percentage points.

Bill Clinton made history by being the second president to be impeached. His offense was lying under oath about having had sex with a young woman working on his staff. He claimed later that oral sex did not constitute sex. At the height of that controversy, the *Journal of the American Medical Association* published a study showing that many young people agreed with Clinton's definition (Sanders & Reinisch, 1999), and the journal editor was fired. Overseas audiences snickered at American expense: A popular Israeli joke ran: "The polls show that 12 percent of Americans think that oral sex isn't sex. I think probably they're just doing it wrong!" Clinton was acquitted. The young woman sold her story to the media for big bucks.

Many politicians and social scientists have complained about the rise in economic inequality in the United States. By many measures, the rich grow richer, while the poor remain poor. Half of all the wealth in the country is owned by only 20 percent of the people. Yet two statistical sociologists concluded that sex is even more inequitably distributed than income (Robinson & Godbey, 1998): Half of all the sex in America is had by only 15 percent of adults; a mere 5 percent of Americans have 30 percent of the sex.

Much of the scientific writing about sex has focused on the inner, biological processes, on clinical problems and their treatment, and on the similarities between human sexuality and that of other species. We can readily see the importance of that work, but we think that there is a missing dimension. *Sex is social.*

Sex is a form of human interaction that provides purpose and structure to a great many human interactions (and not just the few minutes spent together in bed now and then). Many sex acts are shaped by broader social contexts, in the sense that their meaning depends not just on what two people do together but also on how those acts compare with what others do and what message they convey to others about the relationship between the two people. Several acts of copulation might seem identical in terms of the body movements and exchange of fluids—but one of them is an expression of love, another is a business transaction, another is a breach of trust, another is illegal, and another is an exploitation.

This book is devoted to a playful exploration of the social dimension of sex. We intend to trot out assorted ideas, some of them perhaps bizarre. We want to toss them around, look at them from different angles, and unfold their possible implications. We also tend to look soberly at research findings and hope to find that they shed valuable if sometimes unexpected light on these ideas. Let us try an example.

Multiple Wives

Why don't women campaign to legalize polygamy in the United States?

Polygamy has been fairly common through most of world history. It seems likely to benefit women if there are far more women than men in a society, because insisting on monogamy leaves many women without spouses. This assumes, at least, that women would prefer to be married than remain single, but that is a fair assumption: Research consistently finds that nearly all young people want and expect to marry eventually. If there are twice as many women as men in a given society—for example, after a major war in which many men were killed—then it seems reasonable and rational for each man to take two wives.

On the other hand, in most societies (including today's United States), there are roughly equal numbers of men and women. In these cases, polygamy would simply redistribute the women. For every man with two wives, there would be another who has none. Rich, successful men would therefore be likely to end up having several wives, while the down-and-out men would go wifeless.

Polygamy has been gradually eliminated from the modern Western world. Normally this progress has been attributed to feminist movements, on the assumption that polygamy caters to male fantasies and exploits women. This analysis is highly questionable, however. As long as women can choose whether to marry, there is no a priori reason why polygamy should be to their disadvantage. A woman would know if she's marrying a man who's already married, and she could decide whether to marry him or an unmarried man.

Outlawing polygamy simply deprives women of a choice. To the extent that feminism (as being broadly and literally "pro-choice") seeks to increase the range of choices and options that women have, it should perhaps try to restore polygamy.

The female dilemma can be presented this way. If polygamy is permitted, then a woman may choose to become a rich, successful man's second or third wife. If it is outlawed, then as soon as a particular man marries, he is removed from the pool of potential spouses, and the single woman must find her mate from among those who remain unmarried. Her options are thus restricted.

Outlawing polygamy does not increase the number of single men, obviously. In fact, it reduces that number: Polygamy allows the most desirable men to marry multiple wives, leaving other men single, thereby increasing the pool of single men. If Sally and Betty both marry Gerald, then Tom remains single, but if Sally marries Gerald and Betty marries Tom, then Tom is not single. When Francine comes looking for an unmarried man, Tom would be available only under polygamy. Hence *even a woman who wants to marry a single man and be a monogamous wife is better off if polygamy is allowed.*

If a woman doesn't mind being a second wife, she has far more options under polygamy, including some very attractive ones. Put more simply, some women might prefer to be Leonardo DiCaprio's or Bill Gates's second wife rather than the only wife of some unknown store clerk. Making polygamy legal gives them the opportunity to make this choice.

Naturally, it is necessary to consider the wishes of the first wife: Not every woman would be happy about seeing her husband marry a second wife. But if the laws are designed to benefit women, the crucial point should therefore be that a man cannot marry a second wife without the first wife's consent.

Why would a first wife permit her husband to marry a second? She seemingly would lose a fair amount, as his time, energy, intimacy, and money have to be shared with someone else. Yet there may be some consolations and benefits. In some polygamous societies, the wives of the same husband cooperate and get along well. In modern life, where multiple careers are the norm, the second wife may provide another income, or she may do housekeeping chores so the first wife can concentrate on her career.

Plus, in the final analysis, sharing a husband may be preferable to having none. The bottom line is this: Plenty of women these days do see their husbands marry someone else, but the man has to divorce the first wife in order to do so. Some first wives might prefer to be kept on as wives rather than being dumped. This is particularly true insofar as a very common pattern these days is for couples to divorce at midlife and for the man but not the woman to remarry. Legal polygamy does at least give her options too.

What about the man? At first blush, polygamy sounds like every man's dream: multiple women to have sex with him. The reality is less idyllic, however, at least in many cases. Altman and Ginat's (1996) study of modern polygamy as practiced by Mormons in Utah showed that the men did not fare very well. The most common system there was for men to have different wives in different houses, with each wife living with her children. The man would rotate among them, sleeping with different wives on different days of the week. It may sound appealing, but the net effect was often that the man ended up living out of the trunk of his car. "Many participants described life in a plural marriage as an unending struggle" (Altman and Ginat, 1996, p. 437).

Any possessions the husband wanted to have with him regularly had to rotate with him. In principle, he could duplicate them, but this proved quite expensive, and for these men the financial pressures of multiple households were punishing. Imagine having all your rent or mortgage payments, plus all your utility bills, and grocery bills, and so forth, tripled, and suddenly the idea of having three wives loses some of its charm. Few men even had their own rooms in any of their houses. In essence, the man had no private space to call his own. He did not even have much say about how the homes were furnished and decorated, because each wife claimed the initiative for making the decisions about her home—which seemed only fair, since she lived there all the time, and he only sometimes spent the night. As for items like clothing, well, one wife would get jealous and angry if the man kept all his clothes at another wife's house, because that symbolically implied a preference for the other wife. His only solution was to keep his clothes divided among the several homes.

Practical concerns were also quite stressful. The wives would work out a plan to share the man. On Sunday and Monday he stays with Charlotte; Tuesday through Thursday, Jennifer; Friday and Saturday, Ellen. So far, so good. But Ellen's son is having a birthday on Monday, and the father's presence is needed even though the man is supposed to spend that day with Charlotte. Jennifer's washing machine breaks down on Saturday, and she needs his help, even though he is supposed to be spending that day with Ellen. Tuesday morning Charlotte's oldest daughter is sick and has to go to the hospital, and he must either take the child or stay at her house to watch the other children, even though he was supposed to be moving to Jennifer's place that day. And so on. The men thus suffer considerable stress.

These data are not the last word on the subject of polygamy in Western history. Undoubtedly there are special circumstances that make polygamy look as unappealing as it does to some people. Still, these data do place the burden of proof on the other side. In theory, polygamy might work to everyone's benefit, but we do not see much evidence that this actually happens. Advocates of polygamy might point out that it is hard for them to provide the needed proof, given that polygamy is illegal. They have a valid position. Yet possibly premarital polygamous cohabitation could get around the legal problems and show some workable arrangements, but to our knowledge that has not yet happened in the United States on any large scale.

The purpose of this section was not to advocate or condemn polygamy. We wanted only to illustrate the approach we wish to take in this book in order to explore the social dimension of sex. We want to raise ideas and consider possible variations and implications. And then we intend to look at the data to see how those ideas stand up when the facts and figures are known.

What Is Needed?

The goal of this book is to merge two fields: social/personality psychology and sexuality. The focus will be on sex. The ideas will come mainly from social and personality psychology. For the sake of convenience, we will refer only to social psychology.

We are hardly the first to suggest that such a cross-fertilization is desirable. Writing in 1977, in the lead article of the third volume of *Personality and Social Psychology Bulletin*, the highly respected social psychologist Donn Byrne stated that the study of sex spans many fields but that social psychology has been a late arrival to the party. He went on to make many observations that are still relevant and true today. In particular, he said that the study of sex is lacking in integrative theory. He argued that unless social psychology takes an important role, the study of sex will be left to animal researchers and clinical/abnormal psychologists, who are likely to miss the positive and distinctive aspects of normal sexuality. He added that although social psychology's studies of attraction and aggression extend naturally to studies of sexual attraction and sexual aggression, these seemingly obvious extensions had not yet been fully realized, and thus the marvelous knowledge that social psychologists have acquired so painstakingly has not reached its potential in terms of shedding light on sex. And sex, he pointed out, is undoubtedly one large sphere of behavior whose importance can be recognized by almost anyone, from a high school dropout to a professorial expert. Social psychology cannot afford to ignore such an important slice of life.

More recently, the need to borrow from social psychology to understand sex was emphasized in 1994 by the authors of the influential study, *Sex in America*, also known as the National Health and Social Life Survey (NHSLS). Their work is highly respected by nearly all sex researchers, and we shall refer to its many findings repeatedly. Their own view was that Americans too readily succumb to the popular myth that sexuality is determined by a person's inner nature, whereas in reality "sexual behavior is shaped by our social surroundings" (Michael, Gagnon, Laumann, & Kolata, 1994, p. 16). They called vigorously for more theorizing based on social psychology.

As an example of the need to appreciate the social dimension of sex, the authors of the NHSLS pointed to the power of sexual networks. Among all the couples who ever have sex, only about a third start out with one person introducing himself or herself to the other. Moreover, these self-introductions tend to be associated with relatively brief romances rather than durable, successful relationships. And even many of those occur in a situation where people have been screened to have something in common, such as a church, a private party, or a class, so there is still a social network at work. If we look at the sexual couplings that are most purely a result of one person approaching someone else, without any such screening situation—specifically, people who introduced themselves to someone in a bar, on a vacation trip, or through a personal ad in a newspaper—we find that they make up only about 4 percent of all marriages (Laumann, Gagnon, Michael, & Michaels, 1994). In contrast, couples who are introduced by family members or friends make up half of all marriages, slightly over half of all couples who live together, and nearly half of the other sexual relationships. (Actually, introductions by family tend *not* to produce short-term sexual affairs, although they do lead to stable relationships and marriages.) Thus, people depend heavily on friends and family to help them find their sex partners and especially to find the people with whom they will have long-term, lasting sexual relationships.

In emphasizing the social dimension of sex, we are not dismissing the role of biology and other factors. As will quickly become obvious, we think that any adequate social theory has to have some understanding of the influence on sex of physical and physiological variables as well as innate predispositions and motives. Without physiology, and in fact without some very specific physiological responses, sex would be impossible. Our point is only that since the physiology of sex is better understood than the social psychology of sex, we are addressing our efforts to the aspect that has lagged behind the others.

The need for an influx of social ideas to explain sexual behavior is greatly increased by the state of theory in the field of sexuality. The landscape of ideas was assessed in a special issue of the *Journal of Sex Research* in 1998, and the consensus was that new concepts are badly needed. The most precise survey was described by Weis (1998), in the article the editors selected to lead off the special issue. Weis reported on a content analysis of a large sample of articles in the sex field's two main journals (*Journal of Sex Research* and *Archives of Sexual Behavior*). The conclusion was that three-quarters of the articles simply reported data, without presenting any genuine theories or ideas. A surprisingly large number of the articles (53 percent in the *Archives* and 31 percent in the *Journal*) did not even make any effort to pretend they had ideas: They just described their research methods and reported some numbers.

Anyone familiar with the philosophy or politics of science might well ask how is this possible. How can a field blunder ahead, collecting data without having any ideas? The nature of research is supposed to be that an individual (or a team) first gets a general theory, translates it into a specific hypothesis, and then goes out and collects some data to test it. How can such a large chunk of researchers continue to publish if they are skipping the thinking stage and just mindlessly collecting data? Hardly any other fields are so atheoretical, especially in their premier journals.

There was no clear answer in the special issue, but we have one hunch why theory development in sexuality research may lag behind that of other fields: gender. With sex, one can always just look for gender differences. Do men like oral sex more than women? Do men have their first intercourse earlier or later than women? Do women have more orgasms than men? Do women have more worries about sex than men? It is possible for sex researchers simply to collect (and publish) data bearing on these questions, without needing any clear theory about the basic and essential differences between men and women.

Thus, gender is always ready for use as an independent variable. It has the advantage that, at least in connection with sex, there are often differences. The ready availability of such a "default" independent variable means that researchers can make their careers—by publishing studies and getting tenure—without needing a strong theory. As a result, the implications for the higher levels of theory are never very clear, because there are always so many ways to explain any single gender difference. Although there are in fact several competing major theories about gender differences, the field of sex research does allow researchers to publish gender differences without having to establish firmly which of the various theories is correct in their case.

Regardless of whether the mindless focus on gender has been the cause, the conclusion remains that the study of sex is rather weak in theories and ideas. This book is based on the assumption that one place to start remedying that problem is social psychology. By treating sex as a form of human interaction and applying what is known about human interpersonal processes, we can generate some ideas that can at least be tried out as possible keys to understanding sexual behavior.

Men and Women

Many researchers are skeptical of the study of gender differences in general, and we think they have good reason (Baumeister, 1988c). Despite the popularity of simple-minded works like Gray's *Men Are from Mars, Women Are from Venus* of 1993, the facts show that men and women are far more similar than different. Sometimes there is a mean difference, but this difference conceals substantial overlap. One of the largest and most consistently found gender differences, for example, is in physical height: Men are taller than women. Yet even on height there is ample overlap. There are plenty of women who are taller than plenty of men.

An important book by Aries (1996) reconsidered the extensive research literature on gender differences with a novel twist by using new statistical techniques that study effect sizes. She was thus able to ask not only "Is there a difference between the average man and the average woman?" but also "How big is that difference?" She discovered that many reports find differences, but that they are usually tiny: "Typically less than 5 percent . . . of the variance in social behavior is accounted for by gender" (Aries, 1996, p. 7). The small size of these differences tends to get lost in the publicity surrounding various findings, leaving the impression that men and women are, if not from entirely different planets, at least quite meaningfully different.

These misleading conclusions can be destructive. The stereotype that girls are not good at math has persisted for decades. Careful comparison of test results across the United States shows that, yes, girls do not perform as well as boys—but that the difference is only about 3 percent of the variance. The national publicity over the sex difference in math achievement failed to mention how small it really is, thus furnishing a misleading impression (Eccles, 1982). In fact, the difference is hardly worth talking about, and certainly shouldn't be extrapolated to any particular girl in making her plans. If we steer girls away from math courses, or even if we design special remedial courses in math for girls, we are operating on the basis of a stereotype that has only a tiny kernel of truth behind it.

With sex, however, there is more reason to think that there would be large and meaningful differences. Sex is a special case. After all, why would you expect females to be less able to do math than males? Regardless of whether you think the two genders were designed by natural selection or by divine creation, the ability to solve calculus problems was not likely to figure prominently in the process. But there are plenty of strong and compelling reasons to expect some differences in sex. Math relies on the brain, and biologically speaking, men and women have very similar brains with similar parts and functions. Sex, on the other hand, relies heavily on the sex organs, and men and women have radically different sex organs. Women get pregnant, men don't. Some men suffer from premature ejaculations, women don't. Some women can have multiple orgasms, but hardly any men can. Men have a refractory period, women may not. And so forth.

The biological differences are accompanied by severe social role differences in sex. These persist today despite all the movement toward gender equality, and it is fair to assume that they were much bigger throughout most of history than they are now. Men initiate dating, while women wait to be asked. Men initiate sex, and women accept or refuse. Some men pay some women cash in return for sex, but the opposite is extremely rare. And so on.

It would be absurd to try to write a theory of sex without considering the differences between men and women. We have only two points to make about this. First, there is an obligation to ground these differences in coherent, systematic theories about how men and women differ. Second, the emphasis is not simply on saying that there are differences but in providing a separate understanding of each. In a sense, what is needed is two social psychologies of sex, one for men and one for women. Of course, these psychologies will overlap, because men interact with women during sex (in most cases). But one cannot simply reverse the genders in a given sexual interaction without running the risk that the meanings and implications will change.

A note on terminology: We reserve the term *sex* to refer to sexual activities, such as sexual intercourse, sexual arousal, and orgasm. When we want to talk about the differences between men and women, we shall use the term *gender*. Some researchers use the terms in different ways and speak freely of *sex differences*, but we think our discussion of human sexuality will be clearer if the term *sex* is used only for sexual activity.

Regarding Feminism

The feminist movement has done much toward reducing inequality between men and women. In bygone centuries, women were not permitted to vote in elections, to own property or manage money, to preach, to obtain higher education (or in some cases any education at all), to pursue professional careers, to sue someone in a court of law, and in some cases even to testify. The feminist movement began with the belief that women were people on an equal basis with men and therefore should have the same rights and opportunities as men. We, the authors of this book, agree emphatically with that view. We are feminists, at least in the sense of supporting equality and opportunity.

Feminism has not confined itself to political reform but has also spawned a major intellectual movement. In its early days, it was closely linked to the quest for political equality, but over the past couple of decades there has emerged a more radical line of feminist thought that has rejected gender similarity and sought instead to depict women as having different and special psychological abilities. Books like *Women's Ways of Knowing* (Belenky, Clinchy, Goldberger, & Tarule, 1986) and *In a Different Voice* (Gilligan, 1982) proposed that female thought operates in fundamentally different ways than male thought. Scientific data do not support these conclusions, but many feminists angrily reject scientific data and claim a right to believe whatever their own experiences and beliefs may indicate, regardless of proof and evidence.

The split between these two views has been analyzed and documented in Sommers's 1994 book *Who Stole Feminism?* Sommers showed that feminism cannot be reduced to a single body of thought or even a single movement. There are equity feminists, who promote equality of the sexes and want to advance knowledge, even if it means occasionally acknowledging women's faults and failings. And there are radical feminists, who want to advance the cause of women at all costs. For them, politics is more important than truth, and they will work to suppress any ideas that do not advance the cause of women as they see it. Sommers stated that feminists urged her not to publish corrections to false claims that had been made in the mass media, because the false claims were beneficial to women.

Equity feminists may love our book. Radical feminists will probably not. We have to discuss gender differences, because sex is full of them, and it is simply impossible to make women come out on top in all phenomena according to all possible value judgments. Many radical feminists want to depict men as evil oppressors and to blame all misfortunes on them. We cannot cater to that view.

If you believe in the equality of the genders, you will find our book quite agreeable. Equality does not mean sameness. But in our analysis, men and women are adapting to their slightly different situations and slightly different needs, and usually they do so in fairly reasonable and understandable ways. No doubt a male chauvinist will think we have been too critical of men here and there, just as a radical feminist will think we have not always presented women in the best possible light. But we think the two genders come off about equally well in our analysis.

Truth Is a Big Pie

Thus, a problem with the field of sexuality is that there are not enough theories to structure debate and give researchers ideas to prove and disprove. The two major theories—the *essentialist* and the *social constructionist* perspectives (DeLamater & Hyde, 1998)—are to some extent just broad frameworks that can be used to interpret a great many findings, instead of being sources of ideas that can be tested. The essentialist view argues that sexuality is largely a matter of the way one is born. It emphasizes biological processes such as genes, hormones, and evolution. By contrast, the social constructionist position examines how culture and society shape sexuality.

Although the debate between the essentialists and the social constructionists is often bitter, we think there is room for their peaceful coexistence—and indeed for more theories to join the party. The bitterness of the debate comes from the assumption that any victory for one side is a loss for the other, and that ultimately only one can win. We don't think that's right.

By saying that "truth is a big pie," we mean that reality is complex and multiply determined. Yes, hormones and genes can influence sex, but that doesn't deny that society and culture can play powerful roles. When you think of all the sexual behavior that occurs in the world, there is plenty for different theories to claim. Part of the behavior is due to nature, other parts to culture. The evolutionary theories can be correct about a large part of sexuality, even while the constructionist theories are also simultaneously correct about a different part. And a few more theories may be available to claim their parts.

We think, therefore, that more theories are needed. The state of sexuality theory is not a final battle to the death between essentialism and constructionism, with one of them fated to be utterly discredited. Rather, each has part of the puzzle, and there are probably several other theories waiting to be introduced and claim their part too. In the next section, we will offer one theory that seems to be missing from the current picture and may have some validity. But we do not plan to feature it at the expense of other theories, nor do we think it is better than the others. We do not even want to assert that it is correct. We just think it deserves to be considered alongside the other major ideas in the field. All the main theories may be right to an important extent, and all may help explain some part of the vast spectacle of human behavior.

Sex as Social Exchange

This book is explicitly trying to milk social psychology for ideas that can be imported into the study of sex and used to analyze sexual behavior. These should not be treated as proven facts or truths but rather as possible ideas or extensions that deserve to be considered and tested.

One very simple approach to understanding social behavior is *social exchange theory*, which is sometimes considered part of a broader view called *interdependence theory*. The essence of this approach is to understand social and interpersonal behavior in terms of seeking rewards and avoiding costs. These are not just monetary costs and rewards but also purely social ones, such as the approval of others, attention, and acceptance. People want others to treat them in certain ways, and so their interactions with them will be guided by the pursuit of such favorable treatment. At the simplest level, people will try to get others to like them, and they are willing to do other things in return for being liked.

Social exchange theory has its roots in sociological analyses and group dynamics work. Homans (1950, 1961) analyzed social interactions in terms of the exchanges of rewards between people. He discussed how supply and demand principles affect how people treat each other. Likewise, Blau (1964) proposed that two concepts—power and exchange—could explain a very broad set of social interactions.

Waller and Hill (1938/1951) offered the beginnings of an exchange analysis of love and sex. They proposed the "principle of least interest," which is that whoever cares less about a relationship has greater power. If the man loves a woman more than she loves him, she can get him to do many more things than he can get her to do. Conversely, if he is less in love than she, then he can call the tune. Holding back your love is a source of power. Simply not caring about the relationship (or even just caring less than the other person cares) is to your advantage, at least in terms of giving you a certain degree of power over the other person.

The same applies to sex. Whoever wants sex less has a certain amount of power in the relationship. Being the one with less sexual inclination gives you a major edge. You're doing the other person a favor whenever you have sex, if you want it less. In terms of who owes what to whom, this is a better situation for you than the other way around.

The broader context was articulated by Thibaut and Kelley (1959) as *interdependence theory*, which analyzes how much each person can control the other's rewards and benefits. In an intimate relationship, for example, each person has considerable power to hurt the other or to make the other happy. These powers are not necessarily equal. For example, if the romance is taking place on an isolated college campus, where there are three times as many men as women, the women have considerably more power, because the men have fewer choices available. Even if a particular man and woman have equally strong desires for a good, loving relationship, the woman may be in a stronger position, because if this relationship fails she can easily find another man from the large pool of unattached men. He, meanwhile, cannot easily find someone else, because there are relatively few unattached women, and they are much in demand (because lots of men are after them). In such a situation, the man will work harder than the woman to make sure the relationship succeeds.

Ironically, selective infanticide can produce just such an imbalance. Of course we do not approve of infanticide, but it is possible to look at it not as a moral issue but simply as a social science pattern of behavior. Infanticide frequently victimizes one gender by killing off babies of one gender and not the other. But when those babies grow up, the gender that suffered worse losses in infancy is suddenly much more in demand and can dictate the terms of heterosexual relations much more effectively than usual.

Social exchange theory can be applied to sex in a variety of ways, but we want to feature one cluster of ideas in particular. These ideas were implicit in several of the writings of the social exchange theorists, but they did not articulate them precisely, possibly because sex was not a central concern of their work.

The core idea is this: Women give sex to men. That is, sex is a kind of resource that women control and that men want. To get sex, men have to do things that will please women, by and large. They must offer women something in exchange. The opposite arrangement, by which women must give men something in order to induce men to have sex with them, will be much rarer.

This view flies in the face of the current emphasis on equality of the sexes and the view that men and women are equal partners in bed. It even seems to run against some of the positions in women's liberation, which sought to put women on an equal footing with men and to regard sex as a mutual display of affection and possibly commitment. These alternative views have considerable appeal, and so we do not want to claim that the exchange view of sex is the only view or even the correct view. It does, however, have some potential importance for theoretical understanding, and thus it is worth considering from time to time as we study various patterns of sexual behavior.

According to the exchange view, when a man and woman make love, they are not giving and getting precisely the same things. The woman is bestowing some positive benefit on the man. In a sense, therefore, he owes her something in return. If sex were simply an act of pleasure between equals, there would be no debt or obligation connected with it for either party. But if women give sex to men, the man has to earn it or pay for it in some way.

This is where the "principle of least interest" comes in. Since, according to the original presentation by Waller and Hill (1938/1951), withholding love is a form of power, we would add that withholding sex is also a form of power. If men want sex more than women, women gain power by withholding sex. If women lack other sources of power, this one could be crucial to their prospects in life.

Hence various sexual interactions can be analyzed in terms of women having something that men want and men trying to get it. At one extreme, there would be a direct exchange of sex for money (prostitution). At another, men might "steal" sex, as in taking it forcibly from reluctant women (rape). In between those extremes lies the vast majority of sexual interactions, in which some more subtle but still important form of exchange takes place. In between, in most relationships, men see sex as a benefit they gain more than women do (Sedikides, Oliver, & Campbell, 1994).

Turning back to the general point that women give sex to men, we must next inquire why that might be true. Social exchange theorists typically focus on supply and demand. Again, if there is a surplus or shortage of one gender relative to the other, then the gender that's in the majority is ironically in the weaker position (because the demand for them is less than the supply). In the monogamous marriage market, the principle of majority rule doesn't apply! It is the minority that has the power to make the rules. But supply and demand could be affected even more strongly by other factors. In particular, if women want sex less than men, or even if women generally *pretend* that that's how they feel, men will be the ones who will have to offer something in return.

Evolutionary psychologists offer one (albeit controversial) basis for arguing that women give sex to men. In their view, which we shall examine at several points in this book, men have evolved to want more sex partners and more frequent sex than women. This is allegedly because evolution depends on reproduction, and because the difference between male and female sex organs creates different selection pressures.

A classic study by Bateman (1948) on fruit flies demonstrated the difference. The more often a male had sex and the more sex partners he had, the more offspring he produced. A female, however, needed only one sex partner and an occasional bit of sex to reproduce, and any more sex beyond that was useless in reproductive terms. The same logic applies to human beings, of course: A man can in theory father dozens of children every year, if he copulates with enough women, but a woman can only get pregnant about once a year, regardless of how many men she sleeps with and how often she does so. As Ridley (1993) puts it, let's assume that the notorious Italian lover Casanova and the Whore of Babylon both set records for the number of sex partners, and that it's hard to say which one slept with more members of the opposite sex—but it's easy to say which one had more children: The superpromiscuous man produces far more offspring than the superpromiscuous woman.

According to this line of thinking, women did not crave a great deal of sex. But since men were often so crazy for it, the women could use sex to gain things they wanted from the men. One thing they wanted was something great to eat. (These days, it is sometimes easy to forget that for most of human prehistory and history, most people were in danger of going hungry much of the time.)

Accordingly, the argument goes, there developed a pattern of trading meat for sex. Men were hunters who could run fast, throw spears, and kill big animals that made good food. Men could do this better than women, having slightly greater strength and no nursing babies to carry around on the hunt. The men might have kept all the food for themselves, but instead they were likely to use some of it to persuade women to have sex with them. The evolutionary psychologist David Buss thinks that such patterns still apply to dating today, and he tells a story in his lectures about a woman who decided to have sex with a man and told her friends about her intention. They thought she should not simply go to bed with him: "Make him buy you a steak dinner first," they advised!

Whether the meat-for-sex trade has been a common and overt feature of human sexual exchange, it is clear that men have often exchanged various kinds of rewards for sex. The simplest exchange is cash, of course, and throughout history far more men have paid women for sex than vice versa. Even apart from prostitution, social interactions between men and women have often required the man to bestow some resources on the woman in order to earn sexual favors. At some periods in history, these exchanges have been overtly sensed by men. Homans (1961) quoted a remark (claiming it was fairly typical) made by a man in a New England town he studied in the middle of the twentieth century: "I paid for her dinner and I didn't get a damn thing out of her" (p. 355). Clearly the man thought of sexual favors as something the woman should give him in return for the food he had bought her.

Such a remark strikes us today as archaic and possibly offensive. Apparently the men who made such remarks to Homans were from an era in which sex was a reward women gave to men, but perhaps times have changed. Even if all the men and women in that town understood the rules of exchange just the way that that particular man did, that would not prove that it is true now. Then again, even if no one would say such a thing today, the pattern of exchange might still be lurking beneath the rhetoric about equality and the mutual wonderfulness of sex. Again, we are not claiming that this exchange theory view of sex is the correct one—only that it is a perspective that we can consider from time to time to see whether it fits or explains various patterns of behavior.

Social exchange theorists had one further point that may prove helpful. They noted that when a person gives out social approval freely, it loses its value (Blau, 1964; Homans, 1961). A person who generally withholds approval, however, will find that people place great value on it when it is (occasionally) given. If you pay compliments to everybody all the time, your compliments are not taken that seriously (although people will probably like to hang around with you). Compliments have more weight if they are special, and to be special they have to be unusual, even rare.

This view—that scarcity increases value—can certainly be applied to sex, at least in theory. Blau (1964) applied it to affection generally, using the implicit principle that men want it from women: "To safeguard the value of her affection, a woman must be ungenerous in expressing it and make any evidence of her growing love a cherished prize that cannot be easily won" (p. 80). If a woman has sex with only one or two men in her life, they should in principle regard this as a very high honor and a recognition that they mean something quite special to her. In contrast, if she has sex with dozens of partners, then bedding her will have less value to them.

From that perspective, the woman's situation is different than the man's in a way that might contribute to what has been called the "double standard." The woman suffers a loss of bargaining power when she has many sex partners, because the value of what she has to give—sex with her—is diminished. Hence her self-interest pushes her to restrict her sexual activity, even if she were to feel plenty of sexual desire and to be curious about having sex with various partners.

Although these pressures may incline women toward taking a cautious, even prudish attitude toward sex, they cannot be too restrictive for two reasons. First, if the woman never has sex, then she never reaps the value of what she has to bestow. She has to give sex to some men to benefit from the value she possesses. Being overly prudish would be comparable to being a miser who has lots of money but never spends any of it and as a result lives like a poor person. Second, she has to compete against other women for men's attention. If she dispenses sexual favors (ranging from a kiss on the cheek to full intercourse) at a rate much lower than other women, the men are likely to ignore her and spend their time courting the others.

Thus, the terms of sexual exchange are not likely to be universal or innate (as an exclusively evolutionary or biological analysis would propose) but will depend instead on the current culture. If all the other women kiss on the first date, then the woman who refuses to kiss is giving the man less than he can get elsewhere, and she is likely to feel some pressure to come up to par. If the other women all have intercourse on the first date, then the woman may feel pressure to do the same, or the man might leave her for another. Looking at the couple in isolation misses an important dimension of the context and an important influence on what happens.

To be sure, most theories about sex acknowledge that norms and peer groups play some role. To some extent, people simply conform to what others do and learn their values from others. The appeal of the social exchange theory, however, is that it says peer and cultural influence is mediated by something more substantial than mindless conformity to what everybody else does. The peer group is vitally important (especially to a woman) because it sets the going rate for the exchange of sexual intimacies. Knowing how soon other women go to bed with their new boyfriends is more than simply a matter of prurient, gossipy curiosity: It tells the woman whether she is giving too much or too little in proportion to what the man has offered her in terms of time, attention, money, and commitment. And it is directly relevant to whether her boyfriend is going to be satisfied with her.

Although the social exchange theory depicts women as facing some special dilemmas and problems that men don't (and what is surprising about that?), it also portrays them as having some power and influence that men lack. Men, in this view, are largely at the mercy of women, unless they are willing to do without sex. By controlling access to sex, women can exert considerable influence over men's behavior.

In the social exchange view, men essentially will do whatever is necessary to obtain sexual favors—but not much more. If a man can get sex simply by dating a woman once or twice and showing her a little friendly interest, without spending much money or promising anything, that will be about the extent of what he does. In contrast, if he must spend much of his money on her and promise to marry her, then he will do that.

This view was once expressed rather bluntly for us during a discussion of a female friend's romantic travails. She had made herself available to the man in multiple ways, including sexually, and he had taken advantage of her. This seemed to be a repeating pattern in her life. She bemoaned the perfidy and general badness of men. A man listening to her complaint suggested, however, that she had allowed this to happen to her. He himself professed to be mystified by how women seemed willing to date and have sex with men who acted badly, and he proposed a general hypothesis: "If women would stop sleeping with jerks, men would stop being jerks!"

That remark may be overly optimistic, and without clear-cut evidence we cannot say whether it is entirely true, entirely false, or somewhere in between. But it does fit with the social exchange analysis of sex, and so its correctness or incorrectness may reflect on the validity of the entire analysis. Undoubtedly multiple causes feed into the misbehavior of various men, and not all of it is likely to disappear based on shifts in women's behavior, but there would be some influence.

In particular, the social exchange analysis would suggest that the sexual revolution has radically changed the terms. Far less good behavior is now required of men than was the case prior to the sexual revolution. A man can get sex much more easily than he could fifty years ago, and so he does not have to offer nearly as much in return. Indeed, the sexual revolution poses an interesting problem for the social exchange analysis, because it suggests that women as a group generally accepted a devaluation of their bargaining resource and thus a weakening of their position. It almost seems self-destructive for women to have allowed the sexual revolution to happen. Yet as we shall see, at least some women look upon the sexual revolution in precisely those terms. The feminist author Germaine Greer, who in 1970 wrote *The Female Eunuch*, which contributed to the sexual revolution, returned in 1999 with her summary conclusion. Men won the sexual revolution, she wrote, because "the sexuality that has been freed is male sexuality" (Greer, 1999, p. 10).

Some Words of Warning

We freely acknowledge several features of this book that might surprise or even annoy others. We want to point them out right at the start so as to minimize any disappointment.

First, we are not offering a single, grand theory of the social nature of sexuality. In fact, we shall cover several grand and not-so-grand theories. We think the social dimension of sex is too complex to fit into a single formula. Most of the theories will have their strong and weak moments. The social exchange theory we outlined in this chapter is just supposed to be one of the group. (We had to introduce it because it has not been explicitly advocated among the current theories.)

Second, we are not giving "equal time" to homosexuality. We fully support gay rights, and we recognize the importance of analyzing the special social circumstances that accompany same-gender sexuality. We shall in fact cover it at several points in the book. But the main focus will be on heterosexual sex. Actually, we think our treatment is roughly in proportion to the real world: Probably about 95 percent of sex involves a man and a woman, and about the same proportion of our coverage is likewise devoted to heterosexuality. In any case, because of its majority status, heterosexuality gets first claim on the social scientist's attention.

Third, we do not intend to cover the full range of sexual practices. Again, our focus will be on heterosexual sexuality and what social psychology has to offer toward explaining it. We are not going to cover every possible topic. Other authors might well cover a different list of topics in a book on the social dimension of sex, and we hope they will do so. But we make no promises to say everything that could be said or cover every corner of the domain.

Fourth, we cannot promise to be politically correct. On the contrary, our goal of exploring new ways of looking at things will require us to challenge some accepted and preferred views. Frankly, we admire the values behind political correctness, especially respectful consideration of others and sensitivity to victims, but we deplore the extremes to which political correctness is often taken, especially the suppression of intellectual debate and the refusal to consider certain unpopular facts and theories.

Fifth, we do not regard our conclusions as being the absolute truth. They should instead be regarded as summaries of what ideas provide the best fit to the currently available information (or, at least, our interpretation of the data!). The scientific study of sexuality is still early in its development, and much remains to be learned. We anticipate that in the coming decades further research findings will emerge and overturn some of the tentative conclusions we draw in this book. That is how science works, and we are happy to be a part of it. In fact, we would be quite pleased if some of the ideas we consider will inspire other researchers to collect data that will end up refining, modifying, and even radically revising or disproving them. In the long run, the truth will emerge, provided that scientists are permitted to conduct their research and publish their conclusions. All wrong ideas eventually bite the dust, as long as free inquiry continues.

Sixth, even if our conclusions in this book are perfectly correct, and if all the studies we cite turn out to be thoroughly sound and universal, this is still not necessarily the full story. Most social science theories take the form "*A* causes *B*" (such as, "depression causes suicide"). But the world is *multicausal:* Multiple causes can produce the same effect, either in combination or separately. So even if it is true that "*A* causes *B*," there is also room to show that "*C* causes *B*" as well as that "*A* causes B only when *X* and *Y* are also in the picture." Such is the complexity of human sexuality in particular and of human behavior in general. Although some might be discouraged by this, we think it makes for an exciting field that will be a rich source of ideas and findings for many years to come! Again, the truth is a big pie.

Seventh, we hope people will not infer value judgments from our comments. If we have value judgments to make, we will make them explicitly. For example, it is necessary for us to use the term *promiscuous* in its literal sense of having multiple sex partners, and we will periodically refer to someone as "promiscuous"—but our usage does not convey any implication of moral disapproval or criticism. More generally, we think that critical thinking about sex will be most effective if most value judgments can be suspended, and so we hope readers will enter into the spirit of considering the behaviors and outcomes without constantly consulting a canon of value judgments. There is ample time for value judgments once the basic patterns and phenomena have been understood.

It is essential to try to use social psychology to help us understand sex. Sex is too important a part of life to ignore. Sex brings intense joy and suffering to many individuals. A society's ability to survive depends on sex, and a balance between overpopulation and underpopulation is needed. Sex can mean life and death, as shown in the range of outcomes that include AIDS, jealous murder, and childbirth. In 1990 Paul Abramson, then editor of the *Journal of Sex Research*, wrote that "future generations will find it incomprehensible—and perhaps unconscionably negligent—that so little effort was marshalled to obtain data on and establish a science of human sexual behavior" (p. 162).

We agree. And we hope that our efforts to apply insights from social and personality psychology to the problem of understanding sexual behavior will be a step in correcting the oversight.

We would like to thank the following individuals for their helpful comments in reviewing our draft manuscript: Betsy Bergen, Kansas State University; Robin Kowalski, Western Carolina University; Randy Fisher, University of Central Florida; James Johson, University of North Carolina at Wilmington; and William Rick Fry, Youngstown State University.

CHAPTER

2

How Much Sex Is Going On?

When Americans were first permitted to resume visiting China in the 1970s, a young American academic managed to slip away from the official tour and walk through the city streets unchaperoned. He could speak some Chinese and was able to converse with the people who thronged around him and clearly regarded him as a remarkable novelty. To his surprise, the most frequent question they asked him about his homeland was, "Is it true that everyone in America has sex five times a day every day?" He was uncertain whether that widespread impression was the result of official Chinese propaganda or had somehow been distilled from the U.S. mass media.

Basketball star Wilt Chamberlain boasted after his retirement that he had had sex with about 20,000 women in his lifetime. An incredulous reporter calculated that such a tally would require having sex with three new partners every night, seven days a week, for twenty years, including Christmas vacations and when you had the flu. And that was not counting repeat performances: having any *regular* sex partners would boost the figure needed to four or five women per night, every single night, across the two decades. Confronted with these numbers, Chamberlain is said to have nodded and replied in a serious tone, "That's about right."

Such anecdotes feed the impression that the modern American adult has an extremely active sex life. Undoubtedly most Americans recognize that estimates of having sex five times a day, especially with a constant flow of new partners, are excessive and unrealistic portrayals of what the average person is doing. But by how much do they overestimate? If the average young American adult doesn't have a hundred new partners every year, does he or she at least have twenty? or four? In fact, it turns out that according to the broad averages and national patterns, having even four partners each year would qualify you as quite the social butterfly.

Moreover, such figures are more than mere passing curiosities. People evaluate themselves by making use of information about what others do. An average is, after all, a norm, and most people want to be at least normal where important and desirable things are concerned. Indeed, most people manage to convince themselves that they are above average in a variety of important ways (Taylor & Brown, 1988). They become upset, depressed, or even threatened if they conclude that they are below normal.

That is the essence of *social comparison theory*, articulated first by Festinger in 1954: People compare themselves with others in order to reach an evaluative understanding of themselves. Many realities are not fully objective but rather are social, and evaluation in particu lar depends on one's relative standing. Being able to run a mile in eight minutes is simply a fact, and it only becomes good or bad depending on how it compares with what others can do. Indeed, it depends on what *particular* others do. An eight-minute mile may be a stellar achievement for a middle-aged jogger but a deep disappointment for an Olympic hopeful.

In the same way, people evaluate their sex lives by comparison with others. If you have sex once a day, that may seem like a great deal—so long as you believe the average person has sex only a couple times a month. On the other hand, if you think the average is five times per day, or even twice a day, you may start to worry that your once-a-day habit qualifies you as an undersexed prude.

Two issues raise special difficulties for people who try to use social comparison to evaluate their sex lives. First, sex is a fairly private activity, and so reliable firsthand information is not easy to come by. For height, weight, blood pressure, and similar things, precise norms exist. Tables can be consulted to evaluate your IQ score or cholesterol level. It is easy to see how fast other people run or swim, and you can race against them to ascertain whether your own speed is good or bad. In contrast, you can hardly ever observe other people having sex, let alone gain a clear idea of how often they do it or in what varieties.

Instead of direct observation, one has to rely on verbal reports—what other people tell about their sexual experiences—but these are, to put it mildly, less than fully reliable. Many people try in casual conversation to give an idealized impression of their sex lives. They know sex is important, and they try to present an impression that they are healthy and normal or even above normal, based on whatever their impression of "normal" is. Some people try to portray themselves as paragons, experts, or superstars in the sexual realm. If they have had difficulties or problems, they may conceal them or give misleading hints. A well-known parody of this pattern was presented early in the movie *Sex, Lies, and Videotape*, in which the star's psychotherapist asks her how her sex life with her husband has been in recent weeks. She gives an embarrassed laugh and evasively says, "Fine, fine," to dismiss the question. When the doctor persists, she adds, "Well, it's good, except that I'm sort of going through this thing right now where I can't stand for him to touch me." Apparently everything is far from "fine," but many questioners might have been content with the first answer. If you were a little worried about your own sex life, hearing this woman say that everything was fine might have made you feel your own problems were worrisome. But after you hear that she can't stand to let her husband touch her, any problems you have might seem relatively minor in comparison.

Thus, the first problem with evaluating one's own sexuality by social comparison is that people generally do not know what other people do. This is true in today's United States, and it has been even more true in most other societies in the history of the world. Evaluating one's sex life against the norms is very difficult if one does not know what the norms actually are.

The second difficulty concerns the shifting standards of evaluation. Of course one would like to be better than average when it comes to sex—but what is "better"? With body fat or weight, less is better, at least in today's society. With money, more is better. With sex, the matter is more complex. Prostitutes have sex multiple times each night and gradually may accumulate thousands of sex partners, certainly far far more than the average person, but are they the ideal? Few women would envy them or want to trade places with them, even just in the matter of sex. On the other extreme, nuns may remain lifelong virgins, but most people would not regard that as an ideal sex life either. Still, in the many cultures that have evaluated individual women's sexual experience by a standard of less is better, virginity would look rather virtuous. With regard to sex, in the contemporary United States only the middle is good—some but not too much. Neither prude nor slut: Both tails of the bell curve are bad. And even the middle ground is not considered ideal for everyone. Many people (particularly women) are proud of being virgins (Sprecher & Regan, 1996). Society reserves a host of derogatory labels for women who have far more sex than average. Hence having slightly less sex than average may be perceived by many women, and possibly some men too, as the relevant form of being "better" than average. To others, especially men proud of conquests, a little more than average is desirable, as long as one doesn't have too many. And some men may reject the notion that there is any such thing as having too many partners.

To complicate matters further, standards change across cultural and historical periods. Victorian authorities proclaimed that "the majority of women (happily for society) are not much troubled with sexual feeling of any kind" and that "sexual feeling in the female is in the majority of cases in abeyance . . . and even if roused (which in many instances it never can be) it is very moderate compared with that of the male" (Acton, 1857, p. 163, quoted in Haller & Haller, 1974). Others wrote that "most [women] are entirely frigid, and not even in marriage do they ever perceive any real desire" (Napheys, 1871, quoted in Haller & Haller, 1974, p. 98). Many women who received such advice may have felt guilty about enjoying sex more than that. In contrast, today a woman may feel guilty if she fails to have an orgasm every time she has intercourse, all four times per week, like a healthy young wife is supposed to do (or so she thinks).

These examples involve women, and some may suggest that sexual standards are especially complex and conflicted for women. Even for men, though, matters are not entirely straightforward and simple. True, many men would regard a little more sex than they currently have as an improvement. The more-is-better attitude has its limits, however, especially in an era when epidemics of venereal disease can bring lifelong or even fatal consequences. Many men may give a quick wistful smile at the thought of Wilt Chamberlain's twenty thousand sex partners, but (as we shall see) few seriously want to embark on such a sexual career.

Then again, few men would have the opportunity. Being a national celebrity undoubtedly opens some chances that would not be available to most. It is plausible that most men might say that they would not want to go to bed with that many women, but if they actually had the opportunity, they might change their tune.

Let us therefore consider the actual facts based on recent research findings. Given the wealth of information, it is not difficult to find numbers to answer certain questions. Figuring out which numbers are valid is more difficult, however. Furthermore, interpreting the numbers may also often take more effort than one might assume. It is important to examine each research finding carefully, so as to see precisely what it means and what it does not. The ideal social scientist is neither overly cautious nor overly credulous . Most research findings in the social sciences (even in the best, most selective journals) contain some valid and correct points but may also be subject to some limitations, biases, misleading aspects, and even errors.

One purpose of this chapter is to highlight some of the methodological and interpretive issues with sex. When looking at facts and findings about any social behavior, it is often necessary to remain cautious and skeptical. The truth does exist, but one has to consider each finding carefully before deciding what the truth is.

How Many Sex Partners?

Detailed answers to many questions about sex were furnished by a pair of works published in the 1990s. Both consisted of national samples carefully constructed to resemble the U.S. population as a whole. Both had expert Ph.D. researchers in charge. One of them, the Janus Report (Janus & Janus, 1993), used a team of over two hundred researchers set up specially to investigate American sexual habits. The other, the National Health and Social Life Survey, or NHSLS (Laumann et al., 1994; Michael et al., 1994), used the resources and experience of the prestigious and highly respected National Opinion Research Center to gain answers. Yet the two surveys came to drastically different answers about some of the most basic issues. Depending on which of these two books we consult, we receive a very different impression of the sex life of the average American.

For example, one area of disagreement is the simple number of sex partners people report having had. The Janus Report does not give an exact median, but interpolating from the tables and data it does present suggests that about half of American adults have had nineteen or fewer partners, and the other half have had more than that. (The median was about twenty-four for men, fourteen for women; see Janus & Janus, 1993, p. 95.) The NHSLS, on the other hand, gives a median of three (Laumann et al., 1994, p. 106). That is, the researchers found that half of American adults have had three or fewer sex partners in their lifetime.

Naturally, both these surveys include some young adults who will still go on to have more partners, so the tallies are not final, and one may project that over the course of an entire life the eventual numbers will be somewhat higher. But probably that would just make the estimates from the two different studies diverge even further.

Which is correct? Has the median American had sex with nineteen partners or with three? The two numbers imply very different sex lives for the average American.

The difference between the two surveys can be seen dramatically by comparing their conclusions about what proportion of women have had sex with more than ten men in their lives. Is such double-digit bed-hopping a common experience that is typical of the modern, liberated American woman, or is it reserved for a small minority? The Janus Report concluded that over half the women (55 percent) have reached that level of sexual variety. The NHSLS (Laumann et al., 1994) found that only a small minority (9 percent, or one out of eleven) had had that many partners. Thus, if one were to draw the line somewhat arbitrarily so as to define as "promiscuous" any woman who has slept with more than ten men, the two surveys would differ by more than a factor of six as to how many promiscuous women there are in the United States.

The resolution is probably to be found in the different ways the two surveys obtained their information. The Janus group improved on a standard, familiar (but flawed) method for conducting surveys about sex. The traditional approach was to distribute questionnaires to whomever was willing to fill them out. Their improvement was to build a sample that resembled the U.S. population as a whole on demographic factors such as age, geographical region (home), marital status, and education.

To appreciate the value of this improvement, it is useful to compare it with a well-known earlier survey that relied on a questionnaire printed in *Playboy* magazine (Hunt, 1974). It simply counted every response that was mailed in. *Playboy* readers probably do not resemble the U.S. population as a whole—for example, few elderly women read *Playboy*, let alone mail in a response to a survey about sex printed in the magazine, and thus such people were missing from their conclusions. Plus, a survey in *Playboy* probably elicits at least a few responses that are constructed by a group of slightly drunken male college students who fill it out pretending to be one person (sometimes even a woman) as a lark during a Friday night party.

The Janus group made sure to get responses from elderly women as well as many other groups, in proportion to their frequency in the general population. They were careful that the sample (i.e., the total set of people who gave them information) resembled the American population as a whole in a number of crucial respects. This was clearly much better than relying on something printed in a magazine.

Still, demographic resemblance alone does not make a reliable sample. People who volunteer to answer a survey about sex may be systematically different from people who would not volunteer. Most likely, such volunteers are more interested in sex and perhaps less likely to be ashamed or confused about their sexual habits as compared with people who decline to answer. With sex, it is not safe to assume that people who volunteer to talk are similar to those who refuse.

The effect of volunteer bias has been confirmed in other studies in various ways. People who volunteer to participate in sexuality research tend to have had more experience with intercourse, engage in more masturbation, have fewer inhibitions about sex, and have tried more unusual sexual activities than people who do not volunteer (Morokoff, 1986; Wiederman, 1993). Relying on people who volunteer for research thus gives a distorted picture of sexuality.

The NHSLS claimed to be the only survey with genuinely reliable data, and its authors claim that the other surveys "all are so flawed and unreliable as to be useless" (Michael et al., 1994, p. 12). They derided the conclusions of other groups as "junk statistics of no value whatsoever in making valid and reliable population projections" (Laumann et al., 1994, p. 45). It may seem inappropriate and unprofessional, even arrogant, for researchers to criticize their rivals in those terms. In this case, however, they may be right.

Instead of merely targeting the particular groups to get a broad sample, the NHSLS used the resources and expertise of the National Opinion Research Center, which uses methods similar to those of expert pollsters who are able to predict political elections with high accuracy. (After all, no major election-eve poll has made a false prediction about a presidential election in several decades.) They carefully targeted the entire population of the United States, at least between the ages of seventeen and sixty*. Most importantly, they tried to get everyone they selected to respond. They were mindful of the scientific problems that arise when a sex survey omits people who do not voluntarily come forward to answer the questions. They did quite well, getting 79 percent of the people they targeted to respond. In contrast, the *Playboy* survey got back only 1.3 percent of the questionnaires it printed, the *Redbook* survey (Tavris & Sadd, 1978), 2 percent, and the Hite (1979) report 3 percent. The Janus Report got back 61 percent of the questionnaires it distributed, but this is still well short of the 79 percent reported by the NHSL survey (Laumann et al., 1994).

Moreover, crucially, the NHSLS used selection methods to target a proper and representative sample. (Its 79 percent counts as nonresponders people who could not be located, unlike the other figures for the other reports, which count only people who were actually given the questionnaire. If we throw those out and simply count refusers, compliance rate of the NHSLS was substantially higher yet.) The authors of the NHSL survey noted that the Janus group used a "sample of convenience," which is to say people who were available and willing to respond, whereas they themselves strove to choose a representative sample of individuals and exerted themselves to get all of them to participate. If people did not respond the first time, they followed up with further attempts. They tracked down people who had moved or changed addresses. For people who were reluctant to answer, they explained the importance of broad participation and in other gentle ways tried to convince them of the value of taking part.

For example, the Janus group commendably wanted to include some elderly people in their sample, so they took their questionnaires to where they could find elderly people willing to fill them out. This turned out to be sex therapy clinics treating old patients. Undoubtedly, that was a good way to find old people willing to discuss their sex lives. But patients at such clinics may not be typical of older Americans in general. As the NHSLS researchers pointed out, people who are being treated at a sex therapy clinic are more likely than others to be interested in sex, to have a partner, and to want to have sex.

The Janus group found that over 70 percent of Americans past the age of sixty-five have sex once per week or more often. Wow! Hats off to Grandma and Grandpa! In contrast, a national survey (the General Social Survey described by Laumann et al., 1994) that did not preselect people in that way found that only 7 percent of elderly Americans have sex once per week or more. That difference, 70 percent versus 7 percent, is so large that the two figures suggest radically different views of the sex lives of elderly Americans. The way the Janus group chose their participants seems to have inflated their conclusions about how much sex is going on. The 7 percent figure is probably correct. The 70 percent reflects sampling bias and volunteer bias.

Thus, because the NHSLS data do a better job of approximating the entire U.S. population, they provide the most reliable guide as to sex in America.

Incidentally, the Janus data may still be incredibly useful; they are not really "of no value whatever," as rivals have suggested (Laumann et al., 1994). The size of all the numbers may be inflated and thus unreliable, even meaningless, but the relationships among the variables—for example, whether people who have anal sex also have oral

---

*Noninclusive; therefore, respondent ages ranged from eighteen to fifty-nine.

sex—could still be quite valid, and indeed would be more sensitive than the NHSLS data to some statistical relationships, since the numbers are larger.

Also, of course, the Janus data may be relevant to people who have a high interest in sex. If you would be willing to answer a sex survey (and would actually take the time to complete it), then the Janus Report tells you about the sex habits of people like yourself. This category of people differs as a group from people who would not volunteer, and apparently these differences include having more sexual experiences with more people. Naturally, if you think having more sexual experiences is good, you would rather compare yourself with the findings of the NHSL survey, since its lower norms will make you look (and hence feel) better. The Janus Report instead tells you about what like-minded people have done.

For the purpose of knowing what is going on in the United States, however, the NHSLS provides the most useful data. The picture it offers is that of less sex than people often assume. It differs radically from the images that emerge from the mass media—of young, beautiful people casually and frequently falling into bed with a kaleidoscopic assortment of partners. The average American is not a movie star, nor even the kind of character depicted in the movies. Take a downtown bus ride in a big city and look around at the passengers, and ask yourself what kind of sex lives they have probably had. The NHSL survey includes people like them as well as people like the characters on television.

What about this seemingly low amount of sexual activity? Indeed, low numbers were a recurrent theme of the NHSLS data. It was not just that people have had relatively few partners, but they have had relatively few partners in the past year, have had sex with their main partner rather infrequently, and are unlikely to engage in unusual sexual practices. Few people ever have same-sex experiences, few have group sex or use drugs or alcohol in combination with sex, few engage in bondage games, and so forth. It is commonplace to suggest that Americans are obsessed with sex, but this impression is probably based on the mass media, which are far out of step with the mainstream. To judge by actual behavior, sex is a small corner of American life. It might still qualify as a national obsession in some sense, and it could certainly retain considerable power and importance. But in terms of what the average individual American actually does in bed, the evidence presents a picture that is far from flamboyant or hyperactive. People have less sex, less often, with fewer partners, and in fewer ways than the media images and stereotypes suggest.

Sex remains an intensely personal act that the average person shares with only a few partners across a lifetime. The norm, apparently, is to have sex with only a couple people, including the spouse with whom one settles down for a long time.

Does Average Mean Normal?

The gap between desire and reality is nowhere so apparent as with sex (and perhaps money!). The term *counterfactual thinking* refers to thought processes that focus on things that might or could have happened but didn't. Such thoughts are common with sex: People wish they had slept with someone, or they wish they hadn't, and so forth. Thus far this chapter has focused on what people actually do. That is not, however, a reliable guide to what they would *like* to do. Opportunities, worries, fears, social pressures, and many other factors conspire to separate sexual realities from desires.

Let us reconsider the question of the number of partners from the perspective of what people would want as opposed to what they actually do. The national surveys we considered in the previous section did not include this topic, but other research has. For present purposes, we rely on a survey (Miller & Fishkin, 1997) that asked students at the University of Southern California (USC) how many people they would ideally like to have sex with over the rest of their lives, assuming they did not have to worry about disease, social pressure, fidelity, or other factors.

It must be acknowledged that these college students do not necessarily resemble the entire U.S. population. They are younger than most others, and obviously very few elderly people were included in this survey. The students live in California, which has a reputation for liberal, tolerant, even favorable attitudes toward sexual experimentation. Indeed, Los Angeles is home to the nation's movie industry, and if the screen images of frequent, casual sex are based on the actual experiences of people in the business, it is possible that Los Angeles is indeed more promiscuous than the rest of the country.

Still, the results of the USC survey did not differ much from what other, similar surveys have found. It appears that people may be more similar than different, even when they live in the media centers such as Los Angeles and attend college. On the positive side, though, no one refused to participate in the survey, and so it is relatively free from the volunteer bias that (as we saw) compromises many studies and findings.

For present purposes, its most interesting finding concerns something we have glossed over thus far: gender differences. When asked how many sex partners they would ideally like to have, the women responded with a mean of 2.7. That is, the average response by all the women surveyed was that they would like their lifetime sexual experience to be shared with 2 or 3 partners. Among the men, the mean response was 64.

Before we conclude that men and women are from different planets, however, let us consider a different kind of average: the median. The median represents the midpoint of the group of responses—half of the people responding picked an equal or lower number, and half of the people picked an equal or higher number. In terms of desired number of sex partners, the median response for USC women was one. The median for the men was the same: one.

Thus, once again, the simple facts are not as simple as they may initially appear. It is necessary to consider carefully what lies behind the numbers. The discrepancy is obviously most striking for the men. When asked how many sex partners they would like to have over the course of their lives, the men gave a mean of sixty-four but a median of one. These are worlds apart. A man who has sex with sixty-four different women has clearly lived a very different life from the man who has had sex with only one woman over the same span.

Moreover—and this is quite important—the discrepancy between 1 and 64 has huge implications for the question of gender differences. If one looks at the medians (1 versus 1), men and women seem basically the same. But if one looks at the means (2.7 versus 64), men and women are widely different. These numbers came from the same survey, so one cannot suggest that they reflect different approaches, different samples, or possible biases among the researchers. The same researchers, working with the same people, obtained both sets of numbers.

The key to understanding these discrepancies is to consider how the numbers are calculated. The mean is produced by adding everyone's numerical response and dividing by the number of people. The median is reached by arranging all the numbers in order from lowest to highest and then counting halfway through the list. Thus, exactly half the people in the sample are below the median, and half are above it.

The mean and median can differ widely when there are several extreme scores in one direction but not the other. With number of sex partners, the minimum is obviously 0, and many people in this survey clearly said they wanted only 1 (or 0), so there are no extreme low scores. Among both men and women, there are lots of scores at the low end. High scores are unrestricted, however. A few men who say they want to have 1,000 sex partners can have a big effect on the mean, but they have no effect on the median. In a set of 11 numbers, for example, the median is the sixth highest score, and it makes no difference at all whether the single highest score is 20, 200, or 2,000. The median doesn't budge, but the mean would change radically.

The implication is therefore that the majority of men are basically the same as the majority of women: They want to find one sex partner and settle down for a lifetime of faithful, loving sex. They do not crave a large assortment or variety.

There is, however, a minority of men who desire a broad variety of sex partners. These promiscuously inclined men have relatively few female counterparts. Put another way, there are far more men than women who want to sleep with lots of people.

Are men and women different? From these data, most men are similar to most women—but a sizable minority of men is radically different from most men as well as most women! The answer to the gender difference pattern depends on whether one identifies men with the seemingly silent majority or with the distinctive minority.

The Dubious Gender Difference

To continue this discussion of gender differences, let us now reconsider one of the findings about the number of sex partners. The NHSLS reported in 1994 that the average modern American man, aged twenty to forty, has had six sex partners, and the average woman has had two (Laumann et al., 1994; Michael et al., 1994). This gender difference has been well replicated. Even in surveys with different methods that produced higher numbers, such as the Janus Report, the gender difference has been obtained. (As we saw, the Janus group had medians of fourteen and twenty-four, which are quite different.) These figures are medians, but similar discrepancies are found with means. The conclusion from this mass of evidenc is clear: On average, men have more sex partners than women.

How is this possible? After all, sex typically involves one man and one woman. Each time a man adds a new sex partner to his lifetime total, his partner also adds one to hers. The difference between means and medians is not relevant here. Mathematically, one would strongly expect men and women to report an equal mean number of sex partners. Yet they do not.

Similarly, another recent survey (Robinson & Godbey, 1998) concluded that men have sex 19 percent more often than women. How can this be? If we take these numbers at face value, we must conclude that, at least 19 percent of the time, men are not having sex with women. Does this carry some disquieting insights into the private lives of U.S. farm animals and domestic pets? Or does it mean that 19 percent of the time men are having sex with each other? (Of course, the true rate would have to be higher, insofar as women sometimes have sex with each other too. The men's rate would have to be 19 percent plus the entire rate of lesbian sexual activity.)

It must be acknowledged that this difference fits a broad pattern in which men report more sexual activity than women in plenty of ways. Yet some of these differences are plausible. For example, the influential work by Oliver and Hyde (1993), combining results from 177 studies, found a consistent pattern indicating that men report more frequent sex than women. This too would seem implausible, except for one thing: The difference was negligible among young people but became larger when older adults were surveyed.

The NHSL survey found the same thing: Among older people, women report having sex less often than do men (Laumann et al., 1994). Robinson and Godbey (1998) also concluded that the gender difference is substantially attributable to widows and other older women who have no sex partners and hence have no sex.

Thus, the broad average difference in frequency of sex seems to conceal an age effect. Plenty of older women are having very little sex, or none at all, but older men are much less likely to fall in this category. For example, by age fifty, 22 percent of women (one in five) report having had no sex at all for at least a year, whereas only 8 percent of men (one in twelve) say that they have not had sex in the past year.

This is plausible because this figure, unlike the lifetime sex difference tally, assesses current behavior. There are two reasons that older women may not have sex. One is that men die at younger ages than women. Men begin to die off in their forties, and in some groups, such as poor minorities, crime and violence take a disproportionate number at even younger ages. Across the United States, there are only 88 men per 100 women in the age range of 60–64, and past the age of 75 there are only 55 men per 100 women (Michael et al., 1994; based on the *Statistical Abstract of the United States*, 1992). Thus, among older people, there are two gals for every guy. Because there are fewer men to go around, many older women will be left without a sexual partner of their own age.

In theory it would be possible for women to find younger partners for sex, but this brings up the second reason older women may not have sex: Among couples who have sex, usually the man is older than the woman. Older men in particular may seek out much younger women as sexual partners, particularly if these men are interested in having children (since women become infertile much earlier than men), but even just on the basis of attraction to physical beauty. If a couple gets a divorce when both are in their fifties, the man will often find a younger woman for a sex partner, but the woman will not. If she looks for an older man, which is consistent with the standard mating pattern, she will find potential partners to be in very short supply because of the greater (i.e., earlier) mortality of men.

Thus some studies will find women having less sex than men, on average. The average for women will be brought down by the many older women who find themselves without a sex partner. In short, it is plausible that women report having less sex than men, especially among the elderly and other groups where women outnumber men. But it is not plausible that men have more total partners than women over a lifetime, as long as men and women are equally represented in the entire population (which they approximately are).

Let us therefore critically consider this consistently found but logically implausible discrepancy between men and women in terms of the number of sex partners. As it happens, researchers have not yet provided definitive proof about what explains it. But social psychology offers powerful clues about how it could arise from such factors as biased reporting and self-deception.

Unequal Populations

Men and women would have different tallies of sex partners if there were far more of one gender than of the other. Imagine an island, for example, on which there were fifty men and one hundred women. The men would average twice as many sex partners as the women. This would happen even if there were no divorce, no premarital sex, and no extramarital sex—or, at the opposite extreme, if everyone had sex with every possible member of the opposite gender.

To be sure, there have been times and places in which the genders were severely unequal in number. These will be the focus of Chapter 4. But the modern United States is not one of them. Slightly more males than females are born, and slightly more males than females die young, but these roughly cancel each other out. Females make up about 51 percent of the population, which is quite close to equal. The difference in number of sex partners thus cannot be explained on the basis of a surplus of women (except, as we noted, among the older segment of the population, in which women do start to outnumber men by significant numbers).

Homosexuality

Another way that men could honestly have more sex partners than women would be for them to have sex with other men. Each first-time sex act between two men boosts the average number of sex partners for men without affecting the average for women.

Could homosexuality explain the discrepancy between male and female reports of number of sex partners? Several factors speak against it. Certainly sex between males does occur, but sex between females occurs too, and lesbian sex would work against the discrepancy. To be sure, there is more male-male sex than female-female sex, but the male-male sex can only be counted toward the implausible discrepancy after it has offset the totality of female-female sex. It will contribute a small amount, but it is not enough to produce the entire discrepancy between men and women.

Moreover, the amount of homosexual sex going on appears to be rather small. Kinsey et al. (1948) estimated that 37 percent of his sample of men had had at least one homosexual experience and that one out of ten American men went for at least three years having sex exclusively with men. But those numbers are by now generally considered to be serious overestimates (see Laumann et al., 1994). Because Kinsey was not systematic about how he collected his data, and because he actively sought to interview homosexuals his results probably overrepresent homosexuals.

More recent and careful studies give much lower estimates. The NHLS survey (Laumann et al., 1994) found that only 9 percent of males had ever had a sexual experience with another male since puberty, only 5 percent had done it at least once since they turned eighteen, and that less than 3 percent considered themselves to be either homosexual or bisexual. (The Janus Report [Janus & Janus, 1993] found that 22 percent of men had ever had a homosexual experience. It found that 4 percent of men described themselves as homosexuals, which is actually the figure that Kinsey himself put forward; the Janus group found another 5 percent considered themselves bisexual. As suggested, however, the Janus figures are generally high because of their sampling methods.)

So, can homosexuality explain the discrepancy in sex partners? If homosexuality can account for the fact that the average man has had four more sex partners than the average woman, then the average man would have had sex with four other men. The actual number would have to be even higher in order to offset female homosexual activity. (The NHLS survey [Laumann et al., 1994] found, for example, that there were about half as many lesbians as gay males.) In other words, if the average woman has had one male and one female sex partner, then the average male can only have had one female partner, and so to reach a total of five partners he would have had to have sex with five males. This seems quite implausible, and the general frequency of homosexual activity found in recent studies is far less than that. The average man has certainly *not* had sex with five other men.

Before writing homosexuality off entirely, however, it is necessary to acknowledge that it does make some contribution to the discrepancy. The fact that there are twice as many gay males as gay females already means that men will end up with slightly more sex partners than women, on the average. Moreover, some gay males accumulate very large numbers of sex partners, and as we have seen, a few extreme values can affect a broad average.

Thus, homosexuality probably plays a small part in explaining the discrepancy in number of sex partners between men and women. It is not a sufficient explanation of the discrepancy, but it is a small contributing factor.

Uncounted Prostitutes

Undoubtedly the people who have had the highest tallies of heterosexual partners are prostitutes. Women who exchange sex for money on a regular basis often have multiple new sex partners every working night. At 10 men per night, 5 nights per week, 50 weeks a year, for 10 years, a woman could accumulate 25,000 sex partners. At 4 men per night, 4 nights per week, only 40 weeks per year, for 5 years, a woman would still have over 3,000. Even if repeat customers and slow nights reduce that figure by half, it is still far beyond what most other women could even imagine doing. A few prostitutes could certainly affect the average for many women.

Of course, the fact that prostitutes exchange sex for money does not change the mathematics of calculating sex partners. Ultimately men and women must have the same average number of opposite-gender sex partners, regardless of whether the sex is performed for love or money.

The implausible discrepancy could emerge in the data, however, if the researchers failed to include the prostitutes in their sample. This could occur for several reasons. Possibly some researchers would see their task as studying the average woman's sex life, and they thus would regard prostitutes as a special, unusual group who should not be included. Possibly prostitutes are harder to find than other people, especially since their profession is illegal (so they are reluctant to respond to surveys) and since they usually work evenings and nights (so they are unavailable when most surveys are being conducted). Perhaps some prostitutes take part in the surveys but are unable to give honest, correct answers. After all, most people probably lose count of the number of sex partners when they get to around twenty—so who would keep an accurate count when the number runs into the thousands?

In any case, failing to include the prostitutes (or even simply undercounting them) could conceivably boost the discrepancy between males and females in number of sex partners. Sex acts between men and prostitutes would show up in the male averages but not in the female ones.

For example, consider again our hypothetical island, and assume this time that there are a hundred men and a hundred women. Everybody has one premarital sexual relationship and then marries and remains faithful, so everyone has two main lifetime sex partners. Three of the women, however, each have sex with every single man on the island, once each, for money. Hence the men have all had five sex partners, and most of the women have had two each (except for the three prostitutes, who each have a hundred partners). If researchers start interviewing people about their sex lives, they might well settle on the five-and-two results, unless they happened to include the three prostitutes and get honest answers from them. If those three women are treated badly by the others and are forced to live in a separate, hidden, unattractive part of the island, the researchers might never come across them.

But can prostitution or indeed a handful of "hypersexual" women really explain the discrepancy? This was the focus of a study by Einon (1994). She concluded that the answer was no. First she analyzed national samples from Britain and France, which included prostitutes as well as women who had had sex with lots of men without being paid to do so. She did not find any signs that there are more women than men who claim to have had large numbers of sex partners. Then she calculated how many prostitutes would have to be active, with how many clients, in order to produce the difference in reported numbers of sex partners (assuming that all these prostitutes had not been included in the surveys), and these estimates went far beyond what the most liberal estimates of prostitution suggested. The numbers simply don't add up.

Likewise, Phillis and Gromko (1985) found that men reported more partners than women even in a setting where the researchers were careful to sample thoroughly. They found no evidence that prostitutes or a few highly promiscuous women contributed to the difference.

Thus, the idea that a handful of highly promiscuous women account for the higher numbers of sex partners reported by the average man appears to be false. The explanation based on prostitutes, who are omitted from sex surveys themselves but are counted as sex partners by their male clients, also does not seem to work. At least, it is not plausible as a full explanation for the discrepancy. Perhaps it makes a small contribution to the difference. As we said, truth is a big pie, and so part of the gender difference in promiscuity could be accounted for by prostitutes. But expert opinion and statistical calculation suggest that this is only a fairly small part. We must keep looking for the answer.

Social Desirability

Thus far we have concluded that two factors (homosexual activity and uncounted prostitution) may make a small contribution to the implausible gender discrepancy in number of sex partners, but even together they seem inadequate to explain it. Therefore let us turn to another class of explanation: Possibly people's reports are not to be taken at face value. Most sex may indeed involve one man and one woman, so that total sex partners are equal in reality, but people's reports are distorted.

Researchers have long known that answers to personal questions are subject to bias because of concerns over social desirability. That is, people want to present themselves as being good, and thus they may conceal or gloss over some undesirable facts about themselves. Certainly sex is an area in which social pressures and standards are strong, and so people might conceivably be subject to motivations to distort their answers.

In order for social desirability biases to account for the discrepancy between men and women in the number of sex partners, it is necessary to assume that these biases operate differently for men and women. Either one gender is more susceptible to social desirability bias than the other, or the biases push the two genders in opposite directions. The latter assumption is fully plausible: Regarding sex partners, many women may feel that fewer is better, while men may feel that more is better.

Hence men might exaggerate, while women might undercount. Social pressures have long urged women to limit their circle of sex partners, and indeed sexual chastity and (later) monogamous fidelity have generally been prominent among the virtues extolled by many cultures as ideals that women should strive for. For men, in contrast, the values of chastity and fidelity have been less strongly and less uniformly promoted, and to some extent they are often offset by a competitive prestige that accompanies having had a high number of sexual conquests. Many men admire the macho "stud" who has bedded several dozen women.

We shall return at several points in this book to consider the meaning of these gender differences in attitudes about having multiple sex partners. For now, it is sufficient to note that if the ideals differ, then men want to have more sex partners and women fewer, and their answers to survey questions could be biased by these motivations. This is, after all, consistent with the social exchange theory of sexuality we explained in Chapter 1. If sex is something that men get from women, then men should be proud of how much they have gotten, while women may be proud of how little they have given up.

On the negative side, however, it seems doubtful that large numbers of people would simply lie about their sex lives on a lengthy, important survey. In the NHSL survey, Laumann et al. (1994) included several checks to try to verify that people were telling the truth (such as asking the same question with different wording at widely different points in the interview), and they concluded that people were giving sincere, reliable, consistent answers—which does not quite guarantee truthfulness but comes close.

If people were sincere and consistent as opposed to untruthful, then the only way their answers were biased would be if their own beliefs were themselves biased. That is, maybe people gave what they thought were honest answers, but their own views and recollections were distorted by norms, expectations, and other motivating factors associated with gender roles. This brings up the possibility that people lie to themselves, a phenomenon known as *self-deception*. Social psychology has furnished several ideas about how that might happen.

Sorry, That Doesn't Count

The notion that wishful thinking can result in erroneous judgments is deeply embedded in folk wisdom. Psychoanalytic theory (based on the work of Sigmund Freud) proposed several ways in which thought processes could be distorted by motivations, such as repression and wish fulfillment. More recently, social psychologists have provided strong laboratory evidence for multiple ways that people can arrive at distorted, even false beliefs, and some of these could well apply to sex. Let us consider a couple of the key ones.

First, people often manipulate the criteria they use for making judgments, thereby helping themselves to get the answer they want. Dunning (1999) and his colleagues have shown ways that people use elastic criteria. For example, everyone wants to be a good parent or a good leader, but it is not entirely clear how these roles are defined, and so people can rely on criteria that suit them best. Generous people think that good leaders are generous; strict and stern leaders think that good leaders are strict and stern. In that way, most people can think they are above average and thus end up thinking well of themselves.

This process of manipulating the criteria could be crucially important with sex, because there are many borderline cases and gray areas. What qualifies someone as a sex partner? Undoubtedly one should count someone with whom one has repeatedly had genital intercourse with orgasm. But what if there was only one time, and no orgasm occurred, and the penetration was only momentary? What if only oral sex was involved? Does a handjob count? If so, is orgasm required? Does it matter if you performed the handjob (or oral sex) or received it? There are no definitive answers to these questions, and so people may prefer to interpret the borderline cases as they choose. That could well differ by gender: Men may count more of these situations than women.

Could biased counting explain the discrepancy between men and women? Clearly some sexual experiences are beyond misconstrual (although they could be forgotten), but it is possible that the average person has had a few experiences that could go either way. If these constituted the sole sexual contact with that particular partner, then men and women could well honestly arrive at different tallies despite having had similar actual experiences. If someone went to a party, got drunk, met an attractive person, began necking, partly undressed, had some contact with the person's genitals, and then stopped without going further, this might be an encounter that a man would remember and count as sex but a woman would not. A few such occurrences could contribute substantially to the discrepancy.

In 1999, President Bill Clinton was impeached for having lied under oath about his sexual relations with Monica Lewinsky, a young intern working with him at the White House. He insisted on national television (as well as under oath) that there had been no sexual relationship. Further questioning and evidence revealed, however, that on multiple occasions the two had had oral sex plus some other acts—but they agreed they had not actually had genital intercourse. Clinton was decried in some circles for trying to claim that oral sex did not count as sex. Clearly in his case, he did not want it to count, because having sex with a female subordinate would be regarded by many as inappropriate for the American president, not to mention the fact that he was married and adultery was illegal. Clinton's opponents insisted, however, that "everyone knew" that oral sex was sex.

A study published that same year indicated that people do in fact differ in how they count certain acts as sex. Sanders and Reinisch (1999) surveyed college students with a series of questions beginning, "Would you say you had 'had sex' if . . . ?" Although everyone agreed that vaginal intercourse was sex and that mere kissing was not, there were genuine differences of opinion with regard to the intermediate acts.

More to the point, men and women differed in how they rated these acts. In particular, significantly more men (44 percent) than women (37 percent) said they would regard performing oral sex as having sex, and likewise more men (44 percent) than women (38 percent) claimed that receiving oral sex counted as having sex. Although the difference is not huge, it may be sufficient to contribute to differences between men and women in how they count their sex partners. About 7 percent of the time, when a man and a woman engage in oral sex, he will count that as sex whereas she will not. Similar patterns are found with hand-to-genital encounters: Men are more likely than women to count them as meaning that they had sex.

Those differences could even snowball into a relatively large difference in the tally of sex partners, if some women use the "not sex" definition of oral sex as a justification for performing the act with a large number of partners. The movie *Clerks* presented a humorous rendition of this discrepancy. The main male character and his girlfriend were having a quiet discussion, and she asked him how many sex partners he had had. When he said a dozen, she slapped him and called him a pig, claiming that she had only had three partners. Later on, however, he asked her about oral sex, and she confessed to having performed fellatio on thirty-seven fellows—which to her had not counted as having sex. To him, however, oral sex had counted, and he was shocked to think of his girlfriend having had that much experience. He could not look upon any of the male acquaintances of his girlfriend without wondering. He was so stunned by her revelation that he blurted out to the next customer in the convenience store where he worked that his girlfriend had performed oral sex on thirty-seven guys, to which the startled customer replied, "Wow, in a row?"

Selective Forgetting

A second way that self-deceiving biases could alter the numbers is through selective forgetting. People are better at remembering ego-boosting experiences than unpleasant or degrading ones (see, e.g., Crary, 1966; Mischel, Ebbesen, & Zeiss, 1976). Things that reflect badly on the self are "conveniently" forgotten more often than things that flatter the self. We already noted that many men may regard each new sex partner as a conquest of which to be proud, and so men may want to remember every one. Women, in contrast, may prefer to forget some experiences, especially ones that are brief or that do not turn out well. A minor, mediocre sex act may offer the woman neither pleasure nor pride, and so it could be far more forgettable to her than to the man.

Some indirect evidence for this view was provided by Downey, Ryan, Roffman, and Kulich (1995) in an article called "How Could I Forget? Inaccurate Memories of Sexually Intimate Moments." They had people keep diaries of their sexual activities, which were collected by the researchers regularly. At the end of three months, people were asked to summarize their sexual activities during that period. These retrospective summaries contained a surprisingly high number of inaccuracies, especially considering that everyone was recording every sex act in the diaries. (Each time you think about something, it creates a new memory trace. So doing it once creates one trace and thus one chance of being remembered; doing it once and then writing it down creates two traces, and hence two chances of being remembered. This is why many students find that taking notes in class helps them remember the material, even without studying the notes.) It is necessary to assume that in everyday life, inaccuracies would be even larger, because people are not normally writing everything down.

Of particular interest to Downey et al. (1995) was the pattern for undesirable activities, such as having unprotected anal sex (which carries probably the highest risk of AIDS of any activity). These showed a strong tendency to be omitted from the three-month summaries. Clearly, people tended to selectively forget some the most foolish and ill-advised things they did.

Moreover, this forgetting went contrary to the pattern in the rest of the data. Downey et al. found that the three-month summaries tended to exaggerate the frequency of relatively rare events and to underestimate the frequency of highly common activities. In other words, retrospective summaries tended to drift from both extremes toward intermediate numbers. Yet the undesirable acts constituted a significant exception to this general pattern. The undesirable acts tended to be rare, and so the normal pattern would have been to remember more of them than had actually happened, but in fact people remembered fewer of them than had actually occurred. This suggests a pattern of motivated forgetting. When people *regret* some sex act, they gradually delete it from their memory.

These findings converge with more general patterns in social psychology. A study of biased memory by Stillwell and Baumeister (1997) found much more evidence of selective forgetting than of biased fabrication. Although there was some evidence of the fabrication, forgetting was more common. It is probably true that it is easier to distort by forgetting something that did happen than by coming to believe in something that did not happen.

This line of reasoning suggests that women are mainly responsible for the gender discrepancy: Men will accurately remember how many sex partners they had and will probably not make up sexual experiences that they did not have (at least not in their own genuine memories), but women may conveniently forget a couple experiences, especially ones that they regret. In other words, women may recall fewer sexual partners than men because women selectively forget the experiences they regret. Men have fewer regrets, so they do not erase them from their memories.

How Did You Get That Number?

Another line of reasoning, however, points the finger at men as being more responsible for the discrepancy. In fact, Wiederman (1997), who explicitly sought to ascertain whether men or women are more responsible for the discrepancy, concluded that men are the main culprits, not because they lie, but because they tend to base their answers on estimates that have rounded up the true number.

In his first study, Wiederman asked people to write down how many sex partners they had had. Then he asked them whether they had given a number that was not true. Some admitted that they had in fact given a wrong answer. He dropped these individuals from the sample and repeated the analyses, but the numbers did not change: Men still reported more sex partners than women. Dishonesty was apparently not responsible.

Next, he asked people to rate their certainty that the number of partners they gave was correct on a 10-point scale. Wiederman tried the novel approach of dropping everyone who gave an answer less than 10 (i.e., less than absolute, maximum certainty). When he did this, the average number of partners reported by the males dropped substantially. In other words, some men were completely sure their answers were correct, and these men reported fewer partners than the men who were not absolutely certain.

What about women? The difference between the absolutely certain and the not-so-certain rememberers was not significant for women. Moreover, the uncertain ones tended to give higher numbers of partners than the certain ones, which goes in the wrong direction for explaining the gender discrepancy.

Wiederman concluded that some men know exactly how many sex partners they have had, and that these men report relatively low numbers. Other men do not know exactly, and these men report higher numbers. He suggested that the gender gap is due to inflated estimates by these men.

A follow-up study confirmed the pattern of estimating. Wiederman noted that most men who reported more than 20 sex partners gave a round number (i.e., one that ended in 0 or 5). In fact everybody who reported more than 35 gave such a round number. For example, a man might claim to have had 50 sex partners, but no one claimed 49 or 48 or 51. These answers reflect the fact that the men do not really know exactly how many partners they have had and so they estimate the number; in the process they may give a generous estimate, because they want to think they had plenty of partners.

Wiederman also noted that the round numbers contradict the view that the men are simply lying. If they wanted to tell a lie to impress someone with how many sexual conquests they had had, they would probably make up a nonround number, such as 47, rather than something suspiciously round, such as 50.

Thus, the estimates were probably made in good faith, but they ended up inflating the numbers. Wiederman suggested that most people lose count of the exact number of sex partners they have had when the tally gets into the teens, and so after that it becomes necessary to estimate.

One might argue, though, that even this explanation is not fully satisfactory. If people have to estimate because they have had too many partners to count, and if men are more likely to be in this category, we are back to the initial problem: How can more men than women be in the category of having had too many to count? This might work, however, in combination with some of the other factors. If men count a few questionable cases (e.g., oral sex, or hand-to-genital contact), for example, this might boost their tallies to a point at which the exact number is difficult to know, and so they estimate, which inflates the number further.

The influence of estimation was examined in a systematic way by a team consisting of both a social and a cognitive psychologist (Brown & Sinclair, 1999; Sinclair & Brown, 1999). They asked people how many sex partners they had had and how they had arrived at that number. This method seemed very promising, although in many cases people gave the answer zero or one, and so the question "How did you get that number?" seemed foolish. Still, they did get some interesting findings among the minority who had higher numbers. (Specifically, they conducted separate analyses on the 10 percent of their sample who claimed to have had eight or more sex partners.) They found that women tended to rely on counting how many sex partners they could remember, whereas men tended to rely on estimating. As they noted, estimation tends to bias the result toward a higher number (because people round up), whereas counting tends to bias the result toward a lower number (because people forget some).

The use of different reporting strategies is especially revealing, because it indicates how men and women could really end up with discrepant numbers. Although Sinclair and Brown presented their findings in terms of cognitive strategies, there is ample room for motivation. After all, women might rather count than estimate because they prefer a strategy that yields a low number. Likewise, men might prefer to estimate rather than count because estimating will give them a higher number.

Implications for Social Exchange

In Chapter 1, we laid out one theoretical basis for analyzing sex as a social transaction: Women give sex to men. The distortions we have seen here could be linked to that basic pattern.

If women give sex, and by giving lose something of value, then logically they should desire to underestimate how much they have given. We noted that several theorists of social exchange insisted that social rewards have the highest value when they are rare. Each woman's sexual resource can be a precious gift, but if she gives it away too frequently, it loses its value. Hence she would want to maintain the view that she has given relatively little, and she will lean toward ways of calculating sex partners that yield relatively low numbers. She might also be quite willing to forget a few episodes and to dismiss others as not counting (e.g., by setting restrictive criteria for what counts as sex).

Men, meanwhile, may believe that they gain something of value by having sex, and so they would wish to believe they have gotten a great deal. They will lean toward ways of counting that yield relatively high numbers, which will make them feel successful in the sphere of sexual transactions.

In terms of actual interactions, men may often find themselves trying to persuade reluctant women to do sexual things. These will include cases in which the man really wants sex and the woman does not, so he tries to persuade or influence her. Afterward, she may regret the episode, whereas he might be proud. As we have seen, people tend to forget sexual events that they regret, so women may particularly delete some of these persuasive episodes from their memories. Men, in contrast, may tend to inflate and exaggerate the same episodes.

Conclusion

Social psychology has inherited its notions of causality from the physical sciences and medicine, and these conform to the simple model of "*A* causes *B*." Many psychologists are, however, coming to recognize the pervasiveness of *multicausality*—that is, the fact that many phenomena are the result of multiple, combined causal processes. The difference in the tallies of sex partners reported by men and women is probably multiply determined.

The purpose of this section has been to demonstrate the need to evaluate sexual statistics critically. Many studies generate numbers, and it is easy for a reader to take them at face value. The critical approach here benefited from the fact that the available numbers are logically implausible: Men cannot have more heterosexual sex partners than women have, yet nearly every study finds that they do report more.

The implausible discrepancy suggests a need to consider what else (other than the raw truth) goes into the answers that people give to sexual questions. Probably there are several factors that contribute to the durable finding that men have more partners than women. Some of these are methodological, such as the notion that some men have sex with prostitutes and that the prostitutes are often not included in the sex survey. Moreover, most surveys have not limited the tallies to heterosexual sex, and so the male average may be inflated by the well-established pattern that gay males have more sex partners than gay females. Age may also contribute, and the gender gap is sometimes found to be much bigger among older people, among whom the unequal sex ratio guarantees that more women than men will have no current sex partner.

Still, the greater part of the difference is probably due to biased counting by individuals. As we have seen, more men than women want a multitude of sex partners.

These opposing wishes may cause men and women to use different methods (without really lying) for coming up with their answer as to how many people they have slept with. Men and women may differ as to whether borderline sex acts, such as oral intercourse, count as sex. When the exact answer is not immediately known, men and women may follow different mental procedures for giving an approximate answer. Men tend to estimate, which typically yields a relatively high number, whereas women tend to count, which yields a relatively low number. By manipulating the criteria and the cognitive strategy for generating it, individual men and women can reach answers that drift toward the answers they prefer and desire—thereby causing the male and female averages to drift apart.

CHAPTER

3

Sex, Self-Esteem, and Self-Awareness

From Conquests to Spanking

Long before the sexual revolution and the women's movement, men regarded sex as a conquest. Back then it was hard to persuade women to have sex, and indeed in many circles it was assumed that most decent girls wanted to remain virgins until their weddings, or at least until they became engaged. For a man to have sex was thus a credit to his powers and a reflection of his prowess: It showed that a woman was willing to abandon her normal reserve and caution in order to experience sex with him. Men bragged about these rare conquests with each other, and some adopted illicit techniques (such as getting a date drunk) in order to have sex with her and boost his tally. The man's number of sex partners was seen as a sign of his manhood: The more the better, just like with salary.

One might assume that those attitudes reflect an obsolete stereotype and certainly nothing that would be found among today's young men, who have been raised (often by a single mother rather than a father-dominated, patriarchal household) to respect women and see sex in a totally different light. But that assumption is probably why contrary evidence gets publicity. Such a story (Faludi, 1993) erupted on the national scene in 1993, when it emerged that one group of young men had not only persisted in such exploitative and egotistical attitudes toward sex but had even formalized the male competition with a point system. This group took the name the "Spur Posse." The "Spur" part came from the San Antonio Spurs, since some of the boys were sports fans. The "Posse" part was of course one term for a gang, but in fact was probably chosen for its resemblance to the sexual goal of the group.

The group came to public attention when the police arrested nine of the young men, ranging in age from fifteen to nineteen, on suspicion of various sex crimes. After further investigation, the charges were almost all dropped, because the sex acts were apparently consensual. But the young men reveled in the attention they received.

Their competition reportedly awarded each member one point for every woman or girl he had sex with. Scores varied, but the four-year winner had amassed a total of sixty-seven points—supposedly meaning that he had had sixty-seven sex partners. This young man, named Billy Shehan, was not one of those who had been arrested, but he became the media darling. Several talk shows invited him to New York, all expenses paid. "Here I was in this limo in this giant-ass city, and it was like I owned the taxis and the cars, I owned the buildings and all the girls in the windows in the buildings. I felt like I could do whatever I wanted," he said on his arrival. He gloried in the attention. When a mugger took his wallet one night, he demanded that the *Maury Povich Show* reimburse him, and when Povich's group declined, he responded by refusing to appear on their program. On another show he boasted that he had gotten his sixty-seventh point on that very trip, seducing a New York woman in his hotel room. Later, though, he admitted he had not succeeded in having sex with that woman. He said, however, that the talk show producers had urged him to claim that he had scored that very night. He felt bad about the lie, which amounted to cheating, and he even composed a song: "Everyone thought I was a sixty-seven, when I was just a sixty-six."

For such young men, sex was clearly not a way to express their love for a special young woman but an ego trip. The competition among the men was simply a codification of the view that having sex with a woman was a way of establishing the value of the self—and of showing oneself to be better than other young men. Some men use the slang term "scoring" to refer to having sex with a new partner, and the Spur Posse were merely a bit more systematic about keeping score and comparing degrees of success. The young men based their self-esteem on how often they made sexual conquests, in comparison with each other. That the national media would publicize the winners in their competition seemed only fair to them. "I felt they owed me something," said Shehan about his insistence that the Povich show cover his expenses even to the point of reimbursing him for the mugging.

The nature of the self, along with strivings for self-esteem, have been studied extensively by social psychologists. Their findings have a variety of implications for sexuality. This chapter will examine a series of them.

Self-Esteem and Sex

The topic of self-esteem has been of central concern in American society in recent decades. Part of this comes from the self-esteem movement, a collection of efforts by various groups and individuals to elevate self-esteem, based on the assumption that high self-esteem will produce many benefits and advantages. The higher a person's self-esteem, the better adjusted that person is assumed to be. Self-esteem guru Nathaniel Branden (1994) asserted that "self-esteem has profound consequences for every aspect of our existence" (p. 5). The Internet site "self-esteem.com" tells all visitors that low self-esteem is "society's most devastating emotional virus."

One high point of the self-esteem movement was the formation of an official state task force in California that embraced the mission of boosting self-esteem. The task force asserted that "lack of self-esteem is central to most personal and social ills plaguing our state and nation" (California Task Force, 1990, p. 4). If self-esteem could be raised throughout the state, it was hoped, its social problems would go down, and citizens would live happier, healthier lives. The state would thrive and flourish not only because the costly social problems of crime and addiction would be reduced, but also because people with high self-esteem would earn higher salaries and hence generate more tax revenues. Self-esteem would help balance the state's budget, as Assemblyman John Vasconcellos asserted: "People with self-esteem produce income and pay taxes. Those without [self-esteem] tend to be users of taxes" (quoted in Winegar, 1990).

At the same time that the task force's initial manifesto was issued, however, an edited book was published in which California professors reviewed various research on the possible links between self-esteem and major social problems (Mecca, Smelser, & Vasconcellos, 1990). Despite the pressure to form positive conclusions, the evidence suggested that self-esteem had only small and erratic relationships to these problems. The self-esteem movement did not have a solid research justification.

Still, there is little doubt that high self-esteem feels good and is associated with more benefits than drawbacks. Does self-esteem have any relevance to sex? A survey of the research literature yields mixed results.

Self-Esteem and Sexual Practices

People with high self-esteem have more sex. A smattering of studies has yielded a variety of correlations between self-esteem and various sexual behaviors. The correlations are mostly positive. Young people with high self-esteem are more likely to have safe sex, that is, more likely to use condoms (Hollar & Snizek, 1996). Then again, they are also more likely to have unsafe sex (Hollar & Snizek, 1996). Underlying both of these findings is the fact that they may be having more sex in general (Strouse & Buerkel-Rothfuss, 1987), which means that having more safe sex may simply be a result of having more sex.

People with high self-esteem may be more likely than others to have abortions (Plotnick, 1992), too, which casts doubt on the safe-sex point and favors the conclusion that people with high self-esteem just have more sex. After all, if you're using more condoms, you should have fewer unwanted pregnancies and hence fewer, not more abortions. But if high self-esteem simply equals more sex, then there would be all the consequences of increased sex, including more condoms *and* more abortions.

Still, why do people with high self-esteem have more sex? With correlational data, it is important to be careful about drawing causal conclusions. In principle, the arrow can point in either direction. High self-esteem might perhaps lead people to have more sex because they are more confident or feel more entitled to do what they want. On the other hand, having more sex might lead to higher self-esteem, especially if having sex is a point of pride or an ego boost. (Clearly the Spur Posse were getting their high self-esteem from sexual conquests, although some modicum of high self-esteem probably was necessary to enable them to get started.) And there is also the possibility that some third variable causes both the high self-esteem and the increased sexual behavior.

Another aspect of self-esteem is self-acceptance. This can be studied by examining the role of self-esteem in connection with homosexuality. In a study of bisexual men, those who had higher self-esteem were more likely to shift toward a full homosexual identification than men with lower self-esteem (Stokes, Damon, &McKirnan, 1997). These data point to the fact of self-acceptance that seems central to self-esteem. If you like yourself in general, you are more willing to accept your own sexual orientation, whatever it may be (especially among males; see Savin-Williams, 1989). Some gay movements have used the slogan "We're here, we're queer, get used to it," which clearly implies and indeed *asserts* self-acceptance! Although many bisexual individuals may be bisexual because they simply like to have sex with both males and females, bisexuals may often be people who are trying to decide what their true and proper sexual orientation is. Self-esteem helps them be comfortable with a gay identity.

On the other hand, accepting oneself as gay is not necessarily the same as being accepted by others. Many gay people suffer victimization by bigots and others who dislike homosexuality. Not surprisingly, one's self-esteem tends to drop if one is victimized for being gay (Waldo, Hesson-McInnis, & D'Augelli, 1998). This shows how social approval or disapproval can influence self-esteem, a topic to which we now turn.

The Sociometer

An important theory about self-esteem has been put forward by Leary and his colleagues (Leary, Tambor, Terdal, & Downs, 1995). This theory started with the point that self-esteem actually has not been shown to have very many positive benefits in terms of making people healthier, richer, or more successful. Yet people are very concerned about their self-esteem. Since it seems implausible that people would be so concerned about something that matters so little, self-esteem must be linked to some powerful need that does have strong benefits.

A leading candidate for such a motivation is the need to belong. Pretty much all human beings are strongly motivated to form and maintain close, communal relationships with at least a handful of other people (Baumeister & Leary, 1995). Throughout our evolutionary history, being alone in the world was associated with lower survival and lower reproduction, and so natural selection would favor people who remained together in groups. Even today, across the entire population at large, people who have a handful of strong social connections are happier in life and physically healthier than people who are largely alone in the world (e.g., Baumeister, 1991b; Campbell, 1981; Myers, 1992).

Self-esteem, in this view, is your own measure of how well suited you are to attract and maintain some close relationships. Low self-esteem essentially means "no one will want to hire me, date me, or be my friend." Consistent with that view, Leary et al. (1996) showed that experiences of social rejection tend to reduce self-esteem. And, conversely, experiences of social acceptance boost and strengthen self-esteem.

Leary has coined the term *sociometer* to capture the central idea of his theory: that self-esteem is a meter that keeps track of social success and failure (and eligibility for more of the same). Self-esteem is not important in and of itself; rather, it is a meter that keeps track of something very important.

Applied to sex, sociometer theory suggests that popular kids will tend to have high self-esteem, because popularity carries the reassuring message that everyone likes you and wants to be associated with you. Popularity is also likely to lead to relatively higher amounts of dating and romance. This can explain several of the findings about sex without assuming that self-esteem is itself either a cause or an effect of sex. It is hardly surprising that the people who have more dates and more romantic relationships are more likely to have sex—including both safe sex and unsafe sex. More condoms, more abortions.

Other hidden variables that may produce misleading correlations with self-esteem are anxiety and inhibition. For example, among women, there is a significant correlation between having self-esteem and performing fellatio, such that women with high self-esteem perform more oral sex (Herold & Way, 1983). It seems doubtful on an a priori basis that performing fellatio causes a typical woman's self-esteem to increase by a significant amount, but neither does it seem very likely that having high self-esteem causes a woman to start performing fellatio.

Yet high self-esteem is linked to lower anxiety and fewer inhibitions (e.g., Leary & Kowalski, 1995). Probably there is a group of women who have high levels of anxiety and inhibition about both life in general and sex in particular. These feelings cause the women to have low self-esteem and make them less willing to engage in certain sexual practices.

The link between self-esteem and masturbation may also be relevant. Some studies find that they are unrelated, while others find a small correlation. For example, Hurlbert and Whittaker (1991) found that women who masturbated had higher self-esteem than those who did not. Again, we doubt that masturbation causes high self-esteem. Possibly self-esteem causes masturbation, as if loving yourself makes you want to have sex with yourself, but we doubt that most people perceive masturbation as a highly expressive act of love to oneself. People don't express gratitude and appreciation to themselves by bringing themselves flowers the day after masturbating, for instance. Instead, it seems most plausible that high inhibitions and anxieties lead to low self-esteem and low masturbation in some people, thereby generating that correlation. The small size of the correlation is also consistent with the view that it is not a direct effect but rather mediated by something else.

The Conquest Mentality

One implication of the sociometer theory for sex is that people might get a self-esteem boost from sex. If someone has sex with you, that is one sign that you are desirable as a sex partner. Just as sexual rejection can involve a blow to self-esteem, sexual acceptance could carry a very positive message.

The two genders are likely to differ on this. In Chapter 1, we outlined the basic assumption of a social exchange theory of sex, namely, that women give sex to men. Sex is therefore likely to yield a bigger and more reliable ego boost to men than to women. Egotistical competitions (such as that of the Spur Posse) are likely to be more common among men than women. Women may even lose esteem by certain sexual episodes.

The data support these views. Strouse and Buerkel-Rothfuss (1987) and Walsh (1991) found that self-esteem was positively correlated with number of sex partners for both men and women—in other words, the more people you've slept with, the higher your self-esteem—but that the effect was stronger for men than women. Newcomb (1985) found a significant positive correlation for men, but a nonsignificant and negative correlation (i.e., higher self-esteem went with having had fewer sex partners) for women. A larger subsequent investigation by the same researcher (Newcomb, 1986) found that higher self-esteem was linked to having had more sex partners in both younger and older men, with the difference greater among older men past the age of thirty. For women, meanwhile, the young women showed no significant correlation at all, and past the age of thirty there was a weak negative relationship, indicating again that lower self-esteem went with having had more partners. For women later in life, having shared your bed with a relatively large number of men is not associated with high self-esteem but rather with lower self-esteem, although the total effect is not large, which suggests that other predictors of self-esteem should be mainly considered.

Why the difference? Simply finding someone to have sex with is a much more impressive accomplishment for the average man than for the average women, because of differences in availability of partners. A woman can find someone to sleep with simply by inviting a relative stranger or someone she has just met, but this strategy does not work for heterosexual men (Clark & Hatfield, 1989). In other words, for the average women finding someone willing to have sex with is not much more of an accomplishment than finding someone willing to give directions to a restaurant. (And, sad to say, probably many women would prefer the restaurant.) For men, however, there is a vast difference, and each new sex partner may be regarded as a rare and precious accomplishment.

Men could, of course, use prostitutes. Yet most men do not consider prostitutes a viable option for various reasons, including fear of crime and disease. We also suspect that having sex with a prostitute would not boost a man's self-esteem, simply because it is relatively easy to do (assuming you have the money) and therefore not an accomplishment. Having sex with a hooker probably does not constitute a genuine conquest for those men who keep score.

Because of this difference, having sex is not much for a woman to be proud of, whereas it is for a man. If a man succeeds in having sex with a new partner, he may feel his self-esteem rise, because he has in a sense beaten the odds. Hence many men may approach sex with a "conquest" mentality. Each new sex partner increases the tally and enables at least some men to feel pride. Men may compete among themselves, implicitly or even explicitly, to score with as many women as possible. The very term *to score* reflects the conquest mentality, because it treats making love with a woman as a competitive achievement and as a basis for pride. A man who has bedded several dozen women is likely to be respected and envied by at least some other men. No wonder the leader of the Spur Posse felt that appearing on national television and having his expenses covered was his due! Meanwhile, a man who has remained a virgin untill age thirty, or who has had no more than two sex partners in his life, may be pitied in some male circles.

These attitudes may well be deplored because they cheapen sexual intimacy, reduce women to the status of sex objects, and promote casual promiscuity that can foster disease and other social problems. But it is hard to deny that many men feel those attitudes. Quite probably these views were even stronger prior to the sexual revolution, when most men had very few opportunities to have more than a small number of sex partners.

For a woman, there is much less reason to feel proud about accumulating multiple sex partners. As we saw, some findings even indicate that a woman may lose self-esteem if she has had many partners. Traditional values have emphasized that a woman's virtue and good reputation depended on sexual purity. Although the modern sexual revolution may have changed attitudes and reduced or eliminated the double standard (e.g.,

Sprecher, 1989), these views may persist to some degree. Certainly it still seems unlikely that a woman would boast about having had twenty sex partners, whereas a man might. Such a tally does not really demonstrate anything very positive about her, because many men will copulate with seemingly almost any willing partner.

These attitudes may well be based in biological patterns favored by evolution. In an evolutionary perspective, the most successful males had sex with many women, and as a result male sexual desire may well incline toward promiscuity and brief sexual liaisons. The man who boasts about multiple conquests may simply be proud that he has been able to do what he believes nature shaped him to do. (He might still deserve to boast, nonetheless, because other men with similar desires are unable to carry them out.) The alpha male had sex with every female in the tribe, which reflected and rewarded his superiority, as well as producing many children to carry his genes into the next generation. Women, meanwhile, did not gain any biological advantage from having multiple partners and may even have paid a price for doing so. One good regular partner was better for her, if only because it meant ongoing support.

Women, however, did benefit from having high-quality partners, as both evolutionary and social construction analyses of sex have emphasized. Having sex with the king was better than having sex with a peasant, partly because the king could better provide for the woman and her offspring. Being the king's wife was better yet, because he would almost surely be a good provider.

The social exchange theory of sex might also apply. One key point of this theory is that a person's approval rises or falls in value depending on how frequently it is given. Someone who praises everybody cannot confer a really strong value by his or her praise. In contrast, someone who hardly ever says a kind word to anyone can make a huge impact with one compliment because it is so unusual.

Applied to sex, this suggests that a woman should maximize the value of having sex with her by giving it out only in small doses or only to a few partners. She shouldn't be totally abstinent or celibate, because then she never gets to benefit from the high value she can confer. Staying a virgin forever amasses great power that is never used. But if a woman has only a few men, then each should be highly appreciative, because having sex with her is quite special. If she's had the whole football team, on the other hand, her favors (although still appreciated, no doubt) do not constitute a great honor for each new gentleman caller.

In any case, the sexual sociometer is likely to operate somewhat differently for women than for men. For men, simply finding sex partners may be enough to provide an ego boost. For women, any possible ego boost that might come from finding a new sex partner would depend on who he is, and accumulating too many partners may even have a negative rather than a positive effect on her self-esteem.

The Social Role of Attention

Attention paid by others might conceivably be a prominent way of estimating a man's value as an esteem-boosting sex partner, although we cannot find much in the way of relevant data on this hypothesis, which remains entirely impressionistic and speculative. Derber (1979) has written an important analysis of the *social* nature of attention, including the rules and implications of who pays attention to whom. Attention is often a powerful sign of a person's importance. When everyone pays attention to a certain man, it is usually a sign that he is powerful or successful. The attention he pays to a woman gains or loses value by how much attention everyone else pays to him.

The "groupie" mentality might begin to make sense in this context. Objectively speaking, musicians seem like poor choices for mates: They have unstable careers, take drugs, think they are creative geniuses almost like gods, sweat a very great deal, and are often immature or weird in other ways. But they do have high status, as may seem particularly vivid when they are on stage and everyone is looking at them. Performers are the centers of attention, and so when they themselves focus their attention on a woman, she may be thrilled.

The notorious groupie Pamela Des Barres (1987) described one of her early affairs with a musician. He was married, so she could not have much of a relationship with him, and he rarely even spoke to her, but he did like to have her perform fellatio on him backstage before each concert. This small act filled her with gratitude: "And I still felt like he was doing me a favor," she remembered later (p. 45).

According to the social exchange theory, the man is not normally doing the woman a favor by allowing her to perform fellatio on him. But given this performer's high status as the concert's center of attention, his attention to her became imbued with high value, and so she did end up feeling that she was getting the benefit.

A colleague of ours once briefly dated the coach of a professional basketball team. She described one incident that vividly captured the powerful role of attention for the sexual sociometer. She went with the coach and some of his friends to a nightclub. They sat to the side and had drinks. When the disc jockey put on some music she liked, she took the coach by the hand and led him to the dance floor, and they began to dance. After a few minutes, however, a large spotlight came down on them, and the public address system announced to all patrons that the club was honored to have the coach as a guest. Everyone applauded, but the coach made no response and kept dancing. Yet the experience was a vividly remembered moment of pleasure for the woman. As she described it, it was extremely exciting to think that "everybody in the place was looking at him, and he was looking at me." His attention to her seemingly gained in sexual power because of all the attention that everyone else paid to him.

Self-Esteem and Sex Appeal

On Australia's beaches, it is acceptable for women to sunbathe topless, although naturally not all women take advantage of this legal permission. One team of researchers gave questionnaires to a broad sample of sunbathers and found that women with high self-esteem were more likely to go topless than women with low self-esteem (Herold, Corbesi, & Collins, 1994). Self-esteem produces bare boobs, as it were.

This finding is most plausibly explained by putting self-esteem in the causal role: Having high self-esteem makes women more willing to display their breasts in public. In theory, the correlation could be explained by the opposite direction of causal influence, but that would mean that sunbathing topless causes a woman's self-esteem to rise, which seems unlikely. If it were that easy to raise self-esteem, clinical psychologists by now would probably be using a therapy in which women achieve higher self-esteem by baring their breasts in public. This technique would no doubt be very popular all around if it really succeeded at boosting women's self-esteem. But don't bet on it.

Men, too, undoubtedly have some links between self-esteem and body image, especially where the penis is concerned. According to anecdote, Sigmund Freud was once accosted at a social gathering by an argumentative student who said, "Isn't it true, Dr. Freud, that the way a man feels about himself depends on the size of his penis?" As was typical, Freud took a puff on his cigar to give himself a moment to reflect before answering. Then he said, "I would prefer to think that the size of the penis depends on the way a man feels about himself!" (Reuben, 1969, p. 25). Regardless of which of the two was correct, the issue they debated was whether self-esteem was cause or effect, and this issue remains troublesome even today.

This raises the broader issue of how self-esteem is linked to sex appeal. Harter (1993), a developmental psychologist and an authority on self-esteem in children, noted that across many of her studies there was a consistent strong and positive relationship between physical attractiveness and self-esteem. In fact, the relationship is so strong—the correlation was .85 out of a maximum possible value of 1.00—that it leaves very little room for any other influence. Still, this conclusion fits well with sociometer theory: Because people want to associate with attractive people, the most attractive are likely to end up with high self-esteem. The only refinement that sociometer theory needs is to suggest that, at least among children and adolescents, physical attractiveness is almost the only key to the sociometer, and hardly anything else matters. Physical beauty leads to social acceptance, which in turn produces high self-esteem. Period.

There is, however, one question surrounding Harter's conclusion. Her studies relied on asking people how attractive they were. This is, after all, a standard method, and certainly such self-reports are almost the only way to measure self-esteem. But it was just possible that people with high self-esteem merely overestimated how attractive they were, thereby inflating that correlation. High self-esteem means thinking you're great, after all, and that could indicate a slightly conceited outlook. Maybe high self-esteem doesn't go with actually being gorgeous—only with *thinking* that you're gorgeous.

There are ample precedents for this. Our own research has included dozens of studies of self-esteem and task performance. We have consistently found that people with high self-esteem perform no better than people with low self-esteem. But they *think* they perform better. In terms of task performance, the superiority of people with high self-esteem exists mainly (but quite strongly) in their own minds. Could it be the same with physical attractiveness?

Given that concern, other researchers have tried a more methodologically difficult approach, which is to have a panel of supposedly objective judges rate the physical attractiveness of various people (either in person or in pictures), and then match those ratings with self-esteem. When this is done, the correlation between self-esteem and physical attractiveness dwindles dramatically, and in some studies ceases even to be significant (e.g., B. Major, personal communication, 1999).

Even on issues such as weight, the crucial issue is self-perception, not reality. Miller and Downey (1999) reviewed many studies on the relationship between body weight and self-esteem. Among white women (and to a lesser extent in other groups), *believing* oneself to be heavy was associated with lower self-esteem, and the effect was fairly large. The link between actual weight and self-esteem, however, was small. It was not how fat the woman actually was, but how fat she thought she was, that determined her self-esteem.

Thus, people with high self-esteem aren't necessarily any more attractive than other people: They merely *think* they are more attractive. High self-esteem, after all, means taking a generally favorable attitude toward yourself, and so it is not surprising that this carries over into beliefs about your good looks.

And this conclusion fits well with the topless sunbathing point. After all, whether you display your breasts on a public beach is probably not determined directly by how attractive your breasts actually are, in an objective sense. Instead, it depends on how good you think they are. High self-esteem women probably have a more positive view of their bodies in general, and so they ought to be more willing to display them. Low self-esteem women might in fact look equally good, but they would probably be disinclined to think so, and therefore they would not take the chance.

Who is correct? It is generally believed that women underestimate their physical attractiveness. Men tend to be fairly comfortable with their physical attractiveness, but women are frequently dissatisfied with their bodies. They often believe they are too fat or otherwise deviate from ideal proportions. This probably contributes to a gap in self-esteem between the two genders. A recent meta-analysis (Kling, Hyde, Showers, & Buswell, 1999) found a consistent but small difference in self-esteem between men and women, with men generally having higher (but only very slightly) self-esteem than women. We would speculate that the difference in body image may account for this entire gap. Women do not think they are less intelligent, or competent, or socially skilled than men. They do, however, think their bodies are less than ideal. In particular, many women think they are too fat, or at least not thin enough.

Although thinness is the main focus of women's negative body image, the dissatisfaction with one's physical self does pertain more explicitly to sexual attributes as well. Reinholtz and Muehlenhard (1995) compared men's and women's feelings about their sex organs. Although both men and women were moderately positive, men were more positive than women. That is, men had more positive feelings about their penises than women had about their vaginas. Lest this be taken as some sign of inherent superiority of the penis over the vagina, it must be added that men also rated their partners' genitals more positively than women rated their partners'. In other words, men liked their girlfriends' vaginas more than women liked their boyfriends' penises. Men just generally hold somewhat more positive attitudes about all sex organs.[1]

This is consistent with the view that women have lower self-esteem regarding physical attributes. As research has shown, people with low self-esteem are critical not just of themselves but of other people as well (see Baumeister, 1993; Brown, 1986;

---

[1]Perhaps not other men's penises; no evidence was included on that question.

Crocker & Schwartz, 1985). Low self-esteem often reflects a generally negative attitude toward others as well as the self. Women are critical of their own bodies and of other people's bodies, whereas men have a more positive attitude toward both.

The Thinness Craze

Thus, women are critical of their bodies, and in particular they tend to think they are not thin enough. An important reason for this is the images of women displayed in the mass media, although this too is not an independent cause and probably reflects public appetites. Models, movie stars, and beauty queens tend to be extremely thin, and most women cannot conform to those images. The trend in recent decades has been an increasing emphasis on thinness. Several important studies have tracked Miss America contestants (and winners) and *Playboy* centerfolds from the 1950s through the 1990s (Garner, Garfinkel, Schwartz, & Thompson, 1980; Spitzer, Henderson, & Zivian, 1999; Wiseman, Gray, Mosimann, & Ahrens, 1992). The shift toward thinness was reflected in the measurements of all the women in both venues. The average measurements of Miss America contestants and *Playboy* centerfolds became progressively thinner over the years. Moreover, during the 1950s the Miss American winner typically had body measurements that were about average among the fifty state champions who competed for the crown, but by the 1970s the winner was typically among the thinnest of the contestants—a sign that being thin counted for more even among the nation's most beautiful women.

The concern with thinness has an even darker side. Eating disorders have been on the rise during this period, as more and more women try to starve themselves into conformity with the ever receding ideals of thinness. As the media hold up ever higher standards of thin female bodies, women find it harder and harder to meet those standards, and their efforts to do so lead to incessant dieting and an epidemic of anorexia and bulimia.

Some feminists have protested that the obsession with thinness is caused by men. In this view, men want women to be thin, perhaps just because men happen to find thinness sexy, or possibly because thin, hungry women can be dominated more easily than other women. African American women, for example, have not generally embraced the idea that they should want to be thin, and they are often quite assertive as well as relatively free from the widespread mild depression that afflicts white women. Seligman (1994) believes that the female depression rates are linked to the thinness craze and the general result that women are chronically underfed.

But are men to blame? In reality, many men find a slightly fuller figure attractive. Marilyn Monroe was regarded as one of the sexiest movie stars ever, and men still admire her pictures, but most modern women would consider themselves horribly fat if they looked like Monroe.

Meanwhile, many men actually prefer plump and sometimes even fat women. The Amsterdam Sex Museum (1999) noted that pornography featuring plump and fat women has been on the rise throughout the world for several decades, presumably reflecting a large minority of men who like to look at nonthin women.

An even more relevant study was done by Fallon and Rozin (1985). Women were asked how thin they would like to be and how thin their boyfriends wanted them to be. The researchers then also asked the boyfriends how thin they wanted their girlfriends to be. The results showed a dramatic progression. The boyfriends' preferences were the least thin. The women believed their boyfriends wanted them to be thinner than the boyfriends actually wanted, and the women wanted to be even thinner than they believed their boyfriends wanted. Thus, the female concern with thinness went far beyond what the men actually wanted and somewhat farther than even they believed the men wanted. Men are apparently not to blame.

Are the media to blame? Undoubtedly the media play an important role in furnishing images of female beauty to the public. Yet the power of the media is often overstated, and we are skeptical of attempts to identify it as a sole cause. The media give the public what they want. When the ultrathin model Twiggy appeared on the scene in the 1960s, she was quickly embraced as an appealing icon by many—a sign that there was a predisposed readiness to endorse a very thin model of female beauty. In contrast, when the heavy comedian Roseanne came to national prominence in the 1980s, there was not corresponding rush among women to gain weight. If the media alone could manipulate appetites, it would be a simple matter to end the epidemic of eating disorders by simply putting plump women on television all the time. But we doubt it would really work. The media do not have that much power.

We favor an explanation that is, at present, rather speculative and in need of further research, which is that the thinness craze reflects an excess of female egotism and competitiveness, not unlike some of the destructive competitiveness that the male ego has been known to cause. Both genders compete to be attractive to the opposite sex. For men, as we have seen, status is an important component of attractiveness, and so men battle each other for dominance and high status. In the extreme, men become workaholics or vicious competitors, seeking to outdo other men by any means possible. They may not always be able to explain why they are so insistent on outdoing other men, and some can even recognize that their drives produce irrational, excessive behavior. But probably underlying much of that behavior is the belief that if a man reaches the top, he will be appealing to women. Both nature and culture have prepared him to believe that.

Status and dominance don't work in the same way for women. If anything, high-status women have a relatively harder time finding suitable mates (although, in some societies, a female's high status may increase the survival of any offspring she might have). Competitive striving for dominance is therefore irrelevant to the female competition for mates. Instead, what matters most is physical attractiveness.

Yet there is something cruelly unfair about this, even if it is instilled by nature. Women cannot really control their physical attractiveness in many respects. Certainly women cannot control their beauty as much as men can control their status in today's open and socially mobile societies.

But thinness does give women something that seems, at least, to be controllable. A woman may be able to outdo other women by dieting more assiduously and becoming thinner. Plump women know they are plump and, by implication, feel inferior (at least in attractiveness) to other, thinner women.

Hence the anorexic may resemble the workaholic: Each has gone to an irrational, possibly destructive extreme in what would otherwise be a normal quest for superiority. The motivation started with a valid basis in mate competition criteria, but probably it began to lose touch with actual mate competition. (We doubt that either workaholics or anorexics actually go out on many dates!) The competitive striving for thinness (or work success) became an end in itself, tied to the inner quest for self-esteem. The anorexic may feel superior to other women insofar as she practices greater self-control and self-denial, and achieves a greater loss of weight, than the others. By eating less and becoming thinner, she becomes the winner of the implicit competition she perceives among women.

This view is not proven, as we said. It does, however, fit our general belief that men and women are more similar than different. Men and women both want to compete successfully to attract desirable mates, and their own feelings about themselves may be shaped by these considerations. Men's and women's strivings may take different forms, as do their destructive excesses, but the underlying motives may be quite similar.

Self-Esteem and Not Having Sex

Probably there are some areas of sex in which self-esteem does play a causal role. After all, self-esteem gives you confidence that you can succeed and a sense of entitlement that encourages pursuit of what you want. This might lead people to perform certain acts.

One of the best-established effects of self-esteem is that people low in self-esteem tend to be more vulnerable to external influence. Brockner (1984) reviewed a broad variety of studies and concluded that people with low self-esteem are more susceptible to advice, persuasion, and other forms of influence.

In sex, susceptibility to influence could lead to being talked into doing things that one does not want to do. This may be particularly an issue for women, insofar as men often try to persuade women to have sex. Does high self-esteem enable women to resist such influences?

There is some evidence that the answer is yes. Although (as we saw) high self-esteem among women is linked to performing more fellatio and having more sex in general, that does not necessarily signify that those acts went against the women's wishes. When researchers have explicitly studied the willingness to say no, they found that women with higher self-esteem were more assertive. For example, Abel (1998) found that women with high self-esteem were more likely to have had only one sex partner. In plain terms, it is harder to seduce a woman with high self-esteem than one with low self-esteem, unless she wants to be seduced.

Thus, high self-esteem enables women to say no. Men may not feel a need to refuse sex as often, or they may not want to refuse, and so the issue is less relevant to them. Still, this raises the broader issue of how virginity is linked to self-esteem.

Researchers who have examined virginity find that it has strikingly different meanings depending on gender. For women, virginity is often a positive status, and they may take pride in it (Sprecher & Regan, 1996). This is consistent with the point we just made about high self-esteem and the willingness to say no. To remain virgins, most women must be willing to refuse invitations, and even passionate exhortations, to engage in intercourse. Women with low self-esteem, being more susceptible to such influences, will find it harder to remain virgins. (To some extent, however, this may be offset by the link between self-esteem and popularity described earlier; popular women will have more active social lives, which may lead to more sexual opportunities, including, presumably, some ones that will appeal to them.)

For men, virginity is quite a different matter. Male virgins often are unhappy about being virgins, especially when they reach an age where most of their peers have had sex and are in long-term relationships (Sprecher & Regan, 1996). They may feel that they have failed in their efforts to appeal to women. Virginity may therefore feel like a badge of shame to some men, which in turn could lower their self-esteem. Sure enough, some evidence indicates that virginity is associated with lower self-esteem among men but not among women (Walsh, 1991).

This all can be understood in terms of the social exchange theory. As we outlined in Chapter 1, the idea is that women give sex to men. By giving sex, women lose something, and so they may feel some loss of self-esteem. In contrast, men gain something by having sex, and so sexual activity reflects favorably on them.

Yet the hope that boosting women's self-esteem will reduce teen pregnancy by making women more willing to refuse sex does not seem well supported. The most thorough data suggest that there is no relationship either way: Self-esteem level is unrelated to the likelihood of becoming pregnant, and getting pregnant does not affect self-esteem (Oates, 1997). Occasional bits of evidence has suggested a weak correlation (e.g., Herrenkohl, Herrenkohl, Egolf, & Russo, 1998), but the main factor appears to be having been mistreated during childhood, which leads to both low self-esteem and early pregnancy. In other cases, low self-esteem may be the result rather than the cause of teen pregnancy. When your life takes a turn for the worse, including loss of educational opportunities and peer group contacts, your self-esteem drops.

A related point concerns erectile dysfunction, also called impotence. At various points in their lives, particularly in old age, many men lose their ability to respond and perform sexually. In particular, they may cease to have erections. In most cases, this is caused by some physical problem rather than a purely psychological one. Surgery, drugs, alcohol, diabetes, and other factors affect the body in ways that can impair sexual response (Reinisch, 1990). These changes often have a negative impact on how the man views himself. Self-esteem is sometimes low among men with erectile dysfunction (Herer & Holzapfel, 1993), but our understanding of the data is that the low self-esteem is usually the result rather than the cause. When the penis doesn't work, self-esteem goes down.

A theoretically interesting extension of this work has examined sexual response in unemployed men, who have relatively high rates of impotence and erectile dysfunction (Morokoff & Gilliland, 1993). In most cases, the unemployment clearly preceded the sexual problems, so it is reasonable to assume that the unemployment was the cause rather than the consequence. (The possibility that some third variable contributed to both the job loss and the impotence is difficult to rule out, but it seems less plausible.) Why? To be sure, unemployment raises a host of practical problems that in principle might take one's mind off of sex. Yet any rise in daily hassles was not an explanation for the loss of erection. If anything, unemployed men who had more daily hassles had more sex than other unemployed men.

Self-esteem does seem like a potential mediator here: Losing one's job might undermine a man's self-esteem, impairing his ability to respond and perform sexually. Several factors could be involved as well, such as a drop in testosterone that could be caused by job loss and that could lead to lower sexual arousal. The man may also feel that unemployment makes him less appealing to women, insofar as women judge men by their status and resources, and the loss of confidence could impair his sexual response. Until more studies are done, we will not know the precise explanation for this finding, but it does at least raise the possibility that some aspects of self-esteem could take on a causal role in sexual response, at least for mediating between unemployment and impotence.

An Epidemic of Low Self-Esteem?

One of the ironies of the self-esteem movement is that, just when the United States seems most concerned with a putative epidemic of low self-esteem and the need to boost positive feelings about ourselves, the rest of the world perceives Americans as being full of themselves and more prone to being conceited. Which view is correct: Do many ordinary Americans suffer from low self-esteem, or do they think very highly of themselves?

The answer to this is clear from many studies: Americans in fact think quite positively of themselves. In fact, most people seem to have somewhat inflated views of themselves, a pattern that has sometimes been called the "Lake Wobegon Effect" in honor of the mythical community described by humorist Garrison Keillor, where "all the children are above average." The average American does in fact regard himself or herself as above average. In one study of self-reported driving ability, for example, 90 percent of the people rated themselves as being above average (Svenson, 1981). In a survey of ability to get along with others, no students at all rated themselves as below average, and an amazing 25 percent rated themselves in the top 1 percent (College Board, 1976–1977; see Gilovich, 1991).

Meanwhile, studies of self-esteem tests reveal a consistent pattern that likewise points to high self-esteem. When researchers collect self-esteem scores from modern American adults, the scores range from the top down to a little below the middle, but hardly anyone scores at the low end. Nearly every study shows the same pattern, regardless of which of the many self-esteem scales is used. The average self-esteem score is almost always higher than the middle of the scale (for a review, see Baumeister, Tice, & Hutton, 1989).

Thus, it is clear that there is no epidemic of low self-esteem afflicting today's Americans. Does this signify that Americans are pathologically conceited and narcissistic? Are they in danger of ruining their lives through reckless overconfidence? An influential article by Taylor and Brown (1988) concluded that the answer was a firm no. In Taylor and Brown's view, mental health does not depend on seeing the world (or yourself) accurately. Instead, the optimum is to see the world distorted in a positive direction. These "positive illusions" include exaggerating your good qualities, overestimating your control over your fate, and maintaining some degree of unrealistic optimism. Happy, healthy people see the world in those positive terms. Depressed and other unhappy people tend to see the world in a more accurate, objective fashion.

It Will Never Happen to Me

Still, there are certain risks that accompany positive illusions and disregard of reality, and some of these can be seen in the sexual arena. After all, someone who is unrealistically optimistic and who overestimates his or her own control might take unwise chances in sexual behavior that could lead to venereal disease or pregnancy.

Several investigations have shown precisely that point. Burger and Burns (1988) found that sexually active female college students rated themselves as less likely than several other groups of women (including other women students, other women their age, and women of childbearing age in general) to get pregnant. On a scale running from 0 (no chance) to 100 (guaranteed), they were asked to rate the likelihood of becoming pregnant in the next twelve months. Their own chances, on average, were rated under 10, whereas those of other students were rated at 27 and those of American women in general in the 40s. In reality, of course, the estimates should have gone the other way, because all women in the sample were themselves sexually active, whereas many of the women in the comparison group were not active. Because having sex is usually necessary for getting pregnant, the women in the sample should have rated their own chances of pregnancy as higher than the chances of other women. But instead of the objectively correct high rating, they gave an implausibly low rating to their own chances of getting pregnant. The researchers borrowed the term "the illusion of unique invulnerability" from Perloff and Fetzer (1986) to describe this pattern of believing that bad things happen to other people but are not likely to afflict oneself.

Did these illusions have any real meaning, or were they just check marks on a questionnaire? Burger and Burns asked the women in their study whether they had used contraception during their recent sexual experiences. The more the woman indulged in the illusion of thinking "It can't happen to me," the less likely she was to use contraception. This pattern is especially ironic, because not using contraception should obviously make you think you are more likely to get pregnant! But somehow the women who were least likely to use contraception were also least likely to think they would get pregnant, relative to other women.

Those results suggest that some women apply the unrealistic, unwarranted pattern of personal optimism to their sex lives. They somehow believe that they will not get pregnant, and so they fail to take adequate precautions. The result is likely to be a rush of unwanted pregnancies, and in fact Burger and Burns found that almost one-fourth of the women in their sample did become pregnant (usually when they did not want to). Personal illusions of unique invulnerability can be costly.

The risk of AIDS in particular has sometimes been downplayed, especially by people whose risk is high. In fact, the journalist Randy Shilts (1987) described America's initial response to the danger of AIDS as "denial on all fronts, leading to stupid mistakes that would costs thousands of lives in the short term and tens of thousands in the long term" (p. 224). He claimed that some gay men increased their activities in promiscuous sex, thereby increasing their own risk of contracting the fatal disease.

The sense of being personally immune from disease is fairly strong. Hansen, Hahn, and Wolkenstein (1990) asked people to rate their own chances of getting AIDS. Some men in their sample had not had sex with anyone for a long time and had engaged in no risky behaviors. Others had had sex with multiple partners in the past year and had failed to use condoms on numerous occasions. These groups are objectively quite different in their level of risk—but amazingly both groups rated their own risk about the same! And the rated risk was quite low: Both groups of men thought their own chances of getting AIDS were about one in a million. Nor did this reflect a lack of awareness of AIDS: These men rated other men's chances of getting AIDS as about one in nine hundred. This fits "the illusion of unique invulnerability" pattern described by Burger and Burns (1988): AIDS is something that can happen to other people, but not to me.

The only group who seemed to recognize that their own risky behavior posed a serious danger to them were women who engaged in high-risk practices such as having multiple partners and not using condoms. Yet even they believed that other women were more vulnerable than they were themselves.

How are these illusions sustained? A fascinating exploration of rationalizations about AIDS was undertaken by Offir, Fisher, Williams, and Fisher (1993), who interviewed gay men. Most of the men they interviewed believed in the danger of AIDS and believed it was desirable to take precautions and practice safe sex, yet most of them did not regularly do so. In particular, nearly all of them expressed a strong dislike of condoms, and hence many of them said they had occasionally (or in some cases frequently) failed to use them. Perhaps ironically, many men said they were least likely to use a condom when having sex for the first time with someone they did not know well, which is precisely when the risk of AIDS and other disease is greatest.

The gay men offered a wealth of rationalizations. Some men said that they were relatively safe because they had not been the one who had been penetrated by the partner's penis. Those who had been penetrated said that their risk was lower because the partner had not ejaculated. If the partner had ejaculated in their mouth, they said their risk was low because they had not swallowed the semen. Those who had done that said that at least they had not done it as much as other gay men, so they were relatively safe.

Others claimed to be able to tell whether a partner (even someone they had just met) was likely to carry the AIDS virus. Many of the men had theories about what someone with AIDS or HIV looks like or acts like, and so they felt fairly certain that their sex partners were free of the virus. Such assumptions are probably invalid; there is no way to tell whether someone is carrying the HIV virus until he or she becomes seriously ill, which is often years after first contracting the virus. Others believed that their partners were not promiscuous. Although promiscuity is certainly a risk factor, it is questionable whether people can really know whether their sex partners have had many partners. Many people would not reveal such information, particularly when preparing to have sex for the first time with someone new.

Some men did not bother to rationalize. "You have to live a little," said one man to the interviewers, in response to the question about why he had had unprotected sex with a new partner. Condoms detracted from the pleasure as well as interfering with the romance and adventure of the moment, and of course raising the specter of possible death is likely to dampen erotic spirits.

High self-esteem contributes to this view that "It could never happen to me" and the consequent willingness to take risks. Smith, Gerrard, and Gibbons (1997) found that women with high self-esteem are more likely than others to underestimate their chances of becoming pregnant by having unprotected sex. Even when women wrote down a list of their sexual activities and precautions, those with high self-esteem saw less risk. The actual behaviors were no safer among women with high self-esteem, but they perceived them as safer. The implication is that high self-esteem is associated with a mental style that distorts the world in a favorable, desirable direction and hence assumes that bad things will not happen to the self.

The denial of personal risk fits that pattern we have already seen: High self-esteem goes with an objectively unwarranted exaggeration of oneself. People with high self-esteem think they perform better than others, but they don't really. They think they are much more attractive than others, but the difference is small or nonexistent. And they think they are safer than others from the dangers of unprotected sex, but they are not.

Self-esteem is hardly the only culprit, however. Other factors cause people to disregard risks and take foolish chances. Prominent among these are alcohol and drugs. Leigh (1990) found a strong relationship between using alcohol or drugs prior to sex and engaging in risky sexual behavior. That is, people who drink or take drugs are more prone to skip the condoms and go to bed with people they do not know well.

To be sure, self-esteem may play some role even in that link. There is some evidence that self-esteem goes up when people are drunk (Banaji & Steele, 1989). Other drugs, perhaps especially cocaine, may produce similar reactions, but these have not been studied as thoroughly, because researchers cannot as readily administer them legally. In any case, alcohol intoxication causes people to feel good about themselves and rate themselves more positively than they would normally do.

Still, the relationship of alcohol and sex depends on far more than self-esteem. The next section will take a closer look at what alcohol does to the self and how this can alter sexual behavior. First, however, it is necessary to consider the role of self-awareness in sexuality.

Self-Awareness and Sex

One of the most important events in the history of sex in the United States was the publication in 1970 of Masters and Johnson's *Human Sexual Inadequacy*. This book was based on years of clinical and laboratory work and offered a much more scientific approach to sex and sexual problems than had marked most of America's discussions about the subjects.

Masters and Johnson were sex therapists, and they used their understanding of sexual problems to develop methods to treat them. One pattern they found that contributed to sexual problems in both men and women was what they called "the inner spectator," which made individuals feel as if a part of their mind were off watching them during sex. Nor was the internal spectator a supportive fan or even quiet observer: Instead, the inner spectator would often make judgmental, critical, discouraging observations.

For example, a man with erectile dysfunction might try to have sex with his partner. He'd be worried that he might not be able to get or sustain an erection. His inner spectator would watch him try, all the while prompting thoughts such as, "That's sure not hard enough," or "Looks like it's starting to wilt." These discouraging thoughts would magnify his difficulties.

By the same token, during intercourse a woman who had difficulty achieving orgasm might feel that her inner spectator was saying things like, "Hurry up, this is taking way too long," or "This isn't working," or "Pretty soon he will be getting annoyed at you!" The more intently she watched and judged her efforts to reach orgasm, the more the goal eluded her.

The inner spectator refers to a phenomenon that social psychologists have called self-awareness. Influential works by Duval and Wicklund (1972) and Carver and Scheier (1981) laid important foundations for understanding self-awareness. One important point is that self-awareness is typically more than just a matter of turning attention toward or thinking about the self. Instead, self-awareness usually invokes some *standards* of good and bad, so that attending to the self often involves evaluating how you are doing.

Hence arises the judgmental attitude of the inner spectator. It doesn't just watch the person having sex, but it compares performance to some notion of what would be optimal. Because people often fall short of their ideals, self-awareness is likely to set off unpleasant emotions such as anxiety, discouragement, guilt, and regret, which can interfere with sexual pleasure and performance. For that reason, Masters and Johnson (1970) tried to develop techniques to get people to tune out the inner spectator. Lovers will perform better without self-awareness.

Why would nature instill in human beings a pattern (self-awareness) that mainly functions to make them unhappy? Carver and Scheier (1981) explained that self-awareness is part of the process of self-regulation. In many respects, people are able to change and improve themselves if they engage in self-regulation, but in order for that to happen, they have to recognize what they are doing and perceive the discrepancy between their current status and what they ideally might be like. Self-awareness can help motivate people to try to change for the better.

Some of these positive effects might be seen in sex, although they tend to discourage and prevent rather than promote sexual pleasure. For example, if someone were about to have unprotected sex with an unreliable partner, or even if the person were simply going to be unfaithful to a long-term, valued, trusting mate, self-awareness might help the person avoid the mistake by saying, "Hey, what am I doing?" Self-awareness would help the person compare his or her current actions to ideal standards (such as safety or fidelity) and avoid behaviors that will be regretted later.

Self-awareness can thus prevent various sexual misdeeds. Perhaps unfortunately, self-awareness seems to be mainly useful for stopping behavior rather than facilitating it. As a result, it can interfere with proper, desirable sexual behaviors too. Sexual inhibitions depend on self-awareness, because they involve comparing one's current or desired behaviors to standards such as morals and prohibitions. A person might want to please a beloved partner by performing oral sex, but inhibitions might interfere by saying, "That's wrong," or "That's dirty," or even "That's disgusting, and you should be ashamed." Self-awareness plays a central role in such inhibitions.

Another way of looking at this situation is that self-awareness helps turn behavior over to the conscious mind instead of letting it flow along in an automatic or natural fashion. That pattern can be very useful in preventing mistakes, because the conscious mind can accomplish many things—like telling you to put your pants back on and to get out of there before you do something you'll regret.

There are some severe limits to what the conscious mind can accomplish, however, and in those cases self-awareness may be useless or even counterproductive. The conscious mind cannot (typically) cause the penis to become erect, the vagina to lubricate, or an orgasm to occur. Those things depend on automatic and natural responses. When the conscious, self-aware mind takes over, the process breaks down (if it hasn't already). Self-awareness can thus interfere with good sex just as easily as it interferes with bad sex.

It is quite possible that the sexual problems of unemployed men involve self-awareness as much as or even more than self-esteem. Loss of employment makes a man question himself and doubt his manhood (Newman, 1988). It is possible that he might feel such doubts at many times, including during sex. He might regard it as especially important to perform well in sex to offset any question about his masculinity. Unfortunately putting such pressure on himself is likely to increase self-awareness (see Baumeister, 1984); which may cause the inner spectator to make disparaging, judgmental comments about the man's erection and performance. The outcome would almost certainly be bad for the sexual response.

There could well be another contributor to the unemployed man's sexual problems, however: alcohol, which tends to interfere with sexual response.

Self-Awareness and Alcohol

Getting a woman drunk is a technique familiar to most men who devote a great deal of effort to getting different women to have sex with them. As we shall see in Chapter 9, sexually aggressive men (such as date rapists) tend to belong to groups of men friends who spend a lot of time talking about obtaining sex. This includes giving each other crude tips for how to elicit cooperation from women, such as, "Candy is dandy, but liquor is quicker." The essence of that particular phrase is that if you want to get a woman into bed, the admirable and classy approach is to buy her gifts (such as candy) and to romance her in elegant ways, but getting her drunk is often an effective shortcut.

Why? One reason is that alcohol reduces self-awareness. This has been shown in an important program of research by Hull and his colleagues at Indiana University and Dartmouth College (see Hull, 1981; also Hull & Young, 1983). People who have had even a few drinks pay less attention to themselves and are less likely to think through the implications of events for their self-concepts. That is one reason that people get drunk following a blow to their self-esteem, such as a job setback or a romantic rejection: Alcohol cuts short the process of analyzing what a failure you must be. It also explains the use of alcohol in celebrations and parties: Alcohol makes you forget about your dignity and inhibitions, so you can cut loose and have some fun. Sure, you may say or do things that you'll regret in the morning, but at the time they'll seem like a great idea.

But doesn't alcohol just make people do crazy things? Doesn't it give rise to all sorts of strange impulses and desires? The simple answer is no. Alcohol does not make people want much of anything. It does not have the power to create new desires or motivations. Its main effect is to remove inhibitions and other internal barriers that might prevent you from doing what you already want to do. In simple terms, alcohol undermines self-control—so you act on desires you already had (but were restraining).

This conclusion was supported in an important article by two social psychologists, Claude Steele and Lillian Southwick (1985). Combining results from many studies, they showed that alcohol does not simply increase all sorts of wild and crazy behavior. Instead, alcohol produces wild behavior only in cases where there was an inner response conflict—that is, when the person both wanted to do something and wanted not to do it. Alcohol undermined the restraining part, making the person more likely to act on the positive urges. Thus, you need not fear that alcohol intoxication will cause you to want to have sex, or have homosexual sex, or indeed commit violent actions—unless you already want to commit them. If you already have those desires, alcohol may make you feel more willing to act them out.

This view of alcohol as something that "inhibits the inhibitors" meshes well with what we have seen regarding self-awareness. Self-awareness is often central to inhibition and self-regulation. It keeps you from doing things that you will be sorry about. Reduce self-awareness, such as by consuming alcohol, and such actions become all the more likely.

Alcohol's effect on self-awareness and the resulting effect on inhibitions help explain its popularity with seducers. A man who wants to convince a woman to have sex with him will find her resistance increases as she reflects on what she is doing, on her sexual standards, on her risks and costs, and on other factors. All these reflections involve self-awareness. Alcohol will help reduce self-awareness and make her less likely to consider those restraining factors—and hence more likely to comply with his wishes. Nor is this pattern confined to men who want to seduce women. When women want to get men to have sex, they likewise find that getting the man drunk is an effective strategy (e.g., Anderson & Struckman-Johnson, 1998).

Thus, alcohol lowers self-awareness and thereby impairs self-regulation and other prudent behavior. This probably contributes to the risk-taking patterns we already covered. As Leigh (1990) showed, intoxicated people engage in riskier sex, including promiscuity and failure to use condoms. After all, most people believe in the desirability of using condoms, especially when going to bed with someone who may have had many prior sex partners. A sober person would probably consider the personal standard of taking precautions and possibly the potential costs and dangers to the self that might attend being negligent. But a drunk person would not think through those implications and contingencies and may therefore just go ahead and take the risks.

Infidelity is another relevant pattern, because most relationships hold some ideal of sexual monogamy. There is some evidence that alcohol is involved in infidelity. The NHSLS found a higher rate of alcohol use during sex with people's secondary partners than with their primary partners (Laumann et al., 1994). In other words, people who do not drink during sex with their main relationship partner are more likely to drink when having sex with someone else. Probably that indicates that being intoxicated makes people more willing to have sex with the secondary partner. And the psychological mechanism behind that is likely to involve alcohol reducing self-awareness and thereby removing inhibitions and impairing self-control, so that people do things (such as commit adultery) that they would not do if they were sober.

The risks seem to extend even beyond venereal disease, AIDS, and pregnancy. For women, one of the serious risks in sexual behavior is rape. As Chapter 9 on rape shows, victims of sexual coercion often suffer considerable and lasting distress as a result of their victimization. To the extent that rape can be prevented, women will be happier and healthier as well as better able to enjoy good relationships (including good sex) with men.

There is some evidence that alcohol intoxication increases a woman's chances of being raped. This is particularly true of date rape and acquaintance rape, which are far more common than rape by strangers. Women's stories of victimization often make reference to drinking, frequently by both themselves and their dates. In some cases, the woman becomes so drunk that she is unable to resist the man's sexual activities or is even unconscious when the man initiates copulation. One study concluded that alcohol use by one or the other person was involved in over half the cases of rape, and that both the man and the woman had been drinking in 36 percent of the cases (Abbey, Ross, McDuffie, & McAuslan, 1996). Still, there were only 3 percent of the cases in which the woman victim had been drinking and the male attacker was completely sober. Moreover, alcohol is consumed on plenty of noncoercive dates and prior to many instances of consensual sex, so perhaps the appearance of alcohol in the date rape stories is not so remarkable. There are certainly no controlled studies that randomly assign couples to drink or not drink and then assess whether date rape occurs.

Clearly, there are multiple ways that alcohol increases the risk of rape, and those with the most impact involve the man instead of the woman. Alcohol reduces the man's inhibitions just as much as the woman's, and so he may be more willing to perpetrate rape if he is intoxicated. Moreover, some men regard alcohol use by a woman as a sign that she intends to have sex. In one study, men listened to a tape in which a couple was on a date and the woman resisted the man's sexual advances. Sexually aggressive men were more willing to discount the woman's negative comments and to think she was actually willing to have sex—but the difference was only significant when the the listener believed the woman had been drinking. Thus, sexually aggressive men think it appropriate dismiss a woman's sexual refusals and continue to persist, and they do this most strikingly when she has had alcohol (Bernat, Calhoun, & Stolp, 1998).

Although we have emphasized the various ways that alcohol contributes to sexual behavior and misbehavior, it must be acknowledged that there are direct physiological effects of alcohol that impair sexual response, perhaps especially among men, for whom getting and maintaining an erection can be difficult or even impossible in a highly intoxicated state. As the night watchman said in Shakespeare's *MacBeth*, referring to alcohol, "It provoketh the desire, but it taketh away the performance." (Strictly speaking, it does not increase desire; it merely removes restraints and barriers against desires that are already present. But that may seem like an increase in desire to the man himself.) Alcohol removes one's inhibitions, thereby making people more willing to do certain sexual things—but alcohol may also impair their physical ability to do and enjoy them.

Escape from Self-Awareness

There is yet another way that one could consider these effects of alcohol. We have emphasized the dangers of intoxication in terms of making people more willing to do things that they may regret. One could, however, put alcohol in a more positive light. In particular, when people want to do something but lack the courage or are held back by inhibitions, they may consume alcohol as a way of escaping from self-awareness and its restraining influence.

Alcohol has long been used to overcome fears, anxieties, and inhibitions. The military historian John Keegan (1976) reported that it has been a common practice over many centuries to give alcohol to soldiers to prepare for battle. The term *Dutch courage* expresses the idea that alcohol makes people braver, and when a soldier is preparing for battle he (or she) may welcome this extra boost. For the first day of the battle of the Somme during World War I, for example, thousands upon thousands of British soldiers rose before dawn to line up during a horrifically loud artillery bombardment of the German trenches. While they waited, they were served their ration of grog, and by accident the first wave of attackers received both their own ration and the second wave's ration. Most of the young men drank this on an empty stomach, having skipped breakfast in order to reduce the danger of infection from a stomach wound. Between the lack of sleep and the unfamiliar hour for drinking, not to mention the double dose of alcohol for the first wave, the lads became shockingly drunk. No doubt this helped make them willing when, at first light, the cannon fell silent and they got the order to charge across no-man's-land toward the enemy machine guns, which they did, until so many had been shot down that the remaining ones turned around and staggered back.

Sex is certainly a far cry from charging against machine guns, but some people are nervous or scared anyway, and they may use alcohol to increase their courage. In particular, losing one's virginity is often a somewhat worrisome, daunting event, and people may desire a little Dutch courage to help them through it and ease their fears. Sprecher, Barbee, and Schwartz (1995) found that about a third of their sample of both men and women reported drinking alcohol just prior to losing their virginity. According to people's retrospective reports, the alcohol was not a big help in this domain: People who consumed alcohol reported less pleasure, more guilt, and no difference in anxiety, as compared to people who did not report drinking. It is, however, not entirely safe to assume that the two sets of experiences (i.e., those of drinkers and nondrinkers) were exactly the same in all other respects. Possibly people who drank were facing a less appealing or more nerve-wracking experience to begin with, which is why they chose to drank. Certainly if you were preparing to lose your virginity under ideal conditions, with a passionate, caring lover in a committed relationship and mutually positive attitudes about sex, you would probably not want to be drunk for that moment. But often circumstances fall short of that ideal. In any case, Sprecher et al.'s findings cast serious doubt on the helpfulness of alcohol for improving first-time sex.

Undoubtedly people use alcohol to escape from self-awareness in many other contexts, as we have suggested (Hull, 1981). Alcohol is not alone as a means of such escape, however, and even some sexual patterns may revolve around the loss of self. Let us turn to examine one in particular, namely sexual masochism.

Masochism: The Joy of Being Spanked

Masochism is one of psychology's oldest puzzles. At first blush, masochism runs contrary to several of psychology's most basic assumptions and principles. It is well established, for example, that human beings, like almost all other creatures, seek pleasure and avoid pain. Why, then, would someone want to be spanked or whipped?

Psychology's theories about the self are particularly at odds with the phenomena of masochism. Nearly all experts agree that human beings have a strong, deep-seated striving to gain control. But masochists often desire to be deprived of control: to be tied up, given commands, and in other ways rendered helpless and vulnerable.

Likewise, the desire for self-esteem is a powerful and pervasive human motivation, but masochists seem to thwart it directly. Many masochists desire embarrassing or humiliating experiences, including both physical and symbolic indignities.

How can these contradictions be reconciled?

Theories of Masochism

There have been several noteworthy attempts to explain sexual masochism. Freud's (1938, 1924/1961) views have long been influential. He proposed that people primarily want to dominate others for various reasons—because they have aggressive instincts, because others annoy and frustrate them, or simply because they enjoy power. Dominating and hurting others can, however, cause people to feel guilty. As a result, some people go through a psychological defense mechanism by which they switch roles, so that the desire to dominate is somewhat mysteriously converted into a desire to submit to domination by others. Voilà, said Freud, that is where masochism comes from.

In Freud's view, thus, the wish for dominance is the primary force, and masochism is a secondary or derivative pattern. Sadistic inclinations should therefore far outnumber masochistic ones. Unfortunately, the data point strongly in the opposite direction: Far more people have submissive or masochistic desires than sadistic or dominant ones. In fact, S&M clubs typically have problems caused by the imbalance of members: Usually there are two, three, or even four submissives for every one who wants to play the dominant role (Scott, 1983). Prostitutes get far more requests from clients who want to be spanked than from clients who want to deliver a spanking (Greene & Greene, 1974; Janus, Bess, & Saltus, 1977). Researchers have regularly found that submissive fantasies outnumber dominant or sadistic ones by three or four to one (Baumeister, 1989; Friday,

1980). The preponderance of masochists suggest that masochism, not sadism, is the primary desire.

Furthermore, when people play both roles, the typical pattern is to start out as a submissive and then move on to playing the dominant role (Califia, 1983; Kamel, 1983; Lee, 1983; Scott, 1983). The reverse is rare or even nonexistent. If masochism comes first, it should be assumed to be the primary form, not the secondary or derivative one. So the original Freudian theory, although interesting and inherently plausible, does not really fit the facts very well.

A variation on the Freudian theory is that masochists suffer from guilt about sex, and thus they desire to be dominated as a way of being freed from guilt. By being tied up and helpless, they escape from responsibility for their actions, so they do not need to feel guilty. By being spanked or otherwise punished, they work off their guilt feelings. Either way, masochism allows people to enjoy sex without the guilt they normally have.

The guilt theory is plausible, but again the facts speak against it. Most tellingly, therapists (Cowan, 1982) report that masochistic clients come to them wanting to be restored to desiring only normal sexual activities, not the masochistic pleasure, which they fear is sick or dangerous (a view that is not surprising, considering what many books have had to say about masochism!). Thus, they do not have guilt about normal sex—only about masochism. Masochistic sexuality is the source of their guilt problems, not the solution to them.

Indeed, looked at another way, the guilt theory rests on a highly implausible mechanism. If you really felt guilty about normal sex, would you be likely to engage in kinky sex? Most people who have high sex guilt are highly averse to trying new, deviant sexual activities.

Another explanation of masochism is based on opponent-process theory (Solomon & Corbit, 1974), which argues that the body's steady-state (homeostatic) mechanisms set off opposite reactions whenever the body departs from its normal condition. For example, when you run up a flight of stairs, your heart starts beating faster and you breathe more heavily, but soon the body's opponent processes work to slow down the heartbeat and return the breathing to normal.

Applied to masochism, this suggests that the body's response to pain would set off some contrary response that might be felt as pleasure. The spanking hurts, and to counteract the pain the body may release endorphins or other chemicals that induce a good feeling. As a result, people may start to seek out controlled doses of pain, such as in masochism, in order to enjoy the pleasure that follows.

This theory has some appeal but also fails to fit the known facts about masochism. For one thing, it works too well: If feeling pain were that reliable a source of pleasure, the majority of people would seek out pain on a regular basis, whereas masochism remains the practice of a small minority. For another, opponent processes tend to grow slowly from very weak and tentative initial reactions, but masochists often have vividly pleasant first experiences, and their most common reaction to their first time is a desire to do it again (Spengler, 1977). For these reasons, Baumeister (1997) concluded that opponent-process theory can explain sadism better than masochism.

Also, explanations that are based in the biological facts of human nature, such as opponent process theory, have considerable difficulty accounting for substantial cultural differences. Masochism is very culturally relative. It was first noted in Europe around 1500 and until quite recently was mainly known only in modern Western countries (for a review, see Baumeister, 1988b, 1989). For example, the sex historian Reay Tannahill (1980) noted that the sex manuals of ancient China cover almost exactly the same sexual practices as one would find in a modern American book on sex—except masochism, which she said was conspicuous by its absence from the Chinese books. Likewise, ancient Greek literature was full of sex scenes, containing a broad variety of practices—but again no sign of masochism (Licht, 1934).

The medieval Christian authorities wrote extensively about sex, debating the sinfulness of many practices and discussing their scriptural and theological implications. They too cover nearly all the sexual practices known to modern man, except masochism (Bullough & Brundage, 1982). These patterns suggest that masochism was largely unknown in most of human history and most societies and is somehow a special product of modern Western culture.

Escaping the Self

These cultural differences played a central role in stimulating a recent theory of masochism by Baumeister (1988b, 1989, 1991a). According to this view, masochism appeals to people as a way of escaping from self-awareness (not unlike alcohol). Individuality and selfhood acquired a special, overgrown, burdensome nature in modern Western societies, and so modern Western individuals periodically have the need to escape from self-awareness, a need that is different and stronger than what it has typically been in other cultures (see Baumeister, 1986, 1987; Markus & Kitayama, 1991; Triandis, 1989).

The theory that masochism involves escape from self also addresses the paradoxes that we saw earlier. The psychology of self emphasizes that the self is mainly designed to maximize esteem and control, whereas masochism revolves around efforts to relinquish esteem and control. Those masochistic desires are thus not illusions or superficial contradictions—rather, they reveal the essence of masochism, which is an all-out attempt to erase (temporarily) who you are.

For example, one study of high-class call girls in Washington, D.C., found that they received a surprisingly high rate of requests to dominate their clients, who were typically the rich and powerful men in the city (Janus et al., 1977). Requests to be beaten outnumbered requests to deliver a beating by about eight to one. Why did these federal judges, senators, and other powerful men have such a high rate of wishing to be dominated?

To hold such a prominent, powerful job, especially in modern America, it is typically necessary to have an elaborate and autonomous self that can take responsibility and make decisions. Elected officials, in particular, must maintain a highly favorable public image of self in order to get reelected, even while political opponents and the mass media are always looking for opportunities to make them look bad. The stressful burden of maintaining such a powerful, magnificent image of self can become severe, and it would not be surprising if these men wanted occasionally to be relieved of the burden.

And that's where masochism can help. Consider a man who is tied up on the floor, having received a whipping on his bare bottom, now kissing a prostitute's feet and awaiting permission to move his mouth up between her legs. In everyday life he may be a senator, but these submissive actions are so contrary to the self he must display during Senate debates that he cannot maintain that identity. Senators have responsibility, power, authority, and dignity, but he has none of these when he is shackled and blindfolded and kissing a prostitute's feet, or when he is nude and bent over to meekly accept a paddling on his bare behind. The loss of control and the humiliation prevent him from being who he is. In the process, he can forget all the cares of his office and his life and concentrate intensely on the immediate moment, with its measured doses of pain and pleasure.

The issue of pain raises the central paradox of masochism, however: Why would anyone ever desire pain? Pain is by definition unpleasant. Some people believe that under some circumstances, pain turns into pleasure, but there is not much evidence for this, and in fact most masochists say that pain is actually painful, not directly pleasant.

One thing pain does very effectively, however, is grab attention. (Indeed, that is one of its main biological functions.) A thoughtful book on pain by philosopher Elaine Scarry (1985) concluded that physical pain tends to banish meaningful thought from the mind. Pain is itself hard to describe, and when you are in pain it is hard to talk about anything else. It grabs attention and directs it to the here and now, and all else recedes from the mind.

Scarry illustrated her point by considering the role of pain in torture. A person will enter a torture session as a fully adult, complex human being with a sophisticated identity, many personal relationships, strong opinions and beliefs, and other symbolic investments. The pain of torture will, however, cause the person (eventually) to abandon all of those aspects of self. The victim will often say and do anything to escape the pain, including giving information that will betray the person's cause or country or that may cause valued colleagues and loved ones to be captured or killed. Scarry says that these facts suggest a remarkable capacity for pain to tear down the entire symbolic structure of the self, at least for a short time.

And that is precisely what masochists want. In a sense, pain has great potential as a narcotic. It grabs the mind's attention and blots out all else, enabling one to forget oneself entirely apart from the here-and-now sensation of pain. By stripping away the meaningful aspects of identity, it reduces the self to being nothing more than a body. That is a powerful aid to the process of escaping from self-awareness.

Are Masochists Merely Self-Destructive Perverts?

Even if one can understand the psychological mechanisms by which masochism helps people escape from self-awareness, one may still ask: Why? Why do people want to escape from self-awareness so badly that they would engage in such painful and embarrassing practices?

A standard answer is that they are self-destructive. In ordinary language, people sometimes use the term *masochistic* to refer to someone who seems to want failure or suffering and who may well be bringing misfortune and ruin upon his or her own head. Clinical psychologists also briefly used the term *masochistic* to refer to self-defeating personality disorders (Franklin, 1987).

Masochism is, however, not self-destructive in a strict sense. Research studies suggest that masochists are usually very careful to avoid any harm (Lee, 1983; Scott, 1983). They do seek pain, but they seek it in situations and ways that ensure that no injuries are caused. They often take precautions to prevent any chance of injury, such as arranging special code words that they can use during an episode to signal the partner to stop. They avoid any partners known to engage in dangerous activities.

Another surprising fact is that most people who engage in masochism seem to be quite normal and successful in their lives (Cowan, 1982; Scott, 1983; for a review, see Baumeister, 1989). Masochism is thus not usually a part of a pattern of mental illness, self-destruction, or other pathology. Masochists are not found among society's losers but among its more prosperous and successful citizens. As we saw, prostitutes who cater to the rich and powerful clients in the federal government get many requests to administer spankings and other domination. Prostitutes who cater to poor or working-class clients get far fewer such requests.

Is masochism nonetheless a perversion? The traditional judgment about people who enjoy deviant sexual activities is that there must be something wrong with them: They are "sick, sick, sick," in the words of advice columnist Ann Landers (Cowan, 1982). But when their sexual tastes are balanced against their apparent success in other spheres of life, masochists cannot be pronounced sick overall, but one may still judge and condemn the sexual masochism as immoral or unacceptable in itself.

One popular rule of thumb that goes back at least to Freud is that the term *perversion* should be used when any activity (other than arousal or intercourse) becomes *indispensable* to sexual pleasure. By that criterion, masochism may or may not be a perversion, depending on whether the particular individual finds it indispensable. It is fine to enjoy being tied up, spanked, and the rest, as long as this is only an occasional aspect of your sex life and you are fully able to enjoy normal intercourse without masochism. But if you find that you can only reach orgasm by way of masochism, you have a problem. By this criterion, most masochists are not perverts, and masochism is not inherently perverse—but masochism will qualify as a perversion in some individuals. The crucial test is not whether you like to be spanked, but whether you enjoy other, more conventional forms of sex too.

Why, then, would people want to escape the self in masochism? There are several possible reasons for wanting to escape awareness of self, as we saw with alcohol use (see also Baumeister, 1991a). One reason is simply that because events cast the self in a bad light, it is unpleasant to be aware of the self. This explanation, however, does not seem to fit most observations about masochism, although it is plausible that some people would desire masochistic experiences when they feel bad about themselves.

A more likely reason, however, is that the modern Western self is stressful to maintain, and so people desire a periodic escape from it. This desire may be especially strong among the people with the most elaborate requirements for selfhood (such as politicians, as we suggested). Stress research has concluded that even mild stress can become extremely unpleasant and harmful when it is uninterrupted, whereas an occasional break or safe period can bring immense relief. In this view, there is no particular occasion or urgent need for a masochistic experience, but the person would simply like to have one now and then to enjoy a relieving break from the burden of being oneself. This fits what is known about masochism, although the data are far from clear about this.

A final reason is that self-awareness seems to reduce many forms of enjoyment and fun. The word *ecstasy* comes from Greek roots meaning "to stand outside oneself," and it is used to refer to intense bliss that accompanies forgetting oneself. Religious experiences, artistic pleasure, "flow" experiences, and other intensely positive moments are often marked by a loss of self-awareness (Csikszentmihalyi, 1990). Hence some people may feel that escaping from self-awareness is an important means of achieving greater pleasure. That brings up the bigger question of whether masochism enhances sex, to which we turn in the next section.

Does Masochism Improve Sex?

Many masochists claim that their sexual experiences during S&M scenes are more intense and bring more pleasure than during normal, "vanilla" sex. If these claims are accurate, then perhaps many people would want to try engaging in masochism, simply out of the desire to feel intense sexual pleasure. Then again, on an a priori basis it seems questionable that being spanked or bound would contribute to bringing about sexual bliss.

Another reason to question such claims of great sex was emphasized by Baumeister (1989) in his critical study of masochism. Masochistic activity is condemned and stigmatized by society at large, and so masochists may feel a need to justify or rationalize their activities. Claims that masochism produces exceptionally intense sexual pleasure may simply be self-serving rationalizations for engaging in deviant activities.

Yet there are some data that make it at least plausible that masochistic experiences may bring a more intense form of sexual pleasure than conventional sex. Many of the methods used by sex therapists to intensify sexual pleasure have parallels in masochism. If these methods work for sex therapists to increase sexual arousal and pleasure, they may work for masochists too. Let us briefly consider several of the main methods that Masters and Johnson (1970) pioneered for enhancing sexual response.

First, social isolation helps remove a couple from their daily cares and worries, so they can focus their attention fully on each other and their sexual expression. Masters and Johnson would sometimes require the couples they treated to stay at a hotel, even if they lived nearby, so as to remove them from their ordinary lives. As we have seen, masochism also uses techniques that strip away the everyday world and create a small fantasy realm in its place.

Second, Masters and Johnson emphasized what they called the "sensate focus," which means confining attention to immediate bodily sensations. Symbolic issues such as evaluating one's performance or thinking about expectations were discouraged, and the patient was encouraged just to notice how the skin felt. Masochism promotes a sensate focus by use of pain and other activities, which forcibly direct attention to immediate sensations.

Third, Masters and Johnson focused on the relationship rather than the individual. They insisted on treating couples rather than individual patients. Masochists also seem very couple-oriented. They prefer stable, committed relationships (even with prostitutes, if those are the only partners they find), and they use the sadomasochistic sex scenes as part of a highly intimate togetherness.

Fourth, Masters and Johnson would restrict the sexual activities of their patients (for example, by forbidding them to touch their genitals without permission). Even sexual intercourse would often be prohibited during the early stages of sex therapy. This liberated the couple from feeling obligated to perform certain acts, and in some ways the restrictions seemed to increase the desire for what one could not (temporarily) have. This too has obvious echoes in masochism, insofar as many masochists like to be told that they may not perform various sexual activities until given permission (or even commanded) by the dominant partner.

Fifth, enforced passivity was useful in many sex therapy cases. As Masters and Johnson pointed out, a man cannot will himself to have an erection: He has to let it happen. In the same way, a woman cannot force herself to have an orgasm but instead must yield to it. In Masters and Johnson's therapy, the patient was therefore often deliberately confined to a passive role in which he or she was not permitted to initiate any activity or even do anything, but could only let things happen. Passivity is of course central to the masochistic experience as well.

Many of these therapy techniques were designed to get rid of the "internal spectator" that Masters and Johnson felt was so responsible for many sexual difficulties. As we have seen, the internal spectator is simply another name for self-awareness. If masochism does in fact reduce self-awareness, it would have the same effect as these techniques and thus might well enhance sex.

Taken together, these parallels do lend some credence to the claim that masochism enhances sex. It is difficult to conduct fully controlled experimental studies to ascertain whether the claims are true, and there continue to be reasons for skepticism and doubt. But at least they might be true.

Are Women Naturally Masochistic?

Before we leave the topic of masochism, it is worth considering briefly one of the more controversial issues that has bedeviled masochism theory for decades. Freud observed that masochists were submissive, passive, and dependent, and he saw the same traits in the women of his time, so he concluded that women are by nature more masochistic than men. Some of his followers, notably Deutsch (1944), emphasized masochism as a central feature of the psychology of women.

Others have, however, objected strongly to any proposed link between masochism and femininity. Feminist scholars did not want women characterized as masochistic, because this might imply that women are partly responsible for being oppressed and victimized (e.g., Caplan, 1984). Meanwhile, observers such as Reik (1957[1941]) observed that more men than women engage in masochistic sex, leading to the opposite suggestion that men are more masochistic than women.

This contentious issue can be resolved by attending carefully to the facts and findings. For one thing, the theory of feminine masochism was so bitterly resented by feminists mainly because it represented a potential justification for political exploitation and other forms of victimization. To feminists, the idea that women are masochistic invoked views that women are self-destructive. But as we have seen, masochism is mainly a sexual pattern that does not carry over or generalize easily to nonsexual spheres, and in particular masochists are not self-destructive. If the political and everyday issues are stripped away, and the issue is simply whether masochism represents a form of sexual pleasure that appeals to women, there is much less to fight about.

It is also clear, however, that masochism is practiced by only a minority of both sexes. Masochism is thus atypical. It is simply wrong to generalize that men or women are masochistic, because the majority of both genders is not masochistic.

Still, is there any basis for saying that either gender is "more" masochistic than the other? Men participate in masochism more often than women, leading some experts to conclude that men are more masochistically inclined. Then again, men engage in most sexual variations more than women (a pattern that will be addressed at several points in this book). Men might simply have stronger sexual desires or be more willing than women to act them out. The higher number of male than female masochists is therefore not very convincing.

To address the possible difference in initiative, one might consider the question of masochistic desire: Do women have more submissive desires than men, even if women do not act on them? It is difficult to get direct measures of sexual desire. One method is to look at sexual fantasies, because those reflect safe and convenient acts of the imagination, so people can do them without worrying about all the obstacles that may hamper actually taking part in masochism, such as finding a willing partner, letting the partner know that you have those wishes, and making sure that things are done safely.

There is some evidence that women have more masochistic fantasies than men. An authoritative review of the research literature on sexual fantasy concluded that more women than men have and enjoy submissive fantasies (Leitenberg & Henning, 1995), such as being tied up or being someone's sex slave who must cater to that person's every sexual whim. In some studies, close to half the women surveyed reported some such submissive fantasy. That finding lends support to the view that some degree of masochistic inclination is relatively common among women. Nor can one dismiss this finding as part of a general pattern, as one could question the male participation in masochism, because overall women have fewer and less varied sexual fantasies than men (Leitenberg & Henning, 1995). The female penchant for submissive fantasy bucks the general trend.

That particular review by Leitenberg and Henning (1995) also included rape fantasies (i.e., being forced to have sex) in this category, and women have more such fantasies than men. Of course, most women who have such fantasies do not actually desire to be raped, which raises some questions about the link between fantasy and desire. The rape fantasies do not resemble actual rapes, however. In fantasy, the woman feels mutual attraction with a man who is off-limits (for example, because she is married), and she imagines him overpowering her token resistance to bring about a sexual experience that is pleasant for both. This may or may not qualify as masochistic.

In any case, the best available evidence shows that women have more masochistic fantasies than men, while men are more likely to actually engage in masochistic sexual behavior. And in either case, only a minority of men and women are at all masochistic. Thus, it does not seem correct to label either men or women as masochistic.

Let us look at the problem another way, however. Women are not masochistic—but is masochism feminine? After all, the masochistic role of being an obedient servant who caters to the partner's needs does bear some resemblance to the traditional female role. Perhaps Freud and others had it backwards when they thought they saw a link between femininity and masochism. There is nothing in the psychology of women that is inherently masochistic, but there may well be something feminine in the psychology of masochism.

Some support for this can be found in cross-gender practices during masochism. Male masochists often describe (and presumably enjoy) being feminized. They may be required to dress in women's lingerie and other clothing, may be given a female name, and may be asked to perform traditionally feminine tasks such as housework. Female masochists are almost never masculinized, however, such as being dressed in men's clothes or instructed to perform traditionally male chores (Baumeister, 1988a, 1989). If anything, female masochists are sometimes subjected to feminizing treatment. For example, stories about lesbian masochism sometimes feature a "butch" woman who, as part of submission, is dressed in frilly dresses and high heels, which she would never wear under normal circumstances (Alexander, 1982; Barker, 1982).

The discrepancy in cross-gender behavior during masochism raises the further issue of whether there are other differences between male and female masochists. Only one study has examined this systematically (Baumeister, 1988a), but it did find a host of small differences. Male masochism revolved around loss of status, and such men often enjoy being reduced to something less than a man—such as being put in diapers and treated as a baby, or being put on a leash and walked like a dog. Verbal insults were also more popular with male masochists.

Female masochists, in contrast, favored experiences that emphasized embarrassment more than simple humiliation. In particular, being displayed naked in a public or semipublic fashion was a more common desire among female than male masochists. For example, one woman fantasized that she would lie naked and spread-eagled on the snack table during a cocktail party, and people would reach across her naked limbs to get some crackers or cheese dip. Another liked to be told to go out in public wearing a miniskirt and no panties, so she was constantly in danger of having strangers be able to see her sex organs under her skirt. She described the nervous thrill of walking up the steps in a crowded auditorium before a lecture, not knowing who could or would see under her skirt.

Other differences involved pain. Male masochists seemed more willing to dispense with pain altogether, and so being spanked tended to be more common among female than male masochists. When men did want pain, however, they tended to desire stronger doses of it, so male masochism might involve paddling or whipping instead of the relatively mild hand-spanking that female masochists favored. Female masochists also preferred to elaborate some context or significance for the spanking, such as if they had misbehaved (usually just as part of the sex game) and were being punished, whereas many male masochists would simply describe being spanked or whipped for no apparent reason.

What about sex itself? A big difference emerged: Female masochists usually ended up having genital intercourse with their partners, but male masochists generally did not (61 percent versus 27 percent [Baumeister, 1988a, 1989]). This supports the social exchange view that women give sex to men. The submissive gives to the dominant, which is the point of the episode. So if the dominant one is a woman, she doesn't give sex to the man, because that would contradict her dominance (which is what many people in those situations reportedly actually say). But if the woman is the submissive one, then she does give genital intercourse. When the man is the submissive, he does usually give her cunnilingus, however, which is regarded as more in keeping with his role. The dominant partner does not usually reciprocate with fellatio or indeed any other stimulation.

Thus, although neither masculinity or femininity is inherently masochistic, there is some basis for arguing that masochism itself is more feminine than masculine. Moreover, men and women practice masochism in slightly different ways and with different emphases, even if the central themes are quite similar.

To conclude: The psychology of self has ample insights to share with the study of sexuality. Self-esteem, self-awareness, and other self processes contribute to sexual behavior. Ultimately this should not be surprising, because the self can seek expression in its sexual behavior just as well as in other behavior. Many possible sex acts gain or lose in appeal depending on their implications for the self.

CHAPTER

4

Nature, Culture, and What If There's No One to Marry Me?

Human reproduction differs radically from that of other animals. Most sex between humans involves women who are unable to conceive at the moment. Unlike most other species, humans have sex for recreation, not just for procreation (Abramson & Pinkerton, 1995). Human beings have sex in private (mostly), human females are receptive to sex at all phases of the reproductive cycle, human females undergo menopause, human beings have long-term sexual partnerships and have them in close proximity to other humans, and both human parents contribute to raising the dependent offspring. In addition, ovulation is concealed not only from the males but even from the female herself. As Diamond (1997) says, "It's especially paradoxical that in *Homo sapiens*, the species unique in its self-consciousness, females should be unconscious of their own ovulation, when female animals as dumb as cows are aware of it" (p. 67). Although a few other species might engage in one or another of the practices described above (bonobos and dolphins engage in recreational sex, for instance, and many species of birds practice coparenting), no other species remotely resembles the very unusual sexual style of humans. We are unique and highly bizarre in the world of animal sexuality (Diamond, 1997). Because we are so wildly different from animals in our sexual behaviors, does that mean that nature has played little or no role in shaping our sexuality? Is our sexual behavior determined solely by culture?

One of the great, perennial questions in the social sciences is whether human behavior is mainly caused by innate, biologically determined forces or by the socialization patterns and normative pressures of culture. Aggression, intelligence, helpfulness, competition, egotism, and many other human phenomena have been the foci of arguments as to whether nature or nurture is decisive. Not surprisingly, sex is likewise open to this debate.

In fact, with sex the debates are especially sharp and nasty. To theorists who favor biological, evolutionary explanations for behavior, sex is a crucial battle to win. Reproduction is central to evolution, and if sexuality is not determined by biology, then perhaps nothing is. On the other side, many people are dissatisfied with current sexual practices and arrangements, and it is vital to them to believe that culture can change them. For feminists, appeals to biological determinism seem like thinly veiled rationalizations for the status quo and the continued oppression of women. More broadly, utopians and idealists of all stripes wish to believe that human sexuality can be changed by culture and socialization. Any society has trouble when its broad control over sexual behavior breaks down, because the consequences (such as unwanted children and derailed adult lives) are a drain on society's resources.

Most theories about sex have recognized that actual sexual behavior reflects some mixture of nature and culture. But the recipes for the mixture vary widely. In an important article on the history of theorizing about sex, DeLamater and Hyde (1998) explained that two poles have dominated theorizing. On the one hand, *essentialist* theories have explained sexual behavior as the reflection of some innate essence, usually dictated by biology and evolution. You are born a certain way, and socialization can only make small differences. In contrast, *social constructionist* theories (including most feminist views) treat biology as merely the basic raw ingredient and insist that most sexual behavior is a result of social and cultural factors such as communication, rules, norms, expectations, approval, relationship status, and social roles.

The underlying assumption is often that what is biological cannot be changed. That is an overstatement, but clearly it is harder to change things that are in our genetic blueprint than things that we pick up by watching television. Body height, for example, is highly determined by one's genes. To be sure, getting proper nutrition early in life can make a difference in how tall one grows. But once you've reached your adult height, it is futile to wish to be taller or shorter.

The nature-versus-culture debate is also a sensitive one with respect to behavioral patterns such as sex, because it carries powerful implications for individual moral responsibility. In 1994, for example, a book received international media attention for its conclusion that patterns of promiscuity and marital infidelity were genetically heritable (Wright, 1994a). *Time* magazine featured the research on its cover with the headline "Infidelity: It's in Our Genes" (Wright, 1994b). Undoubtedly one reason for the huge wave of interest in this finding (the *Time* article drew over eight hundred letters from readers) was that it offered many people an excuse for their behavior. When accused by their spouses of betraying a sacred trust or breaking their marital vows, they could shrug and say, "I can't help it—it's genetic."

Such arguments take an even darker turn when applied to the most sinister sexual behaviors. One might ask, for example, whether it is fair to punish a serial rapist or child molester if his (or, in rare cases, her) crimes arise from an innate genetic predisposition? He might well plead that he should not be held responsible for his actions, and indeed he might sincerely regret them, but biology forces him to act that way. (Then again, if the biological predisposition were that strong, then there would be no chance of rehabilitating him, and if allowed to go free he should be expected to rape again—so society might be best served by removing him permanently from contact with potential victims.) If crimes are determined by genetic, unchangeable dispositions, then punishment loses not only its moral justification but also its value as rehabilitation and deterrence.

One standard criterion for settling nature-versus-nurture arguments is cultural variation. When the same pattern is found over and over, in nearly all cultures, one is inclined to suppose that biology is playing a strong role. In contrast, if a behavior or pattern changes from one culture to another, explanations tend to favor socialization, because people presumably have the same biology everywhere. By the same token, if behavior changes across historical periods within a culture, one again assumes that cultural factors and socialization are mainly responsible for it, because evolutionary change in human biology takes extremely long periods of time, whereas historical change is relatively fast.

Cultural and historical variation seems like a simple rule to use, but it is not. Hard-core believers in biological determinism contend that the cultural patterns are themselves derived from biological factors that adapt to local conditions (such as temperature and disease). Die-hard believers in cultural determinism sometimes reject as unacceptable the view that universal patterns are innate. For example, in all known societies, men have higher status and prestige than women, but feminists and others are loath to accept the implication that nature has genetically instilled guarantees of male superiority (or needs for and feelings of superiority). Still, the search for cultural variation provides one helpful clue to resolving the question, and that clue is probably accurate in the majority of cases, even if it is far from infallible.

With sex, as we shall see, there are plenty of cultural and historical changes, but there are also some patterns that seem universal. One might try to sort each aspect of sexuality according to its cross-cultural universality. Then again, recent theorizing has begun to make more creative and constructive use of the obvious fact that both nature and culture influence human sexuality. The challenge is then to understand how these forces interact.

Culture Scores

Afghanistan spent most of the final years of the twentieth century locked in bitter civil war. It began as rebellion against the Soviet occupation, and it continued interminably after the Russians left. After many years, a new force called the Taliban entered the fray. It consisted mainly of young men with devout Islamic faith and strong discipline. Many had been students. Because the Taliban appeared to be motivated by religious ideals rather than power-grubbing ambition and greed, it attracted popular support, which helped it gain the upper hand.

Once in power, the Taliban remained true to their religious ideals by imposing strict Islamic law. This included severe measures to prevent women from stimulating men sexually. Women were required to cover themselves from head to foot so that no female skin would be visible to inflame male desire. Because the sound of a woman's voice might arouse prurient interest among men, it became necessary that women be accompanied in public by a male relative or guardian to whom the woman would whisper whatever needed to be said (e.g., for making purchases) so that he could speak it aloud. Finally, the sound of women's footsteps was deemed to pose the threat of drawing men's thoughts to female feet and legs, and so this noise was prevented by insisting that women wear only quiet slippers, even when walking in the city.

The penalties for violating this system of sexual control could be severe. Women with uncovered skin were threatened and sometimes beaten. In 1997, the newspapers reported the following incident, which had occurred shortly after the Taliban takeover and before the full restrictions had been imposed. A young married couple, each around twenty years old, was bicycling along the street. A young Taliban guard raised his hand and stopped them. He asked the woman why she was breaking the rules to ride the bike, especially since the action of pedaling revealed her ankles to sight. The woman answered: "I am with my husband. It is not your wish for me but his wish for me, and if he does not mind, who are you to say?" An older Taliban guard came by and joined the argument, saying, "I will deal with this shameless woman." He pointed his rifle down at the husband's foot and fired it once, blasting a bullet through the man's foot. Then he pointed the gun at the woman's heart and fired, killing her instantly (O'Kane, 1997). This happened in a public place, and there were plenty of people around. When they heard the shots, the people took off running, trying to put as much distance between themselves and that incident as possible.

Under the Taliban, even private behavior fell under strict control. Sex was permitted only inside marriage. Premarital sex between single persons was punished by severe, painful whippings to both parties. Adulterous couples were put to death in gruesome fashion: Each person was buried alive, neck deep, leaving the head sticking out but the person unable to move. Then heavy stones were dropped on the head until the sinner was smashed to death.

Contrasting such practices with modern Western countries provides undeniable evidence of cultural variation in sexuality. Afghan women under Islamic law must never show any skin or hair in public, including their faces, whereas on U.S. beaches women wear only skimpy bikinies, and in Australia and some parts of Europe women routinely and legally go topless on public beaches. The notion of concealing one's hair or ankles so as to avoid provoking despicable sexual urges in men has probably not occurred to most American women.

But even among modern Western countries, there are variations in the laws concerning sex and, to some extent, in the actual practices. In some places, homosexuals are permitted to marry and raise children. In others, even performing homosexual acts is illegal. A celebrated case in Virginia in 1993 involved a gay woman whose mother took custody of the gay woman's young child. The woman sought to prove in court that being gay did not disqualify her as a fit mother, and many eminent authorities (including official representatives of the American Psychological Association) supported her. Unfortunately all forms of oral sex (including heterosexual acts) were felonies in Virginia, and insofar as lesbians have few alternatives to oral sex, the woman had to admit to felonious behavior; thus, as a convicted felon, she was unsuitable to claim custody of her child. (Imagine if this rule were applied uniformly, so that every woman in Virginia who had ever performed or received oral sex had her child taken away from her for that reason!)

The sex industry likewise varies widely from place to place. Cincinnati, Ohio, gained national notoriety for suppressing an art exhibit that included nude photos by Robert Mapplethorpe, and more generally the town prided itself on the absence of pornographic material and other commercial sex. Across the state, however, Cleveland permitted sale of a wide variety of pornography in neighborhood stores, licensed clubs where women danced fully naked for paying customers, and contented itself with only occasional and half-hearted efforts to cut down on prostitution. Across the border in

Ontario, Canada, nude dancers performed intimate personal acts and occasionally even allowed customers to touch their bodies, but some forms of erotica were aggressively suppressed. For example, Ontario subscribers to U.S. sex magazines such as *Penthouse Variations* sometimes received their copies with entire pages obliterated with black ink.

Across the ocean, a Czech television station fired the dowdy old weatherman and began having the weather forecast delivered by beautiful, stark-naked young women. The station was run by a former dissident intellectual, whose intellectual pals had thought his station would provide stimulating and uplifting fare, but the man himself said that "we just show what the market wants." The success of his methods was confirmed when his station became the most popular one in the country. The Czech citizens who preferred the naked forecasters contrast strikingly with the Afghan zealots who would beat or murder any woman who went out in public with her ankles showing.

One could go on, but the fact of cultural variation in sexuality seems indisputable. Nor do the variations refer only to abstract matters such as laws: Actual attitudes and practices vary too (although perhaps less than the laws do, since one doubts that Virginians really refrained from oral sex as scrupulously as the laws stipulated). To deny the reality of change in sexual behavior is, among other things, to deny that the sexual revolution ever took place.

The so-called sexual revolution in the 1960s was not the only historical change in sexual behavior in Western history. Historian Lawrence Stone (1977) observed that in recent centuries Western sexual practices have followed approximately 150-year cycles between license and prudery. Thus, the sexually open peak of the 1960s and 1970s contrasted with the restrained sexuality of the Victorian period (the late 1800s), which was itself a contrast to the more permissive times of the Romantic era (the late 1700s and early 1800s).

Nature Claims Its Due

Thus, cultural variation and historical change in sexual matters are genuine. But does this mean that sex is totally determined by culture? Undoubtedly sex has its natural side too. Let us do a survey of some of the consistencies in sexual behavior that may indicate the influence of natural, even biological aspects of human psychology. Sure enough, there seem to be plenty of universals with regard to sex that suggest natural or innate roots. One may start with the obvious: orgasm, pregnancy, and similar physical aspects of sex that are familiar everywhere. But even sexual behaviors are often quite similar across cultural and historical boundaries.

Sexual Practices

Sexual practices do not vary as widely as one might think. In the previous section, we noted that cultures vary in how they regulate homosexuality, prostitution, pornography, oral sex, and the like. Yet this very variation in laws indicates an underlying sameness in practices. All cultures seem to recognize that those varieties of sex exist and must therefore either be tolerated or regulated. Scholars who examine sexual practices in widely different historical and cultural contexts note a remarkable sameness to the list. For example, Tannahill (1980) observed that the ancient Chinese sex manuals included essentially the same practices as would be found in the how-to manuals on sale today in an American bookstore, despite the vast separation by miles, language, and centuries. In a similar vein, Bullough and Brundage's (1982) survey of medieval theological writings about sex found that they discussed almost all the same practices known today, despite the radical difference in attitudes and tolerance: The theologians were opposed to most practices, and their debates often focused on the effort to develop a hierarchy of sinfulness of the various sexual acts.

Thus, the sexual horizon does not actually change very much. Penis in vagina, penis in anus, mouth on genitals, hands on genitals, same versus opposite gender partners, masturbation, sex with animals or mechanical devices—these have been known everywhere, and there is not much else. With the important and remarkable exception of sadomasochism (and one might add phone and Internet sex), cultures have been unable to invent new sexual practices that previous eras or other cultures lacked. The sexual landscape is apparently set by nature, and culture can only try to alter attitudes, preferences, and choices. Culture can place the order, but nature has already written the menu.

Even permissiveness does not vary as much as one might think. Heise (1967) classified 116 societies as to their levels of sexual permissiveness for infancy, childhood, adolescence, and adulthood. Each society (and each age group within that society) was coded in one of three categories: permissive, restrictive, and semipermissive. The total number of possible variations in the sequence was 81, and so if cultures varied widely there could be up to 81 different patterns found across all those societies. In fact, however, Heise found that only 14 different combinations existed, and there was no sign of the other 67 possible combinations in any of the 116 cultures. Something is clearly limiting the degree of variation among cultures. One might propose that the limiting factor would be a tendency for adult sexuality to be permitted more latitude than child or adolescent, but that was not the explanation either: Most of the societies restricted adult sexuality (such as by prohibiting extramarital sex), and in general adult sexuality was given less freedom than adolescent sexuality.

Love

Passionate love is a strong emotional experience that many historians and anthropologists have regarded as culturally constructed. Evidence for major historical variation in passionate love has come from many sources. Yet in a recent compilation by Jankowiak (1995), most participating scholars concluded that romantic passion is familiar to all cultures. What varies (widely) is the culture's attitude toward it. Some cultures belittle it, others regard it as a dangerous form of mental instability, and still others idolize it as a supreme form of human bliss and fulfillment. But the psychological experience of falling in love is familiar everywhere.

Moreover, historians may be correct in suggesting that the opportunity to experience romantic love and, in particular, to pursue it and act upon it, may vary widely, with high levels of individual choice and freedom at one extreme and with arranged marriage, sexual segregation, and restrictive control at the other. But the phenomenon appears to show up everywhere as a possibility.

Thus, again, nature has instilled the basic tendency and the possible experience. Culture can transform it, build on it, fight against it, or use it in the service of other ends.

Cross-Cultural Differences

Socialization theories of sex received great encouragement from anthropologist Margaret Mead's (1935) *Sex and Temperament in Three Primitive Societies*, which contended that those Pacific islanders were free of the guilt, shame, and other problems that plagued Americans' attitude toward sex. In her account, Samoans regarded sex as a pleasant fact of life and did not try to restrict the sexual activities of others, including extramarital relations involving their spouses. The notion that Samoans were free from sexual jealousy and possessiveness provided a powerful stimulus to views that culture determines sexuality.

Sadly, subsequent work by other anthropologists failed to confirm Meade's idyllic picture. She sought to depict Samoans as radically and fundamentally different than Americans, but closer looks concluded that the similarities outweighed the differences. Guilt, shame, jealousy, and the rest of the problems existed in Samoa after all.

Jealousy

Is jealousy natural or cultural? The highly respected sexological sociologist Ira Reiss (1986b) reviewed all the published evidence he could find and concluded that some sexual jealousy exists in all known human cultures. Many particulars vary: where people draw the line, how they express jealousy, how they treat unfaithful spouses, whether the interloper or the unfaithful spouse merits the greater punishment, and so forth. Moreover, individuals vary within cultures as to how they feel and react. But in every society on earth, most people object to letting their spouses copulate with other partners.

Thus, sexual possessiveness may be rooted in nature, not culture, given that it seems to be a universal feature of human life. Moreover, the universality of jealousy goes beyond the mere fact that jealousy is found everywhere. Apparently female infidelity is condemned more strongly than male infidelity in pretty much all cultures. That is, no known cultures are more forgiving of straying wives than of straying husbands (Daly & Wilson, 1988).

This difference is important to the biological and evolutionary theories about sex. According to such views, evolution has gradually favored patterns of behavior that have produced viable offspring, which means making babies and raising them to adulthood (so that they can reproduce too). Because a couple can only raise a few babies, each one is precious from a genetic point of view. Infidelity is seen as a threat insofar as it interferes with passing on one's genes.

One crucial difference between men and women is that women can be certain who their babies are. Because the baby comes out of the woman's body, she can be sure it is hers (although hospitals have been known to make identification errors and send babies home with the wrong parents, for most of our evolutionary history, women had babies at home, where there was little opportuntiy for intentional or inadvertent switching of infants). Even if her husband has had sex with ten other women during the past year, a woman still knows who her own baby is. In contrast, a man must fear that if his wife has sex with someone else, the baby she delivers may carry the other man's genes rather than his own. Only by strictly preventing wifely infidelity can a man be certain of raising his own children.

Thus, nature may well have instilled an attitude among males to want to prevent any sexual infidelity among their wives. Men who didn't care about this were less likely to pass along their genes, as compared to men who made sure their wives were faithful. Women don't like partner infidelity either, but the threat is only that the male will leave her or at least divert some resources to the other woman and away from herself and her own children. Hence letting your spouse have an occasional bit on the side is not as thoroughly or fundamentally opposed to the woman's genetic goals as it is to the man's. For that reason, presumably, all cultures have imposed stricter penalties on wifely than husbandly infidelity.

The argument is logically sound and fits the facts, but that doesn't quite guarantee that it's correct. In all known societies, men have had more power than women. Maybe the greater penalties for female than male adultery follow simply from the political realities: Men have more power, and so men reserve their right to play around, while they insist that women behave properly. As women gain political power and the power gap diminishes, the society seems to relinquish its sexual double standard somewhat (a pattern that will receive closer scrutiny in Chapter 5). Culture clearly makes some difference, even if nature has instilled the original pattern.

Promiscuity and Sexual Strategies

An important crucial step in describing sexual goals and strategies was the recognition that males and females have different reproductive goals (Trivers, 1972). However similar we might wish men and women to be, and however similar they actually are in most respects, there are some irreducible differences. Prominent among these is that sex makes women pregnant, not men. The process of reproduction requires the man to participate for about five minutes, and within half an hour he is ready to start fresh with a new partner, even if he never sees the first woman again. In contrast, once the woman gets pregnant, she is more or less committed for nine months of gestation. In fact, her commitment is often much greater than the nine months, for when the child appears she is usually tied to it regardless of whether the man is there.

And there are other risks for women as well. Throughout most of our evolutionary history, childbirth was often fatal. A careful composite estimate is that before 1800 in Western history, about 1.3 percent of birthings killed the mother (Shorter, 1982). Put another way, if a woman knew about fifteen other married women, she very likely knew one who died in childbirth. Even apart from venereal disease (which also tends to affect women more than men), women have always run significant risks with each act of copulation—risks that are simply not there for the men.

These differences meant that women would logically become more cautious about sex than men. Consider the costs of a mistake, such as copulating with a poor quality partner. If a man makes such a mistake, he loses nothing but one night and a load of sperm, and he has plenty more of both of those. In contrast, a woman may lose an entire year of fertility if she becomes pregnant. She may be stuck for years afterward with the offspring of her poor quality mate, which means she will be working to raise a poor quality offspring. And she may not even get that chance, if she dies in childbirth.

One gender difference is therefore likely to be in the standards people hold for choosing sex partners. There is little need for men to be choosy, because little is at stake (at least in evolutionary terms; modern laws and paternity lawsuits make men somewhat more accountable for their behavior). Women however should be much more cautious about their sex partners.

Evidence supports this. Studies by Buss and his colleagues, for example, show that women want to know their potential sex partners for a longer period of time and to know more about them than men do (Buss & Schmitt, 1993). In one study, the researchers asked people to assume that they were unattached and mutually attracted to someone else (also unattached). Would they have sex with this person if they had known each other for five years? one year? one month? one week? and so forth. Although both men and women generally said they would have sex with someone they had known for a long time under those conditions, their responses differed severely regarding the briefer intervals. Relatively few women said they would have sex with someone they had known for only a day or a week, even if there were strong mutual attraction, whereas most men were willing to have sex with someone they had known for only a few minutes.

Likewise, interest in casual sex has proven to be one of the largest and most reliable gender differences across many studies. A meta-analysis by Oliver and Hyde (1993) combining many findings showed that men consistently express much more willingness and desire to engage in casual sex than women. This fits the evolutionary view: Sex cannot be so casual when each act carries the risk of a nine-month pregnancy, plus having to raise the child afterward, not to mention the chance of death.

Interest in number of sex partners may also differ. Suppose men and women started out with equal proportions of promiscuous and monogamous (faithful) people, back in the primeval forest. Over many generations, the men who had sex with more partners were likely to have more offspring than the monogamous men. Hence the male gene pool would gradually shift toward favoring promiscuity.

In contrast, a woman can only have one baby per year, regardless of whether she has sex with one man or a hundred men. Promiscuity does not increase a woman's reproductive success, except in an occasional small way or in exceptional cases (e.g., if her mate is sterile).

There is an important further twist to this line of argument. Recall that reproductive, evolutionary success requires not just producing children but enabling them to survive to adulthood so they can reproduce too. Children need a great deal more than just to be born, and their survival depends heavily on how well they are cared for and protected for many years. These facts produce advantages for monogamous people: Couples who stay together can provide better care for their children. For the men, the advantage may be offset by the greater number of babies that promiscuity can yield (as long as someone else takes care of their offspring), but for women the advantage is clearly on the side of being monogamous and keeping the main man around.

Consider it this way: What happens to the promiscuous woman who has three children and is now six months pregnant with her fourth? At this point, she is not physically very attractive, so she is unlikely to have any men coming to bring her dinner or provide for her children. Nor can she hunt and gather effectively herself when she is handicapped by the burden of pregnancy. Under those circumstances, she and her children run serious risks of starvation or falling prey to wild animals. In contrast, the monogamous woman who likewise has three children and a fourth on the way—but who also has a husband around—is likely to be fed and protected, along with her offspring.

Thus, even if men and women started off with the same sexual motivations, evolution would gradually produce a tendency for men to want to be promiscuous and for women to prefer to be monogamous and faithful. Research has repeatedly confirmed that this difference is alive and well today. Men want to have many more sex partners than women, on average (Buss & Schmitt, 1993; Miller & Fishkin, 1997; see also Oliver & Hyde, 1993).

Although men could potentially conceive more offspring if they were promiscuous than if they were monogomous, there may have been at least two restraining factors that suggest that what might have evolved over time is more of a compromise for men than for women. Because reproductive success depends on the survival of one's offspring, and because the offspring's chances of survival are better if two parents contribute, men who were highly promiscuous may not have been able to support all their offspring and thus may not have been as genetically successful as more monogamous men. The issue of male coparenting is especially a problem for humans because of the extra-long period the young are dependent on the parents for food and education. By some estimates, a child cannot function on his or her own for more than a decade after birth (Diamond, 1997). Human men provide their families with resources to an extent that is unprecedented among primates. In most other primate species, for example, males usually do not share their food with their mates; females must rely on their own efforts to obtain food.

A second possible restraining factor on male promiscuity is the question of whether the male really can get a lot of potential mates if the females won't consent to mate with him. Many animal models suggest that female preferences weigh heavily in determining a male's opportunities to mate (e.g., Collias & Collias, 1970; Le Boeuf, 1974; Trivers, 1985).

Thus, men with no predisposition to mate in stable, long-term relationships might not have left enough offspring for a totally promiscuous genetic tendency to proliferate in the species (as compared to some species, where no long-term bonding occurs), even among males. Males thus evolved to mate in long-term relationships to raise their children to adulthood, but they appear to have also evolved (or to have not completely lost in evolution) some tendency to be more open than females to a wider variety of mating opportunites. Perhaps this greater need for compromise between monogamy and promiscuity can also explain why men have a greater variety of sexual practices and interests than women.

It is possible that both human genders (like some primates) were promiscuous at the dawn of humanity. As our ancestors became more human, the dependence of childhood became greater, creating evolutionary pressure for both males and females to form monogamous pair bonds to support offspring over a long term. The families with long-term bonding and highly dependent children became more successful and passed on more genes than individuals who did not put as many resources into child-rearing. Although both males and females may have evolved genes for pair bonding, the selection pressure may have been more intense for females than for males, due to the greater costs from women in casual sex. Thus, men may have retained more promiscuous tendencies than women.

Gender Differences in Partner Choice

A final emphasis of evolutionary theory has to do with what people seek in their sex partners. Remember, the evolutionary approach treats people as carriers for their genes, and they will evolve in ways that will pass along their genes most effectively. Both males and females will want high quality mates, such as those who are healthy and intelligent, because that way their children (who carry the genes of both partners) will be more likely to survive and flourish.

Again, though, men's and women's reproductive goals differ to some extent, and so they will emphasize different things in a partner. Men will presumably be most successful if they mate with a young, healthy woman who is most likely to be able to bear and raise many children. After all, suppose that back in the primeval forest there were many men who were only sexually attracted to relatively old women. Old women (past menopause) cannot have any babies, and women approaching menopause have reduced fertility and more pregnancy failures, so these men would quickly remove their genes from the gene pool. In contrast, men who preferred younger women might produce many children. Physical beauty is widely regarded by evolutionary theorists as a sign of good health. That is, good health can be reflected in several physical traits that are associated with being beautiful, including shiny hair; clear, supple skin; good posture and bone structure; clear, bright eyes; and energetic response. To a man, therefore, a young and beautiful woman would be a prime choice as a sex partner.

To a woman, meanwhile, partner age is less relevant. It is her body that has to withstand the strains of pregnancy and childbirth. His body only has to be able to furnish a load of sperm, and most men can accomplish that well into old age. No menopause occurs to mark the end of men's fertility. Hence youth and physical appearance are less important to a woman than a man, and women who were attracted to older men would be fully able to reproduce. What does matter for a woman, however, is how well the man can provide for her, and that depends on his social status. The higher the man's status, the better he can provide. In group hunting, for example, men took turns getting food from their kills, and the turns went in order of status—so the highest ranking man got the best food to take home to his woman. In a study of 5,000 college students on desirable qualities in a mate, women listed status (as in rank, position, power, standing, and station) as being much more important than men did (Langhorn & Secord, 1955). In a more recent sample of 10,047 people from 37 cultures, women all over the world

men-attracted to attractive woman because they will bear the healthiest children

women-can be attracted to older guys because they are powerful & resourceful desired financial resources in a marriage partner more than men did (on average, about 100 percent more [Buss, 1989; see also Kenrick, Sadalla, Groth, & Trost, 1990]). Recent reanalyses of data by Eagly and Wood (1999), however, suggest that these patterns are greatest in cultures with the greatest gender inequality.

In many respects, men and women want the same things in their mates: intelligence, trustworthiness, honesty, sense of humor. But they do differ in the relative emphasis of physical beauty versus social status. To an evolutionary psychologist, the goings-on in a singles bar or a Saturday night dance are based on the same principles that can be seen in the wild: Women compete for men's attention by trying to look young and beautiful; Men compete for women's attention by trying to look rich and successful.

Integrating Natural and Cultural Causation

Neither side is going to claim complete victory in the theoretical battle over sexuality. That is, neither nature nor culture is likely to provide a full explanation, and each has a substantial amount to contribute. Accordingly, we can expect that when the truth does emerge, it is likely to emphasize how nature and culture combine and interact to produce the many forms of human sexuality. Let us start to consider how nature and culture might be understood as working together rather than competing against each other as rival theories.

Morals as Adaptations

A first consideration for integrating evolutionary and socialization arguments is how to understand sexual morality. In this view, people are born with certain innate tendencies. To some extent, acting on these tendencies would undermine group harmony and interpersonal relations. Morality is thus a set of rules that will allow people to live together.

Understanding morals in this way allows one to appreciate both the broad similarities and the diversities among different cultures' moral systems. Many moral theories have struggled with one or the other (i.e., with either the similarities or the differences). Thus, some views of morality have tended to treat moral rules as innate properties of the human mind. This was the essence of Kant's (1787/1929) influential philosophy of morality, and it has been revived in Kohlberg's (1981, 1984) account of moral development: All minds will eventually converge on the same moral judgments, except insofar as they are hampered by inadequate thinking. But such views have difficulty explaining why different cultures would end up with different moral systems, because eventually people should all reach the same universal, innate conclusions.

In the twentieth century, moral relativism has been more popular than absolutist views such as Kant's. According to moral relativism, different cultures invent different moral systems based on various accidents of culture, such as the whims of the ruling class or the personal convictions of influential religious figures. In this view, nothing is absolutely or inherently right or wrong, and the moral judgments people express reflect merely the biases with which they were brought up. These views lost ground after World

War II, however, when the widespread revulsion against the Nazi genocidal projects left theorists unwilling to claim that such moral objections are merely historical accidents. More generally, broad agreement among different moral systems raises a problem for the view that morality is simply a product of a particular culture, because otherwise one would expect different cultures to be more different than they actually are.

Both problems can be solved by seeing morality as a set of solutions to common problems. Cultures essentially provide frameworks to enable people to live together, and human coexistence presents similar problems everywhere. Morality thus offers the society solutions to these problems. There are two kinds of moral solutions.

One is to prevent behavior that is hopelessly antisocial and disruptive of social groups. Examples of this first kind of solution include prohibitions against murder and theft. No culture has yet been found in which arbitrary, premeditated murder is morally acceptable, and this is because that sort of murder is socially disruptive everywhere. People could not live together if they killed each other on impulse. Likewise, some form of respect for personal property is necessary if a society is to hold a concept of ownership and private property.

The other solution is to offer a common approach when agreement is needed, even if various different solutions would be possible. Sexual morality mostly falls into this category. There is no single system of sexual activity that every society must adopt. But sexuality must be regulated to some degree, because people have desires and emotions, and they are upset when their expectations and understandings are violated. Hence sexual morals vary from one culture to another far more than moral rules about murder and theft. Society has to impose some controls over sexuality, and there are various ways of doing this, all somewhat viable. Different cultures will therefore have different sexual moralities.

In particular, moral rules about premarital sexual activity vary widely. It is, after all, possible for a society to function if everyone has plenty of premarital sex, and it is also quite possible for it to operate on the basis of expecting everyone to be a virgin on his or her wedding day. It is, however, much more difficult for a society to operate smoothly if half the people follow the one rule and half follow the other, because there will be conflicting expectations and disappointments (both during the dating phase and on the wedding night!). Hence society must set some rule in order to secure broad agreement and establish legitimate expectations.

To be sure, if either sexual license or its opposite, sexual prudery, were the perfect system, it is likely that most societies would converge on it. But both have drawbacks. When people engage in ample nonmarital sex, society has to struggle with the resulting problems of out-of-wedlock babies and, sometimes, epidemics of venereal disease. Prior to the modern era, contraception was only erratically effective, and so nonmarital sex carried substantial risks of unwanted pregnancy. Even today, many people become pregnant who do not want to be and are not in a position to offer a child a stable, well-appointed home or nurturing environment.

A restrictive sexual morality avoids the problems of sex, but it has costs too. For one, people continue to have sexual desires, and so restraining these desires entails frustration and personal dissatisfaction, thus ultimately lowering the quality of life, at least as compared with the blissful, trouble-free existence that sex-starved people imagine a rich sex life would offer. For another, regimes of sexual repression are generally less than fully effective, and thus it becomes necessary to punish offenders. The punishment process puts some burden on society as a whole and of course is particularly onerous for the individuals involved.

An additional problem is that one of the benefits of sexual restraint is ironically diminished by success. We mentioned venereal disease as one of the costs of sexual indulgence, because when everyone engages in free and easy sex, such disease gradually spreads through the population (if the population is large enough or porous enough to sustain or introduce them). When prudish morals reign, venereal disease cannot spread effectively, and it gradually disappears from much of society. But the very disappearance of venereal disease (from major parts of society, at least) removes one of the reasons to restrain one's desires. After all, fear of disease ceases to be a reason to avoid sex if there is hardly any chance of getting the disease.

Venereal disease may be a crucial reason behind the 150-year cycles of sexual morality in modern Western history cited by Stone (1977). Stone himself pointed to cycles of religious belief as factors that drive the waxing and waning of sexual morality, but it is far from clear why religious beliefs should conform to a 150-year cycle. In contrast, venereal disease could well follow such a pattern.

Thus, in an era of sexual restraint, venereal disease is relatively rare. Hence people begin to realize that they can engage in nonmarital sexual activity without fear of being infected. As they begin to indulge their desires, some form of sexual revolution occurs, and the prudish era is replaced by a more permissive phase of sexuality. This is probably the most pleasant time in the cycle, and people should regard themselves as lucky if their youth coincides with this phase!

Next, however, the permissive sexuality begins to spread venereal disease in its wake. As more and more people engage in promiscuous sex, venereal disease is transmitted among networks of partners. Eventually the risk becomes serious. Parents and other agents of socialization seek to instill a more prudish, restrained approach to sex in the young generation, in order to discourage the sexual indulgence that is now spreading such diseases. They may turn to religious indoctrination to furnish the desired messages, which could be why Stone suggested that religious passions drive the cycle of sexual morals. But it seems more likely that people invoke religion simply in order to have a ready-made justification for the message of sexual restraint that they feel is warranted because of the rising dangers of unfettered sexual indulgence. Nobody wants his or her kid to get VD.

And so a new phase of sexual restraint settles in. Promiscuity is condemned, virginity is respected, and fidelity is prized. The new limitations on sexual activity disrupt the spread of venereal disease, sex gradually becomes safe again, and the cycle can be started anew.

More generally, then, culture and nature probably pull in opposite directions with regard to sex. Nature instills in people a desire for sexual activity, and culture regulates it and pushes people to restrain their desires. Where nature does not instill sexual desire, it is possible that culture sometimes steps in and tries to produce it, but this is not likely to be very effective. For example, some people find themselves with patterns of sexual desire that they want to change, such as homosexual feelings or sadomasochistic inclinations, but therapists are not terribly successful at causing these people to give up those desires in favor of others. Transforming a thoroughgoing homosexual into a practicing heterosexual is quite difficult. In societies where a period of adolescent homosexuality is institutionalized, most males willing leave this stage for an exclusive heterosexual marriage after the birth of their first child (Herdt, 1981), suggesting that even long-term cultural indoctrination doesn't seem to change sexual orientation. And if all the accumulated expertise and techniques of psychotherapy find it hard to create new patterns of sexual desire, it is doubtful that the vaguer and more diffuse pressures of cultural socialization can create desires where nature has not supplied them.

Indeed, the partial successes of therapy lend further support to the argument that culture operates mainly by restraining rather than by encouraging. It is somewhat possible for therapists to destroy a pattern of sexual desire, such as by using classical conditioning to pair the desired sexual object with something aversive or disgusting. In this way, for example, one may possibly condition a homosexual to find homosexual desire unpleasant or disgusting. To cause that person to feel heterosexual desire instead, however, is much more difficult. However, studies of attempts to reorient the sexual preferences of pedophiles suggest that the opposite is true: Sexual desire for adults could be added, but the attraction to children was difficult to eliminate (Schwartz & Masters, 1983).

It is surely an overstatement to propose that all forms of sexual desire are natural. Quite possibly people can have their sexual patterns warped (or otherwise transformed) by powerful experiences early in life. The so-called sexual perversions may be caused in such ways, although the etiological roots of such sexual problems are not well understood at all, and the possibility of genetic predisposition probably cannot be ruled out. Socialization can, at least by accident, transform the focus of sexual desire and redirect it away from its original, natural goals.

By and large, though, it seems fair to conclude that sexual desires are instilled by nature and that the restraints are promoted by culture and socialization. Calling something "natural" should not be viewed as a blanket endorsement, however, as if people should throw off all the inhibitions they have been taught and engage in unrestrained sexual activity just as nature has supposedly decreed. Venereal disease is natural too, after all. Moreover, people must live in a society with other people who may be hurt or angered or may even take lethal action if their sexual expectations are violated (e.g., in cases of jealousy over partner infidelity). To give oneself over to unbridled sexual indulgence on the grounds that doing so is "natural" is to accept the fact that nature has also set up the world so that we might contract dangerous venereal diseases or fall into dangerous interpersonal conflicts. The restraints promoted by cultures are generally well founded.

Mate Shortages

For anyone interested in the interplay of nature and culture, one of the most fascinating works was a book on sex ratios by Guttentag and Secord (1983). They pointed out that cultures change in predictable ways when there is a surplus of one gender in the

in mate shortages, the sex who is in the minority has the most power because of limited resources

population. The changes depend heavily on which gender is in the majority. Those differences thus suggest standard ways that culture responds to nature.

The notion of a surplus is based on the fact that men and women generally mate in a one-to-one manner, so the number of marriages can be no higher than the number of whichever gender is in the minority of adults. If there are twice as many women as men, half the women will go without husbands (unless the rules of marriage change to permit polygamy).

A key point of Guttentag and Secord's research was that sexual morality changes with the sex ratio. When there is a surplus of men and a shortage of women, the culture tends to put women on a pedestal, and sexual prudishness reigns. A double standard of sexual morality that puts higher expectations for sexual restraint and purity on the female is common when men are in the majority.

In contrast, when there is a surplus of women and a shortage of men, society is much more permissive about sexual activities and practices, and women are devalued. Strong family values and traditional sex roles go with surpluses of males; a rejection of traditional values, high divorce rates, adultery, illegitimacy, a feminist movement that challenges or rejects traditional sex roles (including rejecting the double standard), and similar patterns prevail when there is a surplus of females.

Why might these patterns obtain? Readers accustomed to democratic thinking might assume that the majority would rule. This has rarely been the case where the genders are concerned, however, and in fact males have enjoyed superior political power over women in all societies in the history of the world. Thus, it is not that women prefer promiscuity and choose it when they are in the majority, accepting prudish restraint only when it is foisted on them by a male majority. Indeed, the value judgments about women contradict the majority rule theory: Women have lower prestige and status than men even when the women are in the majority, although women probably do fare somewhat better politically when they are in the majority rather than in the minority.

Instead, it appears that gender interactions follow supply-and-demand rules, by which scarcity confers power. Women are treated with respect and become precious, admired members of society when they are in short supply. When they outnumber men, they lose value and hence are treated with disrespect.

The changes in sexual morality are of particular interest. They suggest that men desire promiscuity and commitment-free sex, whereas women desire stable, committed relationships. The gender that is in the minority has the power to call the shots in this.

Thus, when men are in the majority, opportunities for casual sex are limited. At most, prostitution may flourish as a way of providing an outlet for these men. (Another way of looking at this is that prostitution is an opportunity to make money off the deprivation that these men suffer due to the shortage of women and their lack of access to unpaid sex.) If a man does manage to find a woman, he is probably quite willing to marry her. Moreover, he had better treat her well, because if he loses her, the odds are against him being able to replace her easily. Powerful men, who often have better chances of marrying women than poor or powerless men, may even favor a restrictive pattern of sexual morality, because they do not want their wives to become involved with other men.

In contrast, when women are in the majority, it is they have who have to make the greater concessions in order to attract partners. Men desire sex early in the relationship, and so a woman must comply with these wishes or risk having the man move on to another woman. A man does not have to treat a woman particularly well, because if she becomes disenchanted with him she will have a difficult time finding another partner, whereas he can easily move on to someone else if she does leave him. He does not need to offer her much in order to gain sexual favors: Indeed, she may feel she has to use sex in order to compete successfully against other women to retain his affection.

Why would a society have an imbalance in the sex ratio? There are many reasons. Throughout history, shortages of women have been caused by many factors, such as selective infanticide of female babies. Nowadays, infanticide has declined significantly, but in some countries a similar effect is achieved by selective abortion. Modern China, for example, is enforcing a one-child policy to control its population, and many couples feel that if they are only to have one child, they want a boy, because boys traditionally support their parents in old age, whereas girls traditionally support their in-laws. Hence when the wife becomes pregnant, they test the fetus for gender, and if it is a girl they have an abortion. The news magazine *The Economist* reported a study in the city of Shanghai. The researchers found that out of approximately eight thousand abortions in which the child's gender was previously known to the parents, only one was a boy. Clearly, the one-child policy coupled with the desire for sons is in danger of brewing a heavily unbalanced population full of extra males. That generation of young males is not to be envied: The shortage of girl babies will eventually translate into an inability of many young men to marry.

Another historical reason for shortages of women is selective migration. Throughout most of its history, the United States had more men than women, simply because men were more likely to move here from Europe. Even within the United States, men were more likely to migrate to the frontier than women. In fact, the so-called Wild West of the United States was marked by consistently high sex ratios that averaged twice as many men as women, and in some places and groups (such as Chinese Americans), approached two hundred men per every woman. The often-repeated advice, "Go west, young man," may have been good in terms of finding opportunities for business or adventure, but it carried severe costs in terms of any chance for romance or marriage.

Shortages of males occur for other reasons as well. Although slightly more boys than girls are born, boys are more likely to die of infections and diseases. More importantly, social events often prey heavily on young men, and in particular death by violence has always been a much greater threat to men than women (not counting infanticide). After a major war, the male population is often severely depleted, and so the return to peacetime follows the pattern of sexual permissiveness that is found when men are scarce. In Europe after World War II, for example, men were in short supply, and sex was probably much more available to the young men than at other times.

In today's United States, war has not contributed in any significant way to the sex ratios, but there is a slight surplus of females across the population as a whole. In some sectors, the deficit is much more pronounced. Young African American men, particularly among the poorer classes, are in a distinct minority as compared to African American women. For unknown reasons, African Americans conceive more female than male babies. Furthermore, the frequent poverty among African Americans results in a higher rate of fetal and infant mortality, which affects male babies more than females. Then violence and similar social problems take a heavier toll on young males than on young females: One-third of black men in their twenties are in the criminal justice system, either in prison or on parole ("A social profile," 1998). As a result of these trends, the marriageable adult African American population is disproportionately female.

Hence many young African American women are unable to find men of their own race to marry. Since they do not marry outside their race very much (a surprising fact to which we shall return in Chapter 10), they are often faced with the prospect of remaining single for most of their lives. Meanwhile, they suffer the devaluation (evident in the much discussed misogyny of rap music) and lack of sexual bargaining power that characterize female surpluses wherever they arise.

Sexual Orientation and Homosexuality: The Gay Gene Versus the Domineering Mother

Let us now examine another creative integration of natural and cultural processes: the causes of homosexuality and, indeed, of sexual orientation in general.

The causes of homosexuality pose problems for both biologically, evolutionarily oriented psychologists and for those who stress the influence of culture and socialization. Biological explanations of homosexuality incline toward the assumption that people are born with genetic predispositions toward being homosexual. Yet why would such genes survive? Homosexual intercourse does not lead to reproduction, and in fact being exclusively homosexual is a guarantee of having no offspring. If there were a "gay gene," one would think that it would be quickly eliminated from the gene pool, because it would not be passed on to further generations.

Meanwhile, culture-based explanations of heterosexuality have a milder version of the same problem. Given that most cultures have strongly favored heterosexuality (again, if only because that is the only way for a culture to produce future generations), why do people become homosexual? One has to assume that certain formative experiences cause people to reject their society's dominant model of sexuality and prefer their own gender.

Those views depict homosexuality as a result of some problem in development. Such things might happen, and indeed many older theories about homosexuality have taken the form of trying to analyze "what went wrong during childhood?" For example, Freud and his followers proposed that boys who fail to resolve the Oedipus complex (i.e., a phase of childhood marked by love for the mother) might become homosexual. Conversely, girls who were too successful at resolving their version of the Oedipus complex, such as by replacing their mother as the objects of their fathers' affection, were seen as being on a path toward lesbianism. Other views have simply assumed that children who were too close to the opposite-sex parent and identified with that person were likely to become homosexual. Thus, a "Mama's boy" might adopt his mother's outlook, and because his mother sees men as sexually attractive, the boy might end up doing the same.

is homosexuality a genetic or social choice? some may be biological some may be social

These are fine, logical theories, but as so often happens in the social sciences, the data fail to provide support. A large research project in the San Francisco Bay area interviewed a thousand homosexuals and five hundred heterosexuals, and then employed advanced statistical techniques to search for any relationships corresponding to what the leading, culture-based theories of sexual orientation predicted. The results were profoundly disappointing to anyone who wanted to believe those theories. The authors concluded, for example, that the statistical link between how a boy related to his mother and whether he became homosexual or heterosexual was "hardly worth mentioning" (Bell, Weinberg, & Hammersmith, 1981, p. 184). Identification with opposite-sex parents also failed to show any significant relationship. In fact, essentially nothing about the family background showed any link to adult sexual orientation (Bell et al., 1981).

Many people believe that someone might become homosexual by virtue of having been seduced by a practicing homosexual. People might presumably learn to be gay as a result of an influential and satisfying encounter with a member of one's own gender. This might explain how homosexuality could survive despite opposition in the broader society, because active homosexuals might initiate younger people to become like them. This theory, too, failed to find support in the San Francisco study. Most gay people recognized their own same-gender feelings and desires well before they actually had any sort of physical, sexual experience with someone of their own gender. In fact, usually the feelings preceded the behavior by about three years (Bell et al., 1981).

There is some support for the biological, even genetic transmission of homosexuality. Yet that evidence falls far short of the essentialist theory that genes dictate sexual orientation and that nothing can be done about it. For example, in a study of gay men who had an identical (monozygotic) twin, 52 percent of the twins were also gay (Bailey & Pillard, 1991). That is certainly far above the base rate of homosexuality among males, which is under 5 percent (Laumann et al., 1994). But it is also far below the level that a direct genetic path would predict. Identical twins, after all, share 100 percent (or very close to that) of their genes. Identical twins always have the same eye color and height, but apparently they do not always have the same sexual orientation—which implies that sexual orientation is not nearly as direct a result of genes as eye color or height. Moreover, evidence for genetic bases for homosexuality is even weaker in women than in men.

A creative solution was proposed by Bem (1996, 1998). He makes use of both genetic, biological tendencies and social experiences, and so his theory is a commendable model of the integration of nature and culture. It fits what is currently known, although it may be another decade or two before we know whether his theory is a full and accurate account of the roots of sexual orientation.

Bem starts with the reasonably safe view that genes dictate temperament, which refers to characteristics such as level of energy and disposition. Most parents will agree that their children seemed to have temperamental patterns very early in life, certainly before the parents had any awareness of being able to shape or influence them. Naturally, any child or even any adult may become grumpy when frustrated or punished, and that is not what is meant here by temperament. Rather, some children seem just to wake up happy, to smile a lot, and to feel good when there is no apparent reason to feel any particular way, whereas other children are notably different.

Thus, Bem thinks that the pathway toward homosexuality may begin with genetic influence, but that this influence is merely on temperament and other broad, general factors rather than on sexual orientation per se. His theory then leaves genetic factors behind. The next step in his argument refers to childhood play activities and peers. The roles and rules for childhood games tend to be the same everywhere. Boys like rough, aggressive play, whereas girls prefer more gentle activities. Boys prefer competitive, adversarial games, while girls prefer to socialize in harmonious ways.

But not every child fits those patterns equally well. What happens to the boy who, by virtue of his gentle or harmonious temperament, doesn't really like the boys' games? Or the girl who is bored with pretending to have tea parties and prefers to climb trees, play ball, or shoot guns? In Bem's theory, such children are likely to end up playing with children of the opposite sex. If this pattern persists, they may end up having most of their friends among the opposite sex, while members of their own gender may seem different and foreign.

In adolescence Bem, says, it is the *unfamiliar* gender that becomes arousing. People who are different and unfamiliar may make you nervous, in a sense. For boys who have grown up around other boys, girls will be daunting and may make them feel excited, nervous, apprehensive, uncertain, and so forth. For boys who have grown up around girls, however, it is other boys who may have this effect.

The same logic applies to girls, of course. If a girl has spent her childhood playing with other girls, then her discovery of boys at adolescence may lead to excitement at how different they are. In contrast, if she has grown up playing with boys, then the girls will seem different, and she may find them exciting.

How does Bem get from excitement over differences to sexual orientation? One of social psychology's enduring, influential theories has held that people's reactions depend on how they label their bodily reactions. This theory, first put forward by Schachter in the early 1960s (e.g., Schachter & Singer, 1962), depicts emotion as consisting of two parts. One part is bodily arousal, and that is essentially the same for most emotions. (Thus, the physiological response is basically the same for anger, joy, grief, and other emotions, according to this theory.) The other part is the mental label that people put on the arousal, and the type of label will depend on how the person interprets the situation.

When an adolescent feels a nervous, confused excitement around certain people, he or she may learn to label that feeling as sexual attraction (or merely romantic passion), which, according to Bem, is the proximal cause of sexual orientation. The feeling itself is most likely to occur in the presence of the less familiar gender.

Bem has called this theory *EBE*, which stands for "exotic becomes erotic." What is exotic is exciting because it is different and unfamiliar. The childhood experiences dictate which gender is more unfamiliar and hence more likely to seem exotic. The arousal state that arises in such people's presence then becomes labeled as attraction, and so what was initially exotic gradually becomes erotic, in the sense of sexually exciting.

As we said, the EBE theory provides a good fit to what is currently known, but there are many gaps in the existing knowledge and so it would be premature to pronounce it as true. In its favor, however, is its sophisticated mixture of nature and nurture. At present it looks highly unlikely that sexual orientation will turn out to be a direct, exclusive consequence of one's genetic blueprint or the result of formative experiences independent of biology. When the field of sexuality does eventually arrive at its final, correct theories, these are likely to invoke complex interactions between biological foundations and social experiences. Even if Bem's theory turns out not to be precisely and fully correct, it will probably be remembered as a large step in the right direction.

Adoption

Many evolutionary theorists place a great emphasis on paternity certainty because male animals, including humans, want to pass on their own genes and do not want to contribute to the support of another male's offspring. A number of evolutionary theorists refer to a parent (usually a male, but sometimes a female as well, such as a cowbird, who lays her egg in another bird's nest) who raises a child who is not genetically related as being "duped" (e.g., Buss, 1994) or as having "lost the evolutionary race" (Diamond, 1997). Yet while there is considerable evidence that parents do give preferential treatment to juveniles who are more likely to be their genetic offspring, there is also considerable evidence of foster care that is provided even when no clear genetic link exists. So, although if forced to make a choice between saving their own child or a stepchild, humans will usually choose their own child, the majority of decisions may not involve such a drastic choice or such extremely limited resources.

Adopting or fostering children is universal among human cultures. If raising another individual's child is the equivalent of losing the evolutionary race, why is it so common? There may be multiple answers: The first answer (and most important one in terms of integrating nature and culture) may be that the desire to pass along our genes is joined, in humans, with the desire to pass along our culture. We may be programmed by our genes to want to pass along our DNA, but we may be programmed by our cultures to pass along our values and goals. If enough resources are available to support children who are not their genetic offsping, humans may be willing and even eager to raise them because of a strong, fundamental need to pass on their own view of their culture (this may be similar to the generativity need in older adults identified by Erickson [1954]).

Adoption may also be universal among human cultures because we are genetically programmed to support dependent juveniles if resources are available. The "selfish gene" arguments for the existence of altruism (E. O. Wilson, 1975) suggest that for most of human evolution, we lived in small, highly related bands or tribes. Being altruistic to others is genetically adaptive if one shares a high percentage of one's genes with them. Thus, we evolved to be altruistic to others (including fostering their offspring) because these others shared many of our genes, and our genes were likely to survive and reproduce if we helped these related others.

Although current views emphasize that we reproduce to pass on our individual genes, not to ensure the survival of the species, if is also clear that our only evolutionary rivals are not intraspecific (or at least were not so in our long evolutionary past). Thus, for many millions of years, protohumans and humans may have been in danger of becoming extinct. Some of the greatest rivals to human genes might not have come from sexual rivals such as other humans, but rather from the evolutionary success of other rival species (such as hyenas that may have scavenged the same food). By the same logic that one favors one's relatives because they share a large portion of one's genes, raising an orphan passes on all the genes one shares with humanity (or one's race, in the case of most adoptions).

Conclusion

Although some theorists have pitted nature versus culture in an attempt to explain human sexuality (as well as other human characteristics), the final answer is surely more complicated than that. Not only do nature and culture both affect our sexual behavior, but they interact and effect each other in complicated ways.

A society that lasts and passes on both the genes and culture of its members must harness the forces of both nature and culture to accomplish a number of goals, such as creating stable families that support children until they are able to support and reproduce themselves. Both evolutionary and cultural theories of behavior attempt to describe how people adapt to environmental conditions. Evolutionary psychologists suggest that males and females faced different selective pressures when the human species was differentiating from other species (during the environment of evolutionary adaptedness loosely defined as the Pleistocene epoch for humans). Because males and females have different reproductive constraints, they developed different sexual goals and strategies. Social structuralists (e.g., Eagly & Wood, 1999) maintain that the the situations faced by men and women vary widely across different cultures, and that differences between men and women in their sexual strategies and goals reflect differing restrictions and opportunites that cultures offer men and women.

There is some asymmetry of the nature-versus-culture debate: Some role for biology is almost assured. Few social structuralists would deny the biological roles of men's greater strength and size and women's childbearing and lactation. But many evolutionary theorists can and do ignore the role of culture almost entirely. This may be partly because training in evolution emphasizes the role of genetic evolution in animals, where cultural input may be minimal. However, ignoring the importance of culture to human sexuality may miss much of the picture. As stated at the beginning of the chapter, human sexual behavior is highly unusual in the animal kingdom, and animal models alone may not capture its full richness or diversity.

As we said in the opening chapter, truth is a big pie, and there are many slices to go around. A full account of human sexuality must recognize the powerful input of natural, biological patterns as well as the profound impact of culture. Even more importantly, it is not enough just to acknowledge the operation of both nature and culture: Probably what is most needed is the emergence of a sophisticated understanding of how nature and culture interact. Cultural programming builds on natural inclinations. We suspect that culture can shape and refine behaviors to a great extent, such as by accentuating or diminishing them—but probably it cannot very well reverse the natural, biological patterns, in the sense of producing the opposite. Thus culture's attempts to override biological tendencies (such as the Victorian campaigns to eliminate masturbation among young men) are not likely to be successful, whereas culture can have a significant impact when it capitalizes on the biological foundations (such as occurred during the sexual revolution).

CHAPTER

5

Do Women Have a Milder Sex Drive Than Men?

Chris looked at Pat and felt affection, which included a physical stirring. Chris wanted Pat, wanted to rub both hands all over Pat's body. Chris felt such strong love that Chris felt a desire to serve Pat sexually, to submit to Pat's desires. Chris thought about performing oral sex on Pat, carefully and thoroughly. Chris yearned for the oral touch and the taste of Pat. Chris also yearned for the physical union, the joining of genitals in the ultimate symbol of merging of human souls, in intercourse. Chris vividly thought of lying entwined in Pat's arms, gently moving in slow copulation while gazing into each other's eyes, missionary position, and kissing each other, passionate kissing.

But Pat was not so eager to do this. Pat did not feel the genital stirrings of desire for contact and penetration. The offer of oral sex was sweet, but Pat wasn't sure yet about the general desirability of getting naked with Chris. Chris seemed overly passionate and romantic and all, and there was a danger of the whole involvement going rapidly too far, with the potential for a blowup and disaster. Somebody else might even find out about it, which would not be good (public humiliation). Pat liked Chris, but Pat did not feel the physical yearning for intimate body contact with Chris that Chris seemed to feel toward Pat. Pat was not averse to sex in general, but Pat had already had enough sex partners to reach the point where one can recognize when it would be a bad idea and make everybody sorry eventually, and where one can refrain from getting carried away.

Naturally, Pat wanted to avoid hurting Chris, but perhaps the least hurtful approach would be to say no immediately, rather than to give Chris a little joy and then break it off. Pat thought that any partial acts of sex might cause Chris to start falling in love and talking about long-term plans and immediately wanting to have complete physical intimacy on a regular basis. Who knows, if Pat were to go along with Chris on this, the two might rapidly end up as the married parents of a small brood. This seemed far beyond what Pat was ready to contemplate at this point. Liking somebody versus seeing somebody as a long-term companion and mate are two very different things, and it is important to avoid mistakes in this area.

In many relationships, sex is a source of conflict. Like Chris and Pat, a couple finds that one person wants sex earlier in the relationship, or more often, or in different ways, than the other. Such differences are to be expected as long as two people differ with regard to sexual motivations and feelings. Choose any two people at random, and one is likely to want sex more often than the other, and so if they were sex partners, they would have to negotiate or compromise to find a mutually agreeable pattern.

The differences are not entirely random, however. When most couples negotiate or argue about sex, it is usually the man who wants more sex. If the story about Chris and Pat made you imagine that Chris was the man and Pat the woman, your imagination was in line with the more typical pattern, even though the story was carefully worded so that Pat might have been the man and Chris the woman. There are certainly some cases where it is the other way around, when the woman is the one who wants sex more, but those are less common. Most commonly the man is the one with the greater appetite. Some social scientists have concluded from these patterns that men simply have a stronger sex drive than women. Indeed, the stereotype that women desire sex less than men is commonplace in modern Western culture.

Stereotypes are of course not always true, and some of them are thoroughly false. In fact, social psychologists in recent decades have struggled to ascertain whether stereotypes tend to be close to the truth, or consist of kernels of truth that have become exaggerated and blown out of proportion, or are almost entirely fictitious. There seem to be some instances of each, and so perhaps we cannot even form an accurate stereotype of stereotypes!

With gender, for example, there is some evidence that people's stereotypes are fairly accurate in terms of knowledge about the differences between men and women and about the size of those differences (Swim, 1994). Yet even that research-based impression of accuracy may be misleading. Swim's research was based on college students, whose views tend to be egalitarian and based on current patterns in the culture. It is quite possible that older or less educated people may retain more pronounced and biased stereotypes rooted in traditional patterns that have become obsolete (e.g., believing women are not suited for higher education, especially in fields such as mathematics or medicine). It is also possible that a few sexists or other bigots can do a substantial amount of harm based on their distorted views, even if such individuals are too small in number to have a discernible effect on the average beliefs that researchers might find when making a survey of the entire population.

The belief that women have a milder sex drive than men is not universal. In fact, at some points in Western history, some groups have held the opposite stereotype—that women are more sexual than men (Tannahill, 1980). The basis for the latter stereotype is not clear, although there are several obvious possible explanations. For one thing, women have no refractory period (unlike men) and can have multiple orgasms, so in theory most could desire to keep going in sex indefinitely. Alternatively, it could be that men simply associated sex and sexual temptation with women. It could also be that the culture assumed that women had a weaker moral character than men and so were less able to restrain their sexuality. It could be that men did not understand female sexuality and simply noticed that after they (the men) had had their own, rather rapid orgasms, the women were wishing for intercourse to last longer so that they could achieve orgasm too, and the man thus inferred that women were insatiable. Then again, perhaps it was true back then that women wanted more sex than men.

Evidence of cultural or historical variation would give pause to any who might argue that women innately or biologically have a milder sex drive than men. If in some cultures women desire more sex than men, it would be difficult to make a strong case for any such biological arguments. But no modern cultures in which women want sex more than men have actually been identified. Ancient stereotypes are not exactly proof of anything, because they could have been based in ignorance or devised to fit the interests of the ruling class.

Then again, what about the sexual revolution? There is little room to doubt the fact that female sexuality changed substantially during the twentieth century. The sexual revolution did more than just give women permission to enjoy sex: It seems to have produced a fundamental change in the way women felt about their bodies and desires, and in how they made decisions about their own sexual activities. If women did in fact have less sexual desire than men before the sexual revolution, the sexual revolution brought about a substantial change.

Some feminist writers have angrily rejected the belief that women lack sexual desire compared to men. They suggested, instead, that the seeming deficit in female sexuality reflects the oppression by the male-dominated culture, which causes women to end up alienated from their own sexuality. In this view, society tells girls and women not to attend to their sexuality, fails to teach them to masturbate or enjoy sexual pleasure, and punishes women who had too many partners or who simply enjoyed sex too much. When the female potential for multiple orgasms became scientifically established in the 1960s, feminists used this to argue that female sexuality was actually superior to male in the sense of being more powerful rather than less.

Under feminist assault, the view that the male sex drive is stronger than the female has become viewed as obsolete and discredited. As Sherfey (1966) asserted, "Our myth of the female's relative asexuality is a biological absurdity" (p. 100). More recently, a leading sexuality textbook opens its section on gender differences in sex drive by stating that "a long-standing assumption in many Western societies is the mistaken belief that women are inherently less sexually inclined than men" (Crooks & Baur, 1999, p. 68). In another influential textbook, Hyde and DeLamater (1997) note that several experts have speculated that women may actually have a stronger sex drive than males. The authors themselves were sympathetic to this view: They devote a section to the idea that women have a stronger sex drive than men but do not even consider the opposite possibility, that the male sex drive is stronger. Hyde and DeLamater conclude that "perhaps, as restrictions of female sexuality lessen, future generations will regard women as having the greater sex drive" (p. 360). They do point out, however, that such ideas are mainly speculative at present.

The experts cited by Hyde and DeLamater as being in favor of the theory that the female sex drive is stronger, who included the reigning experts Masters and Johnson (1966) as well as Sherfey (1966),* pointed to women's lack of a refractory period, their ability to have many consecutive partners, and their capacity for multiple orgasms. Hyde

---

*Hyde and DeLamater claimed Masters and Johnson (1966) developed this argument, but we have been unable to find it in their book.

and DeLamater said that the weaker sexual response of women compared to men found in their studies and therapeutic work could be an artificial situation resulting from sociocultural pressures on girls and women. In other words, the lessons and influence of society may have transformed women from the more sexual to the less sexual of the two genders. If that is correct, the historical suppression of female sexuality would be an extraordinarily persuasive and powerful instance of sociocultural causation, and so it would generate great theoretical excitement. Understanding how women's sexuality was suppressed and turned from being stronger into weaker than men's would be a high priority, because it would teach us a great deal about how socialization and social pressure can radically transform behavior.

The views of Sherfey (1966) are especially strong on this point. Women are sexually insatiable, she said, in view of their multi-orgasmic capability. Sherfey described primate sexual behavior as indicating that a female during estrus will have intercourse twenty to fifty times per day, going from male to male and exhausting each one. She wrote, "I suggest that something akin to this behavior could be paralleled by the human female if her civilization allowed it" (p. 99). She suggested that prehistorical human females were equally voracious in their sexuality, but that the rise of civilization and in particular patriarchal rule (i.e., domination by men) required the "ruthless subjugation of female sexuality" (p. 119).

It would, after all, be of great practical value to learn how society could accomplish such a change in female sexuality. If this view is correct, then society found female sexuality problematic and was able to effect a change of such magnitude that the female sex drive switched from being stronger than men's to being weaker. By learning how that was accomplished, society might become able to effect similar changes on other forms of sexual behavior that it deemed problematic. For example, it would be of great value to society to learn how to prevent pedophilia.

In any case, as a result of this view, many authors have come to accept implicitly that female sexual desire is inherently no different in strength from male sexuality, and there are probably a strident minority who sincerely believe that female sexuality is actually stronger. Hardly anyone seems willing to propose that men have more sexual desire than women.

When researchers do find differences, they sometimes present them apologetically. For example, Leigh (1989) asked a sample of celibate people (including virgins) why they weren't having sex. Although she actually found about equal numbers of men and women in this virginal status, the genders differed in their reasons for not having sex. The women were significantly more likely than the men to say the reason was a lack of interest or enjoyment of sex. Hardly any men (but some women) said they weren't having sex because they didn't like it or didn't want it. Leigh described this result by saying that "this finding (at least superficially) conforms to the usually discredited stereotype of women having a weaker sex drive than men" (p. 206). In other words, the researcher could not accept at face value the finding that these women desired sex less than men, because it was politically incorrect and even contrary to prevailing scientific opinion. Many researchers face such pressures nowadays, and certainly it is reasonable to expect that evidence going against the currently popular opinion whould be subject to some suspicion and scrutiny.

These competing views make it difficult to ascertain what is correct. This chapter will begin by considering the issue of whether men and women have different levels of sexual desire—first on a theoretical basis, and second in terms of what facts and findings have shown. After that, we will return to the issue of why women's sexuality was seemingly stifled prior to the sexual revolution, as well as why that revolution brought about such a sweeping change.

What Exactly Is Sex Drive?

Before beginning, it is important to consider briefly what is meant by sex drive. In fact, we think that the question of gender differences in sex drive has been made more controversial and confusing because several different concepts have been mixed together.

By sex drive, we mean the motivation to engage in sexual activity. The general desire for sex is thus the essence of sex drive. If Bill has a stronger sex drive than Al, this would mean that Bill wants sex more often, more urgently, in more varieties, with more partners, under more circumstances, and the like.

A second concept to consider is sexual capacity. This refers to how much sex a person can potentially take part in. If Bill has a greater sexual capacity than Al, that means that Bill can engage in more sexual acts, over a longer period of time, with more partners, than Al.

The third concept is sexual enjoyment. This refers to the quantity of pleasure that a person gets from engaging in sex.

Any differences (including gender differences) on one of these variables might be completely unrelated to differences on any other. For example, men are probably just as capable of dieting as women, but men have less desire and motivation to diet. In the same way, differences in sexual capacity do not necessarily tell us anything about differences in sex drive.

The gender difference in sexual capacity seems well established. A woman can have sexual intercourse with a room full of men on the same day, but a man is unlikely to be able to have intercourse with very many different women (and certainly not to orgasm). Some women but hardly any men can have multiple orgasms. Women can continue having sex after orgasm, but men cannot. Thus, the potential capacity of women is clearly superior to that of men.

Sexual enjoyment is difficult to assess, because it is quite subjective. Men have orgasms more regularly than women, and women report more negative sexual experiences than men, so perhaps men get more enjoyment overall from sex than women—if one includes acts of bad sex. If the analysis is restricted to good sex between people who are in love and trying to please each other, however, it is questionable whether there is any difference in enjoyment.

The question of sex drive, however, focuses on motivation and desire. This is the most complex and controversial question. Let us therefore take a long and careful look.

women have no w/ lots of men b/c of multiple orgasms

men come once then refractory period

Why Should Women Want Sex Less Than Men Do?

Let us begin by asking why it would even be plausible that women would desire sex less than men do. Whether human nature was designed by God or by natural selection, it would seemingly be optimal for men and women to desire the same amount of sex. We noted at the outset that many couples end up having conflicts over how often to have sex. If men and women had identical desires, such conflicts would be mostly eliminated. That would be ideal. Why wasn't the human race designed that way?

In many species, females do not even seem to have orgasm-producing organs such as clitorides. Human females are special because of this. The clitoris makes the woman receptive to having sex at all times of the year, instead of for only a few days of heat (estrus). One can easily understand, however, that once the clitoris began to show up in evolution, it would spread rapidly through the population. Females with a clitoris would probably reproduce more often than females without one, especially in a species such as our own, where there is no obvious estrus phase and where indeed women do not even typically know for certain that they are ovulating. Still, the clitoris and its attendant sexual pleasure seem to be a relatively recent biological innovation. In most species, the female has little or no interest in sex for most of the year (Diamond, 1997).

Evolutionary theorists can, however, offer rather convincing arguments for a gender difference in strength of sexual desire. In fact, the female orgasm seems to be nonexistent in most species, and more generally across most species there seems to be far more evidence that male animals enjoy sex more than female animals (Gould & Gould, 1997). Even though pleasure and orgasm are undeniable in human females, they may not have closed the gap entirely in terms of catching up to the males.

There are solid reasons for expecting there to be a gender difference in sexual desire. As we outlined in our discussion of nature and culture in Chapter 4, men and women have different reproductive goals and contingencies. In order to reproduce at all, it is necessary to have sex. But a male of most any species can reproduce many times by having frequent sex with many partners, whereas a female cannot. Very high levels of desire have helped males reproduce more, but they would not have been much use to females in that regard. Hence we are probably descended from more oversexed males than oversexed females.

One may also point to patterns observed in other species, although it is always a little risky to generalize from nonlanguage-using animals to human beings. In many species, males compete for top status, and only the top-ranking male gets to have sex with the females. (Actually, there tends to be some degree of cheating and sneaking around, but there is still a big difference between the alpha male and the rest of the guys.)

Moreover, because competition is intense, the alpha male can usually stay on top for only one or two seasons, after which he is replaced by a stronger, younger fellow. That one season may therefore be his only chance to reproduce, and to take full advantage he has to copulate with as many females as possible and as often as possible. No such urgency besets the female. If she fails to conceive during one season, she can do so the next time. Females tend to spend their adult lives reproducing in small amounts each year. Males have to think in terms of the one championships season and that's it.

In fact, the male animal's options are even more limited than one might realize. First, his breeding rights are limited to the brief period when he is the alpha male. Second, he can only exercise those rights when the female is in heat, which is relatively rare. Thus, even an alpha male with a harem of females may only get to have sex a few times a year. So he had better be in the mood when the rare chance arises!

Hence each female can accomplish her full reproductive potential with only a few acts of intercourse—and so she does not need to have very much sexual desire in order to succeed at reproduction. The male has to have sex every chance he gets during his window of opportunity. For him to produce the highest number of babies—and that is precisely what natural selection will favor—he has to have the most powerful, relentless desire; to be ready at any opportunity; and to be able to go repeatedly during a short, intense interval. In short, the female would require less desire than the male for optimal reproduction.

There are also social reasons for a gender difference in sexual desire, whether these are instilled in one's biological nature or shaped by social experiences. One theme of this book has involved considering sex in the framework of the social exchange theory, which is based on the assumption that women give sex to men. That usually happens as part of a basic bargain, which is one source of benefits to women, including material gain such as food (as in the meat-for-sex trade). Women, as the physically weaker gender, may have spent much of prehistory and history having an ongoing need for such benefits. With the removal of restrictions on careers, modern women may need them less than in the past, but up until quite recently women probably needed to obtain resources from men.

The meat-for-sex (actually meat or whatever else) trade only works, however, if the woman wants sex less than men do. More generally, it is to women's substantial advantage to have less sexual desire for men than the men have for the women.

Consider it this way: If the woman desired sex more than the man did, then whenever they had sexual intercourse, he would be doing her a favor, instead of it usually being the other way around. It's a big, meaningful difference of who owes whom what. If she wanted sex more than he did, and they had sex, she would owe him something in return. But if she wants it less, she should be able to extract some benefits from him. He owes *her* something.

Hence it is vital to women's negotiating strength to have less sexual desire than men. It does not necessarily have to be a large difference. Women could even have very strong sexual desires, as long as men's desires are still stronger.

But the line of equal sexual desire is something that women can only cross at substantial cost. Women can be free to have more and more sexual desire, up to a point: the point of wanting it just as much as men do. When they cross that point, they shift the balance of power into men's favor. That is too big a sacrifice.

Imagine being a woman, especially in a traditional society where you would lack political and economic power along with being physically weaker than men. And imagine that at the same time your desire for sex (like other women's) is stronger than men's. What could you possible give men to gain some consideration? How could you influence them to take care of you financially and socially, provide you with benefits, and do what you wanted? How could you even manage to get them to have sex with you, if they didn't want it as much as you did? You'd need to have some alternative resource to offer them in exchange for sex.

These explanations focus on the individual and the payoffs males and females get from sexual desire. Factors external to the individual may also be considered. As we have seen, feminists have suggested that society sought to control women's sexuality and created a false appearance that women did not seek out sex. We shall return to these external causes in the second part of this chapter, but it is useful to keep them in mind when considering the evidence about whether the individuals themselves start off with different levels of sexual desire.

Evidence of the Gender Difference in Sex Drive

Do women have a milder sex drive than men? There are many different ways to look for relevant evidence. Any category of people with a relatively low sex drive would be expected to exhibit a host of signs of it, and so we could test the theory by looking for differences in how often people want sex, think about sex, have sex, ask for sex, exchange other goods for sex, and the like. Let us proceed through a broad assortment, because no single fact is likely to be fully convincing.

One sign of motivational power is how often a person spontaneously thinks about something. People who love baseball, for example, think about it often, whereas people who don't care about baseball or don't like it probably devote relatively little time to thinking about it.

With regard to sex, men clearly think about it more than women. In a national survey, Laumann et al. (1994) found that over half the men think about sex every day, but less than one out of five women think about it that often. Of course, in principle it is conceivable that men think about sex because they loathe it (and are therefore thinking about how awful sex is), but this seems doubtful. Most likely, they think about it every day because they want it.

Still, given the ambiguity of thought, it is perhaps better to use a measure of how often the person feels sexually turned on. Men have spontaneous sexual arousal more frequently than women (Beck, Bozman, & Qualtrough, 1991). The typical man has sexual arousal several times a day; the typical woman, only a couple times per week (Knoth, Boyd, & Singer, 1988). These findings suggest men have more frequent sexual arousal, if not necessarily more intense arousal.

Sexual fantasy is another sign, given that fantasies presumably spring from desire or interest in sex. A large review of many research studies on sexual fantasy yielded a consistent pattern: Men have more frequent sexual fantasies than women, as well as fantasizing about more different partners and acts (Leitenberg & Henning, 1995). Ellis and Symons (1990) asked people whether in their imagination they had had sex with over a thousand different partners. Men were four times more likely than women to say yes.

In a way, it is remarkable that anyone would say yes, especially someone in a young population such as college students. To imagine a thousand partners would require imagining a new and different one every day for three years. Hardly anyone meets that many people, even to the point of shaking hands or saying hello once. Maybe the only way for the young man to get to a thousand is to imagine having sex with about a dozen women every day, which would have to include pretty much every woman he encounters, excepting only the absolutely least attractive ones. Most of these would be repeats, of course, but possibly he might be able to average one new one every day, especially if he interacts with the public in his work (e.g., customer service department). Otherwise, maybe he imagines having sex with every woman he sees, even just a total stranger sitting on the bus or standing in the subway. That might get him to a thousand imaginary partners before he's twenty. Still, is that really a normal way to spend an entire year, or two or three, of your adult life?

Turning from fantasy to desire, the evidence points in the same direction. Men want more sex partners than women. As we reported in Chapter 2, Miller and Fishkin (1997; see also Buss & Schmitt, 1993) asked a sample of college students how many people they would ideally like to go to bed with for the rest of their lives, under ideal circumstances (i.e., not having to worry about practical things such as disease). The average woman wanted to have two or three sex partners, while the average male response was sixty-four.[†] That discrepancy points toward a stronger sex drive in men, at least in the sense of desire for a variety of partners.

Women actually report having fewer sex partners than men, although as noted in Chapter 2, this finding suffers from being logically and statistically impossible. Nearly all surveys find that men report having had more partners. The same goes if one restricts the count to extramarital sex: In both heterosexual and homosexual relationships, men seek out more partners than women (Cotton, 1975; Lawson, 1988; Spanier & Margolis, 1983; Thompson, 1983). Even if one merely counts minor infidelities in dating relationships, such as necking with someone other than your steady partner, men are more likely to say they did this (Hansen, 1987). For whatever reason men report more partners than women, although whether this is the result of style of counting or wishful thinking, it still seemingly points in the direction that men desire sex more than women.

The sexual practices of high school students were classified by Buzwell and Rosenthal (1996) into five categories of escalating interest and activity: sexually naive, sexually unassured, sexually competent, sexually adventurous, and sexually driven. The lowest category, sexually naive students, consisted of people who showed minimal sexual activity. Three-quarters of these people were girls. The second highest category, sexually adventurous, in contrast, was defined by high comfort with sex, high confidence, and high exploration. The members of this category were mostly (85 percent) boys. The top category, sexually driven, was composed of people who seemed obsessed with sex,

---

[†]We did note in that chapter that the medians were the same (1) for both genders. Thus, there are in fact many men who do not have highly promiscuous inclinations, like most women. But there were enough men with very strong cravings for promiscuity to bring the men's mean far above the women's. Thus because the total level of sexual desire throughout the population was higher among the males than the females, the conclusion here is still valid.

and it consisted almost entirely (97 percent) of males. This pattern again suggests higher sex drive among males than females.

Desire can also be reflected in favorable attitudes toward the sex organs. Reinholtz and Muehlenhard (1995) showed that men have more favorable attitudes toward their penises than women have toward their vaginas. That could certainly arise from several possible things, but if it does have anything to do with strength as sex drive, it would certainly be another sign that men desire sex more than women do. Reinholtz and Muehlenhard also found that men liked vaginas more than women liked penises. Thus, both genders' sex organs are more appealing to men than women. This is important converging evidence that the sexual response is stronger in the male.[‡]

Within dating relationships, men want more sex than women. We already cited findings that men want sex earlier in the relationship than women. When a dating couple isn't having sex, it is far more often because the woman doesn't want to than because the man doesn't (Sprecher & Regan, 1996). In a large Australian sample of dating couples, McCabe (1987) found that the men (at all stages of relationship and sexual experience) often wanted more sex than what they were having, whereas the women were quite satisfied with the amount of sex they had. This doesn't reflect a difference in love. Men and women reported equal amounts of desire for affection, companionship, trust, security, and caring. But women didn't want any additional sex, whereas the men did. Furthermore, there was a very revealing category of people in long-term dating relationships who wanted sex but weren't having it. The researcher labeled this category "reluctant virgins"; it consisted almost entirely of men. Apparently the poor bastards already had a long-standing steady, monogamous relationship and had reached the stage of wanting full intercourse, but the girlfriends weren't ready to go all the way. Some of the unfortunate men had probably been holding wistful, yearning, but so far futile hopes for months. In other words, women are not usually stuck with their virginity. Many men are, however.

Even in long-term marriages, the same patterns are found. In a study of couples who had been married more than twenty years, Ard (1977) found that husbands wanted sex more often than wives wanted it. Both men and women agreed that the men wanted more sex. The average answers to "How often would you like to have sex?" and "How often do you have sex?" were almost identical for women. For the men, the desired frequency was about 50 percent higher than what they were getting. This fits the view that men have more sexual desire. Within the same marriages, the wives saw the rate of sex as just about right, while the husbands perceived a significant margin of disappointment.

Converging evidence comes from same-sex relationships. Within long-term relationships, lesbians have sex less often than gay males (Blumstein & Schwartz, 1983). Thus, when sexual frequency is determined entirely by women, it is lower than when it is determined entirely by men.

[‡]We did not consider whether other men's penises would have an effect, although that would seemingly be a rather unfair test. Probably men would not have a positive attitude toward other men's penises, although pornographers seem to think they do.

Men initiate sex more often than women in heterosexual relationships (Byers & Heinlein, 1989; O'Sullivan & Byers, 1992). Women refuse sex more often than men. Within a marriage or committed relationship, this second finding is not always found (i.e., men and women refuse equally, although men still initiate more). But outside of the relationship, the refusal rates diverge sharply (Clark & Hatfield, 1989).

One team of researchers came up with a list of nineteen strategies for avoiding or obtaining sex. Then they showed this list to a sample of subjects and asked them to rate whether each strategy was more typical of men or women. Both men and women respondents gave essentially the same answers. All ten of the strategies for obtaining sex were rated as more typical of men than women. All nine of the strategies for avoiding sex were rated as more typical of women than men (Mercer & Kohn, 1979). Clearly, the participants in that study perceived that the majority of sexual negotiations involve men trying to obtain sex and women trying to avoid it. The men are seen as acting like they want sex more than the women. Both men and women see the same gender difference on that point.

Masturbation is another very revealing and important indicator of the sex drive, because it is not severely constrained by opportunity, interpersonal concerns, love, romanticism, fear of venereal disease, fear of pregnancy, or other issues. It is a fairly pure and unhindered measure of sex drive. Men masturbate more than women. This is true by two different ways of counting. First, men are far more likely than women to masturbate at all. In other words, a higher percentage of men than women ever engage in masturbation.

Second, among masturbators, men masturbate more often than women (Laumann et al., 1994; Oliver & Hyde, 1993). The incidence difference is one of the few gender differences to reach what statisticians call a large effect size. There are many gender differences, but most are officially small or medium, although they can still be quite important. Only a few are large. Masturbation is one of the few large differences, and that also it means that masurbation is one of the biggest differences between men and women across all possible ways of being different.

Within either gender, masturbation is related to the strength of the sex drive (Abramson, 1973), which provides further reason to think that the difference between men and women also shows a difference in sex drive. In other words, within gender, the effect is consistent: Men with higher sex drives masturbate more than other men. The same holds true among women. The higher your sex drive, the more likely you are to masturbate. The direct link to strength of sex drive is another reason to think that the masturbation gap between men and women is in fact a result of weaker sex drive among women.

Among people who don't masturbate, it is reasonable to ask why. Multiple potential reasons exist, of course, including guilt and lack of privacy. Perhaps surprisingly, the male non-masturbators were most likely than women to mention guilt as a reason. The crucial point, however, was that the women mainly cited lack of desire as their reason (Arafat & Cotton, 1974). Many women apparently regard masturbation as not worth the bother. But few men feel that way.

We mentioned that some feminists have blamed societal teachings, including the fact that society does not teach girls to masturbate, for the lower rates of masturbation among women. Technically it is true that society does not teach girls to masturbate—but no one actually teaches the boys either. Most boys and girls who learn to masturbate figure it out (or discover it) by themselves (Arafat & Cotton, 1974). An equal number of boys and girls learn it from peers and siblings. Thus, lack of female masturbation doesn't reflect the fact that society teaches boys but not girls to do it; it instead reflects the fact that many females simply don't have the inclination because they have fewer or less frequent sexual impulses. Most people who get horny enough to masturbate manage to figure out how to do it, sooner or later.

Along the same lines, women spend less money on sexual aids and devices and are less likely to purchase any such sexual products (e.g., Laumann et al., 1994). The same goes for pornography. Even when men and women are presented with erotic stimuli under identical laboratory conditions, women usually report less enjoyment, although the differences are fairly small in fact (e.g., Reed & Reed, 1972; Sigusch, Schmidt, Reinfeld, & Wiedemann-Sutor, 1970; Schmidt & Sigusch, 1970; cf. Fisher & Byrne, 1978).

It could be argued that pornography is generally produced for men rather than women, so naturally women would enjoy it less. Then again, if there were a large, viable market for female-targeted pornography, the products would probably be available. In any case, the opposite is true for sexual stimulation devices: The vibrator for women seems to be a superior, more effective device than anything that is available to men (on satisfaction with vibrators, see Davis, Blank, Lin, & Bonillas, 1996). But most women don't purchase vibrators.

Another very important indicator is how many sexual practices people enjoy. In the NHSLS, people were presented with a list of fifteen sexual practices and asked how many they found appealing. Across all categories, men liked more practices than women (Laumann et al., 1994). Also, almost every practice was liked more by men than women, although not all the differences were significant. Still, the overall composite certainly was significant: Men like more different sexual acts than women.

Most modern American married couples practice fellatio and cunnilingus, at least occasionally. Even so, women rate these activities less appealing than men. Researchers have suggested that many women seem to perform these more out of a sense of obligation than out of genuine desire and enjoyment. The men were more prone to really like them.

Last, when people rate the strength of their sexual urges, women give lower ratings than men (Mercer & Kohn, 1979). Among people who are not having sex, more women than men cite lack of desire as the reason (Leigh, 1989). When married couples are asked to indicate whether they are having as much sex as they want, far more men than women express the wish for more sex (Ard, 1977; Julien, Bouchard, Gagnon, & Pomerleau, 1992).

Those are the main relevant findings. In our view, they provide more than enough proof that men have more sexual desire than women. To avoid that conclusion, you would have to define the sex drive in a way that does not involve thinking about sex, feeling sexual desire, desiring different partners, enjoying different activities, wanting to have sex often, having frequent sexual fantasies, having more variety of sexual fantasies, masturbating, and self-reporting desire. Such a definition would be absurd. You can't sensibly talk about sexual desire if you throw all those things out.

[handwritten marginal note:] pornography produced for men because men are the ones that watch/buy it

How could anyone have believed otherwise? We suspect that some researchers were misled by two observations, both of which have been repeated at least since the influential first book by Masters and Johnson (1966). First, some women are capable of having multiple orgasms, whereas men generally aren't. Second, women can continue copulating after orgasm, but men must usually stop. This, however, reflects capacity, not the sex drive per se. Yes, a woman is physically capable of having more orgasms than a man—but that doesn't mean that the average woman typically wants or tries to have them. Women *can* do more; men *want* to do more. The wanting is the sign of the drive for sex.

Another possible source of confusion is that during the height of passionate love, women may well desire sex just as much as men. In other words, when the female sex drive is fully aroused, it does not seem any milder or weaker than the male. We shall return to this point in Chapter 7. The observation may well be true (although we do not know of clear data), but it too is beside the point. Perhaps men and women are equally sexual when fully aroused, but men reach that level of arousal more often and more easily than women. Ultimately this too refers to the potential level of female eroticism, which may be as high as (or even higher than) men's. The sex drive question is, however, a matter not of erotic potential but rather of strength and frequency of desire. Clearly, men are blessed or cursed with stronger, more frequent desires.

Taken together, the evidence is thus essentially unanimous and unambiguous: Women do have milder sex drives than men. Women surpass men on sexual capacity, and enjoyment of good sex is probably quite similar in men and women, but men desire sex more than women.

Does this mean something bad about women? There is nothing inherently wonderful or superior about wanting more sex. In fact, in Chapter 8 we shall suggest that the strength of the male sex drive is a source of problems and unhappiness for many men. We suspect that the obsolete value judgments from the 1970s, at the height of the sexual revolution, may have caused women to think it important to believe that women have as much sexual desire as men, but we also think that those value judgments need to be reassessed. More sexual desire is not always better, especially when one considers the wide range of personal and social misfortunes that can be traced to sexual excesses. A moderate sex drive is probably best. Women should more likely be pleased and proud, rather than offended or defeated, about having a moderate sex drive.

We cannot entirely rule out the possibility that the gender difference in sex drive reflects cultural influence, and so it would be going beyond the data to insist that the unchangeable biological nature of women dictates that they have a sex drive weaker than men's. That view may, however, be correct, and unless the field can clearly identify some societies in which women consistently desire sex more than men—reflected in more frequent masturbation, desire for more sex acts and more partners, and so forth—then we should probably assume a biological basis as a reasonable working hypothesis.

Even if there is a biological foundation for the different strength of sex drive, however, there is ample room for culture to exert some influence. Even the most ardent supporter of biological determinism must seemingly concede that different cultures and historical eras have exerted different degrees of pressure on women to control their sexuality. Let us now leave the basic question of differences in strength of sex drive and turn to the fascinating problem of cultural suppression.

The Suppression of Female Sexuality: Four Theories

Regardless of whether women are innately less inclined than men to seek out sexual stimulation and pleasure, there can be little doubting the fact that many individual women have often felt pressure to curb and inhibit their sexual desires. In a word, women have often felt that they were not allowed to seek or even enjoy sex. The sexual revolution was one important indication of this pattern. As Chapter 6 will discuss at some length in connection with erotic plasticity, the sexual revolution was primarily a change in female sexuality (e.g., Ehrenreich, Hess, & Jacobs, 1986). The revolution was in particular a change that liberated female sexuality from the stifling constraints of previous eras (at least to some degree). If we go back to the nineteenth century, especially among the middle class, it is easily apparent that women faced considerable social pressure not to acknowledge themselves as sexual beings—that is, as people who want sex, enjoy sex, and think about sex frequently.

The suppression of female sexuality can be regarded as one of the great crimes or tragedies of history, among other ways of looking at it. Countless women have had their life's sum of pleasure reduced substantially by it. To the extent that sexuality figures in personal fulfillment and self-expression, the stifling of female sexuality has prevented many women from being themselves and reaching their potential. Even after the sexual revolution, some of these processes are probably still at work today. The relative mildness of female sexuality (compared to male), which the first part of this chapter examined at length, could be at least partly due to social pressures that induce girls but not boys, and women but not men, to hold back the sexual aspect of themselves.

Why did the historical suppression of female sexuality happen? And why did it let up? This chapter will consider several intriguing theories. To foreshadow, we shall consider two conspiracy theories as well as two more boring null hypotheses. The conspiracy theories emphasize that it was the men, or the women, respectively, who undertook to curtail sexual behavior among women. The null hypotheses claim there was no actual pattern of suppressing female sexuality. Instead, one view is that women simply desire sex less than men, so the appearance of suppression is an illusion. The other is that because the costs and dangers of sex (particularly the nonsocial costs and dangers) have generally been greater for women than men, individual women sometimes avoid sex out of pure self-interest, rather than as a result of societal pressure.

Let us briefly present these four theories. Because the null hypotheses suggest that there is no need for further explanation, we shall review them first.

The Mild Female Sex Drive

The first part of this chapter presented abundant evidence that women desire sex less than men. To push this theory to an extreme, you could argue there was no historical suppression of female sexuality at all. It is not necessary to suppress female sexuality, because women don't want sex very much anyway.

We think this view clearly falls short of explaining the full historical record. The evidence does indicate that women have less sexual desire and motivation than men, but

[handwritten marginal note, rotated vertically:] sexual revolution is a sign that there had been some suppression of female sex drive – chastity belts, reputations

that does not rule out the possibility that further suppression occurred. The very fact that the sexual revolution occurred looks like pretty strong proof that some suppression had been going on; otherwise there would have been nothing for the revolution to accomplish.

There are plenty of other signs of suppression of female sexuality. From bad reputations to chastity belts, from live burial to gossip, societies have used various weapons to restrain female sexuality and punish women who went too far. To be sure, societies have also punished sexual misbehavior by men, but the punishments for women have sometimes been more severe and more extensive. So some suppression has definitely been going on.

The suppression of female sexuality is thus not entirely an illusion. The relative mildness of female sexuality should, however, be kept in mind when considering various pieces of evidence, because it can perhaps account for some of them. Simply finding that women are less permissive than men, for example, is not enough to constitute evidence that female sexuality has been suppressed, because in the absence of any suppression, women may still be less inclined to do as many sexual things as men.

The Costs and Dangers of Sex for Women

A second null hypothesis focuses on self-interest of individual women. Perhaps society did not really suppress female sexuality; perhaps women suppressed their own sexuality out of a prudent awareness of the costs and dangers in sex.

There is little room to dispute these dangers. Pregnancy is the most obvious one. A man can engage in sex without fear of pregnancy. Even if a pregnancy occurs, he can deny that he was involved. The pregnant woman cannot deny that she had sex, nor can she escape the consequences. At minimum, she faces the hazards and emotional distress of going through an abortion, which are bad enough today and were far worse through most of history (before modern medicine and legal approval). If, as in most cases, she does not choose abortion, she faces months of at least some physical inconvenience and discomfort, followed by the painful experience of giving birth, and then years of being tied down to care for a needy, dependent child. That is a huge risk to take for five minutes of joy.

For most of history (and prehistory), the dangers of pregnancy went beyond having a child and extended even to premature death. Shorter (1982) estimates from extensive data that in traditional Europe before 1800, about 1.3 percent of live births caused the mother's death. Assuming that the average woman gave birth six times in her life, she ran about an 8 percent risk of dying in childbirth. Nowadays the link between sex and death is mostly understood in terms of AIDS, but the chances of getting AIDS are quite small (and shared by men) in comparison to the mortal risk that sex carried for women alone throughout most of world history.

AIDS is a recent development, but venereal diseases have been around for a very long time. Such diseases carry significant risks to both men and women. Although both genders can get them (clearly), the costs may be greater to women. For one thing, women are more vulnerable infection than men. Male-to-female transmission is physiologically more effective than female-to-male transmission (which is true for AIDS as well). There are several reasons for this, including the fact that the woman tends to keep at least some of the man's goop inside her after intercourse, whereas the man does not take in any bodily fluids from the woman, and the fact that sex sometimes causes small tears in the vagina that can create access to the bloodstream for nasty germs.

The sex-is-dangerous theory has an advantage over the mild-sex-drive theory in that it can offer a potential explanation for the sexual revolution. Modern medicine and birth control technology have substantially reduced the costs of sex for women. Death during childbirth has not been completely eliminated, of course, but it has become so rare that it is not usually a factor that enters into women's thoughts about sex. (In contrast, it was customary for the American woman in colonial times to include preparing for her own possible death as part of the final arrangements for giving birth; see Ulrich, 1979.)

Even more importantly, the birth control pill and legal abortion made it eminently possible for women to have plenty of sex without worrying about pregnancy at all. The timing makes it hard to dispute that they had at least some effect on the sexual revolution. The birth control pill became available in the early 1960s, and the sexual revolution was in high gear by the late 1960s. Abortion was legalized in 1973 with the *Roe v. Wade* decision, and the sexual revolution picked up even more steam.

Hence prudent self-interest was undoubtedly an important factor constraining female sexual expression through much of history. Yet was it the only factor? We continue to think that social practices and pressures have conspired to stifle female sexuality. For one thing, the costs and dangers of oral sex were far less than those of vaginal sex, yet through much of history women did not engage in oral sex either. Moreover, many of the reasons women traditionally gave for refraining from sex had less to do with fear of pregnancy and more to do with fear of a bad reputation.

Our conclusion, therefore, is that the sex-is-dangerous view is an important part of the puzzle—but not the full explanation. Again, we must keep it in mind when considering other evidence. But there was some collective suppression of female sexuality, independent of prudence of individual women because of the biological risks.

The Male Conspiracy Theory

Each of the two conspiracy theories focuses on one of the two genders: Either men in general, or women in general, conspired to restrain female sexuality. Because there has been more discussion of the male conspiracy, we present it first, but that should not be taken to imply that it is a priori more or less plausible.

We should add that we do not use the term *conspiracy* to imply some deliberate, conscious plan, as some might interpret it. Although some sources (e.g., Brownmiller, 1975) have insisted that men do consciously and deliberately try to suppress women, we think that those views are unnecessary and excessive. Men may act to suppress female sexuality without necessarily banding together and making a formal plan, and without even being conscious that that is what they are doing. Psychological reinforcement processes, or even biologically prepared inclinations, may shape men's behavior without their realizing it. Hence when we speak of the male conspiracy, we mean only that men are chiefly responsible for stifling female sexuality.

males conspired to restrain female sex drive as a way of controlling them and keeping them from straying - knows that the child is theirs

The view that men have conspired to suppress female sexuality has been asserted in various sources. It is, oddly enough, one of the few areas where both evolutionary psychologists and feminists find themselves on the same side, although, as we shall concede, the alternative female conspiracy theory may also fit major themes in both feminist or evolutionary thinking.

From the feminist point of view, the male conspiracy theory is consistent with the theme that men generally oppress women and are largely responsible for most of women's problems and misfortunes. We shall refer to this line of thought as *victim feminism*, to distinguish it from the alternative, more active feminist version of the female conspiracy (see the next section).

Why would men want to suppress female sexuality? Victim feminism offers several theories. One is that men regard women as men's possessions, and so men do not want women to be autonomous creatures seeking their own fulfillment. In particular, of course, men do not want women to be desiring sex with other men, and so stifling female sexual desire altogether is an effective means of ensuring fidelity. You hope your wife doesn't like sex much so she won't sleep with other guys.

A variation on this is that men want to keep women in an inferior position politically, socially, and economically, and so preventing women from having sexual pleasure may contribute to achieving this goal. (Logically, however, the opposite prediction could be made: If men wanted to exploit women politically, then allowing women to have ample sexual pleasure, as a kind of "opiate of the female masses," might enable men to hog the political power. Actually we'll bet that the alleged conspirators—men—could understand this, because men might well go for it if they had that bargain offered to them. For example, some men might agree to give up the vote if they were promised endless sexual satisfaction for the rest of their lives. If men used this tactic on women, it might be doubly effective, because the extra sex would produce more pregnancies, and so women would be all the more tied down to home and family, leaving men that much freer to run everything and dominate the political and economic spheres.)

Another view is that men are afraid of female sexuality as a powerful force that could undermine the house of cards that is the society men have constructed for themselves. Suppose women really did by nature desire more frequent sex, with more partners and more variety, than men, and suppose they began to act on these desires. Society might degenerate into an ongoing, free-form orgy. Men might lose out in some way in this. (Then again, some men might think that such a state of affairs would be just fine!) "If women are insatiable creatures, their sexuality would, of course, require external constraints, or sexual chaos would reign" (Faunce & Phillips-Yonas, 1978, p. 86). Or, as summarized by Hyde and DeLamater (1997), "in prehistoric human societies, the powerful sex drive of women created havoc—not to mention making the men feel insecure—and therefore societies instituted restrictions on female sexuality to bring it more in line with male sexuality" (p. 360). They added that this argument explains "the restrictions on female sexuality that persist to the present day" (p. 360).

The allusion to male insecurity brings up the related possibility that men envy female sexual power, such as the capacity for multiple orgasms or the ability to copulate nonstop without even any refractory period after orgasms. Suppressing female sexuality would then be a kind of mean-spirited way for men to express their envy. It may also have a practical side: If women do not have sexual desire, then men do not have to bother much about satisfying them, and so a man can just seek his own pleasure in sexual intercourse. In contrast, if women enjoy sex, men have to give them pleasure too.

Yet another variation on this argument is that female sexuality is simply too disruptive of the orderly, peaceful society that men prefer, and so it had to be suppressed. Sherfey (1966) proposed that "it is conceivable that the forceful suppression of women's inordinate sexual demands was a prerequisite to the dawn of every modern civilization and almost every living culture" (p. 119). If women acted out all their innate sexual tendencies, they would have sex with many partners, resulting in confusion about which babies belong to whom and in other forms of social chaos.

The evolutionary argument likewise focuses on infidelity. Because of the bottle-neck of the female reproductive system, a woman can only have one man's baby at a time, and so if she copulates with other men, her husband could end up raising another man's children rather than his own. This would effectively prevent him from passing on his genes. Hence evolution may have selected out men who didn't mind their wives having sex with other men. Instead, the men who did pass on their genes and form the ancestors of modern men were ones who were very possessive sexually.

In principle, if a man were certain that his wife's baby were not his, he could of course reject it or even have it killed. But men do not know: Paternity uncertainty is an inevitable fact of male life, at least until DNA testing becomes common and fully effective. Through most of history, though, men could not be certain whether the children their wives bore were their own. Therefore, they would go to great lengths to prevent their women from straying.

There is little doubt but that men (and women too!) dislike having their spouses have sex with other partners. Reiss (1986a, 1986b) concluded that sexual jealousy and possessiveness have been found in all cultures, which supports the evolutionary argu-ment that some innate pattern seeks spousal fidelity.

The question for the male conspiracy theory, however, is whether this concern is sufficient to prompt men to stifle female sexuality altogether. Is it really necessary or desirable to have your wife lack interest in sex just to improve your chances that the children she bears are yours? Are men really so worried about their wives having someone else's kid that they would want their women not to enjoy sex?

A thought experiment can highlight the dilemma. Suppose it were possible to put something in the drinking water, akin to fluoridation, that would reduce the female sex drive by 25 percent across the entire population of North America. Sexual desire in women would become one-quarter weaker and one-quarter less frequent. Would the men vote for this? Would they celebrate its effective implementation? Men are prone to complain that women don't want to have sex often enough, and a broad reduction in female sexual desire would only aggravate this problem. Thus, men would incur a severe cost to themselves by suppressing female sexuality. It is a serious and theoretically interesting question—as well as an empirical one—whether they would be willing to pay that cost for the sake of being able to think that their wives will lose some interest in other sex partners.

During the historic British election of 1996, Janet Anderson was campaigning for Labour (who eventually won the election). Trying to drum up support for her party, she said, "Under Labour, women will become more promiscuous. That's an election pledge!" ("Perspectives," 1996). The remark was widely publicized, and she later explained that she had just said it as a joke. Still, the premise of the joke was that she would gain votes for her party by promising greater female promiscuity—which implies that she thought men would be in favor of that. We think she is right. If men really preferred a weaker female sex drive, Anderson would have made the opposite promise.

The sexual revolution poses another interesting challenge for the male conspiracy theory. If men suppressed female sexuality, then what happened in the 1960s was that women defeated men and won their freedom to enjoy sex. In plain terms, the men "lost" the sexual revolution, in the same way the British lost the American Revolution. We should be able to find evidence that men deplore the sexual revolution and pine nostalgically for the olden days, before women learned to enjoy sex. The defeated men should be noticeably unhappy about having to satisfy women sexually and having to service women's sexual demands.

A possible explanation for the sexual revolution would be that improved birth control makes men worry less about spousal infidelity. If a man's wife takes her pills scrupulously, she is unlikely to bear another man's child, and so the problem of paternity uncertainty is solved. This view could be supported by any evidence that men have largely ceased to mind their wives or girlfriends having sexual affairs with other men, as long as the the women use birth control.[§] The wife comes home from a business trip, and the husband asks her whether she was good. "No," she says, "I had sex with two different men, and in one case it was a matter of repeated couplings until dawn." "Did you be sure to take your pills?" asks the husband. "Yes, darling, don't worry," she says, with a smile. "All right then," he smiles back, "I'm glad you had a good trip," and he turns back to reading his newspaper.

One important advantage of the male conspiracy view, however, is that men have in fact had the majority of political and social power throughout history. It would probably be difficult to institute any broad pattern of social life that went directly against the wishes and preferences of men. On an a priori basis, ascribing control to men seems the most plausible and logical theory.

The Female Conspiracy Theory

The final approach depicts the suppression of female sexuality as a conspiracy by women instead of men. As with the male conspiracy, we use the term *conspiracy* loosely to refer to the activities of women in general rather than necessarily invoking a conscious, deliberate agreement or plan.

The female conspiracy idea suffers from being implausible right from the start. Apart from the dangers of sex already noted, why would women suppress themselves (or each other)? After all, sex is a main source of pleasure and satisfaction in life. For women to deny themselves this pleasure would certainly seem like a sorry and self-destructive move. Then again, perhaps thinking of sex only in terms of getting one's own pleasure versus not getting it is too narrow a view to take on female sexuality.

[§]We advise you not to bet a large sum of money on this theory.

The social exchange theory offers a strong basis for predicting a female conspiracy to suppress female sexuality. According to this view, sex is something that women give to men, and in exchange men must offer women other valued resources.

As Cott (1979) wrote in her historical analysis of female passionlessness during the Victorian era, if sex is your only bargaining chip, you want its value to be high. Supply and demand come into play here, as in all social exchange analyses: The best way to drive up the price of any commodity is to create a scarcity, which means a situation in which demand exceeds the supply. Generally, the more the demand exceeds the supply, the higher the price will be. Across the whole society at large, women will be best off if they don't give men nearly as much sex as men want.

In a sense, the social exchange view holds that women hold a monopoly on something men desire. The reasons monopolies are illegal in American business is that they can exploit the consumer by driving up the price just to fatten the profit margins. If there is only one source that offers you what you want, that source can name the price. You pay what it stipulates, or you do without.

The advantages of restricting sex accrue to women in two ways. First, since men in general will do whatever is necessary to obtain sex, if women in general make sex difficult to get, they can extract a fair amount in return from men. Second, individual women can exert control over their own husbands and boyfriends by withholding sex. If the man fails to treat her well, she can refuse to bestow favors on him until he apologizes and improves his behavior.

In Chapter 1, we mentioned that the social exchange theory goes beyond just the interactions between an individual man and woman. Sexual exchanges take place with reference to general norms, which operate as more than mere attitudinal guidelines. If a woman refuses to yield as much physical gratification as other women do, her boyfriend may leave her for someone else. In contrast, if she gives more than the others do, she may attract considerable male attention and even steal other women's men from them. This will aggravate the other women and turn them against her. They are likely to punish her in various ways, such as gossiping about her, calling her names, or excluding her from the group of female friends.

That last point is one possible key to the female conspiracy theory: Women must restrain each other's sexuality in order to cut down the risk of having their boyfriends stolen by other women. Consistent with this view, there is some evidence that women who are perceived as sexually very active are seen as highly desirable for dates. Sprecher, McKinney, and Orbuch (1991) spoke of a "reverse double standard" by which men most wanted to date the woman who showed a high level of sexual activity, whereas women most wanted to date the man who showed only a moderate level of sexual activity. (For a spouse, however, both men and women wanted someone with a relatively low amount of previous sexual activity.)¶

¶Some years later, a follow-up by some of the same authors found that both men and women preferred people who had been relatively chaste, regardless of whether the person was to be a date or a spouse (Sprecher, Regan, McKinney, Maxwell, & Wazienski, 1997). The person with the most extensive sexual experience was regarded as the least desirable. There was no gender difference, contrary to what "double standard" theories would predict. Possibly the change from the earlier findings reflects an increasing concern about AIDS and other unsavory consequences of prior promiscuity.

A female conspiracy to restrict sexuality would therefore be something like the actions of OPEC (Organization of Petroleum Exporting Countries): They agree that they each will only pump and sell a certain amount of oil so that the oil-consuming world will be willing to pay a high price for it. OPEC's perennial problem is that any individual country can pump and sell more oil, or lower its price, thereby getting more short-term advantage for itself but reducing the value of what all the other countries have to sell.

In the same way, individual women can attract more attention from men by offering more sexual favors than the going rate. (At least, that is the social exchange argument.) Regardless of whether this is a matter of getting a first or second date, or of stealing someone's boyfriend, sex is a powerful lure that women can use, and it is often effective. The only way for other women to compete is to keep up. If all the women in the broad social group have intercourse by the fourth date, then each new one must approximately do the same, or the men will reject her and date the others instead. If one woman starts having intercourse on the first date, she will get more dates than the others, and so the others will have to change in order to retain male attention. As sexual morals continue to become more liberal, the individual women have to give more and more sexual favors and can ask for less and less in return.

It is therefore in the interests of women in general to restrict the availability of sex by restricting female sexuality. If they do so, they get two benefits. First, they can demand better treatment and possibly other benefits from men. Second, they reduce their worry about having their mates abandon them.

Although this view has not received the official blessing of the feminist mainstream, it is actually consistent with several major currents of feminist thought. It takes women out of the role of passive victims and instead assigns them a prominent, active place in determining their own destiny. In this view, women historically adapted to their circumstances with a rational means of exerting control over men and making use of the few opportunities and advantages they had. We therefore consider the female conspiracy theory to be *agentic feminism*, which emphasizes how women take an active, influential role, as opposed the victim feminist view, which emphasizes male suppression of female sexuality.

The female suppression view could also help explain why men sought to keep women in an inferior socioeconomic position, which is a central feature of feminist thought but not always a well-analyzed one. Why do men want to keep women from having rights and money? Why do men care?

Let us paint an overly simple version of the social exchange, from our possible prehistorical past: Men give food and get sex in return. Both sides would try to improve their bargaining position by keeping the other in need of a good deal. Women want men generally to be somewhat sex-starved, so the men will give a good meal in return for sex. Men want women to be hungry, so that plenty of women will have sex with them and maybe throw in special deals.

The evolutionary approach could also find an echo in this analysis. We noted in Chapter 1 that Buss (1994) and others have described the "meat for sex" exchange as a staple of our prehistorical past. Again, the larger social group most likely sets the going rate of exchange based on supply and demand. The less sex is available, the more meat a man will have to give (and be willing to give) to obtain it. If women can work together to restrict the general availability of sex, then each woman can demand Chateaubriand instead of three bites of dried rabbit.

We started this section by suggesting that it seemed self-defeating for women to restrict female sexuality. The social exchange theory does offer a more positive and understandable reason for women to restrict female sexuality. But if we take the social exchange view seriously, then we have the opposite problem: Why would women ever give up their advantage? The sexual revolution, in other words, needs to be explained in terms of why women would collectively reduce the going price and allow men to have sex with considerably less commitment and less other benefits to women.

The most likely answer is that women can only afford to make sex more freely available to men if women have alternative sources of money, status, power, and other things they want. Return for a moment to Cott's (1979) comment that if sex is your only resource, you want to keep the supply low to drive up the price. A corollary is that when sex ceases to be your only resource, you do not need to charge quite so high a price. Nineteenth-century woman, of whom Cott was writing, had few or no powers to own property, vote, pursue professional careers, initiate lawsuits, and the like. By the middle of the twentieth century, these restrictions had fallen, and women could dictate the terms of their own lives, far beyond what their female ancestors in any era had been able to do. Under women's new circumstances, it was no longer so vital for women to hold sex hostage.

Testing the Theories

Various sorts of evidence can be used to test these theories against each other. The victim feminists sometimes point to an important study by Reiss (1986a) to support the male conspiracy theory. Reiss compared 186 different cultures and found that there was a positive correlation between the gender power differential and the extent of suppression of female sexuality. In other words, the more power men had relative to women, the more female sexuality was suppressed.

Reiss's findings are certainly consistent with a male conspiracy view, and he himself interpreted them that way. If men want to suppress women's sexuality, then they can do so all the more effectively when they hold the bulk of political power. As women get more power, the men can no longer make all the rules, and so men are less able to carry out their plans and wishes—including suppressing female sexuality, assuming that that is one of the main things men want to do.

Unfortunately for the sake of this debate, Reiss's findings fit the female conspiracy theory just as well. If women suppress each other's sexuality as a way of improving their social exchange power in relation to men, this will be something that is most likely to happen when women have few other sources of power or benefits. The less power women have in most sociopolitical and economic spheres, the more they need to get a high price for sex—and so the more they need a general scarcity to keep the price high. In contrast, as women move toward greater equality with men, they can relax and make sex more readily available to men.

Some data within a culture question the link. Kelley (1978) found that people who favored wives having careers were also more permissive in their sexual attitudes toward both men and women. But more thorough data by Reiss, Anderson, and Sponaugle (1980) suggested that the link is indirect at best. That is, they found a weak correlation between believing in gender equality and having permissive attitudes toward sexuality, but the correlation was due to other variables, and when those were controlled there was no direct correlation left. For example, people who believed in gender equality reported less happy marriages, and lower marital happiness was associated with greater permissiveness. But controlling for marital happiness reduced the link between gender equality and sexual permissiveness.

Reiss's data do speak against the two null hypotheses. The dangers of pregnancy and childbirth, and the relative mildness of the female sex drive, are likely to be constant across cultures. Reiss has shown that cultural context makes a significant difference. Hence one or the other conspiracy theory has to be correct. The only problem is that his findings do not help us determine which one it is. (It could also be both.)

A better guide is to look at power in respect to sex and relationships specifically. This is often linked directly to availability of partners. When there is a large surplus of one or the other gender, the minority gender is in high demand and can exert more influence. We can compare the degree of suppression of female sexuality in situations in which there is a shortage of women so that women can demand that men please them however they want, as opposed to situations in which there is a surplus of women so that men can have their pick.

Guttentag and Secord (1983) compared different societies and groups with different sex ratios and concluded that there was a clear general pattern: When women had the advantage, sexual morality was relatively restrictive; there was not much premarital or extramarital sex, and so forth. In contrast, when there was a surplus of women, so the men can call most of the shots, then sexual morality became highly permissive.

These results fit the female conspiracy view a little better than the male conspiracy view, because they indicate that sexuality is suppressed when women (rather than men) have the edge. Still, they are not strongly convincing. For one thing, they could be explained simply on the basis of the milder sex drive. If women desire sex less than men, then when women have the power to dictate the terms of the relationship, they shift society toward everyone having less sex. When men are in control, they push for more sex all around.

The social exchange theory says that one reason for women to suppress each other's sexuality is to reduce the danger of having one's mate stolen by another woman. If there is a shortage of women, this danger would presumably be reduced: A woman can find another mate easier than a man could. It is possible that competition among women for mates would be reduced when there is a surplus of men. Then again, women do not necessarily want just any man, but rather they want the most desirable man they can get. If there is a surplus of men, women can make more advantageous choices than they would otherwise, but the same men are still desirable to other women, and so women may still worry about losing their mates. Thus it is possible that women might still suppress female sexuality when the sex ratio is in their favor.

The social exchange rules would still apply even when men are in surplus, of course (according to that theory). A woman gives sex to a man and gets various benefits in return. The surplus of men simply means that the woman can generally get a very high price involving plenty of benefits to her, such as serious long-term relationship and financial commitments from the man. Creating a shortage of sex for the men is what puts her in this position. If those few women were to have lots of sex with lots of men, this would reduce their advantage.

Meanwhile, the male conspiracy theory might be stretched to fit the loosening of sexual morals when there is a shortage of men. Men might be less concerned to maintain their ownership and control over individual women if there were plenty of women available. At the very least, the dangers of losing one's woman to another man and of having to raise another man's children would be somewhat lower if there are relatively fewer other men around.

Thus, the evidence based on differential power is not entirely conclusive. The female conspiracy theory scores a tentative victory from the evidence that sexuality is most suppressed when women are in the minority and therefore have the edge in the supply-and-demand market for sexual partnerships. But either theory might be stretched to fit the findings or to predict the opposite. Moreover, the null hypothesis of the milder female sex drive could account for the sex ratio patterns. Let us therefore look at other sources of evidence from Baumeister and Twenge (1999).

Direct Influences on Adolescent Female Sexuality

A good place to start is to see who are in fact the primary agents that put pressure on young women not to have sex. Although there are certainly possibilities for indirect influence and background machinations, the two theories make clearly discrepant predictions. If the suppression of female sexuality stems from a male conspiracy, then men should be found to be the main sources of antisexual pressures. In contrast, a female conspiracy would predict that females will be the primary sources.

Probably most girls' first lessons about sexual morality come from their parents. Parents do not want their daughters to become pregnant or get venereal disease, and for these (and possibly other) reasons they may teach the daughters to avoid sexual activity. But which parent?

The answer, apparently, is that the mother is the primary source of antisexual messages for daughters. DeLamater (1989) found that daughters' sexuality was mainly influenced by mothers, whereas sons' were influenced by fathers. Libby, Gray, and White (1978) found that mothers were the main influence on both sons and daughters. Werner-Wilson (1998) computed correlations between adolescents' attitudes about sex and their parents' attitudes. The daughter's attitudes correlated significantly with her mother's attitudes, but the daughter's attitudes did not have any significant resemblance to her father's attitudes.**

**Werner-Wilson did, however, find that greater communication with the father was correlated with more conservative sexual attitudes in the daughter.

Although transmission of attitudes from parent to child can occur by a variety of means, including modeling, the most relevant factor for our debate about direct influence is communication: In the overworked parental cliché, parents want children to "do as I say, not as I do." Several researchers have examined communication patterns. Nolin and Petersen (1992) found that mothers communicated a great deal about sex to their daughters, whereas fathers communicated relatively little. For example, 61 percent of mothers had talked to their daughters about birth control, as compared to 2 percent of fathers. (These do not count the additional cases in which both parents talked to the daughter.) Similarly, 35 percent of mothers had communicated about pregnancy and 37 percent about sexual morality, in contrast to 0 percent and 2 percent of fathers, respectively. Apparently the daughter does not get much direct information or influence from her father. Some fathers join in the mother-daughter discussion, but if the influence comes from only one parent, it is almost invariably the mother.

Similar findings emerged from a Dutch sample studied by du Bois-Reymond and Ravesloot (1996). Neither mothers nor fathers made controlling demands with regard to their daughters' sexuality, but mothers were much more likely than fathers to negotiate with their daughters about sexuality. Fathers were more likely than mothers to feel incompetent to deal with the issue and hence as staying out of it. The fathers' own self-reports confirmed these views: They avoided talking about sex with their daughters and left the whole business to the mother.

The influence of these communications is also relevant, as studied by Kahn, Smith, and Roberts (1984). The more mothers communicated with their daughters about sex, the later the daughters began having intercourse. No effect was found for fathers. A similar study by Lewis (1973) studied adolescent promiscuity at a fairly early point in the sexual revolution. The item "not close to mother during high school" correlated significantly with promiscuity among daughters, indicating that having a close relationship with the mother helped prevent sexual activity.[††] The corresponding item about being not close to the father during high school failed to have a significant effect. Thus, again, female sexuality is suppressed by the mother, not the father.

Peer groups are a bit more difficult to assess than parents, mainly because research has mainly focused on same-sex peer groups. The focus of research may reflect the realities of adolescent life: Relatively few adolescents have significant numbers of opposite-gender friends, and if they do have them, they may not discuss sex very much because of various awkwardnesses. Rodgers and Rowe (1990) were one of the few to compare same-gender versus cross-gender effects on sexual behavior, and the same-gender influence was much more powerful. The link between sexual behavior of female friends accounted for 22 percent of the variance, as compared to only 5 percent in male-female friendships.

In any case, the female peer group does appear to be a restraining influence on sex in many cases. Carns (1973) found that young women were slower than young men

---

[††]Because the finding is correlational, one could argue in the opposite direction, namely that having sex during high school has a negative effect on closeness to the mother (but not to the father). Even if that were correct, it would still put the mother in the position as the one who is mainly involved in shaping the daughter's sexuality, because she is the one who is mainly bothered by the daughter's promiscuity.

to tell their friends about losing their virginity. These women also expected less approval from their peers. Maticka-Tyndale, Herold, and Mewhinney (1998) found that peer groups tended to make "pacts" when going on spring break. The young men's pacts usually involved trying to have sex, whereas the young women's groups involved promising to refrain from sex and even helping each other avoid sex (such as by helping a woman escape from male attention if she got drunk).

Similar conclusions emerged from a large study of late adolescents in Holland during the late 1980s by du Bois-Reymond and Ravesloot (1996). They too found that adolescents mainly discussed sex with their same-gender peers, although many also mentioned their relationship partner as a main confidante. The authors noted that the peer group discussions differed by gender. The males said their peer groups put pressure on them to have sex and experiment with various activities. The female peer groups, in contrast, put pressure on the individual young women "to behave decently and to 'look after their good names'" (p. 181). The women said their female peers cautioned them against the dangers of a bad reputation that would come from too much sexual activity. The researchers quoted a young woman named Monique, eighteen years old, who said: "My best friends do not allow me to date every boy. . . . Each week another one is not done. . . . We think that's stupid. . . . Moreover, my friends are often jealous" (p. 181). Thus, Monique felt pressure from her female friends to avoid promiscuity, and she even felt that they would be jealous if she were to sleep with many young men. This fits the social exchange view that female peer groups perceive it as a threat if one of their number goes too far sexually.

Several other studies have found that a young woman's sexual behavior tends to conform to that of their female peers, which is a key point in the social exchange analysis. Women are mainly competing against other women similar to themselves for men and are mainly in danger of having their mates stolen by other, similar women, and so the terms of social exchange need to be regulated among groups of similar women. Billy and Udry (1985; see also Mirande, 1968; Sack, Keller, & Hinkle, 1984) found that women tended to go as far as their friends had gone.

An alternative explanation for some of these findings would reject the view that the female peer group determines the young woman's sexual limits. Instead, perhaps each young woman decides her sexual level herself and chooses female friends who think the same way. Billy and Udry (1985) were able to address this problem by studying adolescent friendships and sexual behavior over time, to see which changed first. There was no tendency for women to abandon their virgin friends when the women lost their virginity, although they were a bit more likely to add new, nonvirgin friends. The selection of friends based on sexual status thus received mixed support. In contrast, there was clear evidence that the peer groups had influence. A virginal young white woman was six times more likely to lose her virginity by the end of the study if her best friend had been a nonvirgin than if her best friend had been a virgin. In short, the friends came first, and the sexual conformity came later.

Thus, the female peer group and the mother have clear and direct effects on female sexuality, and these effects often involve restraining sex or setting the limits. In contrast, the father's influence seems to be relatively small, and the young woman's male peers are largely out of the picture.

Influences on Adult Female Sexuality

If we turn to late adolescence and adulthood, it is useful to examine broader norms. Large samples were surveyed by King, Balswick, and Robinson (1977) and Robinson and Jedlicka (1982). The crucial question was whether a woman who engaged in premarital sex was immoral. The most important data for our purposes are from the first survey by King et al. (1977), taken in 1965, because that was before the sexual revolution had wrought its changes, and when the suppression of female sexuality was still in more or less full bloom. This can help indicate where disapproval would come from.

Who was most disapproving of women who had premarital sex? King et al. found that 42 percent of the men condemned these women as immoral—but that 91 percent of the women did. These figures strike a serious blow against the male conspiracy theory and in favor of the female conspiracy theory. Clearly, women were much more unanimous than men in their disapproval of other women having premarital sex. The pattern of greater disapproval by women remained the same in all subsequent years surveyed, although as the sexual revolution progressed the proportion of peopled disapproving dwindled, and the gap between men and women narrowed.

The only other figure to consider is the boyfriend (or several of them). Probably these have some effect on a young woman's sexual behavior too, and so they count as perhaps the only meaningful male source of influence. Unfortunately for the male conspiracy theory, their influence tends to be in the opposite direction: Young men often pressure their girlfriends to have sex with them, rather than to refrain from sex. The influence of the boyfriend thus runs directly contrary to the theory that men try to suppress female sexuality. And it seems to be the only significant direct male influence on the young woman's sexuality.

Infibulation and Subincision

In some cultures, the suppression of female sexuality goes far beyond social pressures and gossip. Young girls are subjected to an operation, called infibulation or subincision, that involves sewing up the vagina and/or removing the clitoris. Because the clitoris is the main source of a woman's sexual pleasure, this operation is likely to exert a powerful antisexual influence on women.

These operations are most common in Muslim countries, especially ones in which men hold the reins of power. Yet as we saw, male political and economic power is not itself revealing, because it is compatible with either the male or the female conspiracy theory. One must again ask, who is responsible for subjecting the girls to infibulation?

The weight of the evidence again points to the women. The girl's mother or grandmother decides whether and when the operation will be carried out (Hicks, 1996; Lighfoot-Klein, 1989). In some cases, the operation is a mark of status in the female peer group, and the other girls tease and put down anyone who has not yet had it (Lightfoot-Klein, 1989). The operation is performed by a woman such as a midwife. "Men are completely excluded" (Boddy, 1989, p. 84).

The women offer various justifications for the practice, but most of these are dubious if not wrong. They claim, for example, that the operation improves health (whereas actually it increases health risks), that it is required by the Koran (it is not), or that no one will marry the girl if she has not had the operation.

Shandall (1967, 1979) studied three hundred Sudanese husbands, all of whom had two wives, one who had had the full operation and the other who was intact or had had only a limited operation. The mere existence of all these husbands is enough to contradict the generalization that "no one will marry you if you have not had this done." On the other hand, Forni (1980) asserts that "very few men would marry a girl who has not been excised and infibulated" (p. 26). Then again, Lightfoot-Klein found that European women were in especially high demand among these men, for both sex and marriage, because of their higher sexuality, which seems directly contrary to the view that African men prefer women who are sexually stifled.

Moreover, nearly all of the men said they preferred the wife who had escaped the genital surgery. In cases where both wives had had some surgery, the men expressed preference for the one with the lesser surgery. These data make it difficult to argue that the men are behind the practice or even that they will refuse to marry a woman who has not had this genital surgery. "Something other than men's sexual satisfaction must be at stake in continuing the practice," commented Shandall (1967, p. 93).

Women also appear to be the main defenders of the practice, as many observers report (e.g., Boddy, 1989, 1998). There is a growing group of women in these societies with Western educations and values who have begun to speak out against the practice, but women are also the strongest supporters. Men seem indifferent, and some fathers object to the practice, but they are overruled by the women, who insist on having it done (Lightfoot-Klein, 1989). Hicks (1996) reported several studies finding that men pushed (often unsuccessfully) for less severe surgical practices against determined resistance by the women.

An interesting study by Williams and Sobieszczyk (1997) examined parental attitudes toward the practice. There is usually some similarity between marital partners in values, so these cannot be assumed to be fully independent. If the father wanted his daughter to have the operation, 100 percent of the mothers said they would have the daughter have it. If the father was opposed to the operation, 41 percent said they would make the daughter have it anyway. When the husband had no opinion, 97 percent planned on infibulating their daughters, and the women who claimed not to know whether their husband had an opinion were likewise very likely (79 percent) to have it done. These findings suggest some degree of paternal influence, but clearly the mother was in charge and was willing to go against her husband's wishes in a significant number of cases. Thus, these data too depict infibulation as rooted in and controlled by the female culture.

The feminist author Germaine Greer (1999) commented on this pattern in Western society. "Male genital mutilation is considered trivial; female genital mutilation is considered devastating" (p. 103), she wrote, even when the female mutilation involved little more than making a slight nick to promote ritual bleeding. In the West, physicians who perform genital-mutilating surgery on females are ostracized and can be prosecuted, whereas those who perform such surgery on males, whether circumcision or other procedures such as piercing, are not punished. To Greer, these asymmetries make it difficult to argue that genital mutilation is a crime by men against women. More to the point, she explicitly rejected the view that men sustain these operations against women: "This is indeed a curious explanation of something that women do to women," adding that the idea that women are carrying out men's desires has to invoke male "desires which in these cultures men would never have discussed with [the women]" (p. 103). She herself traveled in countries such as Ethiopia, where these operations are carried out, and she asked men whether they preferred sex with circumcised or uncircumcised women. As far as she could tell, the men didn't have an opinion, and in fact they didn't even know whether the women in their families had had these operations.

Prostitution and Pornography

Another source of evidence is opposition to prostitution and pornography. Pornography depicts women having plenty of sex, and it typically depicts them enjoying it immensely. By the same token, prostitutes are the woman who have sex with the highest numbers of partners and in the greatest frequency and variety of sex acts. Hence the forces that suppress female sexuality are likely to object to both pornography and prostitution.

Consistent with this view, the people of either gender who are most ardent to control female sexuality are typically staunch opponents of both prostitution and pornography. Clergy, moral leaders, and social purity campaigners (more recently, the Moral Majority) have lobbied to curtail the sale of pornography and to stop prostitution by various means.

A central prediction of the social exchange (female conspiracy) theory is that women will perceive prostitution and pornography as a threat to their position. In that view, women are trying to make sexual gratification scarce for men, so that men will be willing to do what women want (such as make long-term financial commitments) in exchange for sex. Prostitution and pornography allow men to obtain sexual pleasure without having to make such commitments. If we return to the monopoly analogy, prostitution and pornography represent the appearance on the market of cheap, second-rate substitutes for the precious but scarce resource. They thus pose a threat to the negotiating advantage that women would otherwise enjoy.

The prediction of the male conspiracy theory regarding prostitution and pornography is less straightforward and perhaps complicated by other issues. Certainly victim feminism may oppose pornography and prostitution on the grounds they exploit women, although in principle one could make the opposite argument that they exploit men, from whom those industries get almost all their revenues. We are not seeking to evaluate victim feminism as a whole, however, but only the specific theory that men are the main agents who have long sought to suppress female sexuality. Multipartnered women and erotica depicting sexually voracious females represent a threat or blow to anyone who prefers to ensure that women do not desire or enjoy sex.

Although both genders have been involved in campaigns against prostitution, women predominate. Also, attitude surveys make it clear that opposition to prostitution is stronger among women than men (Klassen, Williams, & Levitt, 1989). To be sure, male politicians have passed laws against prostitution, and male police have enforced them, so male attitudes are at least divided. But women are more consistently opposed to prostitution.

Similar conclusions emerge with regard to pornography. Both men and women have been active in antipornography campaigns, but if one surveys the full population, men are divided whereas women are more consistently opposed. One might propose that women's opposition to pornography reflects their lesser enjoyment of it. It is, however, quite possible to tolerate something without being opposed to it. For example, women are more tolerant of homosexuality than men, even though men are more likely to engage in homosexual acts. Many women thus feel that homosexuals should be permitted to do what they want, even though the women do not want to have lesbian affairs themselves. Women are particularly more tolerant than men of male homosexuality (e.g., Herek & Capitanio, 1999; Whitley, 1988), which by definition women do not take part in. It is thus a priori plausible that women could tolerate pornography even without desiring to view it themselves. This, however, is not the case.

Fakery

The practice of feigning desire and faking orgasms is potentially relevant to our discussion. Unlike men, women can relatively easily pretend to be aroused or not aroused and likewise can fake or conceal (and deny) having an orgasm. If men generally want to suppress female sexuality, then women would have a reason to conceal their sexual responses from men, and so most fakery would involve having orgasms but pretending not to have them. The opposite appears to be the case, however: Women tend to pretend that they have had orgasms, instead of that they have not had them (Elliott & Brantley, 1997).

The Sexual Revolution Again

The sexual revolution struck a severe blow against the suppression of female sexuality. Whoever had been trying to maintain that suppression was defeated by the advance of women into much greater sexual activity. Hence there is one more way to pit the male and female conspiracies against each other: We can try to ascertain who feels more like the loser due to that revolution.

The results of several national (Roper) polls were compiled by Smith (1994). To determine the dates to use, he relied on the fact that *Time* magazine devoted a cover story to the blossoming sexual revolution in 1964, and then ran another cover story declaring "The Revolution Is Over" in 1984. Hence he used the polls in 1974, presumably right at the height of the revolution, and 1985, after its end. But other, similar dates would probably work just as well and yield similar conclusions.

The Roper polls included the key item: "Do you think society's more widespread acceptance of sexual freedom for people before marriage is a change for the better or a change for the worse, or do you have mixed feelings about it?" By comparing how many men versus women regard the change as desirable, we can get some idea of who benefited more from suppressing female sexuality.

Perhaps surprisingly, both polls show widespread criticism of the new sexual freedom among both men and women. In 1974, when the sexual revolution was at its height, 19 percent of the men expressed favorable views (i.e., it was a "change for the better"), whereas 40 percent held negative opinions. The women, however, were even more uniformly against it: Only 12 percent of women said the new freedom was good, whereas 46 percent were opposed to it. Thus, if we compute a "defeat index" by subtracting the change-for-the-better proportion from the change-for-the-worse proportion, men do report some degree of defeat by the sexual revolution, with an index of 21; the female index, however, is 34. Or, using ratios, men were against the sexual revolution by a 2-to-1 margin, but women were opposed it by a 4-to-1 ratio.

The same conclusion emerged from the 1985 data, although the gap had narrowed somewhat. In 1985, 19 percent of men thought the change was for the better, 37 percent for the worse, yielding an index of 18. Women were 15 percent in favor and 41 percent opposed, furnishing an index of 26.

A more in-depth (but less scientifically systematic) investigation by Rubin (1990) yielded an even stronger but similar conclusion. In her interviews, she found that women were much more likely than men to criticize the new sexual permissiveness.

Thus, opposition to the new sexual freedom is strong among both genders. But if we had to pick one gender as expressing more regret over the sexual revolution, it would have to be women. Greer's (1999) observation that the revolution was won by men and lost by women is close to the mark (although women's sense of loss is apparently more uniform than men's sense of victory).

Converging evidence from a quite different source comes from a study of sexuality in China (Renaud, Byers, & Pan, 1997). China has a rather prudish attitude toward sex, and most forms of sexual expression are not tolerated. Married couples may not even kiss in public. The researchers thought that this prudishness would be associated with low sexual satisfaction for women, but they found the opposite: Women were relatively satisfied, whereas men reported lower satisfaction. Thus, again, men seem more unhappy in a traditional, sexually conservative arrangement as compared with a more permissive society, such as the West after the sexual revolution.

Conclusion

Taken together, the weight of evidence clearly favors the agentic feminist theory over the victim feminist theory. The suppression of female sexuality is far more plausibly explained as a female conspiracy than as a male conspiracy. Young women's sexuality is more consistently restrained by their mothers than their fathers. It is more restrained by female than male peers. Indeed, the influence of male peers seems to be in the opposite direction, in the form of a boyfriend urging the young woman to be more sexual rather than less. In cultures where the suppression of female sexuality relies more on surgical infibulation than attitudinal indoctrination, it again appears that women are the proximal and dominant causes. During sex, women pretend to have more rather than less enjoyment, suggesting that their male lovers are not opposed to female sexuality. They do, however, conceal their sexual activities from other women, consistent with the view that the female peer group might disapprove. Pornography, which depicts women seeking out and enjoying sex, is more strongly opposed by women than men, as is prostitution, in which women offer no-strings sex for cash. Last, the sexual revolution has sparked more regrets among women than men.

Is there anything to contradict these findings? There have been some customs and laws that penalize female sexual misbehavior more than male. Female adultery has sometimes been subject to more severe legal condemnation than male, and Christian theologians have sometimes condemned female sexual misbehavior more strongly than male. These differences are not much proof of a wish to stifle the desire, however, and they could simply reflect the fact that men have had more power and therefore wanted to impose stiffer penalties on their wives for infidelity than the men were willing to accept for themselves. The greater threat of paternity uncertainty could also contribute to this imbalance. The practice of locking women up in harems also probably indicated male desire to keep their women from having sex with other men. These penalties do not, however, operate directly on the desire for sex, and it seems intuitively obvious that most men have wanted their wives to desire sex with them but not with other men. Apart from these patterns, there is essentially no evidence that even hints at male efforts to suppress female sexual desire.

Frankly we were surprised by the uniformity of the data. When we set out to collect evidence about this issue, we expected to find some support for each side and to have to come up with a compromise theory. Possibly future research will come up with more results that support the male conspiracy theory. For now, however, we must conclude that the female conspiracy theory provides a better fit with the evidence. To the extent that social and cultural forces suppressed female sexuality, that suppression appears to have been directly caused by women rather than men.

These data provide more reason to take the sexual exchange theory seriously. Women give sex to men and get various benefits in return. The more easily men can get sex, the less women can receive in exchange. Through most of history, women depended on sex as a major bargaining chip to influence and control men and extract important concessions. As a result, women sought to restrict the supply of sexual gratification available to men. When women acquired social and political power, they were no longer so dependent on men and could therefore make sex more readily available, but women do nonetheless seem to have some sense of regret over the sexual revolution and recognize that it has hurt them in several ways.

It is necessary to note that the theory that women give sex to men is not a complete explanation of the sexual revolution. If sex were nothing more to women than something to trade, they would have opposed the sexual revolution. They clearly did have something to gain. Sex thus does bring pleasure and satisfaction to women. It is probably more appropriate to depict traditional female sexuality as torn between the positive forces of personal desire and the restraining forces of needing to keep men slightly sex-starved. The sexual revolution occurred because the balance between those opposing forces inside the average woman changed.

CHAPTER

6

The Plasticity of the Female Sex Drive

The sexual revolution was one of the biggest events in the history of sexuality in the Western world. Almost all areas of sex were affected. People started having more sex, especially before marriage. Girls stopped aspiring to remain virgins until their wedding night. Extramarital sex increased too, sometimes with full spousal consent, such as at "swinging" or mate-swapping parties. More people began to engage in a broader variety of sexual practices. Films, novels, and nonfiction began to take ever more explicit looks at human sexuality, and pornography went from a low-quality underground industry to a huge, mass-market affair that made nude and sexually explicit images readily available to adults everywhere.

One vital fact leaps out from the complexity and diversity of the sexual revolution: It was a much bigger change for women than for men, as Ehrenreich and colleagues (1986) wrote. As they saw it, men were not very different in what they felt or desired before and after the sexual revolution, although naturally men had more opportunities to act on their desires afterward. Rather, it was women who changed in more fundamental and far-reaching ways. Women came to want different things, and they sought sexual lives quite different from those of their mothers and grandmothers.

In this chapter, we will examine one possible explanation for the gender difference in the effects of the sexual revolution: cultural and historical events may have stronger influences on women than on men, at least in the sexual realm. The sexual revolution may not be an isolated case. Perhaps all sorts of sociocultural influences—religion, education, politics, and others—affect women more than men.

This idea is quite relevant to the interplay of nature and culture in shaping human sexual behavior, which we examined in Chapter 4. The clear evidence of variation across cultures and historical periods shows how sociocultural factors can influence sex. On the other hand, it is difficult to dispute that innate, biological factors play at least some role in sexuality. Most experts believe that some mixture of nature and culture is necessary for an adequate theory of sexuality.

But what sort of mixture? There is little agreement on the relative size of nature's versus culture's influence on sexuality. The field of sexuality as a whole has been torn by the seemingly endless and unresolvable debate between these two theories and their widely different emphases (DeLamater & Hyde, 1998).

At one extreme, social constructionists have argued that social influences and even free choice are responsible for deciding who feels how much sexual desire for whom and under what circumstances. They point out that sexual practices vary from one culture to another, and that these variations support their argument that sexual desire is a product of learning, socialization, and political influence (e.g., Staples, 1973). Feminist theory, which has long been squarely in the social constructionist camp, has asserted that sexual desires of women and men tend to be shaped to serve the handful of powerful males who make up the ruling class. Some feminists have taken this view to the extreme of insisting that even women's desire to have heterosexual intercourse is simply a product of indoctrinaion by a male-dominated culture that wants to shape women for its own pleasure and exploitation (e.g., Kitzinger, 1987). Hence the slogan "any woman can be a lesbian."

At the other extreme, evolutionary theorists have contended that the role of culture has been vastly overrated. In their view, sexuality is largely determined by innate biological forces shaped by human evolution. They believe sexual desire is formed according to the biological agenda of passing on one's genes (e.g., Buss & Schmitt, 1993; Trivers, 1972). Culture may be no more than a system worked out to accommodate these inborn patterns of desire (see Symons, 1995).

In this chapter, we consider yet another possibility for resolving the nature-culture question: Perhaps the relative importance of nature and culture differs by gender. Although both nature and culture are present in both genders, men's sexuality may be more influenced by nature, whereas female sexuality may be more responsive to sociocultural and situational influences. Put another way, we think that women may be creatures of culture and men of nature, relatively speaking.

In a sense, this could mean that the seemingly contradictory arguments raised by the social constructionists and evolutionary theorists all have some validity. Indeed, the intuitive appeal of those theories may differ by gender. Women may find the social constructionist theories more plausible than men, and certainly feminists have been more often female than male. Meanwhile, men may find the evolutionary arguments about innate sexual patterns more intuitively appealing, and indeed it is commonly remarked that evolutionary theorists are more often male than female. At professional conferences, for example, there are often plenty of pointed remarks about the lack of women among the ranks of evolutionary psychologists. The evolutionary arguments that sexual desire is a strong inborn pattern that is always almost out of control (i.e., you can't stop yourself from wanting; you can only stop yourself from acting on those wants, which leaves you disappointed and frustrated but not in violation of the laws or norms) seem to have more intuitive resonance with men than women.

Erotic Plasticity

The core idea is that the female sex drive is more responsive and malleable than the male (Baumeister, in press). We use the term *erotic plasticity* to describe the degree to which the sex drive changes in response to social, cultural, and situational factors. Thus, the core of the theory is that women have higher erotic plasticity than men.

Is this good or bad? We don't see any clear value judgment. That is, neither high nor low plasticity is inherently better. There are only two small exceptions to the value-free nature of this dimension, and these exceptions point in opposite directions and therefore tend toward canceling each other out.

One exception is that, in life in general, it is often better to be more flexible, because you can thus adapt to new, changing situations more easily. If women have higher erotic plasticity than men, women would be better able than men to adjust to changed circumstances. If there is a change in social pressures, roles, or other factors (such as a big shift in the sex ratios, as described in Chapter 4), men could find it more difficult than women to alter their sexual behavior and still be happy.

The other exception is that a more malleable person may be more vulnerable to external influence. If women have higher erotic plasticity, then it could be easier to talk a woman than a man into doing something sexual that is contrary to her or his best interests. Some people regard being vulnerable to influence as being gullible.

Still, neither of these seems highly important, and they may cancel each other out. We are therefore not saying that either men or women are better in this respect. Their erotic plasticity may, however, be quite different, and indeed their understanding of each other may be hampered by this discrepancy.

Three consequences can be predicted based on the idea that erotic plasticity is higher in women than men, and these can be used to check whether the theory is correct. The first is that individual women will change more over time than men. Greater flexibility will produce greater change as a person moves from one phase in life to another, especially if the situation changes.

The second prediction is that social and cultural factors will consistently have a greater impact on women's sexuality than men's. If men's sexuality is highly innate whereas women's is socially constructed, then social influences will be more successful at changing women than men.

The third is that women will show less consistency between attitudes and behavior than men. The debate over attitude-behavior consistency is an old and important one in social psychology (e.g., Wicker, 1969; see also Ajzen & Fishbein, 1977; Fazio, Powell, & Herr, 1983). Consistency is high when people's behavior is driven from internal factors, but when external factors play a large role, behavior may show little or no relation to attitudes.

Let us spend some time considering data about human sexuality to see whether the findings fit these three predictions. After that, we can turn to the question of why erotic plasticity might be higher in women than men.

Changes in People over Time

A first way of testing the plasticity of the female sex drive is to see whether women's sexual interests, desires, and activities change more than men's over time. If women's sexuality is more responsive to social, cultural, and situational factors, then as women move from one social environment to another, they should change more than men.

The idea that individual women show more change in sexuality than individual men across their adult lives was put forward already in the Kinsey reports (see Kinsey, Pomeroy, & Martin, 1948; and Kinsey, Pomeroy, Martin, & Gebhard, 1953). Kinsey interviewed thousands of people in depth in order to get their full sexual histories. He and his colleagues noted that women showed what they called "discontinuities in total outlet" (p. 681). ("Total outlet" was Kinsey's term for all the sexual activities, especially including orgasms, that the person experienced.) A similar conclusion was reached by Masters and Johnson's (1966) pioneering work on human sexual response: "The mercurial tendency to shift rapidly from peak to valley has been exemplified by female study subjects, while levels of sexual expression that remain essentially constant are observed most frequently in male study subjects" (pp. 314–315).

For example, a woman might have a rich sexual relationship involving regular, satisfying intercourse. Then she might break up with her partner and have no sex at all, including no masturbation, for several months. Then she might find a new partner and resume regular and frequent sex. Kinsey said that such fluctuations were almost never found in men. If a man was having an active sex life with frequent orgasms but then broke up with his partner, he would probably begin masturbating regularly, seeking casual sex, or resorting to prostitutes, until he found another regular partner. The man's frequency of orgasms would thus not change radically. A woman's might, however. These changes suggest greater plasticity on the woman's part.

Other studies have looked at how people's sex lives change from young adulthood to older ages. As people grow old, obviously, many have less energy and less frequent sexual desires, so there is a broad pattern of decline in sex drive, which is not directly relevant to the plasticity issue. To get around that problem, Adams and Turner (1985) looked specifically for any reports of increases in any sexual activities from the person's twenties to old age (sixty–eighty-five). These changes were mainly found among women. For example, women masturbated more in old age than in their youth, unlike the men. (The sample was mainly composed of married couples, so it was not simply a matter of widows resorting to masturbation when their partners died.) Some women masturbated when young and stopped by old age, whereas others only took it up when no longer young, and so the changes in both directions indicated greater plasticity among women, as the researchers themselves concluded.

Another place where individuals may change their sexual wishes and practices is in adapting to a long marriage. Such adaptations were studied by Ard (1977), who interviewed people who had been married for over two decades. He asked people specifically whether they or their partner had changed more. Husbands and wives agreed that the wives had changed more than the husbands.

On a smaller scale, another team of investigators examined how young people changed their sexual attitudes over the course of dating (Harrison, Bennett, Globetti, & Alsikafi, 1974). They failed to find systematic evidence of change among men, but women's attitudes changed as they gained more dating experience.

Change in sexual orientation is another important domain to search for evidence of plasticity. If people are born one certain way and cannot change it, then their sexual orientation should remain fairly inflexible, but if social and cultural factors come into play, then people might conceivably switch back and forth. Is there a gender difference in bisexuality, or at least in switching back and forth between heterosexual and homosexual orientations?

Yes: Study after study has found that far more gay women than gay men have heterosexual experience (Bell & Weinberg, 1978; Kinsey et al., 1948, 1953; Laumann et al., 1994; Rosario et al., 1996; Savin-Williams, 1990; Schfer, 1976; Whisman, 1996). Often the difference is huge: Around four out of every five lesbians have had sex with men, but only around half of gay men have ever gone to bed with a woman. The same result is found if one broadens the scope to look at other categories of heterosexual activity than just intercourse (Bell & Weinberg, 1978), or if one restricts it to only meaningful sexual relationships (Whisman, 1996). Nor is this a matter of women taking longer to realize they are gay: Many lesbians have heterosexual affairs after they have taken on a lesbian identity, and even after they have been firmly lesbian for years (Rust, 1992). Likewise, some women who are quite happy and satisfied with heterosexuality will start having lesbian affairs in addition to their heterosexual love lives (Dixon, 1984).

Indeed, this pattern of plasticity has led to political conflicts. Gay pride and gay rights movements often want firm commitments from their members, and some gay people regard bisexuals as indecisive cowards or even traitors. These conflicts have been much more pronounced in the women's movements than in the men's, partly because the lesbian community has a higher proportion of bisexuals than the gay male community (e.g., Rust, 1993; see also Laumann et al., 1994). Women who have sex with other women are significantly less likely to see themselves as irrevocably, exclusively homosexual, as compared to men who have sex with other men.

We already mentioned that women are more likely than men to commence having same-gender sex during mate-swapping and group sex. A study of a large sample of swingers (Bartell, 1970) concluded that when two married couples get together and exchange partners for sex, the women will have sex with each other about 75 percent of the time, but the men would have sex with each other less than 1 percent of the time. (This pattern of mate-swapping was briefly widespread in the United States but is far less common now.) That huge difference suggests that women are more malleable in their sexual expression.

The main advantage of erotic plasticity is that it allows one to adapt better to changing circumstances and demands. Hence one final way to test the hypothesis would consider whether more males or females change from heterosexuality to homosexuality when they find themselves in a one-gender environment. Of these, prison has been studied most frequently. Although data comparing rates of consenting homosexual activity in prison are not extensive, the signs do indicate that more women than men make this adjustment (e.g., Gagnon & Simon, 1968; Ward & Kassebaum, 1965). This is especially remarkable given that prison's main alternative to homosexuality is to do without sex entirely, which, as noted, Kinsey and his colleagues found to be something women did more readily than men. Heterosexual women may adopt a lesbian orientation during their time in prison and then quickly return to a heterosexual pattern once they are released.

Taken together, all the signs confirm the notion that women change more readily than men in terms of their sexual activities and desires. As a woman moves from one situation to another or from one phase in life to another, her sexuality is more likely than a man's to undergo important changes.

Social and Cultural Influences

The next prediction is that social and cultural factors will have bigger effects on women's sexuality than on men's. We have already discussed the sexual revolution, which was a large social and cultural event that seems to have had a greater impact on women than on men. Research studies provided ample confirmation that women changed more than men. Several sets of researchers compared data from surveys conducted on similar groups (e.g., on the same college campus) before, during, and after the revolution, and they consistently found that women changed more than men. For example, on one typical campus, the percentage of university women who were virgins dropped by half (75 percent to 38 percent) between 1963 and 1978, but the corresponding change for men was slight (40 percent to 34 percent [Sherwin & Corbett, 1985]).

Likewise, the sexual revolution lowered the age of various first sexual experiences more for females than for males, and the women also changed more in reporting positive feelings about these experiences (Schmidt & Sigusch, 1972). Attitudes changed along with behavior, and again larger changes were found in women's reports on attitudes about a broad range of sexual activities, from french kissing to intercourse (Croake & James, 1973).

Another way to study the sexual revolution (without repeated surveys) is to compare young versus old people. Most people who were old in the 1970s and 1980s had come of age before the sexual revolution, whereas young people had passed puberty after it. Not surprisingly, behavior changed for both genders, but again the differences were bigger for women than men. With a national sample, W. C. Wilson (1975) found greater age discrepancies in women than men on issues such as whether the person had experienced intercourse before the age of twenty-one. That is, the percentage of twenty-one-year-old virgin men changed only slightly from before to after the sexual revolution, but in women it dropped substantially.

Even more dramatically, Laumann et al. (1994) found a big change in promiscuity for women but not men. Before the sexual revolution, only a tiny percentage (under 3 percent) of women had five or more sex partners by the age of thirty, but after the revolution a substantial minority of women (22 percent) did. Among men, the corresponding numbers were 38 percent and 49 percent, which is a more modest change. Thus, the sexual revolution seems to have created a large minority of women who went to bed with multiple partners—a pattern that had been quite rare previously.

Cultural differences likewise have a bigger impact on female than male sexuality. Cross-cultural comparisons find that women vary more than men from one culture to another (e.g., Christensen & Carpenter, 1962). In a large sample of 186 cultures from around the world, Barry and Schlegel (1984) found that female adolescent sexual behaviors varied more than male.

One may also look at what happens when people move from one culture to another. Naturally, people differ in terms of how much they embrace the new culture as opposed to retaining their identification with the old culture. This process, called *acculturation*, is a general process and not something that is specifically associated with sex. Researchers have, however, used measures of acculturation in general to see whether immigrants change their sexual practices. In an important study of Latino immigrants to Detroit, Ford and Norris (1993) found that acculturation predicted sexual behavior in many and substantial ways for women, but that the effects on men were either small or nonexistent. The implication is that when a man moves from one culture to another, his sexuality hardly changes regardless of whether he embraces the new culture or maintains his identification with the old one he left behind. In contrast, migration and acculturation make a big difference in a woman's sexuality.

Let us now turn away from historical and cultural differences to look at the effects of two of society's major institutions: education and religion. The church and the school (including the university) are among a culture's most powerful means of socializing people, and so it is useful to consider how big a difference they make. The most thorough data on how these pertain to sexuality are found in the NHSLS, the well constructed national survey about sexual behavior that we have mentioned repeatedly (Laumann et al., 1994). The question is, as one moves from the least educated to the most educated, or from the least religious to the most religious, do men or women show more change in their sexual habits?

By and large, both men and women show more liberal sexual attitudes at higher educational levels (contrary to the asexual stereotype of the brainy nerd that is popular in many Hollywood films!). But the changes are consistently bigger for women than men. For example, highly educated women are almost twice as likely to have performed oral sex as relatively uneducated women, whereas men increase by only about a third. As for receiving oral sex, women again show a bigger increase as a function of education. Parallel differences are found with anal sex (i.e., having tried it or not): Education makes a larger difference in rates of anal sex among women than men.

The researchers presented people with a list of fifteen sexual practices and asked them how many they found appealing. Men of all levels of education liked about the same number of practices, but more educated women found significantly more practices appealing than the less educated women.

Most dramatically, higher education increased the likelihood of becoming gay or bisexual, and again the effect was bigger for women. Getting a college education increased a woman's likelihood of being gay by a factor of nine, whereas for men the increase was only by a factor of two.

It is important to acknowledge, however, that the research findings fall short of proving that college produces change in women. All we know is that there are more gays among college graduates than among less well educated people. In our view, the most plausible explanation is that college changes people through such means as exposing them to new ideas and practices, and causing them to reevaluate their feelings and beliefs. In principle, however, the same result could be produced if being homosexual causes people to obtain more education.

Not all variables in the NHSLS showed effects of education. Masturbation, for example, did not seem to reflect much influence (although when there were effects, they were again greater for women). In general, across all aspects of sexuality, the same conclusion kept emerging: When education did have an impact, it nearly always changed women more than men.

Religion gives the same result. It is noteworthy that the effects of religion are to reduce sexual activity, whereas education seems to increase it. Thus, society's two main institutions seem to operate in opposite ways, but regardless of whether the institution increases or suppresses sexuality, it has more impact and power for changing women than men. In the NHSL survey, the two most extreme groups were usually the people who reported having no religion at all and, at the other end, the people who were fundamentalist, evangelical Christians. In such comparisons, women again differed more than men on many issues, such as oral sex (giving and receiving), homosexuality and contraception.

Other studies have shown similar findings and even extended them to other variables. More educated women report a higher age of first intercourse than less educated ones, but educational attainment has much less of an effect on when men start having sex (W. C. Wilson, 1975). College courses on human sexuality produce greater changes in sexual attitudes of women students than male ones (Weis, Rabinowitz, & Ruckstuhl, 1992). Church attendance significantly and substantially predicts less masturbation among women, but the corresponding difference among men is small and nonsignificant (Adams & Turner, 1985).

Thus, the educational system and the church—two of society's main institutions for socializing people—consistently have greater effects on women than men, as shown by changes in sexual behavior. This seems to be true regardless of whether the institution's effect is toward more liberal or more conservative sexuality.

Politics is another form of sociocultural influence. The impact of political factors on sexuality has not been studied much, but what evidence exists indicates again that women are more affected than men. The main relevant pattern involves people who change their sexual orientation (particularly toward becoming homosexual) for political reasons. Many sources have asserted that the women's movement and related political influences persuaded some women to become lesbian (Blumstein & Schwartz, 1977; Echols, 1984; Kitzinger, 1987; Pearlman, 1987). The sort of influence was articulated in Johnston's (1973), statement that "Feminists who still sleep with [men] are delivering their most vital energies to the oppressor" (p. 167). In this harsh view, men and women are enemies in the battle of the sexes, and so homosexuality is the only politically correct choice for women.

Clear, convincing data on politically motivated sex are hard to find. It is obvious, however, that women are more likely than men to perceive politics as a reason for their sexual orientations. Whisman (1996) found that some women but no men cited political reasons for becoming gay. Rosenbluth (1997) reported that approximately one out of eight women in her sample cited political reasons for becoming gay, and that a similar proportion of women said that political reasons had influenced them to be heterosexual. Among a sample of women who changed from heterosexuality to lesbianism during middle adulthood (i.e., midlife), one-third cited political influences such as feminist writings (Charbonneau & Lander, 1991).

Thus, some women seem amenable to changing their sexual orientation under the influence of external factors, even if they appear to have been quite content with heterosexual sex. Driven by political ideology or even in some cases by the wish to try something new and entertain their husbands at mate-swapping parties (Dixon, 1984), women may start going to bed with other women. For men to show that kind of change is almost unheard of, and the published sources essentially never speak of men turning gay under such influences. That is, the claim that some men would turn away from women and instead start performing sex acts with other men, simply because they had read political articles in magazines telling them to do so, or because they wanted to put on a sexy show for their wives, has not been made.

The peer group is another social institution that can influence sexuality, although one cannot assume that male and female peer groups operate in similar ways and have similar values. Still, it is possible to determine whether someone's peer group approves of a certain sexual activity and to check whether that person engages in that activity. Several such studies have found that peer group approval has a bigger effect on girls and women than on boys and men. Peers who have had sex, who approve of sex, or who encourage sex seem to predict whether girls and women, but not boys and men, have sex (Mirande, 1968; Sack, Keller, & Hinkle, 1984). In one well-controlled study that followed people over time, males' sexual practices were largely unaffected by their peer groups, but females responded significantly to them (Billy & Udry, 1985). A white female virgin whose best friend was a nonvirgin was six times more likely to lose her virginity during the following two years than a white female virgin whose best friend was also a virgin. Males showed no such effect.

To be sure, we tend to choose our friends, and so there is some theoretical possibility that people selected their friends based on their sexual intentions. This problem does not apply to parents, because people cannot choose their parents. The weight of evidence again suggests that parents have more impact on their daughters' sexuality than on their sons' (Miller & Moore, 1990). It is plausible, of course, that parents socialize their sons and daughters differently. But the parental influence goes beyond such direct efforts at education. When parents get a divorce, the effect on the daughter's sexual development is stronger and longer lasting than the effect on the son's (Newcomer & Udry, 1987). Likewise, the parents' own sexual histories and attitudes have more impact on daughters than sons (Thornton & Camburn, 1987).

Thus far we have looked directly at sociocultural factors. Another approach, however, is to look at the problem in an opposite way. If sociocultural factors have more effect on women's sexuality, do genetic ones have more effect on men? Studies with twins (e.g., comparing identical twins reared apart and nonidentical twins raised together) and similar methods have been used by behavior geneticists to assess how much people's lives are shaped by their genes. One such large-scale study concluded that, for people born after the sexual revolution, genes accounted for 72 percent of the variance in males' age of first intercourse but only 40 percent of the variance in females (Dunne et al., 1997). Thus, the age at which people start having sex is more genetically determined for men than for women, provided that they live in a society where opportunities are present.

A similar approach is to examine the role of genetics in homosexuality. The quest for the "gay gene" has been hotly controversial, and even homosexual leaders are themselves uncertain whether they hope the full research findings will depict homosexuality as a choice or as an innate, unchangeable feature of a person. The data, using twins or examining patterns such as whether gay people have gay siblings and cousins, are mixed. Still, a review by Bailey and Pillard (1995) concluded that evidence for a genetic aspect of homosexuality is stronger for men than for women. They observed that many experts have begun to conclude that male homosexuality is more genetically based than lesbianism, although they themselves preferred to wait for more data before drawing a strong conclusion. Still, based on what we know now, it does look like biology has a stronger part in dictating the sexual orientation of males, which makes female sexual orientation more plastic.

Perhaps the maximum level of plasticity would involve people being able to make a free personal choice about what their sexual desires would be. The role of personal choice in sexual orientation has been examined in several studies. The consistent finding is that women report more choice than men (e.g., Whisman, 1996). Ironically, men are more likely to wish they had a choice, possibly because the social stigma and social pressures penalize male homosexuality more strongly than lesbianism. But men tend to feel their sexual orientation is not at all theirs to decide. Some women, at least, do feel they have a choice.

Thus, we have a consistent pattern across many factors. Culture, history, education, religion, peers, parents, personal choice—all major sociocultural factors—have stronger effects on women's sexuality than men's. Male sexuality, in contrast, seems more affected by genetic, innate factors. These patterns provide strong support for the notion of female erotic plasticity.

Consistency Between Attitudes and Behavior

The consistency between attitudes and behavior is an important issue in social psychology, and at times it has even been a sore point. Social psychologists have studied attitudes since the earliest days of their field, and the influential thinker Gordon Allport famously remarked that the attitude is the single most important concept in social psychology. The study of attitudes was, however, justified in part by the assumption that knowing a person's attitudes would help explain and predict how that person would behave. This assumption was questioned in a shocking attack by Wicker (1969), who compiled a large mass of data showing that attitudes predict behavior only weakly. Wicker went so far as to conclude that social psychology should abandon the study of attitudes.

From that moment, the issue of attitude-behavior consistency (known in some circles as the "*A-B* problem") became an urgent, fascinating concern. Social psychologists rushed to show how better connections between attitudes and behavior could be shown. One approach was to look for specific attitudes that might do a better job than broad, abstract attitudes at predicting behavior (Ajzen & Fishbein, 1977). Another was to note that many single behaviors would fail to correspond to attitudes because the person wasn't thinking about the specific attitude at the time of the behavior (Fazio, Powell, & Herr, 1983). For example, if a request for donating blood is seen as a test of your social conscience, then broad attitudes about helping others will predict whether you make a donation; but if that same request is seen as a painful experience or as a risk of getting infected, then your attitudes about helping others won't predict whether you donate.

The key point is that plenty of immediate situational factors and pressures can intervene between an attitude and a behavior. In a vacuum, people probably would act consistently with their attitudes, but behavior rarely occurs in such a vacuum. Instead, personal values and noble intentions may by lost in the shuffle as people respond to their immediate situation in a variety of complex and somewhat unpredictable ways.

Erotic plasticity entails that the person would be malleable in response to situational pressures. Hence if women's erotic plasticity is higher than men's, women should show lower attitude-behavior plasticity than men.

One test of this theory has to do with infidelity. Most people disapprove strongly of infidelity in marriage, and most people in fact are relatively faithful to their spouses, so marital infidelity does not provide enough statistical variance to furnish a good test on whether actions match attitudes. In one study, however, the difficulty was solved by studying much lesser instances of infidelity among dating couples, such as if a person were to kiss or hold hands with someone other than the steady dating partner. These behaviors were compared with the relevant attitudes, especially whether the person disapproved of all such infidelity. The researcher (Hansen, 1987) found that the correlation between the person's attitude and actual behavior was lower for women than for men.

The implication is that men's actions tend to line up pretty well with their attitudes and values. For women, the match between attitude and behavior was much weaker. Some might interpret this to mean that women are fickle and like to change their minds. A more appealing explanation, however, is that a woman's behavior depends on the immediate meaning and context, and so her responses to broad, general attitude questions are less relevant. A woman may disapprove of fooling around in general, but in a particular circumstance it may seem all right to her because of social and situational reasons. For a man, the social and situational reasons make less of a difference, and so the broad attitude predicts behavior more accurately.

Condom use is another area where attitude-behavior consistency is often low: People frequently express strong approval of using condoms, but when they find themselves in the situation of actually having sex with a new partner they don't always manage to live up to their good intentions. Herold and Mewhinney (1993) found that women reported higher intentions than men to use condoms, presumably because the sexual risks are higher for women (and possibly because the decrease in pleasure is less). In actual behavior, however, they found no difference, and both sexes often neglected to use condoms. Thus there was a bigger gap between pro-condom attitude and actual (condom-less) behavior for women.

Homosexual activity provides another sphere in which to examine the A-B problem. The NHSLS (Laumann et al., 1994) asked people whether they found the idea of having sex with someone of their own same gender appealing and whether they had actually engaged in such sex acts. Although women rated the idea of having same-gender sex more appealing than men, they were less likely to have actually done it, indicating a bigger gap between attitudes and behavior. For example, among the men who liked the idea of going to bed with another man, 85 percent had actually done so in the past year. Among women who liked the idea of going to bed with another woman, less than half had actually done it in the past year. Thus, the broad attitude matched up with actual behavior much more closely among men than among women.

Similar discrepancies emerge with respect to sexual masochism. As we saw in Chapter 3, women have more submissive fantasies than men but are less likely to act them out.

Adding It All Up

There are some contrary findings on the *A-B* problem, although not many. Occasionally men have a more positive attitude toward doing something but are less likely to do it. Most of these effects can, however, be chalked up to lack of opportunity. Opportunity is a major situational constraint on men. As Clark and Hatfield (1989) showed, most men will go to bed with a woman who asks—but women don't ask them all that often. In contrast, women have more opportunities for casual sex but do not find them appealing. Apart from opportunity constraints, though, men's behaviors correspond to their attitudes more closely than women's.

Thus, the weight of evidence does point toward female erotic plasticity. In three tests of the hypothesis, women came out higher on plasticity. First, sociocultural factors consistently have bigger effects on women than men, such as showing that women's sex lives change more than men's as a function of education, religion, history, politics, and peer influence. Second, individual women show more change in sexuality over time than individual men. Third, women's sexual behavior is less closely linked to their inner attitudes than men's, which again suggests a greater role for situational factors and a greater degree of flexibility and responsiveness.

There was only one pattern of findings that suggests a real exception. Let us turn to it now.

Childhood Experiences: The Big Exception?

A smattering of findings deviate from the general pattern of female erotic plasticity, and they all point toward one particular source: early childhood. It is quite possible that male sexuality can be shaped by situational and social experiences during childhood in more lasting and far-reaching ways than female sexuality. This is not to say that childhood experiences are irrelevant for girls. But female erotic plasticity may make these childhood influences reversible for women in a way that they are not for men.

Let us start with seemingly the most obvious exception to the principle of female plasticity: Men engage in a broader variety of unusual sexual practices (*paraphilias*, or in the more traditional and pejorative term, *perversions*) than women. Does this mean that male sexuality is more plastic in the sense that it can be molded into weird shapes more easily?

Strictly speaking, differences between different men do not reveal anything about sociocultural plasticity. Such differences could be genetic. After all, men have different hair and eye color, but that does not necessarily reflect any sociocultural influence. Still, it seems odd to suggest that a shoe fetish might have a genetic basis. Could it be learned through social factors? And, if so, do they indicate plasticity?

Research has not yet yielded a clear, meaningful explanation of paraphilias. Yet some facts are clear. For one thing, these unusual sexual tastes do not show much plasticity. Men do not adopt them like they might take up a hobby, nor do they find it easy to get rid of them. Sex therapy can sometimes help a man with a paraphilia begin to enjoy regular intercourse, but these therapeutic methods are not very successful at getting rid of the special desire.

Furthermore, many paraphiliacs are quite particular and inflexible about exactly what they desire. For example, some men find it arousing to be scolded and insulted by a woman prior to sex, and they may pay a prostitute to act out such a script and say precisely the things they want. If the woman deviates from the script, though, the man loses his arousal and gets upset. He wants her to say exactly certain specified things in a particular sequence.

Thus, paraphilias seem to be fairly rigid and inflexible, contrary to the concept of plasticity (but consistent with the general pattern of male inflexibility). They also seem to have their origins in childhood (Money, 1990; Reinisch, 1990). That is, something seems to happen to boys that instills such tastes, which then become enduring themes for their adult sexuality.

The evidence about homosexuality likewise points to childhood influence. As we saw in Chapter 4, Bem's (1996) EBE (exotic becomes erotic) theory places strong emphasis on childhood experiences as the basis for adult homosexuality. Because male homosexuality is more inflexible than female homosexuality, it seems reasonable to suggest that the childhood experiences have a more lasting effect on males.

There are in fact some data pointing in that direction. The NHSLS (Laumann et al., 1994), which, as we have said, provides the best database on sexuality, produced one finding that ran contrary to the female plasticity pattern. It found that the difference between rates of homosexuality in urban versus rural (i.e., city versus country) homes was bigger among men than women. To some extent, the difference reflects migration, since gay people may move from a small country town (where there may be hardly any available partners) to a big city.

Yet the difference remained even when the researchers controlled for migration. Thus, growing up in a city as opposed to the country tended to increase the odds that a boy would be eventually turn out to be gay. The corresponding effect for girls was weaker. Possibly the difference has to do with being exposed during childhood to same-gender couples and seeing homosexuality as a real option. In any case, it had a bigger effect on boys.

A fascinating experiment was recently done in England with goats and sheep, which enabled the researchers to do things that would be impossible with human beings. They took the newborn goats and sheep and swapped them, so the goats were raised by sheep and vice versa. When the animals were fully grown, they were reunited with their own species, and the researchers observed their mating preferences (Kendrick, Hinton, Atkins, Haupt, & Skinner, 1998).

The adult females' behavior fit very well with our general pattern of erotic plasticity. The adult female sheep who had been raised by goats were willing to mate with either male sheep or goats. Likewise, the female goats who had been raised by sheep were willing to mate with either species.

In contrast, the males were not flexible—but in a very interesting way. They would only mate with their adoptive, not their biological, species. In other words, the male sheep who had been raised by goats would only have sex with goats, and the male goat who had been raised among sheep would only mate with sheep.

These male patterns speak against a strict biological explanation of sexual behavior leading directly from genes to behavior, because the males refused to mate with their own species (which is generally the only way to produce any offspring). Instead, it appears that the socialization experiences of childhood had a strong and lasting effect on the males. In the researchers' terms, the males showed "sexual imprinting," which means that the first females they were exposed to (i.e., their acting mothers) determined their sexual preferences for life. In females, sexual imprinting effects were weak and reversible.

Recent evidence on sexual dysfunction provides yet another piece of converging evidence. Using the NHSLS data set, a large study by Laumann, Paik, and Rosen (1999) examined what factors predict sexual problems during adulthood. For the most part, the evidence conformed to what we have already seen in terms of female plasticity: Female sexual dysfunction varied with sociocultural factors such as education, whereas male sexual dysfunction was linked to purely physical issues such as overall health and medical condition.

The one exception to this pattern concerned childhood sexual experiences. To the surprise of the researchers, such experiences had stronger and more lasting effects on males than females. In other words, having been touched sexually before the age of puberty had a strong link to sexual dysfunction during adulthood (and to many specific kinds of sexual problems) for males, but the link was weaker among females.

This does not mean that one can do sexual things to little girls without causing problems. Childhood sexual experiences, especially when initiated by adults, can cause lasting harm to both boys and girls. Still, the issue for the individual victim is whether you can eventually put the bad experience behind you and have a normal, happy sex life. Apparently, adult women can do this better than adult men. Erotic plasticity may be part of the reason. The adult woman can take advantage of female erotic plasticity to experience some growth and recovery of her sexuality during adulthood. The lesser flexibility of adult male sexuality means that the lasting effects of childhood mistreatment are harder to shake off.

The totality of evidence for this exception is not strong, but at present it is the best guess as to the truth (Baumeister, in press). Females have higher erotic plasticity during adolescence and adulthood, but there does seem to be a window of opportunity in childhood during which male sexuality is strongly influenced by environmental factors and socializing experiences. Once that developmental phase is over, however, the male sexuality is fairly permanently stamped and remains inflexible during adulthood, whereas female sexuality can continue to grow and change throughout life.

Searching for a Reason for the Gender Difference

Let us now turn to consider various reasons for the apparent gender difference in erotic plasticity.

The Double Standard

The traditional "double standard" might explain some of these differences in erotic plasticity. In this view, women are held to higher standards of sexual purity than men, and so in a sense the culture tries harder to control women's than men's sexuality. This explanation is especially hard to sort out from others, because if women have higher erotic plasticity than men, it would simply make sense for the culture to aim its controls at women. When a society needs to control sexuality, for whatever reason (such as to restrict venereal disease or to limit the population), it will be more successful if it tries to control women than men, if women are more malleable.

Then again, some thinkers have held that society tries to control women simply because society is dominated by men, and so men want to exploit and subjugate women for men's own sake. It might have nothing to do with erotic plasticity: Men simply got the power and so, to advance their own interests at the expense of women, they invented the double standard and other efforts to control female sexuality.

This view can be made to fit some but not all the findings. First of all, it is hard to find genuine evidence that a double standard exists today. When President Clinton was caught having an affair with a young White House intern in 1998, for example, a series of polls explored the American population's attitudes about sexual morality. One of them asked people whether extramarital sex is ever tolerable for a husband or for a wife. The responses (mainly disapproving) were almost identical, and in fact the tiny and nonsignificant difference that emerged indicated greater tolerance of infidelity by wives, contrary to the double standard theory (Handy, 1998).

More systematic research by Sprecher (1989) looked for double standard beliefs among young people and repeatedly failed to find them. She found that women were less tolerant than men of various practices—but that neither gender said that some acts were more acceptable for men than for women, which is the essence of the double standard. Nor was it that her procedures or measures were unable to detect any double standards. People in her study were quite willing to say that certain sex practices would be less tolerable for certain categories of people, such as their own relatives (especially brothers and sisters) and for younger people. People do make distinctions and are very willing to say that certain acts are OK for some people and not for others. They just don't say that certain things are OK for men and not for women.

Actually, evidence of the double standard even in the past is sketchy. Data from national Roper polls before the sexual revolution were compiled by Smith (1994), and even they showed only a small minority of people endorsing a double standard. Specifically, people were asked whether such activities were always all right for everyone, never all right, or all right for men but not women. The last response is the double standard option, but only 7 percent of the people in 1937 used that response, and about the same percentage (8 percent) chose it in 1959.

Thus, there were some people who held a double standard, but they were only a tiny minority of the population. Possibly there is some other hidden or subtle form of double standard. For example, perhaps some people might believe that premarital sex is wrong for both men and women, but somehow more wrong for women than for men. This might cause the survey to show no difference even if a double standard existed. But this is admittedly groping for a basis to believe something contrary to the evidence we have. The data, even from what were supposedly the bad old days of the flourishing double standard, doesn't give much evidence that many people believed sexual activities were acceptable for men but unacceptable for women.

Why do people believe in the double standard, if the data do not support it? One possible reason is that it is an illusion created by the much more real and durable finding that women are less permissive than men. For example, women in the 1940s may have said that premarital sex was wrong, while men at the same time said it was acceptable.

Although that difference does suggest that there was some form of a double standard, in fact women were saying that premarital sex was not all right for either men or women, and men were saying that it was all right for both. The gender difference in overall permissiveness created a misleading appearance of a double standard.

Another problem for the theory that female plasticity simply reflects a plot by male-dominated culture to exploit women is that the two strongest cultural institutions we covered, namely the church and the university, both affect women more than men—but in opposite directions. Religion makes people less sexually liberal, while universities seem to make them more liberal. If the culture has a master plan for exploiting women, its powerhouse institutions are working in opposite directions.

Perhaps one could counter this view by suggesting that religion enforces male oppression of females, while the university is in fact a renegade, countercultural institution that liberates women from their socialized lessons and lets them discover their true sexuality. This view of the university has both its plausible and its absurd sides, and these can be argued at length. More to the point, however, the view of the Christian church as a tool of male oppression has to contend with some seriously contrary facts. Christianity has generally appealed more to women than men, right from the early days when it rose to power in the Roman empire (Stark, 1996), and the predominance of female over male churchgoers was a powerful factor during the early modern period (Cott, 1977). The same holds today: Women attend church more than men. Thus, if the church is a tool of male oppression, one must apparently argue that women like to be oppressed more than men like oppressing them.

Other institutions, meanwhile, are working in mysterious ways. The female peer group seems to have a strong effect on women's sexual behaviors (and more than the male peer group's effect on men). The exploitation theory has to contend that the female peer group is an instrument of male oppression, which seems doubtful.

Nature's Playthings

Let us leave the double standard and male exploitation theories and consider another perspective on female plasticity. Perhaps, in an important sense, men are nature's playthings while women are cultural creations. That is, in the never-ending process of change due to both nature and culture, nature operates more powerfully on men, while culture operates more strongly on women. This does run contrary to some traditional stereotypes that viewed women as beings who were closer to nature and men as civilized beings whose province was culture. But such stereotypes are not necessarily based on reality.

Why would nature operate more strongly on men? Natural selection functions by creating variation through genetic mutations, and whichever version reproduces most successfully will win out. (The shift from survival to reproduction has been one of the main changes in emphasis in modern evolutionary theory; see Buss, 1994; Ridley, 1993.) To select a new genetic type, then, it is necessary to have variation in offspring. And men have more variation in number of offspring. Throughout world history, and even in other species, most females reproduce, but not all males do. (Hence men need to compete, even violently, against each other.)

Thus, at the low end, more men than women have no babies and hence fail to pass on their genes. At the high end, few women have more than ten children, and it is almost physically impossible to have more than twenty. A man, however, can certainly produce more children than that, especially in polygamous cultures (i.e., where some men can have multiple wives). Powerful men who had several dozen wives and mistresses, without effective birth control, could produce dozens or even hundreds of children.

Is there any evidence to support the view of men as nature's playthings? One sign would be if there is more genetic variation among men than women. A full consideration of this idea is beyond the scope of this book, but at least one important example is familiar: intelligence (IQ). Most researchers currently working on intelligence believe that it has a strong genetic component. Adult men and women have essentially identical mean IQ scores, which is another way of saying that the average man and the average woman are equally smart. But the men have higher variance. In other words, there are more men at both extremes. Both the most intelligent people (i.e., geniuses) and the least intelligent (i.e., the mentally retarded) are disproportionately male (Jensen, 1998; Lehrke, 1997; Roberts, 1945). This fits the theory that nature tends to roll the dice with men more than with women.

A related argument would be that the duplication of the X chromosome in women, compared to men, who have only one, makes women more malleable. Thiessen (1994) reported various findings (including data by Vendenberg, McKusick, & McKusick, 1962) showing that female identical twins differ more in their responses (e.g., to a loud noise) than male identical twins. Among females, one of the two X chromosomes is randomly turned off (that is, it has no genetic effect), and this can produce variability. Thiessen argued that this may be a basis for female variability in sexual behavior.

If this is so, then perhaps women are more affected by culture. This pattern would in fact be quite useful and functional. It would allow both nature and culture to have influence, even if those respective influences were channeled through a different gender to some extent.

Still, that does not explain why women have higher erotic plasticity. Before closing, let's consider three possible answers.

Male Strength and Power

One possible explanation for female erotic plasticity is that men are physically stronger than women, and so women have to adapt to men. Being physically stronger, men do not have to adapt their views to women as much as women have to adapt their views to men. If push comes to shove, men can force women to do things, so women would be better off learning to be flexible enough to go along (rather than letting things come down to a contest of strength). This could apply even if men and women rarely get to the point of physical violence: The threat alone could be enough. Put another way, erotic plasticity could be an adaptation to the age-old problem of having to live and sleep with someone who is bigger, stronger, and more aggressive than oneself.

A variation on this idea is that men have generally held social and political power, and so women have needed to adapt to men. Men could put pressure on women to adjust, using political and financial leverage instead of physical strength. This is hardly an appealing explanation in the context of our ideals about love and romance. Men and women should ideally want to be good to each other, and issues such as physical strength and coercion ideally shouldn't enter into it. Neither is this an explanation that appeals on theoretical grounds. It isn't very elegant and puts things on a very crude, even banal footing. Still, the fact that we don't like a particular explanation isn't enough reason to reject it.

There's not much doubt that men are stronger than women. Athletic competitions are routinely segregated by gender, presumably on the assumption that women couldn't compete on an equal basis with men. Sure enough, the racing times and other objective measures generally show that men can outperform women. If you compare Olympic gold medalists, for example, the men have nearly always swum or run faster than the women. Meanwhile, in sports that depend most heavily on upper body strength and physical aggressiveness (such as football, wrestling, boxing, and weight lifting), women hardly compete at all. Although many women may enjoy lifting weights or boxing, and some women can become better at these sports than most men, the best men in the sport can usually beat the best women, and the average man can beat the average woman. Even in those traditional societies where women are expected to do almost all of the physical labor and provide most of the family's food, the most difficult work of breaking the soil to till the garden is done by men because of their greater upper body strength.

Likewise, surveys of political and economic power consistently indicate that males have the edge. This is still true today, after a century of feminist agitation and many efforts by the male-dominated government to include women on an equal basis. Undoubtedly the difference was much bigger in the past.

Thus, it is clear that men do have more physical strength and aggressiveness, as well as more social, political, and economic power, than women. Whether this difference explains female erotic plasticity is much more difficult to say. It is plausible, but nothing resembling proof of the direct link is available.

One important aspect of the differential strength theory is that it is not confined to sex. If gender differences in plasticity arise because of male advantages, then they should run through all spheres of behavior, and not just sex. In this respect, this explanation differs from the next two, which focus specifically on sex. Hence we have an important question for further research: Are women more flexible and malleable than men in all behaviors, or only in sexual ones?

There are some signs that women are not more flexible overall, although these findings are preliminary. Recent work on aggression has suggested that genetic factors play a stronger role in female than in male aggressiveness, which is directly opposite to the pattern with sex (Eley, Lichtenstein, & Stevenson, 1999; see also Christiansen, 1977). Meanwhile, studies of attitude-behavior consistency have not shown that women are generally lower than men in such consistency, unlike the difference found in sex. These patterns suggest that female plasticity is specific to sex, which casts doubt on male strength and power as the decisive cause.

A Milder Female Sex Drive?

A second explanation for higher female erotic plasticity holds that women have a milder sex drive than men. A weaker drive might be easier to transform, redirect, or stifle than a strong one. Just as an animal is more difficult to tame if its wild impulses are strong, men's sexuality might be more difficult to bring under cultural control if it is inherently more insistent than women's.

We have already examined the idea that women have a weaker sex drive, and we tentatively concluded that it is correct. On every measure of sexual desire and sexual motivation, men score higher than women. Some might prefer to regard this as a result of socialization that stifles women and not men. Although we find this a dubious argument that amounts to simply refusing to take the totality of factual evidence at face value, it is irrelevant for the present argument: Women in fact have weaker sex drives, regardless of whether this is a result of biological evolution, innate endowment by the divine Creator, or the pressures of socialization in apparently all known societies. Whatever the source of the mildness of female sexuality, the mere fact of the mildness is enough to enable us to argue that it is the basis for plasticity. Of course, if the mildness of the female sex drive is part of women's innate or natural predisposition, this would make it an all the more plausible and compelling basis for an explanation of female erotic plasticity. For now, therefore, the question is merely if women do have a weaker, milder sex drive than men, is there any good reason to think that this difference explains the difference in erotic plasticity?

Again, at present there is no good evidence that either supports or refutes the possible link between erotic plasticity and strength of sex drive. This remains a question for future research. This explanation can, however, be distinguished from the physical strength explanation, because this one is specific to sexuality, whereas the physical strength theory should entail that women are more malleable in many spheres. If women are more malleable only in sex, then the mildness of the female sex drive becomes a viable explanation, but if women are more malleable in everything, then the physical strength difference seems more parsimonious an explanation.

The most relevant means of testing this argument would be to see whether erotic plasticity is linked to strength of sex drive within one gender. Instead of comparing men against women, researchers could compare men with strong sex drives against men with weak ones. (The same test could be done with two groups of women, obviously.) If the people with milder sex drives show greater susceptibility to sociocultural influence, greater patterns of change across time, and lower attitude-behavior consistency, it would show that there is a link between plasticity and strength of sex drive. Once that link is established within one gender, it would be reasonable to assume (although not yet entirely proven) that that link exists across gender too.

The Changeability of Women

The third and final explanation for greater female plasticity is far more interesting theoretically than the other two, although that does not make it any more likely to be true. It suggests that change is part of the script for the female sexual role. If change is required of women more than men, then women have to be more capable of changing—and erotic plasticity would be the result.

According to this theory, women are generally more cautious and conservative about sex partners, and so when the possibility of sex arises between a man and a woman, the woman's initial attitude will tend to be more negative than the man's. The man will want to have sex earlier than the woman, and so there is a phase during which she says no. If sex is to happen, then, it depends on her changing her mind (from no to yes). Human sexuality and reproduction thus revolve around the issue of whether the woman changes her attitude, and so female sexuality has this requirement of change built in to it. To make this change possible, women have to have some capacity for changing, and this capacity for change is the foundation of erotic plasticity.

We can put this another way. Many men would like to have sex with plenty of different women. Widespread promiscuity is not that good for women, however. Throughout most of history, effective contraception was rare, so women risked pregnancy whenever they had sex, and casual sex could have long-term costs for the woman—including pregnancy and even death, insofar as many women died in childbirth. Even if pregnancy is avoided, promiscuity carries risks of venereal disease, which are greater for women than for men. In those rare cultures where promiscuity has been the norm for long periods of time, the spread of venereal diseases causes women to become sterile. Bailey and Aunger (1995) reported on such a society in Africa, where premarital and extramarital sex are common—and almost half the women end up unable to bear children.

Hence, among human beings as in many other species, the female is the gatekeeper who restrains sexual activity. It is necessary for most women to refuse most offers of sex. But of course if women refused all offers of sex, the species would fail to reproduce. Women must therefore start off with a "default" attitude of not wanting sex and then, in selected instances, change to a positive desire to have it.

The basic assumptions of this explanation are supported in research findings. In heterosexual romance, men are typically ready to have sex before the women. When people are asked how long they would typically want to know someone before going to bed with that person, men give much briefer intervals than women (Buss & Schmitt, 1993). Both genders agree that men want and expect sex earlier in a relationship than women (Cohen & Shotland, 1996). Men are more willing to go to bed with a partner casually, without a relationship context or commitment (Oliver & Hyde, 1993). Men also fall in love faster than women, which likewise entails that they are ready for loving, committed sex earlier than their female partners (Baumeister, Wotman, & Stillwell, 1993; Huston, Surra, Fitzgerald, & Cate, 1981; Kanin, Davidson, & Scheck, 1970).

There is also some evidence that the woman's change of attitude is associated with a special erotic charge. This finding emerged unexpectedly from an unlikely source, namely research on feminist views of pornography. Cowan and Dunn (1994) showed various erotic films to male and female viewers and asked them which ones were most degrading to women. Nine different themes were used, and sometimes the researchers even explained the theme (with its feminist connotations) to the viewers. People then watched the films, rated how degrading they were to women, and also rated whether they found the films arousing.

One of the films involved the theme of "submission," by which the researchers meant that the story depicted the woman initially resisting and refusing sex but then changing her mind and even enjoying the sexual activity. The researchers' feminist views predicted that this would be rated as one of the most degrading to women, because presumably it plays on stereotypes that women change their minds and are susceptible to external influence. But the viewers didn't see it that way. Neither the men nor the women rated this film as degrading to women.

Even more importantly, the "submission" film received very high ratings for being sexually arousing. Among the female viewers, it was far and away the most arousing of the nine films. It was also given the highest arousal ratings by the men, although this was a close call, because the men had several favorites. (For example, the men liked the movies on the theme "penis worship"—one can only imagine what these must have been like—whereas the women failed to appreciate what was supposed to be so great about them.) Still, the "submission" film was the favorite among both genders.

For present purposes, the important point is that the story in which a woman changed her mind from no to yes was especially exciting to women. Despite feminist teachings that would condemn such a theme, women (and men) found the idea to be a particular turn-on. Quite possibly this reflects the central importance of that change to the female sexual script. In these films, as in the actual experience of many individuals, sexual activity occurred when the woman, who started off not wanting sex, changed her attitude to desire it after all.

Similar evidence comes from research on sexual fantasy. One pattern of sexual fantasy involves a woman initially resisting sex but being overpowered or overwhelmed by the man and forced to have sex with him—which, in fantasy, turns out to be very exciting for her. A review of the research literature on sexual fantasy concluded that the fantasy of being forced to have sex is more common among women than men (Leitenberg & Henning, 1995). In some studies, over half the women report having had this fantasy. In others, where participants are provided with a list of fantasies to choose among, the fantasy of being overpowered and forced to have sex is often chosen first or second (in frequency) by the women. This is also a common theme (perhaps the most common theme) in the so-called romance literature genre, which is written primarily for women readers.

It is important to remember that the fantasy of being overpowered and forced to have sex or to serve a man sexually does not reflect an actual wish to be raped. In many fantasies, the woman puts up only token resistance and then succumbs to the man in a way that brings pleasure and satisfaction to both. Even women who fantasize about being forced against their will to have sex usually say they would never want to have such an experience in reality. They simply find the idea exciting. Again, this evidence suggests that the switch from no to yes (even in a fantasy of coercion) has special sexual appeal to women.

Thus, it is reasonable to suggest that switching from no to yes is an important aspect of female sexuality. Is it, however, the basis for erotic plasticity? As with the other two explanations, there is currently no solid basis for accepting or rejecting this theory as the true cause of female plasticity. Women do change their attitudes in this one way, and this change furthermore seems to have special sexual appeal to women (and men too) in pornography or sexual fantasy. Yet it is far from clear whether this pattern of change creates a basis for other changes as well.

Before leaving this explanation, we want to point out that there are several other ways in which the sexual role of women requires flexibility. One is simply in terms of choice of partner. Throughout most of human history, it has fallen to the male to select the partner he wants;* the female is not supposed to act on her preference other than to say yes or no if the man asks. It has often been strictly taboo for women to initiate romance, such as by asking a man out on a date, and even today that pattern is far rarer than the reverse. The result is that the woman's lot is often a matter of reconciling herself to having a partner who is not necessarily the one she would have chosen. The man at least did make the choice and initiate the romance. Flexibility would thus help the woman adapt to the partner she gets, whether chosen by the man or indeed by her family. The man can, however, cling more to his own actual choice and therefore does not have to be as flexible.

Another area of flexibility concerns timing of sex. The simple theory would be that a loving or married couple has sex whenever they feel desire for it. In practice, however, they might not feel desire at the same time. Recent research has confirmed that the timing of intercourse does not correspond to the patterns of desire for women, and some experts (e.g., Wallen, 1995) have contended that it is inadequate to analyze female sexual behavior solely in terms of desire and that the category of willingness or receptivity may in fact be more important than actual desire.

For example, some researchers have looked for time patterns in sex. Palmer, Udry, and Morris (1982) found daily and weekly but not monthly patterns. That is, couples were more likely to have sex at some times of day (in the evening, obviously) and on some days of the week (such as Sunday). There was no variation across the month, however. In contrast, when researchers ask women to keep diaries of how much sexual desire they feel, these ratings show monthly patterns, indicating that women are more desirous or "horny" around the time of ovulation (Stanislaw & Rice, 1988).

Thus, again, women have to be flexible. Couples don't necessarily have sex more when the woman wants it more. In many couples her level of desire may be irrelevant, and her willingness may be more important than her level of desire. Willingness is itself a form of flexibility, and the sex lives of many couples may require it.

The woman's role in sexual behavior thus seems to hold the requirement of flexibility in multiple ways. Whether the demands of that role produced the high level of female erotic plasticity—or whether the role evolved that way precisely because women were more flexible—is not a question that can be answered with the data available today.

Conclusion

This chapter focused on an important aspect of the female sex drive, namely its (relatively) high degree of erotic plasticity. Women's sexuality seems to be flexible and responsive to social, cultural, and situational influences—far more than men's. Although human sexuality is undoubtedly a mixture of nature and culture, the balance between the two differs by gender: Women seem to be more affected by culture than men.

---

*To be sure, in arranged marriages neither of the prospective spouses initiates the selection, at least in theory.

The basis for this difference cannot be determined given the present state of knowledge, however. We proposed several possible theories. Each has some plausible basis, but there is not yet any good way of determining which of them is correct.

What are the implications of female plasticity? Social psychology is fundamentally concerned with the power of the situation to shape behavior, and hence it requires people to be somewhat responsive to these situational factors. In the sphere of sexual behavior, social psychology will do better predicting the actions of women than men.

One implication is that a culture or society will have more success at altering the behavior (and desire) of women than men. If a society were to need a major change in its sexual habits, it would be most prudent to try to change women than men. Such needs may arise for various reasons. A war or famine might result in underpopulation, so that many more babies were needed to replenish the population. The spread of some venereal disease, such as AIDS, might require a fairly rapid change in sexual mores, such as curtailed casual sex. An imbalance in the sex ratio might require a shift away from monogamy, so that whichever gender is in shorter supply might be permitted to have more partners. Women would adjust to such changes better than men.

Sex therapy might also work better for women than men. Therapy operates to change people's feelings and actions, and in the sexual sphere women are more changeable. They should respond better than men to treatments.

On the other hand, sexual self-knowledge would be more difficult for women than men to achieve. Men could come to understand their sexual selves relatively easily, because their wants and needs seem fairly fixed and stable, whereas women's may shift with circumstances, making understanding more difficult. A woman needs to understand not just what she wants, but how her desires and other feelings may change from one situation to another. There is in fact some evidence that women find it more difficult than men to know and understand their own sexuality (Vanwesenbeeck, Bekker, & van Lenning, 1998). After all, men do not appear to want books such as *Our Bodies, Ourselves* (Boston Women's Health Book Collective, 1976), even though men buy plenty of books about sex.

Another implication is that sexual decision-making will be more complex and difficult for women than for men. To some extent, this is true simply because the consequences of bad sexual decisions have generally been more severe for women than men. Erotic plasticity means, however, that women cannot quickly or easily make optimal decisions, because their wants and needs may change in response to different circumstances. A man can perhaps simply figure out what he wants and follow that guideline in many situations. The difficulty of self-knowledge for women makes it harder for them to follow the same plan.

In terms of the relationship between men and women, the difference in erotic plasticity creates both obstacles and opportunities. Men may find it difficult to understand why a woman's wants seem inconstant and subject to change, and women may be disappointed at how men seem unable to understand the seeming importance of situational and contextual factors for sexual response. On the positive side, greater flexibility creates greater room for compromise, and female erotic plasticity has probably done much to help men and women be able to live together.

Finally, the higher female erotic plasticity means that same-sex relationships will tend to take different forms. If it is indeed true that homosexuality is more genetically determined in men than women, then the issue for men becomes self-acceptance. For women, in contrast, sexual orientation may be continually subject to revision. Choice, politics, and situational factors may play an important role in whether a woman becomes a lesbian. Moreover, as we noted, the gay community suffers more disunity among women than men, because the option of converting back to heterosexuality is far more available to women than men.

The effects of nature versus culture are brought about by vastly different mechanisms. Nature operates by physical and biological processes, which means that sexuality will be influenced by genetically programmed tendencies and by hormones. For males, these factors may play the biggest role in sex.

Social and cultural factors, meanwhile, operate through meanings, that is, through interpretations that can be expressed in language. Norms, rules, expectations, relationship context, communication, and similar factors depend on meanings. Insofar as female sexuality has higher plasticity, it will be more influenced by these meanings.

The question "What does it mean?" is therefore likely to play a central role in the sexual experiences of women. Who the person is, where the relationship stands, what lovemaking may signify or express, how the couple communicates, what other couples are doing, who will know about the lovemaking, what the individuals expect, what the rules are—all these will play a big role. Does sex mean that you are in love? Does having sex mean that you are a slut, or does refusing sex identify you as a prude? Does it signify a commitment? Moreover, the influence of these factors will probably be present before, during, and after the sexual act. (Considering all there is to process, it is not surprising that it takes women longer than men to fall in love and decide to want to have sex!)

For men, in contrast, such meanings will play much less a role. In fact, men may find sex a perfectly fine experience even if it hardly means anything at all. The physical, biological processes such as visual appearance, bodily sensation, and hormone processes will be decisive, not the context or interpretation (although, as we keep saying, men and women are more alike than different and most men may be at least somewhat affected by the meaning of the act).

Hence, as people move from one situation and context to another—in history, in society, in their own individual lives, or in their relationships—women may find their sexual feelings and desires changing much more substantially than men's. These contexts change the meaning of sex but leave the physical reality essentially the same. For that reason, women's sexuality will change more than men's.

7 Limited Resources in Sex

Novelty, Passion, and Intimacy

Old wives' tales are a familiar form of advice, but old husbands have their tales too. One of these, told in some form by many ostensibly worldly-wise old husbands to various young men as they enter the adult social world of dating and romance, is the "bottle theory of marriage." The idea is that a newly married man should take a bottle and place it on his dresser on his wedding night. That night, he should put a penny in the bottle each time he makes love to his wife. He should then continue this practice until his first wedding anniversary. Beginning then, and thenceforth for the duration of the marriage, he should perform the opposite exercise of taking a penny out of the bottle each time he has sex. The key prediction of the "bottle theory" is that he will never empty the bottle.

To articulate the bottle theory in statistical terms, it holds that a married couple will have sex more often during the first year of marriage than in all the subsequent years combined. As we shall see, research suggests that this is somewhat overstated. Still, the bottle metaphor does rather vividly capture a genuine and well established phenomenon, which is the declining frequency of sexual activity over the course of a long relationship. Apparently, physical passion fades.

Part of the fading may be attributed to aging. Older people have less energy and less desire than young people to do many things, including entering dance marathons, playing sports, drinking, partying until all hours, and "pulling an all-nighter" at work or school. Yet this normal aspect of aging does not fully explain the gradual decline in marital sex. In particular, when middle-aged people divorce their spouses and find new partners, they start having sex much more often again (Call, Sprecher, & Schwartz, 1995). Clearly they have not magically become younger. But the gradual decline in marital sex was not specific to the individual, rather was a function of the relationship.

These patterns raise the issue that sex involves some limited resources that become depleted over time. Some are obvious, like virginity. You can only lose your virginity once, and so virginity is a limited resource. Others may be less obvious but in the long run even more important, such as the possibility that a given sex partner may only be able to provoke intense sexual excitement a given number of times, after which sex becomes old hat and only a new partner can really turn you on.

This chapter will look closely at several candidates for limited resources in sex. If there are in fact limited resources, then people may want to consider their long-term approach to sex on that basis. Rushing to get as much sex as possible as quickly and early as possible might ironically reduce one's lifelong yield of sexual pleasure, because the limited capacity for arousal may burn up. Likewise, if a given partner can only be arousing for a certain number of times, then people may face a difficult choice between sustaining a long-term intimate relationship with the same person versus having a series of briefer but more exciting relationships with different partners. Then again, perhaps there is some way to prolong the opportunities for passion within a relationship.

Novelty as a Limited Resource

A famous story about President Calvin Coolidge led researchers to dub a particular finding the "Coolidge effect." According to this story, the president and the First Lady were touring a large farm, and they were led off on separate tours. When the Mrs. Coolidge passed the chicken coops, she noticed a single large rooster roaming the area in a confident manner, all alone among the females. She asked the farmer in charge whether the rooster was able to perform sexually more than once per day. The man replied that yes, the rooster was in fact able to copulate dozens of times each day. "Please point that out to Mr. Coolidge," she said.

The farmer was probably nervous about this, but he could not obey a direct order from the First Lady. And so when the president himself came by, the man stepped forward and dutifully said that Mrs. Coolidge had instructed him to point out that the rooster was able to have sex dozens of times every day. Mr. Coolidge, who was known for speaking as few words as possible, looked at the man and back at the rooster. "Same hen every time?" he asked. The man replied that no, the rooster would actually copulate with dozens of different females each day. "Point that out to Mrs. Coolidge," said the president. End of conversation!

The "Coolidge effect" is a preferential response to novelty. In controlled studies with animals, it has often been found that males will become more aroused (or more rapidly aroused) by a new partner than by a familiar one. Novelty reduces the refractory period: After a male has sex, some time must pass before he is capable of achieving another penile arousal and ejaculation, but the time lapse is shorter if he is getting ready for a new partner instead of the same one.

Coolidge effects have mainly been documented in males. They are probably stronger and more consistent in males than females, although many doubt that they are completely absent in females. Moreover, there is always a question about whether it is appropriate to generalize to human beings from other species, especially because not all species show a Coolidge effect.

Still, let us assume that the Coolidge effect is genuine, is stronger in males than females, and applies to human beings. What are the implications? First and foremost, sexual arousal will be stronger in response to a new partner than in response to a familiar one. Long-term relationships may face a perennial problem of how to sustain sexual passion. In particular, it may be hard to keep your mate faithful to you and interested in you if he or she would have higher sexual arousal to someone else. In a sense, almost anyone except you has an advantage over you in bed, at least once you have become a familiar sex partner. And this problem may be more severe for wives than for husbands, if the novelty preference is stronger for husbands.

Is there a problem? Let us look at the data.

Sexual Frequency in Long-Term Relationships

Is novelty in fact a limited resource? Is the bottle theory correct? If so, one would predict that frequency of sexual intercourse would decline steadily over time in marriage.

There is evidence that frequency of sex does taper off in established couples. Many young couples have sex every day at first, and some even copulate multiple times each day. Such fervent rutting is rare among long-married couples. In one study of couples who had been married for an average of seventeen years, the mean frequency of intercourse was once or twice per week (Mann, Berkowitz, Sidman, Starr, & Wost, 1974). The NHSLS concluded that only 7 percent of all married couples in America claim to have intercourse four or more times per week (Laumann et al., 1994). Twice that many married couples (14 percent) reported that they had had sex only a few times, or not at all, in the entire year!

Some studies have systematically examined how duration of marriage predicts frequency of intercourse. These have consistently found a steady decline (Blumstein & Schwartz, 1983; Greenblat, 1983; Griffit, 1981; James, 1981; Udry, 1980). For example, Blumstein and Schwartz (1983) found that almost half the newlyweds (i.e., those married less than two years) had intercourse at least three times per week, but that less than a fifth of the couples who had been married over ten years had sex that frequently. James (1981) found that the frequency of intercourse declined by half after the first year of marriage, which is reminiscent of the bottle theory and its claims of precipitous decline.

The pattern is familiar enough to joke about. In a recent episode of the CBS sitcom *Everybody Loves Raymond*, for example, Raymond's wife Deborah has a personal conversation with her mother-in-law and discovers that the old couple has been having sex only about once per year for the past two decades. She worries that she and Raymond are headed in that direction. That night, as they lie in bed, she cuddles up to him and kisses his neck, but Raymond is intent on watching a sports event on television. Eventually she grabs the remote control, shuts off the television, and confronts him with her worries and fears. At first he denies there is a problem. But to dramatize it, she points out how he just now brushed off her advances. Earlier in their marriage he was much more ardent for her, with far less encouragement than she had just given him. "Ten years ago, all I had to be was awake," she said—then added, with a stern look of remembering something—"And sometimes not even that!"

Is Marriage Bad for Sex?

Before we can assert that novelty has anything to do with the long-term slump in marital sex, it is necessary to consider some alternate points of view. The decline with aging was already mentioned. As people get older, they have less frequent sexual desires. Even people who remain single for a lifetime tend to masturbate less often as they get older.

Undoubtedly the dwindling of sexual desire with age contributes something to the decline in frequency of intercourse. Yet it is not the whole story by far. When people remarry, they show a big increase in frequency of sex (Call et al., 1995). If age were the sole factor, then second marriages would generally start off with less sex than the first marriage ended with, but this is manifestly not the case for second and third marriages have their honeymoon phases, too. It would seem that something akin to the Coolidge effect operates in middle and late adulthood.

A theoretically more interesting view is that marriage itself is inimical to sexual love: Marriage is the death of passion. This view has been asserted as an argument against marriage from time to time since it was first put forth in the Romantic era. It claims that passion and excitement depend on being spontaneous, on resisting rules and routines. Marriage tries to bottle love up within a stable, predictable framework, and in the process something vital and wonderful tends to be destroyed.

This may sound like an argument better suited to poets and libertines than to psychologists, but in fact social psychology has provided a powerful theory that makes similar points. This theory rests on the distinction between intrinsic and extrinsic motivation (Deci, 1971; Lepper & Greene, 1979). *Intrinsic motivation* is defined as a desire to do something for its own sake—as for the intrinsic enjoyment of doing it. You do it because you like it, because it's fun. *Extrinsic motivation*, in contrast, involves doing something as a means to obtain some rewards beyond the activity itself. You do it because you have to, or because of what it buys you.

For example, an intrinsically motivated worker is someone who really likes his work and would want do it whether he was paid or not. An extrinsically motivated worker may not care at all about the activity itself and works solely for rewards such as salary and prestige.

Then there is another point that is the crux of the whole theory: The extrinsic side wins out. If intrinsic and extrinsic motives are both present, the intrinsic ones die out. In other words, when people receive external rewards, their intrinsic motivation is reduced. An athlete may, for example, enjoy playing a sport simply for fun, but if he becomes a professional and starts receiving a large salary for playing that same sport, his love of doing it for its own sake will be undermined. Many studies have shown such effects: Paying people to do things they like to do reduces the amount they like to do them, so that when the pay stops they are less interested in doing them than they were initially (Deci, 1971; Lepper, Greene, & Nisbett, 1973; for a review, see Lepper & Greene, 1979).

A decisive feature of this "overjustification effect" is that a person must know in advance about the extrinsic reason for doing something. If you're just doing something for fun and then somebody comes along and gives you $25 for doing it really well, your intrinsic enjoyment is not reduced and may even increase. But if you know about the extrinsic reward while you are doing the task, you begin to think that you are only doing it for the reward (Lepper et al., 1973). Similar effects have been found for extrinsic factors other than payment: In one study, simply knowing that one had a deadline led people to enjoy a task less and be less likely to choose to do it again (Amabile, DeJong, & Lepper, 1976). It was not the matter of rushing to meet the deadline, but of simply perceiving that one's work was constrained by the extrinsic limitation, that undermined motivation.

Applied to sex, this theory suggests that marriage is an extrinsic constraint that undermines intrinsic enjoyment of sex. Sex is part of the contract of marriage, and married people are expected to have sex. Hence when they are married they may start to perceive sex as a duty or obligation rather than as something they want to do for the sheer enjoyment of it. As a result, they lose their desire to do it. That's why married people do it less and less often, as the marriage goes on.

It is hard to dispute that sex in marriage can start to seem like an obligation. As a married woman once said to one of us, after she had put the kids to bed and was getting ready to join her husband, "It's a chore like any other." A set of researchers surveyed people over whether they had ever participated in sexual activity without desire. Most people (three-fifths of the men and four-fifths of the women) said yes, usually to please a partner (Beck et al., 1991; see also O'Sullivan & Allgeier, 1998). In fact, nearly all the women past the age of twenty-five reported that they had done this. The researchers did not report an explicit breakdown by marital status, but many women over twenty-five are married, and the nearly universal experience of having had sex when one doesn't want it does probably shed some light on what goes on in marriage.

One way to test this theory is to compare married couples with couples who live together in an unmarried state. Both types of couples have regular access to each other and presumably sleep in the same bed every night. The only difference is that one has an extrinsic contract, whereas the other is there with no legal obligation and has only intrinsic motivation to keep it going. Is there any difference in frequency of sex?

Yes. In one study, for example, people kept a diary of how often they initiated (and/or refused) sex. The cohabiting couples initiated sex more often than the married ones (Byers & Heinlein, 1989). This appears to have been true even if one adjusts for the newness of the relationship, which is an important control (because many marriages go on much longer than cohabiting arrangements, so they would show lower sexual average frequencies even if marriage itself had no effect, simply because the married people had been together longer).

The large study of American couples by Blumstein and Schwartz (1983) confirmed that married couples have sex less often than cohabiting couples, even controlling for how long the couple has been together. For the first two years of marriage, 45 percent of couples had sex at least three times a week, and among couples who had been married between two and ten years, the frequency was 27 percent. For the first two years of living together without marriage, however, 61 percent reported having sex that often, and among couples who had lived together between two and ten years, 38 percent were still having sex that often. Of course, some of the people who were married had previously lived together, and so these numbers may be slightly inflated, but the effect is clear and robust: There is more sex if you live together without being married.

It is of course hard to prove that the marriage contract itself, as an extrinsic constraint, has undermined couples' intrinsic desire to make love to each other. It is possible, for example, that more married than cohabiting couples are involved in pregnancy and child care, which could well interfere with an active sex life. Still, these results do fit the pattern of overjustification.

Still, even if marriage does provide an extrinsic constraint that undermines sexual desire, this cannot fully explain the decline in frequency over time. As the numbers quoted above show, unmarried cohabiting couples show a dramatic decline in frequency of intercourse over time, just like married couples. Passion dwindles over time, with or without a marriage contract.

Marriage is not the only kind of long-term relationship, of course, but similar declines are found in other relationships as well. Blumstein and Schwartz (1983) found that frequency of intercourse declined over time among gay male couples, and (most sharply) among lesbian couples, as well as among heterosexual couples living together. No type of person or couple, apparently, is immune to the waning of sexual frequency over the course of a lasting relationship.

Let us then give some consideration to the central idea that novelty is an important resource in sex—and a limited one.

The Theory of Novelty as a Limited Resource

"I feel sorry for these young guys. They'll never know what a thrill we used to get out of something as simple as a glimpse of a young lady's ankle." These words were written in a letter to a college magazine by an elderly alumnus when the college was undergoing the sexual revolution. He was not objecting to the new sexual permissiveness on moral grounds, or in terms of disease or other practical concerns. His point was simply that the total yield of sexual pleasure is diminished when people rush into intercourse.

The view that sexual novelty is a limited resource needs to be spelled out in reasonably precise terms. Taken literally, the point is trivial: There is only one first time for everything. Once you have lost your virginity, it is gone forever. But this is not the full point by any means.

Rather, a full articulation of the novelty-resource theory begins by noting that novelty has special appeal. In sex, novelty probably produces extra excitement, arousal, and pleasure. In ancient China, upper-class women wore their feet tightly bound until they married. On the wedding night, the man unwrapped his wife's feet, enabling him to see a woman's feet for the first time in his life. According to some reports, many men had a spontaneous orgasm just from this sight. That response, which echoes with the comments of the elderly alumnus about glimpsing an ankle, probably depended heavily on novelty. It seems highly unlikely that the Chinese husband would continue to ejaculate simply by seeing his wife's feet after they have been married for five years and he has seen those feet every day. (If so, the Chinese might have failed to produce any children!) Such a strong reaction would mainly be plausible on the very first time only.

It seems necessary to avoid restricting the concept of novelty to only the first time something happens, although naturally novelty reaches its peak then. A sex partner does not become fully familiar after one act of intercourse. The first time may indeed be special, but it may take a certain number of repetitions before one feels that the novelty is truly all gone.

Certainly the data we have cited about declining frequency of intercourse do not indicate that the novelty is all gone after the first time. Rather, they suggest a gradual decline over time.

Let us then further suppose that all sexual acts have some of the power of novelty. A first date, a first kiss, a first episode of necking, the first time you see someone undressed, and so forth—these are not just milestones of growing up but intense personal experiences that are accompanied by a level of excitement that can never fully be recaptured.

Except, of course, by other and different experiences—on *their* first time. In fact, if you could always move on to another intense novel experience, there would be no long-term loss. But that's the problem: There are only so many boundaries to cross. In sex, for example, what is left after you have had a full sexual relationship with several different people? The boundaries recede into S&M, threesomes, bisexuality, and the so-called perversions. And there aren't that many of them either. Suppose you work your way through the entire sexual spectrum and because a "trisexual" person ("if it's sexual, I'll try it"). Even so, after a certain amount of time you'll have tried everything.

Novelty attaches to the act as well as the partner. Your first kiss ever would have the highest degree of novelty. After you've kissed that person many times, the novelty will have worn off, but kissing someone different would be exciting again.

Probably the new partner excitement wears off too, however. Your first kiss with the first person would provide high excitement. Your first kiss with a second or third person would also be exciting, although perhaps slightly less. Your first kiss with the fiftieth new person probably would be quite a bit less exciting, and indeed the novelty of kissing any new person may eventually wear off entirely. (But probably not; we'd guess there will always be some extra surge associated with it.) The same pattern might well apply to more intimate sex acts, such as intercourse: A new partner may generally be more exciting than a familiar partner, but if someone has sex with dozens of new partners, eventually even the thrill of having a new partner will diminish.

To be sure, novelty is not the only factor that determines arousal, or losing one's virginity would invariably be the most sexually exciting event of one's entire life. In fact, losing virginity is often a less than ideal experience, partly because factors such as awkwardness, nervousness, uncertainty, and guilt interfere with pleasure and excitement (Sprecher et al., 1995). If these are reduced or eliminated later, subsequent sex acts may be more pleasurable than the first one, even though the first might benefit the most from the novelty factor.

Any Evidence to Support The Theory?

This view of novelty as a limited resource has not been systematically tested, and so it will be necessary to wait for more work to be done before we can know whether the idea is true. Still, there are some bits and pieces of evidence that support the novelty hypothesis. As we noted, the Coolidge effect observed among lower animals provides some support for the view that new partners are more exciting than familiar ones.

What about among human beings? Ethical and practical constraints make it difficult to do a proper experimental test of the Coolidge effect among human beings, because that would involve randomly assigning people to have sex with different partners.

Research on pornography provides some relevant evidence, however. In one study, married couples watched a film of people having sex. Before they saw the film, they were given one of three explanations for the story line, by random assignment. One story said the two people in the film were newlyweds; another said they were a man and a prostitute; and the third said they were two single people who had just met at a dance. The couples rated the sex scene as most exciting when it was paired with the third story line (Fisher & Byrne, 1978).

These findings lend some support to the power of novelty. Although the newlyweds had presumably not reached the point at which sex was very familiar, they had presumably known each other for some time and had had sex before. In contrast, the couple who had just met that same evening were clearly having sex for the first time. The man and the prostitute were probably assumed to be having sex for the first time, but one assumes that a prostitute has had many partners (and probably so has a man who frequents prostitutes), so even though they were new to each other, they had likely had many new lovers previously.

Watching pornography can itself be a novel experience with a limited power to excite. An important study by Mann and colleagues (1974) had long-married couples keep diaries of their sexual behavior and then gradually invited them to the laboratory once a week to watch erotic films. This experiment was done before videotape machines were available and before sex movies could be rented, so it is fairly safe to assume that most of the couples had had fairly little exposure to erotica prior to their first time in the laboratory. Probably most had had none.

Sure enough, the first time the couple watched a sex film, it stimulated a great deal of sex, even though they had to travel back home before they had an opportunity to have intercourse. On an average night without pornography, only about one-fifth of these couples had sex, but the first time they watched sex films, fully two-thirds of them did so afterward.

One might explain those results by suggesting that pornography is simply so exciting that it will always stimulate a large increase in sex. But this view was disconfirmed by additional data. The researchers brought each couple back to the laboratory for four weeks, once per week, to watch more sex films. The huge jump in frequency of intercourse from the first time was not repeated. Instead, the increase was smaller each week, and by the fourth week watching pornography failed to increase sexual activity above the baseline rate. In other words, by this point pornography had no measureable effect on sex. The novelty had worn off.

The novelty aspect was confirmed by one other aspect of the research design. The experimenters had carefully planned the four nights of erotica that each couple watched. Two of the nights were devoted to conventional sex, whereas the other two were devoted to more unusual, even "kinky" activities, including threesomes and light sexual spanking. Half the couples watched the conventional films the first two weeks and the unusual ones the last two. For the rest of the couples, the sequence was reversed.

What difference did this make? Among the couples who started with the unusual films and then saw the conventional ones, the impact of viewing erotica diminished steadily across the four weeks. Among the others, it also diminished steadily except for week three, when the data show an increase in sexual frequency. That was the week that the people who had started off watching conventional films suddenly saw kinky films for the first time, which apparently were very exciting to them. Thus, the novelty of switching to unusual sexual activities provided a high level of arousal that reversed the general trend of declining response.

These data do suggest that pornography, at least, conforms to the pattern of novelty as a limited resource. Watching erotic films for the first time is very exciting and creates a high level of sexual desire, even among couples who have been married for many years. However, if one continues to watch erotic films week after week, the novelty wears off, and the films produce less and less arousal. The only exception to this loss of impact is to switch from conventional sex films to more unusual forms of erotica, which may produce high excitement again.

Over time, then, regular viewers of pornography will gravitate toward wanting to see more extreme and unusual sexual behaviors. By gradually escalating the level of erotic depiction in the films, they can achieve higher levels of excitement than they would get by sticking to the same kind of films. But of course this escalation cannot continue indefinitely. There are only so many varieties of pornography (not to mention the fact that many viewers will find many of them unappealing if not downright disgusting). Eventually the capacity to be stimulated by pornography may be used up.

What then? Mann et al. (1974) did cite some further evidence that the satiation effect for erotica will itself wear off. In another study, people watched pornography repeatedly until it failed to have any stimulating effect on them. Then they stayed away from all erotica for a month. The next time they watched erotica after the month of abstinence, it did stimulate them again.

Thus, apparently some (but not all) of the power of novelty can be recaptured. Abstaining from some sexual activity for a period of time can make it seem novel again. Although we do not know of specific data on this issue, it does seem plausible that it would work in matters beyond pornography. For example, the first time one has heterosexual intercourse after being released from prison would probably produce high excitement, even if one had continued to have orgasms in prison by means of masturbation or homosexual activity. The period of being deprived of some type of sexual activity may make it seem novel again when one does finally manage to participate in it again.

Pornography is generally regarded as appealing more to males, although Fisher and Byrne (1978) found no gender difference in arousal ratings. We propose that the novelty effect would be stronger among males than females. Is there any evidence to support this?

Several signs do indicate that novelty is more exciting for a man than a woman. For one thing, males report more pleasure and satisfaction from their first act of sexual intercourse than females (Sprecher et al., 1995), although the two genders' experiences of losing their virginity may be different in multiple ways, including the woman's physical pain of rupturing the hymen. For another thing, males report significantly higher numbers of desired sex partners (Buss & Schmitt, 1993; Miller & Fishkin, 1997). The desire to have sex, even casually, with multiple partners is consistently higher in men than women, and in fact this is one of the largest gender differences in sexuality (Oliver & Hyde, 1984).

Start Slow and Go Far

If sexual novelty is in fact a limited resource, this would have important implications for how to manage one's sex life. The novelty problem puts one kind of limit on how much sexual excitement one can experience in one's life. Hence if one wants to maximize the amount of sexual pleasure over a lifetime, one should think about how to use novelty.

Ironically, the two biggest consequences of the sexual novelty theory point in opposite directions with regard to sexual permissiveness. Sexual conservatives will like one of them but dislike the other; sexual liberals will also find one to like and one to dislike.

With any limited resource, the central challenge for effective management is to design a way to allocate it so that it is available wherever it is most needed. Using it up too fast in one place will cause it to run dry early, being subsequently unable to provide for further demands. Using it up too slowly essentially wastes it. As an analogy, a primitive farm family has to make its supply of food last through the winter. Eating it up too quickly will result in desperately hungry weeks or months just prior to spring. Eating it up too slowly will create the unfortunate consequence that food might be left over at the end of the winter but that people will have starved along the way.

Sexual novelty raises the same challenge. If the stock of novelty is exhausted early in life, then few thrills remain for middle and old age. This may be especially unfortunate, given that young people can typically have strong erotic responses, whereas older people find it more difficult to become aroused, and so the added value of novelty would be especially desirable later in life—if the person has managed to conserve some.

A touching illustration of this was provided in Reuben's (1969) book *Everything You Always Wanted to Know About Sex*, which was one of the best-sellers of the sexual revolution. He described an elderly couple, Henry and Irene, who had to give up sex for six months because of her illness. When they tried to resume having sex, Henry was unable to get an erection. He was very upset about this. Desperate to try anything that might help her husband out of his misery and depression over this problem, Irene purchased some books on sex, which at that time was a fairly unusual thing for an elderly woman to do. The books offered some interesting advice. She said that one thing she was surprised to read was that she could stimulate the man by touching his penis with her hand, something she had apparently never done over the decades of marriage. She had been taught that decent women did not do such things, but she decided that times were changing, and besides she didn't care as much about conforming to an ideal of femininity as she did about helping her husband to be a man again.

And so she tried it. The results were "like magic—it got even harder than it used to get thirty years ago!" (Reuben, 1969, p. 391). Her husband was thrilled, and they were able to enjoy physical intimacy again. She ended her letter by saying she was even thinking of trying some of the other things she read in that book.

Such stories need to be considered carefully. Clearly this couple had had regular intercourse for many years, and clearly it was something that both of them valued. Apparently, however, their sexual activities had not extended much beyond the minimal coital act itself. Possibly they had used some foreplay to arouse the woman, but not much aimed at exciting him—if she had never so much as touched his penis with her hand during their entire marriage.

On the negative side, the couple had probably sacrificed some quantity of sexual pleasure by keeping their sex lives to such a restricted range of activities. Most young people today would not want to wait until their sixties to try manual stimulation, let alone oral sex and other variations.

On the positive side, however, when they did become old and sexual desire waned to the extent that it interfered with their marital intimacy, they were able to draw on the power of novelty to arouse each other. All those years of sticking to a no-frills sex life suddenly paid dividends, insofar as they could start exploring those frills. Had they engaged in the full range of sexual activities all through their married life, they would have had few or no options for rekindling sexual excitement later on, and their so-called golden years would have had to remain empty of sexual intimacy.

That trade-off is a good example of the dilemma: Conserving novelty means sacrificing immediate pleasure. The sacrifice may be considerable, although strictly speaking we do not know whether the couple really lost much pleasure along the way. It is conceivable that they were amply thrilled by their limited sex life for most of the years of their marriage.

Still, if novelty is a limited resource, then one clear implication is that it is best to use it up slowly. Becoming a sexual adult is the end point of a series of first-time steps, and the way to get the maximum yield of pleasure and excitement from each one is to space them out. If one progresses from kissing to holding hands to petting to intercourse all within one year, especially at a relatively young age, then one has wasted some possibilities for pleasure and satisfaction. Young men may envy those of their peers who start having intercourse very young, but the novelty analysis suggests that those people are not to be envied.

One does not have to go to the extreme of the elderly alumnus quoted above, whose youthful sexual experience was so limited that a glimpse of a woman's ankle was a major turn-on. But the optimum is to remain at each stage of sexual contact until most of its novelty is gone. Holding hands, for example, can be quite exciting at first, as long as one is not also having intercourse. In contrast, if you have already experienced oral, anal, and genital intercourse by the age of fifteen, what thresholds are left to cross for the next fifty years?

The slow-progress implication of the novelty theory may appeal to sexual conservatives, but the other side of the argument may appeal more to liberals: To maximize one's lifetime yield of sexual pleasure, it will be necessary to experiment with a relatively broad variety of sexual activities during adulthood, and especially during the course of a long marriage. At some point, such as ten or twenty years into the marriage, the couple may benefit from experimenting with new activities. Exactly what they are will of course depend on what they have not tried yet (and what is therefore still novel). Experimenting with bondage and spanking, having an audience, engaging in anal sex, and even inviting a third person into bed may be powerful ways to use the power of novelty to rekindle excitement.

Start slow and go far! That's the logical recipe for mazimizing sexual pleasure over one's entire life.

Passion, Intimacy, and Time

What we have seen thus far about the course of sexual behavior in long-term relationships raises another big question: If passion dwindles, what about intimacy? After all, the two are widely understood to be related, even to the extent of being almost the same thing. Phrases such as "being intimate" are used to refer to having sex. If a married couple has sex less and less often, does this mean that their marital intimacy is declining?

The issue gets even more confusing when one begins looking at data for how passion and intimacy are related. On the one hand, surveys that ask couples how much intimacy and how much passion exist in their relationship tend to find the two are positively correlated: High intimacy goes with high passion (e.g., Patton & Waring, 1985). On the other hand, following particular relationships over time yields a very different picture. Intimacy tends to increase progressively over long periods (e.g., Acker & Davis, 1992), and depending on the measure it either levels off at a fairly high level of intimacy or even continues to rise indefinitely. Passion, in contrast, shows the pattern that the sexual behavior suggested: It is high early in the relationship and then diminishes over time. Hence intimacy grows into its long-range peak just when passion has dwindled to a relatively low level. From these data, one might infer that the relationship between passion and intimacy is negative, rather than positive.

An influential theory of love was proposed in the 1980s by Sternberg (1986), who argued that love is composed of three ingredients: passion, intimacy, and commitment. The relative amounts of the three may vary independently, so that some love relationships may be full of passion but lacking commitment, whereas others have strong intimacy and commitment but less passion, and so forth. Sternberg stopped short of asserting that passion and intimacy are entirely independent, but he did say that they can vary independently of each other. This theory has the advantage that it can accommodate the seemingly paradoxical pattern of long-term relationships in which passion goes down while intimacy goes up: Sternberg would say that the recipe for love changes over time, emphasing passion early but intimacy later on. Still, if the two are somewhat independent, how can they seem to be related in so many studies?

What Are Passion and Intimacy?

Before we try to understand how passion and intimacy are related, it is necessary to clarify what is meant by the concepts. Unfortunately, the two terms have been used and defined in assorted ways. The use of the term *intimacy* to refer to sex is merely an extreme example of confusing the two concepts. To learn whether sexual intercourse has taken place, it would be more precise to say "Have you been passionate with him?" rather than "Have you been intimate with him?"

Intimacy has been defined in slightly different ways by many different authors (see Clark & Reis, 1988; Hatfield, 1984; Hendrick & Hendrick, 1983; Lewis, 1973; Perlman

& Fehr, 1987; Reis & Patrick, 1996; Reis & Shaver, 1988; Schaefer & Olson, 1981). Several common features of these definitions can be invoked. First, intimacy involves knowledge. People become intimate by disclosing things about themselves, starting off with basic and obvious facts and building gradually to highly personal, emotional material. The partner's response to this is also vital to intimacy: Sympathetic under-standing and acceptance make for intimacy, but critical or rejecting responses do not. Sharing experiences and observing the other person in many settings also contribute to intimacy. Across time, the buildup of sympathetic knowledge and mutual understanding creates a feeling of closeness that is one of the major hallmarks of intimacy.

Second, intimacy involves developing a favorable attitude toward the partner. This includes feelings of warmth and concern. Intimate partners want to protect each other from harm and to help the other, and they become upset if the partner is hurt even by something entirely outside their own control.

Third, intimacy is marked by the exchange of indications of affection. Intimate partners express liking for each other in verbal and nonverbal ways. These verbal ones can range from simple compliments to declarations of undying love. Nonverbal signs include making eye contact, giving gifts, and being physically near the other person. In romantic partnerships, affection is also expressed through kissing, holding hands, and having sex.

Passion, meanwhile, is an emotional state marked by strong feelings of attraction (see Berscheid, 1983; Hatfield, 1988; Hatfield & Walster, 1978; Meyers & Berscheid, 1997). One likes or loves the person. The stronger, more intense, and more frequent the feelings, the more passionate the person is. In love, passion is the subjective feeling of being in love, which for many people provides strong sensations such as warmth, excitement, nervous arousal, joy or bliss, and a constant desire to see and touch the other person. Passion does not have to be mutual, although people much prefer it to be so. One person can have passion alone, such as in cases of unrequited love, love at first sight, or indeed passionate arousal toward a character one has only seen in a movie.

Understood in this way, intimacy depends on knowledge and understanding, whereas passion is essentially an emotional state. As a general rule (in other words, even beyond love and sex), emotions come and go rather fast, but knowledge is built up slowly over time. Achieving an intimate relationship with another person may take many months or years of getting to know the person, learning to empathize with that person and anticipate what the person will think or feel. Passion, in contrast, can arise quite rapidly, but it does not tend to continue for long stretches of time.

How Are Passion and Intimacy Related?

We have seen three possible ideas about how passion and intimacy are related. One is that there is a positive relationship, such that high passion goes with high intimacy, and this is supported by surveys that ask couples to rate their own relationships (e.g., Patton & Waring, 1985). The second is that there is a negative relationship, such that intimacy goes up when passion goes down. This fits what is known about the time course of passion and intimacy across long-term relationships. The third possibility is that the two are not really related at all, so one can go up or down independently of the other. This might account for the conflict and inconsistency among other findings.

There is, however, a fourth possibility that fits all these seemingly inconsistent facts: Maybe there is an *indirect* relationship between passion and intimacy. In particular, passion may be related to change of intimacy rather than to the level of intimacy itself.

In this view, passion is high when intimacy is felt to be rising rapidly. At the very beginning of a relationship, when the couple hardly knows each other, there is likely to be very little of passion and intimacy. Then, however, intimacy begins to rise as the two people find each other mutually attractive and begin to spend time together talking and getting to know each other. Rising intimacy sets off passion. When intimacy takes its biggest steps, such as when the two people start expressing to each other that "I like you better than anyone else," then passion is likely to reach its highest peaks.

If the couple gets married and settles down, intimacy may continue to rise, but more slowly. After a certain point, the two people know most of what there is to know about each other. There is much less room for intimacy to increase further. As a result, passion drops off.

This, after all, is the crucial implication of the idea that passion depends on change in intimacy: When intimacy remains stable, regardless of whether it is high or low, passion will dwindle toward zero. Rising intimacy produces passion, but unchanging high intimacy will not.

The same expressions of intimacy thus gradually lose their power, for their power depends on novelty. The first time someone tells you, "I love you," your heart pounds, your breath comes short, your attention narrows to the immediate present, and (assuming the person's love is good news) you probably feel a wave of affection toward that person. But the two hundredth time that that same person tells you, "I love you," the effect is likely to be minimal. "Yeah, me too, can you get me a beer?" might be a response, or "OK, what do you want?" or just the mechanical recitation of "I love you too" with minimal feeling behind it. The same goes for the first time the person calls you on the phone, the first time you kiss, the first time you are in bed, and so on. These produce the most passion when they signify increases in intimacy. When they become familiar and standard, the intimate message is still implicit, but it has lost its novelty.

For the mathematically inclined, this relationship can be expressed in calculus terms: Passion is a function of the first derivative over time (Baumeister & Bratslavsky, 1999). This could be written as an equation:

$$P = C \times (dI/dt)$$

where P is passion, I is intimacy, t is time, and C is some (positive) constant number that one multiplies by the change in intimacy to calculate passion. (Actually, the correct formula would probably include some additional factors, because passion may depend on a variety of things unrelated to intimacy. So we should write $P = C \times (dI/dt) + R$, where R refers to other sources of passion.)

Social and clinical psychologists have already begun to use rate of change calculations in some of their other theories about emotion. Carver and Scheier (1990) proposed that people feel good or bad about what is happening in their lives depending whether they are moving closer or farther away from their goals. Obviously, reaching goals produces happy emotions, but people are often happy even when they have not just reached a goal. Carver and Scheier proposed that feeling that you are making progress is enough to bring happiness, even if you have not fully achieved the goal. More generally, satisfaction seems to depend on change in outcomes, rather than the outcome itself: Only when things get progressively better do we feel the emotion of satisfaction (Hsee & Abelson, 1991; Hsee, Abelson, & Salovey, 1991; Hsee, Salovey, & Abelson, 1994; Salovey, Hsee, & Mayer, 1993).

Similarly, anxiety has been conceptualized as being dependent on the approach of something bad. Riskind's theory of anxiety emphasizes *looming vulnerability* (e.g., Riskind & Maddux, 1993, 1994; Riskind, Moore & Bowley, 1995; Riskind & Wahl, 1992). In other words, knowing that some danger or threat exists in the world is not enough to produce anxiety; rather, people feel anxiety when the threat is looming, which is to say it is coming at them.

All of these views can trace influence back to Mandler's (1975) theory of emotion, which holds that emotions are caused by interruptions to ongoing activities. This seems to imply that the essential function of emotion is to call attention to some important change. Because emotions come and go rapidly, marked by physiological arousal, they are not good at registering stable, steady conditions. Instead they seem much better suited to respond to changes. Because the quest for a stable, predictable environment has been such a fundamental aspect of human life throughout history, it would not be surprising that people have evolved a physical mechanism such as emotion that essentially calls attention to change.

Hence it is plausible that passion, as an emotion variable, is tied to change. Intimacy, meanwhile, is more a matter of knowledge than of emotion, and so it would not be so strongly based on change. (Instead, it may accumulate over time, just like any other knowledge.) Change in intimacy could be what sets off the feelings of passion.

These considerations also help fill one further gap in the theory: What about when intimacy goes down? In a good relationship, that might not happen, but there is no question that some couples find themselves less intimate after many years together, especially if the relationship is marked by conflict and problems. The change-in-intimacy theory would suggest that some emotions would be caused by any sharp deline in passion. These would of course tend to be negative, unpleasant emotions. In other words, positive changes (increases) in intimacy produce positive emotions, whereas negative changes in intimacy would produce negative emotions.

The Passion Problem in Long-Term Relationships

If passion really does arise from increasing intimacy, then one category of relationships is particularly likely to struggle with the problem of not enough passion: long-term relationships. When you've heard all his stories twice, or when you've seen her nude body often enough that it ceases to be a revelation, or simply when you always seem to know what the person is going to say or do before it happens, intimacy has reached a plateau, and there is little opportunity to increase it further. Passion will therefore be hard to generate.

These patterns suggest a problem of limited resources. Clearly, passion seems to run out on people over the course of long-term relationships, at least to some degree. The first part of this chapter linked the passion drought to some limit on novelty. We can now build on this by suggesting that intimacy is also a limited resource. There is, after all, a limit to how intimate you can be with another person. This is easiest to understand if we go back to the view of intimacy as a kind of knowledge. There is only so much to know about another person. When you first meet the person, it is relatively easy to see how much about the person you do not know. New relationships often include personal conversations that last late into the night and include the sharing of many personal feelings and experiences. Although it may seem that the person you love is an unlimited source of fascination, in reality the source is actually limited. For example, people have only had so many interesting experiences in their lives, and once they have told them to you, the supply is exhausted. Likewise, people may have all sorts of interesting ideas and opinions, but gradually you will have heard all of them too.

That is why intimacy levels off over time. Like knowledge, you may gain intimacy rapidly at first and then retain what you have, but it becomes difficult to get more from the same source. Even in an ideal marriage, intimacy may rise up to a certain point but be unable to increase beyond that. Once the couple understands each other perfectly, is fully attuned to each other's wishes and needs, and empathizes effectively with each other's emotions, what more can be added? Their intimacy may be very high and stay very high in a steady state, but it may be unable to rise any higher.

We have already seen some signs that passion does seem to be in short supply in mature relationships. Frequency of sex is one good sign of passionate love, and all studies find that frequency decreases as the relationship matures. For a less scientific but vivid sign of the decrease in passion, one need only scan the covers of magazines sold to the general public (especially women's magazines) in supermarkets and similar places. Many articles offer advice for rekindling the flames of passion or generating desire in a long-term relationship. Apparently this problem is common and perennial enough that it helps sell magazines.

What can be done?

Evidence suggests that in most cases intimacy does continue to increase, although much more slowly, even after many years of marriage (Acker & Davis, 1992). This may occur because the two people still manage to learn a little more about each other through new experiences.

Furthermore, intimacy seems to be produced by sharing experiences, and so even a couple that has been together for many years can increase intimacy by doing something new and exciting together. Such shared experiences strengthen the bonds between the two people. When these events are happening, passion may be stimulated. It is therefore likely that people will feel more love and passion toward their mates (and probably more sexual interest too) when they are on vacation—not simply because when back at home they are too tired to have sex, but because a vacation produces a new intimacy that the everyday home life does not.

Indeed, some studies have found that couples who share exciting new experiences will end up with more passionate relationships. Couples who engage in shared recreational (fun) activities seem to end up with stronger marriages, and this effect is especially strong for novel activities (Hill, 1988), which is consistent with what we have already seen about the benefits of novelty. An important study assigned couples to do various activities together over a ten-week period, and they found that merely spending time together did not strengthen the relationship, whereas doing exciting things together did (Reissman, Aron, & Bergen, 1993). Norman and Aron (1995) showed that a single experience in the laboratory could increase relationship satisfaction even in couples who had been together for a long time (in fact, the boost was biggest among the couples who had been together the longest, which precisely fits what we have said about the passion problem in long-term relationships), provided that the activity was novel and arousing.

Part of this may be due to the fact that excitement from the experience is physiologically arousing, which may translate into passion and even into sexual activity (not in the laboratory, usually!). Still, it is also likely that these experiences offer the couple new insights into themselves and each other, resulting in a sense of rising intimacy. The result could well be passion.

Some couples report that, after many years of being together, they have their best sex when making up after a fight. This could be another illustration of the power of rising intimacy. A fight is undoubtedly a decrease in intimacy (at least a temporary one). During the fight, the people feel themselves opposed to each other instead of striving and functioning in harmony. Their interests are at cross-purposes, and their feelings toward the other person are hostile, antagonistic, and otherwise negative.

When the fight ends, however, the couple may reconcile by returning to more positive feelings about each other. In particular, if they make up at a particular point, this will involve expressing positive feelings to each other and showing a favorable atittude toward the relationship. This brings them back to a positive state of intimacy. It would therefore be felt as an increase in intimacy from the temporary low point that was reached during the argument. Even if the intimacy level after the fight is the same as it was before the fight, the contrast with the low level of intimacy during the fight will produce a local increase in intimacy, resulting in a feeling of change and hence producing passion.

The more general point is that any temporary interruption in a couple's intimacy may create an opportunity for a rise in passion when the interruption is over. Thus, if the couple is temporarily separated because of a business trip or other travel, seeing each other again may be an opportunity to generate passion by the renewal of intimacy. To be sure, this effect might be easy to spoil. If the couple talks on the phone every day during the separation, then getting back together may not produce much in the way of passion. By the same token, if the couple's reunion after the separation begins with grumpy or accusing complaints, or even sarcasm, the effect of a rise in intimacy may be undermined. Still, it seems quite plausible that a couple will feel more than usual passion when they first get back together after being separated (and out of touch) for several days.

Evidence

Let us consider how the rate-of-change idea can explain some of the facts and findings. As noted, it fits what is known about patterns of passion and intimacy in long-term relationships. When intimacy is rising rapidly, early in the relationship, passion is at its peak. After the relationship has gone on for some time, intimacy has leveled off at a high level, and passion drops off substantially. Intimacy does continue to rise, although more slowly, in an advanced stage of the relationship, and so passion does not shrink to zero in most cases. But passion is low while intimacy is high.

We mentioned that some studies find positive correlations between passion and intimacy. There are two reasons that this could happen. One is that people simply tend to merge all good things together when reporting on a good relationship. They may refer to intimacy when they are talking of increases in intimacy or even "feelings of intimacy," which are probably close to what we are calling passion. Indeed, in ordinary speech it is common to use the phrase "being intimate" to refer to having sex, even though "being passionate" might be more appropriate.

The other reason is that many surveys are conducted at universities, simply because that is where the researchers are. Universities are full of young people (i.e., students), and they are generally in the early stages of a relationship. After all, hardly any college students have had a twenty-year marriage, because most of them are only about twenty years old! Thus, the surveys tend to emphasize people who are in the early stages of a relationship, when intimacy may be rising rapidly and passion may be high—or, in other cases, the relationship is not going well and is headed for a breakup, in which case neither passion nor intimacy is likely to be high. With a sample like that, passion and intimacy will tend to go together.

Social psychology provides other evidence to back up the idea that passion is linked to change in intimacy. Studies by Aronson and Linder (1965; see also Clore, Wiggins, & Itkin, 1975; Mettee & Aronson, 1974) revealed what they called the "gain/loss effect," which indicates that change in evaluation produces a stronger reaction than the evaluation itself. In their studies, participants received a series of evaluations of themselves from another person. In one condition, the other person liked the participant right from the start and gave consistently favorable evaluations. In another, the other person started off disliking the participant and giving bad evaluations, but then gradually switched to giving increasingly positive evaluations. The participant ended up liking the other person more in the second condition than in the first. That was ironic, because the consistently favorable evaluator gave the participant more praise than the one who had started off negative and then became positive. It does, however, suggest that the change in evaluation from bad to good produces a stronger emotional response—akin to passion—than a consistently (but stable) positive evaluation.

Negative changes in intimacy should also set off passion, although not necessarily passionate love. Sure enough, when a relationship is deteriorating toward breakup and the two people are becoming less intimate with each other, people typically experience plenty of distress. This distress does not remain with them forever; like the favorable passion, it is mainly felt at the time that intimacy is changing most rapidly, and then it dissipates gradually (Baumeister & Leary, 1995; Hazan & Shaver, 1994; Price & McKenry, 1988; Spanier & Casto, 1979; Weiss, 1979). Some degree of distress over a romantic breakup seems to be nearly universal, even if the person earnestly desired the split and is glad that it happens. Apparently, then, it is hard to avoid having a strong emotional reaction to a negative change in intimacy.

Comparing extraverts and introverts is another useful way of checking the validity of the idea that passion depends on change in intimacy (for a review, see Baumeister &

Bratslavsky, 1999). It is well known that extraverts become intimate with someone faster than introverts. Indeed, that is central to the very definition of extraversion. Extraverts open up faster, learn about new people faster, perform intimate acts such as gazing into someone's eyes more often and sooner, and so forth, all of which speed up the process of becoming intimate.

If rising intimacy produces passion, then, extraverts ought to show higher or earlier passion than introverts. Sure enough, evidence suggests that extraverts are more sexually active. They have sex with more people and do so earlier in their relationships (e.g., Eysenck, 1972, 1973, 1974, 1976; Schenk & Pfrang, 1986; Schofield, 1968). They also show greater sexual arousability (Harris, Yulis, & Lacoste, 1980). It is not just that extraverts are oversexed or "horny"; on some measures, such as masturbation, extraverts show less sexual activity than introverts (Eysenck, 1972). But they do seem to become passionate quicker, consistent with the earlier rise in intimacy.

The downside of a quick rise in intimacy is that the relationship reaches its plateau stage sooner, and so passion will die down faster. Sure enough, extraverts seem to suffer the problems of this stage too. They break up more often than introverts, and they start new relationships more often (Eysenck, 1980; see also Cramer, 1993).

Of course, introverts will eventually reach that plateau of intimacy too, and so their relationships would also seemingly be vulnerable to boredom and the temptations of other partners. What may save the introvert from infidelity, however, is that even if the introvert meets someone new, it takes a long time for intimacy to start rising, and so passion does not flame up quickly. For an extravert, however, meeting someone new can set off another whirlwind pattern of attraction, romance, and sexual passion. Hence extraverts have less stable relationships.

There is some converging evidence from the data about how fast people have sex after they first meet. The cultural myth of "love at first sight" implies that you need little more than the physical appearance in order to recognize your ultimate soul mate. Couples who have such a rapid awakening ought, then, to show a high rate of successful relationships, as compared to couples who know each other a long time before they develop passion. Hence one might predict that marriages will tend to be between couples who quickly developed a passion for each other, as indicated by having sex soon after they met.

The data are not perfectly clear on this question, but they do point strongly in the opposite direction. The NHSLS compiled rather thorough data on how long people knew each other before having sex, and their data spanned the full range from people who went to bed with each other on the same day they met to people who had known each other for years before they became sexually active. Only 1.4 percent of the marriages in their sample—barely one out of every seventy-one—consisted of people who had had sex with each other the first or second day they knew each other. Likewise, people who had had sex within the first month they knew each other (which is easily enough time for five or even ten dates) made up only 10 percent of all marriages. In contrast, almost half the marriages (47 percent) consisted of people who had known each other for a year or more before they became sexually active (Laumann et al., 1994).

Rushing into bed is thus not correlated with a strong, lasting relationship. Instead, the attraction that leads to rapid sex seems to burn out fairly rapidly.

It is possible that the rapid sex itself did not cause the relationship to fail to lead to marriage. Perhaps the people who started having sex right away were attracted to each other for different (and less durable) reasons than the people who waited for many months before commencing sex. Even if that is true, however, it would still be fair to conclude that linking passion to the slow development of intimacy provides a more lasting basis for a long-term relationship than whatever produces immediate sexual activity.

Revisiting the Gender Gap in Sex Drives

In Chapter 5, we grappled with the thorny question of whether men and women differ in the strength of their sex drives. As we saw, feminists have disputed and rejected the view that women have a milder sex drive than men. Such theorists assert that women have tremendous untapped potential for romantic and passionate feelings. Meanwhile, though, a broad assortment of research findings have shown women to be less interested in sex, on average, on almost every conceivable measure: frequency of thinking about sex, frequency of wanting sex, masturbation, number of partners, eagerness with a given partner, use of sexually stimulating materials, and so forth.

The idea that passion depends on change in intimacy offers another way to understand gender differences in passion. Even if the link between passion and change in intimacy holds true for both genders, it could well be that the formulas are slightly different. It may be that the multiplier C (that is, the number that is multiplied by the rate of change of intimacy in order to produce passion) is a higher number for men than for women, on average. This simple suggestion—that men have a higher value of this multiplier than women—would offer clear implications for how men and women would differ in their patterns of sexual response and passion.

In plain terms, this would mean that the same event—the same increase in intimacy—would normally produce a bigger response of passion in a man than in a woman. To put this another way, it would take a bigger dose of intimate communication to produce sexual passion in a woman than in a man. Hence female sexuality will seem to depend heavily on strong doses of intimacy, whereas male sexual response will require much less.

For the mathematically inclined, we can explain this as follows. We suggested that passion is a function of the first derivative of intimacy over time. The function probably takes the form of the derivative of intimacy multiplied by some constant. The idea here is that men and women have different average values for the constant, with men's being higher.

When talking about gender differences, there is frequently a concern about implicit value judgments. If men do have a higher value, is that better or worse? On an a priori basis, we can see no reason why it would be better to have either a high or a low value of this constant. The only relevant implication is that patterns of sexual response will differ depending on the value of this constant (i.e., the multiplier).

If nothing else, a difference in the size of the multiplier would create the potential for misunderstandings and miscommunications. Certainly no one will dispute the conclusion that such misunderstandings sometimes arise between men and women where sex is concerned! The nature of these misunderstandings can be explained, however, by considering the differences in the multiplier. If a man and a woman have a positive interaction that is somewhat pleasant and warm, such as a friendly conversation in private, both of them are likely to feel some rise in the intimacy between them. This rise in intimacy will, however, produce a stronger response of passion in the man than in the woman, and so he may think the couple is ready for romance when she merely thinks of him as a nice friend.

Research by Abbey (1982) has suggested the prevalence of such misunderstandings. Her work showed that when a woman is moderately friendly toward a man, such as by smiling at him and talking to him in a pleasant way, the man is likely to interpret her behavior as suggesting romantic or sexual interest. The woman may not have intended her behavior as anything more than merely being friendly, but the man interprets it as much more.

Abbey interpreted her research findings to suggest that men misunderstand what women try to communicate. It is certainly possible that men are mistaken. Then again, it is also possible that in many situations men and women perceive their conversation in the same way—but that the man reacts more strongly. It was just a pleasant, friendly conversation to her, but it meant more to him. She walks away thinking, "That was kind of nice, and I wonder if people would think him cute," and he's thinking, "I'm in love—this could be the one."

Shallow, Insecure Jerks or Cold-Hearted Bitches?

If the multiplier that converts rising intimacy into passion is bigger for men, then men should feel passionate love sooner than women. At first, this may seem counterintuitive, because stereotypes hold that women are more "romantic" than men. Indeed, some stereotypes depict men as emotionally inept and finding it difficult to love anyone.

But the stereotype is wrong. (In fact, men score higher than women even on a questionnaire measure of romanticism; see Hobart, 1958.) Several studies have looked at the speed of falling in love, and the consistent finding is that men fall in love faster. One influential study asked people about their current love relationships (Kanin et al., 1970). Over a quarter of the men (27 percent) reported that they had fallen in love within the first four dates, whereas only 15 percent of the women had fallen in love that early. At the other end of the spectrum, nearly half (43 percent) of the females still did not feel they were in love after twenty dates, while less than a third (30 percent) of the men failed to feel love by that point.

Nor was this difference between men and women in speed of falling in love due to "love at first sight." The researchers found that such instantaneous love was relatively rare overall and did not differ in frequency between the two sexes. Apart from love at first sight, however, there was a clear and consistent pattern indicating that men fall in love sooner than women.

Using other methods, several other studies have confirmed that men fall in love faster than women. Men are ready for an exclusive "couple" relationship instead of merely dating after an average of two-and-a-half months, whereas for women the interval is closer to six months, and men are also quicker to reach the point of expecting the relationship to lead to marriage (Huston et al., 1981). This finding also contradicts another stereotype, namely that men want to avoid commitment.

Is there a value judgment here? Probably it would be more rational and sensible to be more choosy about falling in love. Both men and women frequently make bad choices in love, and so the hastier the choice, probably the worse it is. Our culture puts a high value judgment in favor of acting on the basis of love and passion, but probably this is foolish. Moreover, as we have seen, evolutionary theorists emphasize that it is more rational for women than for men to be extremely choosy, because the cost of making a bad decision is higher for females in the vast majority of species.

Those data come from successful relationships, but the same conclusion emerges from studies of unsuccessful ones. Research on unrequited love, in which one person falls in love but the other never reciprocates it, again indicate that the more common pattern is for the man to fall in love and for the woman to reject him. This is certainly more common than the reverse. True, there are plenty of cases in which a woman falls in love with a man and he fails to return her love. But there are far more cases in which the man is the one who gets his heart broken because the woman fails to love him back (Baumeister & Wotman, 1992; Baumeister et al., 1993).

The common view of love portrayed in movies shows a young man falling in love with a woman and trying to win her love. Thus, in the movies, the man tends to fall in love sooner. It is necessary to be suspicious of movie depictions, because movies are often saturated with fantasy and because the movie-making business does not get equal input from both genders (men tend to dominate, and so movies tend to reflect male views of the world). In this book we find a number of occasions to be critical of the way the movies portray life.

In this case, however, the movies seem to have it right. The man does fall in love first, as a rule. And, for present purposes, what matters is that this fits the theory that the same increase in intimacy will produce a stronger reaction in men than in women. Both people may have the same sense of intimacy in terms of how far the relationship is progressing, but while the woman is merely thinking that it is nice, the man is in love.

Who Wants Sex, and When?

The idea that men and women differ in their "passion multipliers" makes clear predictions about differences in men's and women's patterns of sexual desire as a function of stage of relationship. That is, if the same increase in intimacy creates more passion in the man than the woman, the man may end up desiring sex on many occasions when the woman does not.

When the couple first meets, intimacy is likely to be low, although even getting some positive notice from a woman may be pleasant to a man and give him some hope of intimacy. In general, neither will have all that much passion right at the start.

As the pace of intimacy begins to pick up, the first increments are small. Men have the larger multiplier, so small increments in intimacy will be enough to set off their response of passion. Those same little doses won't be enough to produce passion in the woman. As a result, there is likely to be a significant early stage when the man wants sex while the woman does not. Ample research confirms this (e.g., Cohen & Shotland, 1996; McCabe, 1987).

Then, assuming things go well, the couple does begin to rise in intimacy. At this stage, the relationship is blossoming, and it moves into the stage of young love. Intimacy would be felt to be going up palpably at these times, and so passion would be high in both males and females.

As the relationship matures, however, intimacy levels off toward a plateau. This means reducing the pace of increasing intimacy. Only small doses of intimacy continue to come along, for the most part. Still, these would be enough to evoke a passionate response in the man. Hence at this stage the man would be wanting sex more often than the women.

The early and late predictions fit the data well, although they fit several other theories (such as that women simply have a weaker sex drive than men overall) too. More unique is the prediction about the middle part, when female passion catches up to male passion and may even match or surpass it. This suggests an important exception to the general conclusion that women simply have less sexual passion. During the period when the relationship is blossoming, in the sense that intimacy is rising rapidly and both partners feel passion, men and women may both have plenty of sexual desire, and any gender difference may be minimal. Feminists could well point to this phase to suggest that the power and potential of female sexuality are comparable to men's.

Same-Sex Relationships

Another reasonable way to look at gender differences in sexuality is to contrast the gay male and gay female groups. Merely by being gay, of course, a person indicates that he or she is not statistically typical of his or her gender, and so it is risky to generalize from gay men to all men, or from lesbians to women in general. Still, these patterns do show something about what sex is like when only men and no women are involved, and the same goes for what happens when only women and no men take part. Gay people are, after all, undeniably influenced by the gender definitions that their culture creates, and to some extent they live by them. Even gay male and lesbian relationships, for example, sometimes fall into the pattern of having "husband" and "wife" roles.

We are asking whether women require greater intimacy than men require to produce passion. One sign of this in heterosexual relationships was the pattern that wives have less sexual desire than their husbands after intimacy has reached its plateau and only small increments remain. Do lesbian relationships confirm this pattern?

They do. Blumstein and Schwartz (1983) tracked a large sample of gay male, lesbian, heterosexual married, and heterosexual cohabiting relationships. After ten years, when intimacy had very likely reached its plateau for everyone, the lesbian relationships were the least likely to show signs of passion. Nearly half (47 percent) these long-term lesbian couples reported that they had sex once per month or less, and probably many of those have stopped having sex altogether. In contrast, only 15 percent of the heterosexual married couples reported that their sex lives had dwindled to once per month or less, even after ten years.

What about gay males? Blumstein and Schwartz found that their sexual frequency had dwindled too, but not as drastically as the lesbians'. After ten years, 33 percent were having sex once a month or less. Meanwhile, 11 percent of the gay men had sex with their partner three times a week or more, which was the top category of sexual frequency that Blumestein and Schwartz used. The 11 percent figure is closer to what the heterosexual married couples reported (18 percent) than to what the lesbians reported (1 percent).

Moreover, gay males were often finding their passion elsewhere: They had a high rate of having sex with men other than their partner after they had spent ten years together. Lesbians were not having sex with either their partner or other women.

The gay men's passionate attraction to other men may reflect the high multiplier we proposed for males. That is, a small increment in intimacy translates into substantial sexual passion among males, more than for females. The data about new relationships confirm this view. As Blumstein and Schwartz report, gay males had sex with their partners more than any other type of couple in the early stage of the relationship. The only group that came close was the heterosexual couples who were living together in an unmarried state. Within the first two years of the relationship, twice as many gay males (67 percent) as lesbians (33 percent) fell in the top sexual category of having sex three times a week or more.

Thus, the same-sex relationships confirm the patterns we have proposed. The high multiplier we have suggested for males entails that passion will rise without needing a huge increase in intimacy. Consistent with this, all-male couples have sex more often than any other type of couple early in the relationship, when intimacy is still rising. They still have sex more often than lesbians late in a mature relationship, when intimacy has reached its plateau. And when intimacy with the partner has reached a plateau, they tend to have sexual encounters with other men, again indicating that passion can be stimulated quickly and easily.

Lesbians, meanwhile, show patterns of passion that indicate the greater difficulty of generating passion from a given increase in intimacy. They are perhaps slower to become highly sexual early in the relationship. In long-term relationships, after intimacy has reached a plateau, their sexual responses dwindle farther than those of any other couple, and many lesbian pairs seem to stop having sex altogether after intimacy levels off.

Another Kind of Passion

We have focused here on the positive passion of sexual arousal, as stimulated by an increase in intimacy. But what about decreasing intimacy? If changes in intimacy produce more passion in men, would they also suffer more from decreases in intimacy?

It is difficult to answer this question definitively, because couples may experience decreases in intimacy differently. It is even plausible that in some couples, one person may complain about a lack of intimacy and a sense of growing apart even while the other thinks everything is fine.

Despite these problems, the evidence does depict men as suffering more dramatically than females over a decrease in intimacy. The stereotype suggests that women suffer more, but the reality is quite different. The influential, early study of breakups of dating relationships among young adults (mostly college students) found that men suffered more emotional distress (Hill, Rubin, & Peplau, 1976). Other evidence about divorce in adulthood and midlife suggests that men suffer more in a variety of ways, extending even to health and crime problems (e.g., Bernard, 1970). Thus, in general, men seem to have the larger multiplier, which means that they have more passionate reactions when relationships change in either direction—for better or worse.

In summary, passion may derive from changes in intimacy, but the rate at which changing intimacy begets passion is not the same for everyone. The exchange rate seems to be based on a bigger multiplier for men than for women, on average. The same increment in intimacy produces more passion in the man, resulting in his apparent overreaction to a woman's merely friendly behavior, his tendency to fall in love faster, his greater interest in sex at many (but perhaps not all) phases of a relationship, and his greater distress upon breaking up. When intimacy is blossoming rapidly, women are just as passionate as men, but as the increases in intimacy become smaller and less frequent, women's passion drops off faster than men's.

Limited Sexual Resources and the Conservation of Passion

Let us now return to the theme of limited resources in sexuality. Both passion and intimacy have limits. That is, a couple can only become intimate up to a certain point, and they can only experience only so much passion on a given occasion. Let us consider each of these.

The idea that intimacy has its limits follows directly from its basis in knowledge. In an important sense, there is only so much to know about a person. True, there may be hidden details or minor secrets that can still be discovered after many years of living together, but these are typically trivial. Most of the important things about a person are learned fairly early in the relationship.

The other features of intimacy we describe also have limits. One can develop a more positive attitude of warmth and concern toward someone, but eventually this reaches a limit. When you are deeply in passionate love, it may not be possible for you to double how much you care for that person. Likewise, expressions of affection have a well-demarcated hierarchy that starts with the occasional smile or compliment, ranges up through increasingly clear and positive declarations, and reaches its peak with declarations of love, expensive gifts, and wedding vows. Beyond promising (in a church full of witnesses) to spend your life loving and caring for someone, what stronger expression of affection is possible?

Thus, intimacy is likely to reach a full quota. We have described this in terms of the rise of intimacy hitting plateau. The concept of a plateau is slightly misleading, for as we said there may still be small increases in intimacy from time to time, and perhaps even occasionally a large one. But relationships undoubtedly have a powerful phase of rising intimacy that is generally associated with the early part of it, and that does come to an end.

Meanwhile, passion is also limited, although in a different way. There is only so much passion that can be felt on any given occasion. Passion is an emotion, and as such it includes a response by the body (similar to an adrenaline rush). When you have that full adrenaline rush, you aren't likely to be able to have anything stronger.

Sexual passion also has clear limits on a given occasion. A person may be not excited at all, or somewhat aroused, or extremely aroused. Beyond that level, there are no further categories of higher arousal. Most people in the midst of romantic love experience this high level of sexual desire, in which they eagerly or desperately long to make love with the partner. To double that feeling of desire may not be possible.

To get the maximum amount of passion, therefore, you want to reach that high level as often as possible. To do so may depend on increasing intimacy. But intimacy too has a limit. Hence there is an upper limit to how much passion you can generate over time. But even reaching this limit may be tricky.

If passion comes from new intimacy, then disclosing personal things about yourself is a good way to generate passion. The more you disclose, the more passion you create—up to a point. That point is the passion ceiling. Beyond that point, further disclosures of personal information will yield no additional passion.

Suppose, in other words, that you and your romantic partner can create passion in each other by disclosing four very personal things, such as emotionally potent memories or attitudes. This might take place while spending a long evening together early in a love relationship, followed perhaps by passionate love-making. If you disclose twenty very personal things, passion will be no higher than if you had stopped at four. The other sixteen disclosures are useless in passion terms.

Moreover, once you disclose something, you cannot really disclose it again, because the other person already knows it. Each bit of personal information can only increase intimacy with a particular person once. Hence those extra sixteen disclosures may have been wasted. If you get no more passion from twenty disclosures than from four, you have used up the extra sixteen for nothing.

"Wasting" these extra disclosures might not matter if people had an unlimited amount of highly personal material to disclose—but remember that people have a ceiling on intimacy too. They only have so many things to reveal. Those extra sixteen disclosures are thus irreplaceably lost, at least for purposes of increasing intimacy. (To be sure, there may be value in having the other person know those things about you, so they are not entirely lost. Disclosing them may contribute to intimacy, even if the contribution to passion is negligible.)

At some point, then, the stock of material to disclose is depleted. Passion will become harder to generate. At that point, people may wish they had conserved some of their disclosures. That evening when they disclosed twenty things rather than four and effectively wasted sixteen of them—that is something to regret. Those extra sixteen disclosures might have been enough to create high passion on four other evenings. Disclosing twenty instead of four personal things has thus reduced the total number of passionate experiences available to the couple.

The numbers of twenty and four and so forth are arbitrary, and of course some disclosures are more intimate than others. Still, the general principle holds in relative terms. A couple that discloses everything early in the relationship may find that they are quicker to reach the point of dwindling passion than the couple that saves some things to disclose later. The longer you can feel that you are still getting to know the other person, the better the opportunities for passion.

The gender difference we described may apply here too. We depicted women as needing a bigger dose of intimacy than men in order to generate the same level of passion. Women will therefore tend to use up the stock of intimate disclosures faster than men, so a female approach to relationships will run out of fuel for passion earlier than a male approach. The research findings we reviewed about gay and lesbian relationships supported this view: Passion (at least as measured by frequency of sex) diminishes faster and more thoroughly in lesbian than in gay male relationships.

In a heterosexual relationship, therefore, the optimal approach to maximizing passion in the long term will be different for men and women. It would be rational for a man to be slower to open up and divulge personal, emotional material than for a woman. The man can reach the ceiling of passion without a heavy dose of intimate exchange, and so it makes sense for a man to conserve his stock of personal information so as to be able to generate passion on other occasions. The woman may need or want more intimacy to get her level of passion up to the maximum. From her perspective, therefore, "conserving" intimacy by opening up more slowly simply leads to lack of passion at all times. Put another way, a given man and woman are likely to have some disagreement as to how much intimate communication is necessary or desirable on a particular occasion so as to produce a high amount of passion and make for good sex.

Face-to-Face

Let us turn now to a very different and seemingly unrelated question. Why do people have sex using the face-to-face position?

Most other species do not use face-to-face coitus. Rear-entry ("doggie-style") mating is preferred by most mammals. Admittedly, dogs and other four-legged creatures could not easily accomplish face-to-face intercourse. The human upright skeletal structure makes it easier to switch position, but it doesn't require it. Apes and monkeys have fairly upright skeletons, but they continue to favor rear-entry mating (Michael & Zumpe, 1971). The evolutionary legacy is still quite apparent in men. Many men find the view of the female gluteus maximus highly arousing, even though her derriere does not show her sex organs or contribute in any meaningful way to coital pleasure or reproductive success. Probably the "ass man" who prefers to look at women's behinds is an holdover from the long evolutionary experience of rear-entry coitus.

Why, then, did the human race turn the female around to face the man during sex? Sexual ethologists and researchers have long recognized this as a puzzle that is not satisfactorily explained by existing theories.

The passion-intimacy link might just hold the answer to this puzzle. The key would be whether the face-to-face position would facilitate the exchange of intimacy cues so as to increase sexual passion. In plainer terms, sex might be better face-to-face because it enables the people to feel more intimate (and hence more passionate) with each other.

Does facing someone cause people to feel a rise in intimacy? Some laboratory findings by Kellerman, Lewis, and Laird (1989) in social psychology suggests that the answer is yes. In an experimental study, male-female pairs were randomly assigned to gaze into each other's eyes for two minutes at fairly close range. These people ended up having much stronger feelings of attraction, warmth, interest, and even romantic love than did pairs of people who engaged in other procedures (in control conditions). Thus, looking into someone's eyes does seem to lead to feelings of attraction toward that person. Normally we do not gaze into strangers' eyes, although we may do this with intimates. Hence doing it with someone constitutes a signal of intimacy, resulting in the beginnings of passionate attraction. Facing a sexual partner might well therefore produce greater passion.

A face-to-face position for sex accomplishes two other things that could create a sense of rising intimacy and hence stimulate passion. One is that it makes it possible for a man and woman to kiss while they are having intercourse. Obviously, rear-entry mating makes this very difficult, whereas if the partners are facing each other, they can kiss constantly.

Is kissing important? Kissing is an important sign of intimacy in many (but not all) cultures. People kiss those they care about, and kissing increases as they become intimate. We have already noted that the first kiss is an important step in the rise of intimacy. Another indication of the importance of kissing is that prostitutes tend not to kiss, because they want to avoid developing intimate attachments to the men with whom they have sex. In fact, intimacy is a kind of occupational hazard for prostitutes, who have sex with clients they may never see again and who therefore cannot afford to become emotionally involved.

One study of prostitutes found that over half of them reported that they never kissed their clients, and most of the others reserved kissing for special and regular customers (Freund, Leonard, & Lee, 1989). Another researcher quoted one prostitute who alluded to a "code" among prostitutes that included not kissing the clients. This particular prostitute agreed with that policy. As she explained: "Kissing is very intimate. It's a kind of intimacy I don't want to share with my clients" (Chapkis, 1997, p. 121).

Intimacy may be something prostitutes have to work hard to avoid, but most couples who have sex desire intimacy to accompany sex. Moreover, if the change theory is correct, creating a sense of increasing intimacy will make for more passionate and hence better sex. Kissing would therefore improve sex, because it would help people feel intimate. The few people who want to remain emotionally detached during sex tend, like prostitutes, to avoid kissing, but people who want intimacy want kissing (see Blumstein & Schwartz, 1983)—especially women, who as we have suggested require a stronger dose of intimate communication in order to generate maximal passion. It is moreover the women who change position between rear-entry and face-to-face sex, and this fits well with the argument that they benefit most from the heightened passion that the intimate act of kissing produces.

It is also noteworthy that lesbians have an unusually high rate of kissing as compared to other types of couples (Blumstein & Schwartz, 1983). They are not lacking in all physical expressions of affection. Although several possible reasons could be suggested for the lesbian penchant for kissing, one explanation follows directly from the change-in-intimacy theory. It is harder for women than for men to generate a high level of passion, and kissing is an important expression of intimacy that can therefore be especially useful as a way of stimulating passion.

The other bonus of face-to-face sex is talk. Unlike kissing, talking is at least possible during rear-entry intercourse, but it is not easy. Generally people face each other when they speak, if only because it is easier to hear. Talk can be used to communicate many things, but during sex it is likely that talking is used to exchange intimacy cues, such as expressing attraction, love, desire, and commitment. Rear-entry sex must forgo most such communications, whereas face-to-face sex can be accompanied by many such comments. These too could increase passion.

In short, face-to-face sex allows people to look closely into each other's eyes, kiss, and easily speak words of love and intimate caring. If passion comes from rising intimacy, the short-term effect of these intimate communications would be greater mutual passion, and hence better sex. That would explain why the human female, unlike her animal forebears, turned around to face her lover in countless acts of sexual intercourse through the ages.

kissing

intimacy

passion ,etc .

8 The Tragedy of the Male Sex Drive

A₍s₎ men get older, their sexual desires gradually dwindle in strength and frequency. In some cases, as the men reach their seventies and eighties, sexual desire ceases altogether. The guys become virtually nonsexual beings.

A group of researchers interviewed such men about the process of aging and their reactions to it (Shock et al., 1984). Included among the questions was one asking how they would react if it were possible to restore their sex drives to the level they were when the men were much younger. To the surprise of the researchers, the majority of the men said they would not want that to happen and would refuse the offer. Only a third of the men said they would want a full restoration of their sexual vigor.

To be sure, not all men had this reaction, and some seemed quite ready to leap at the chance to be sexually young again. Yet it is surprising that any man would say no to the chance to have his sexuality restored to the condition of youth. Our culture idolizes youth, and Americans spend billions of dollars every year on ways to restore either the feeling or the appearance of being younger than they are. And sex, above all, is central to what many people associate with youth, vigor, and pleasure. Why would any man say no?

Part of the answer is probably that in some way the male sex drive is at best a mixed blessing. Undoubtedly many men get a great deal of pleasure from sex. But perhaps they pay a high price for that pleasure. Perhaps in the relative calm of old age, some men look back and think the price was too high. The Buddhist philosophers described the highest mental state they sought as the absence of desire, and Christian mystics have used similar phrases. Maybe they have a point; inner peace and bliss may require the cessation of desire. The average man spends most of his life far from even the possibility of reaching such a state.

Desire is a state of wanting something one does not have. To have strong desires is to be reminded repeatedly of what you lack. It is no wonder that Buddhism and some other religious traditions emphasize the idea that the best way to be happy is to cease wanting, especially if we consider happiness in the more Asian sense of peace and serenity. Possibly those old men had grasped something of the truth of the Buddhist message: The absence of desire is the best chance for happiness. You're better off *not to want.*

After all, another term for wanting but not having is frustration. There is thus a rather fine line between desire and frustration. If desire is a temporary state leading to satisfaction, then it can be part of a positive experience. Desire can be good when it is followed by the bliss of satisfaction. But if desire is a matter of endless, generally unsatisfied cravings and frustrated wants, it can be hell. Frustration is simply desire that continues for a while, unresolved.

The question for this chapter is therefore whether the nature of the male sex drive produces a greater yield of pleasure or frustration. If there is something in the nature of the male sex drive that leads to endless feelings of wanting what the man does not have, then he is doomed to live out his life in a state of chronic unsatisfaction. If that is man's biological heritage, then he can indeed be said to be cursed. The male sex drive would be a tragedy.

What Men Want

There is a general pattern with a long history in the social sciences of treating men as the norm and women as the exception. Interest in gender usually means studying how women are different. Women are therefore the focus of gender studies, because they are "the Other." When a university starts a program or department devoted to gender studies, the usual result is a group of scholars and classes focused on explaining how women are different. This tradition can easily be decried as sexist, and we agree it is. It may, however, be understandable insofar as most researchers, especially in bygone decades, were men, and so they could grasp the psychology of men intuitively but saw women as the different ones.

Let us try to reverse this pattern for now, because we want to appreciate the differentness of men. Pretend for a moment that you and all other humans were women, but that men had just been discovered as an exotic new variety of human life. How would you describe the sexuality of these creatures? In other words, what is the picture of the male sex drive that the data have painted?

If women are the norm, then men seem to be remarkably centered on sex. An earlier chapter addressed the question of whether women have a milder sex drive than men, and the tentative answer was an emphatic yes. Turning that point around to fit our present goal, the question was whether men have stronger and more relentless desires for sex (again yes). Men think about sex far more often and experience sexual arousal more often than women. They want to have sex with more different partners and in a broader variety of activities. They desire sex far more frequently than is needed for purposes of biological reproduction. They have more (and more assorted) sexual fantasies than women. They spend much more time masturbating than women. Within a marriage or other long-term relationship, men want sex earlier and more often than women.

The stereotype of men as sex-mad creatures is thus not entirely wrong, in this perspective. Compared to women, men spend much more time thinking about sex. They want sex more often and in more variety. The majority of men probably want more sex than they are getting.

Of particular importance is the difference in promiscuity. Men want more sex partners than women want. We already presented the results of one survey showing that the average woman (in a sample of college students in California) wished ideally to have sex with two or three sex partners over the rest of her life, whereas for men the average was sixty-four (Miller & Fishkin, 1997). Similar results are found in other studies (Buss & Schmitt, 1993).

Why that huge difference? We have noted that biological, evolutionary arguments make the strong case that promiscuity has conferred much bigger reproductive advantages on men than women (and indeed has conferred similar relative advantages on males in many other species). Even if men and women started off as being equal in desire for multiple sex partners, evolution would gradually favor the most promiscuous males over the least promiscuous, and thus the species would fill up with the descendants of the horniest males. The female reproductive system would not produce the same result, and if anything it may be that females inclined toward stable, sexually monogamous relationships would be the best bet for producing healthy offspring who would in turn grow up and reproduce.

Hence, over the many centuries of evolution, the promiscuous men and the monogamous women were the ones most likely to pass on their genes. The implication is that today's human race will be descended disproportionately from those. That could be why today's average young man wants to have sixty-four sex partners, while today's average young woman thinks two or three is enough for a lifetime.

Of course, we do not have proof that these differences are innate patterns that are the result of evolution. Some theorists continue to believe that they are the results of cultural conditioning and social learning. But the burden is on them to show more evidence of cross-cultural variation. If men are everywhere more inclined toward promiscuity than women, it is reasonable to assume that that pattern is part of the innate, biological makeup of men, which is the result of evolution. On the other hand, if the opposite is found in significant number of cultures, we should disregard evolutionary thinking and start looking for cultural influences.

Regardless of whether the basis for the difference lies in biology or in socialization, the difference itself is clear: Men and women have somewhat different patterns of sexual desire. Men want more frequent sex with more different partners than women want.

The discussion of erotic plasticity in Chapter 6 lends a further twist to this picture of the male sex drive. Taking the female as the norm (contrary to the way that chapter was set up), we can see the male sex drive as relatively rigid and inflexible. Men's sexual desires seem deeply rooted in their biological nature, and they are relatively unresponsive to social, cultural, and situational factors. If they find themselves in a situation that is not conducive to their needs and wants, they are simply out of luck: They cannot adapt themselves to the situation by changing their own feelings and desires as well as women can.

Doomed to Sexual Starvation

Two facts thus stand out from our consideration of the male sex drive, if we take the female as the norm: Men want a great deal of sex. And they aren't likely to get it.

The crux of the problem, for the average man, is that he wants sex with many women, but almost none of those women want him. Again, this applies in both variety and frequency. He wants to have sex with many women—but women don't desire nearly as many partners, and so far fewer women will want to sleep with him than he desires. A man who wants to have sex with sixty-four women will have trouble persuading them to oblige him, if they each want only two or three partners, and plenty of other men feel the same way he does. He is probably going to have to settle down with one sex partner, because that is the way most women prefer to organize sex.

And, to top it off, when he settles down into a stable, monogamous relationship, it is likely to be with someone who wants sex less often than he wants it. This is not to say he is entitled to more, and the arrangement ought in principle to persuade men to be nice to their wives by and large. But for the present argument, the key point is that even when he gives up the single lifestyle, with its alleged opportunities for multiple partners, and pledges himself to one woman, he won't even get his fill of sex with her.

The result is an ongoing struggle with sexual frustration and deprivation. When Dutch researchers developed a "Sexual Compulsion Scale" to measure how much people battle with inner sexual desires, men scored higher than women (Vanwesenbeeck et al., 1998). Items on this scale included "My desire for sex disturbs my daily life," "I think more about sex than I would like," and "I must fight to keep my sexual thoughts and behaviors under control." These items apparently resonate with men more than women. No wonder that some men don't wish for a full restoration of their sex drive when they are old and finally get some peace!

Across a large number of studies (with results combined by meta-analysis), one of the biggest differences between men and women is in attitude toward casual sex (Oliver & Hyde, 1993). Men like the idea of going to bed with someone just for fun, including someone they have just met and have no intention of pursuing a long-term relationship with. From these men's point of view, sex is enjoyable, and sex with new partners is extra-enjoyable, so why shouldn't people just go to bed together without any strings attached? Unfortunately for these men, most women don't see it the same way.

The difference in attitudes toward casual sex is probably linked to the difference in desire for many sex partners. After all, it is hardly practical to have sex with dozens of partners if this means having a serious, long-term, committed relationship with each one. Life simply isn't long enough for that. For the average man to have sex with sixty-four partners, starting at age fifteen and continuing to his death in his seventies—and to have a monogamous, committed relationship with each woman—these relationships could not last more than a year each. And that's even if women cooperated and were satisfied with having these one-year relationships.

Sexual frustration is thus almost inevitable for the majority of men—and not just occasionally, either. Given the mismatch between men's and women's desires, most men are doomed to experience chronic sexual frustration. They won't have enough partners, or even enough sex with one partner, to satisfy their wishes. They will have to settle for less than they want. Face it, most men have almost no chance of having sixty-four sex partners, unless they spend a lot of money on prostitutes.

Statistically, not all men are doomed to this fate. A few lucky ones may be able to attract enough partners to satisfy them. Rich, powerful, famous men may find that plenty of women are willing to satisfy them. These lucky few men may achieve sexual fulfillment.

Or will they? Unfortunately, men's sexual desires are probably subject also to the adaptation-level effect. This effect, which emerged from research on animals (Helson, 1964), showed that one gradually becomes accustomed to the status quo, and so it ceases to produce much of a reaction. Only changes from the status quo bring a strong reaction. This also bodes ill for men. Their very biological nature has built-in sources working against satisfaction.

The adaptation level effect is often illustrated with salary levels. If your salary is $25,000 per year, even if you are reasonably satisfied with that, you might wish for $30,000, and you think $35,000 would answer all your dreams. When you get a raise to $30,000, you are indeed going to be happy for a while. But the joy wears off, and you grow accustomed to $30,000. Now you wish for $35,000, but you think it might take $45,000 to be the answer to your dreams. The $25,000 that once satisfied you now seems hopelessly inadequate. And if you do reach $45,000, it won't be the permanent answer to your dreams, even though you may be delighted at first. Within a couple years, you'll be wishing for more. Studies have been done with lottery winners demonstrating that even the joy of winning a large amount of money wears off after about a year or so, and people are then no happier than they were before the windfall.

The adaptation-level effect poses a significant barrier to achieving any lasting human happiness. Brickman and Campbell (1971) coined the term "the hedonic treadmill" to describe this problem. On a treadmill, you keep taking steps forward, but you end up in the same place. In much the same way, people may take steps toward fulfilling their dreams, but the joy quickly wears off and they end up no happier than they were. Their net happiness does not change.

On a large scale, this pattern has been repeatedly confirmed. For example, in the decades following World War II, Americans became much richer. Average family income increased by nearly two-thirds between 1945 and 1973, *after* adjusting for inflation. Yet happiness showed no net increase (Campbell, 1981). Most people think that getting more money will make them happier, but events prove them wrong.

To our knowledge, adaptation-level theory has not received a clear and direct test in the field of sexuality, but the pervasiveness of these effects makes it seem likely that sex will show the same effects as all the other behaviors. The implication is that men are unlikely to be permanently satisfied even when they do get what they want.

Let us assume that many men do live their lives in some degree of chronic sexual frustration. When they do gain an increase in sex, they are likely to be happy for a while. But this joy will wear off, and they may revert to wishing they had more. The world of men may consist of many individuals who envy others. The young man who has never had sex wishes to have it with at least one woman. The man who has had one partner wishes for two or three. The man who has had six may wish for ten. The man who has had sex with fifty women may wish for seventy or a hundred. The man who has only experienced oral sex may wish for intercourse. The man who has sex once a week may wish for it two or three times a week.

The result is that satisfaction is likely to be elusive even for the minority of men who do manage to have a relative abundance of sexual opportunities. Most men will not get as much sex as they want. The supposedly lucky few will find that their desires escalate, so getting what they want is not satisfying either, at least not for long. Either way, men seem doomed to live out much of their adult lives in a chronic state of sexual frustration. They are doomed to be horny.

There is at least some indirect evidence that this is what happens. Watt and Ewing (1996) developed a measure of sexual boredom, and they found that men scored significantly higher than women. At first glance, this result is surprising and counterintuitive. The difference in sex drive and other attitudes suggests that men are more obsessed with sex than women, and so one might infer that sex would never become boring for men. But being prone to sexual boredom did not mean lack of interest in sex. In fact, even among just men, high sexual boredom was linked to more (rather than less) masturbation, as well as to more partners. Apparently the male vulnerability to sexual boredom means that men get tired of whatever sexual gratifications are regularly available to them. Soon they want something different.

The negative side of sexual boredom was readily apparent. Watt and Ewing (1996) found that high levels of sexual boredom led to sexual depression (i.e., being unhappy and discontent with one's sex life). It was also linked to taking chances, such as having unprotected sex with casual partners, thereby running the risk of contracting AIDS or some other disease.

Risk-taking has been studied by social psychologists, and it appears that the arousal of bad feelings plus discontent makes people prone to take foolish, self-destructive chances. Leith and Baumeister (1996) conducted a series of studies in which people were first put into bad moods and then given a choice of several lotteries, each of which offered both good and bad outcomes. The lotteries were set up such that one was objectively better, but it required "playing it safe." The other lottery offered a small chance at a very positive outcome but also carried substantially higher risks of having something bad happen (an outcome that in important ways resembles the taking of sexual risks in the quest for a positive, satisfying experience). When people were in bad moods, they were more likely to choose the high-risk option. Happy people, in contrast, favored the play-it-safe course of action, as did people who were in neutral moods. Unhappy people liked the high-risk choices because they were drawn by the chance (however slight) that something fabulously wonderful would happen, like winning a big prize, and they didn't think about how unlikely it was or what bad things would happen if the the perfect outcome didn't materialize as they had hoped.

The male yearning for sexual novelty will apparently lead some men to take foolish chances, especially when that yearning is combined with a feeling that they have not had a satisfactory sex life and would like to have more sexual adventures and fulfillments. This is precisely what one would expect from people who are condemned by their own inner nature and external circumstances to being chronically unsatisfied in sex: discontent, risk-taking, depression, and a relentless quest for any sort of new satisfaction.

Compared to Whom?

Let us turn now from actual satisfaction to self-esteem issues. How do men appraise their own sexuality? Because hardly any man consistently has as much sex as he would like, over a long period of time at least (there are brief spells of sexual satisfaction), men probably seek to know whether they are at least relatively well off in the sexual sphere. The influential social psychologist Leon Festinger proposed in 1954 that many people evaluate themselves not in absolute terms but in comparison with others, a process called *social comparison*. A man may therefore try to comfort himself by ascertaining how his sex life compares with what other men enjoy. No man gets all that he wants in sex, but perhaps a man can pat himself on the back for doing better than most other guys.

Unfortunately, social comparison is not likely to yield much comfort to many men. Men do talk about their sex lives and experiences, but these discussions may inflate the facts, leaving each listener envious of the speaker. As we saw in Chapter 2, many men tend to overestimate the number of sex partners they have had, even if these are honest mistakes. As we also saw, people who are willing to talk about their sex lives tend to have had substantially more sexual experience than people who don't talk about sex, and so everything the average man hears from other men is likely to distort the true picture. Remember the difference between the Janus Report and the NHSLS: When researchers relied on people who volunteered to discuss their sex lives, the average man emerged as someone who claimed he had had twenty-four sex partners (Janus & Janus, 1993). But when researchers carefully constructed a sample representative of the full population, the average was only six partners (Laumann et al., 1994).

Put another way, if you only listen to the men who volunteer to talk about their sexual experiences, you get the impression that most men have four times as much sex as the facts would indicate. Unfortunately the average man has no way of knowing this. The result? He is likely to end up viewing his own sex life as less satisfactory. He may feel what social scientists call *relative deprivation:* He is not getting as much as other men, and so he feels deprived. This feeling of relative deprivation is likely to be piled on top of his feelings of absolute deprivation, in the sense that he is not having as much sex as he would like.

A further complication concerns a kind of sexual grass-is-greener effect, which is another form of social comparison. Research has not clearly confirmed this, although there is some evidence pointing in that direction, but our impression is that married men and single men tend to envy each other. Married men believe single men have great sex lives marked by a revolving kaleidoscope of new sex partners and exciting adventures. Single men envy married men who supposedly have a regular, willing, loving partner who is willing to have sex with them every night, or even every night and every morning too.

Single men may be especially prone to believe in nonstop married sex because their own experience may seem to imply that that is normal. When a single man and woman fall in love, they may well go through a stage of having very frequent sex. Quite possibly they may think that the frequent sex reflects the seriousness of their relationship, so they expect that marriage will be just like that, instead of recognizing the frequent sex as a result of the novelty of the relationship, which would mean that it would not last the course of a long marriage.

Hence the pattern of mutual envy between married and single men. Each thinks he is missing out on the sexual fulfillment that the other is getting. Each may therefore feel all the more deprived and dissatisfied.

There is some justification to these patterns of mutual envy, but again the problem arises that both sets of men focus on what the other has rather than on what they themselves have. Single men do have a valid reason for envying married men, because in fact married men have sex more frequently, averaged over long periods of time (Laumann et al., 1994). Meanwhile, married men do have a valid reason for envying their single peers, because single men do accumulate more sex partners and probably have more varied and exciting sexual adventures.

Of course both married and single men would be happier, and more content with their own lives, if they focused on the other's disadvantages rather than advantages. Married men might tell themselves that they are fortunate to be married because they have more frequent sex than single men. And the single men might console themselves with the greater variety, novelty, and adventure in their sex lives. But they don't.

The differences are thus probably rooted in the situational structure of married versus single life. Married men are tied to one partner who is always there, and even though she may not want to have sex as often as her husband wants it, she does tend to have sex with him on a fairly regular basis. The single man's life, in contrast, is marked by the absence of a regular partner. Periodically he finds someone new to take to bed, and for a period of time he may have very exciting sex with this new person. Married sex is more frequent but also more predictable and familiar (and hence somewhat less exciting). Single sex is more novel and exciting but paid for with long periods of enforced celibacy.

The men seem to find these periods of sexual deprivation more painful than the women. As Kinsey et al. (1953) indicated, some women go through periods with no orgasms whatsoever, in between high-sex relationships. Men find some other way to keep their orgasm rate fairly constant, even if masturbation is the only available outlet.

We must also acknowledge some role of the media. Most people gain a fair amount of normative information from the mass media, including television and movies. As we saw in the discussion of the self in Chapter 3, this information is often distorted in ways that are likely to make women feel inferior, because the movie and TV stars tend to be slim and beautiful to an extent that the average woman cannot achieve. In the same way, the normative information is likely to make the average man feel bad, because there is a great deal more sex (and more exciting sex) on the big screen and boob tube than the average man has in his regular life.

One can blame the media for being distorted, and although there is some truth to this reproach, the media can be defended on two grounds. In the first place, they mainly put on what people want to watch, and obviously people want to watch exciting romantic and sexual experiences. Second, a movie is only a slice out of a person's life, and as such it is likely to be one of the most interesting slices. A film may, for example, depict a passionate love story that is supposedly the one sexual adventure in a character's life. After all, that story makes more interesting (and hence more profitable) viewing than the long years of boring celibacy that came before and after. But viewers may not make this correction in their own minds. They see those adventures and wonder why they are not having similar adventures in their own lives.

For present purposes, all these patterns are likely to intensify a man's feelings of dissatisfaction with his sex life. He probably does not have as much sex as he wants, nor does he have as much sex as he believes—probably mistakenly—that other men have.

The Nature of Tragedy

The term *tragedy* is used in ordinary conversation to refer to almost any sort of bad event. Yet as the great American playright Arthur Miller (1978) wrote in a famous essay, this usage is misleading. The term "tragedy" should be reserved for a highly specific kind of misfortune: One that the person brings on him- or herself, especially in the context of striving for something grand and positive. In Miller's explanation, the deaths of people in traffic accidents or hurricanes do not really constitute tragedy. Those deaths are indeed sad and deserve sympathy, but they should be regarded as misfortune rather than tragedy. In tragedy, a man or woman aspires to something grand or noble and is brought low by his or her inner traits as well as by circumstances.

Central to Miller's analysis is the concept of the "tragic flaw," which refers to some inner aspect of the person that leads to his or her undoing. Ambition is the tragic flaw of Shakespeare's Macbeth, for example. He desires power and glory and lets himself be persuaded (by his wife) to use murder to realize his dreams. His own actions to achieve something grand ultimately cause his own downfall and death.

We have titled this chapter "The Tragedy of the Male Sex Drive" because the nature of that sex drive does fit Miller's notion of the tragic flaw. The male sex drive seems designed to prevent happiness, especially given the hedonic treadmill. Male sexuality may be unable to find permanent satisfaction in almost any sort of system, and certainly in most systems that actually occur. Men want more sex with more partners and in more varieties than they are getting. Actual men may blame circumstances, such as the uncooperativeness of women or the institution of marriage. But it looks as if men are doomed to be discontented with almost any arrangement.

Whatever they get, they soon want more. For men, then, sexual satisfaction is temporary at best. Even if a man manages to woo the woman of his dreams and marry her, his bliss won't last forever. After he has slept with her a thousand times, perhaps, he is likely to start wishing for someone else. And some men may start wishing for someone else after a dozen times rather than a thousand. Even if he likes her and wants to stay with her, he may still desire others too.

If this is correct, then the problem faced by the average man is different than it first appears. He may think the problem is to find a suitable sex partner who will satisfy him, and sure enough that would help make his life better. In the long run, though, the problem of unsatisfaction will resurface. Whatever he gets, he'll end up wanting more. The ultimate problem is therefore to find a way to live with chronic or recurrent unsatisfaction.

Why Don't Women Pay for Sex?

Prostitution is (probably erroneously) described as the "oldest profession," and in any case it is found all over the world and throughout history. Prostitutes provide a broad variety of sexual services. But by and large they provide them to men. Female prostitutes mostly serve men. Male prostitutes also mostly serve men.

One might regard this difference as a reflection of the male-dominated culture, which is only concerned about taking care of men. But in many modern societies, open and free capitalism would almost certainly mean that if women demanded some service, it would become available. There never seems to be much of a market for this, however. The American sex industry has tried offering some services to women, including male strippers, magazines that feature photo spreads of nude men, and the like, but these do not find a market that is anywhere close to what the male-oriented market can expect.

And selling sex itself seems to do worst of all. If a man finds himself needing money and lacking skills, to the point at which he turns to prostituting himself, he must rely on male customers to make a living. There's no way he'll pay off his Mafia debt or support his heroin habit by getting women to pay him to have sex with them. Women in comparable situations who turn to prostitution are hardly to be envied, and prostitution is certainly a less than ideal life, but men who might wish for the same setup don't even have the option.

Why don't women have to pay for sex? Because they can usually get enough of it for free.

Although this point can be documented in several ways, let us use one dramatic experiment, which we have briefly mentioned earlier in the book but is most relevant here. One of America's leading social psychologists, Elaine Hatfield, collaborated with a colleague to perform some experiments that have shaped the thinking of many other researchers in the field (Clark & Hatfield, 1989). Ironically, they encountered resistance when they first sought to publish their work, and the article ended up in a relatively obscure journal. But since its publication, it has often been cited and discussed by many experts. It sheds considerable light on gender differences in sexuality.

In this work, the researchers employed confederates who were themselves college students. Their task was to approach attractive members of the opposite sex and extend an invitation for a date, a visit, or sex. In the last of these conditions, the confederate went up to the person, claimed to have been noticing him or her around campus, complimented the person, and asked, "Would you like to go to bed with me tonight?"

When the confederate was a woman approaching an attractive man with this invitation, the responses were quite favorable. Indeed, in the first study, three-quarters of the men agreed to go to bed with the woman, even though they did not know her at all. The researchers noted that the male subjects did not need a great deal of convincing and in fact seemed generally quite pleased with the invitation and eager to accept it. Some even told the woman that it was not necessary to wait until tonight!

The difference is especially striking when one considers that the confederates were of average attractiveness, whereas the people they approached had been selected to be highly attractive. Most research on sex partner selection emphasizes that people find someone who matches them in attractiveness. By those criteria, the men in the study were not getting a good deal in the sense of an attractive offer: The women who asked them for sex were less attractive than the men were. Despite this, most of the men agreed.

It was a vastly different story, however, when the confederate was an average-looking man approaching an attractive woman. Across two studies, not a single woman consented to go to bed with the man. Zero.

This is a large and quite meaningful difference. Every single woman in these studies refused an average stranger's invitation for sex. In contrast, the majority of men accepted a similar invitation from an unknown woman.

There are important implications of these results, but in order to appreciate them, it is first necessary to consider some other findings, including some not directly concerned with sex. We turn first to stress research.

The Panic Button Effect

Undoubtedly people are affected by things that happen to them. One of the more interesting and thought-provoking patterns of findings in social psychology has shown, however, that people are often affected by things that do not happen. Although there are several such effects, we focus here on one that emerged from research on stress: If people believe they are stuck with the status quo, they may be less pleased with it than they would be if they think they have an alternative.

This effect was first demonstrated experimentally by Glass, Singer, and Friedman (1969). They were conducting a series of studies on how well people could perform under stress, which in their work took the form of random, unpredictable, aversive loud noise. In other words, the people who served as experimental subjects had to work on tasks and solve problems while listening to these randomly spaced blasts of noise. The noises were specially prepared for the experiment and consisted of a variety of super-imposed sounds, including loud machine noises and two people jabbering away in an Armenian dialect. This hodgepodge was blasted at people at 110 decibels, which is quite loud, although not enough to be harmful.

The researchers found that people could cope reasonably well with the noise for a while, but that coping took something out of them. Afterward, when they had more work to do in a quiet setting, they showed low frustration tolerance, poor concentration, more mistakes, and a willingness to give up quickly when they encountered difficulties. In other words, they had used up their capacity to cope.

In another study, the researchers added a crucial condition. Before the experiment started, they told the subjects that there would be a button on the desk, and that if the noise became too aversive or unpleasant, they could just press the button to turn it off. This was false; the button actually did not work. But no one discovered this. The experimenters had told the subjects that it would be best for the experiment if they didn't press the button, and nobody did.

The button was thus a phantom escape option, a "panic button" that was available for instances of dire need. *No one ever pressed the button.*

When people then went on to the second part of the experiment, in the quiet room, a dramatic difference emerged. People who had had the button available to them (even though they had never used it) were able to perform just fine. They did not show the impairments in concentration, persistence, and frustration tolerance that the others did.

It is important to appreciate these results. Everyone in this experiment listened to exactly the same amount of stressful noise. No one really could escape from it, although some people falsely believed that they could have if they had really wanted to do so. This belief was enough to reduce the harmful effects of stress, even though no one ever actually pressed the button. Merely having the belief that they could escape, if necessary, was enough to counteract the effects of stress. People's reactions to what did happen (the stressful noise) were changed by something that did not happen (the option to press the panic button).

One implication is that what is really stressful about stress is not so much having bad things happen, but rather being aware that you cannot escape from them. It is the feelng of being trapped: No matter how bad things get, you cannot get out. The noise was the same for both groups, but only one of them believed they would be able to get away if they wanted. For them, the same amount of noise produced much less harm.

Now apply this reasoning to sex. Let us assume that desiring sex without being able to have it is unpleasant. The popular term *horny* is used to describe the feeling of having sexual desire without any immediate prospect of relief or satisfaction. Believing that one has an escape option would make this sexual desire much more bearable. Without an escape option, it could be far less tolerable.

This is where the results of Clark and Hatfield (1989) are relevant. Remember what they showed: An average woman can approach an attractive man, even a total stranger, and ask him to go to bed with her, and the odds are good that he will accept. Here and there she might encounter a refusal, but since over half the men in the experiment consented, it is fair to predict that if a woman asked two or three men to have sex with her that night, at least one of them would probably agree. Combined probabilities suggest that if she asked three men, her likelihood of getting at least one positive answer is over 97 percent—almost a sure thing.

Sex is thus available to the average woman. Just for the asking, even with a total stranger—and one who is more attractive than she is herself. That's why women don't pay for sex. If a woman's sexual cravings were to become so strong that she wanted to be released from them, she could do so. She can easily find someone to have sex with her. *Sexual desire is not a trap for the woman;* she can escape if she wants to, even if she chooses not to.

In contrast, an average men cannot expect any success at all in the same circumstances. Asking women for sex will get him nowhere (except perhaps slapped or arrested!). The combined probability of getting at least one yes in response to asking three strangers is still 0 percent—a far cry from the woman's 97 percent chances! As we have seen, even if he is in a relationship, he may well not get as much sex as he wants. Meanwhile, if he does not have a wife or girlfriend, the odds are heavily stacked against him. He might well ask fifty women, and all of them would say no.

The man is thus in the no-panic-button condition. There is no escape. No matter how strong or unpleasant his sexual cravings may get, there is little or nothing he can do.

To be sure, he can masturbate. But of course that is not really what he wants. In principle, he could hire a prostitute, but such acts are illegal in most places in North America, and so he would run several risks. Moreover, many men think (probably with good reason) that a prostitute would not be satisfactory anyway. It is simply not regarded by most men as a realistic option. What the man wants is consensual, mutually interested sex with an attractive partner. If he doesn't have a steady girlfriend or wife, he's not likely to get it.

The panic-button effect operates independently of the difference in sex drive, and the combination is a double whammy for the average man. Even if men and women had the same level of desire, it would be worse and more stressful for men, because of the panic-button effect. Women can escape from sexual frustration if they want to, but men cannot do so very well. Thus, men would be worse off even if men and women started off with the same amount of horny sexual desire. As we have seen, though, men have more frequent and stronger cravings for sex, and so their lack of opportunities makes it that much worse. The combination makes the tragedy of the male sex drive acute.

An additional irony is that even though men are far less selective about sex partners than women, they still have fewer opportunities. The Clark and Hatfield study showed that most men would be happy to have sex with a woman who approached them almost at random. The implication is that many a man would often settle for nearly any woman, or at least any one of a large category of women (e.g., roughly his own age or a bit younger, and not wildly ugly). Many a horny young man would be happy just to have a warm female body to share his bed. Almost any woman would do, or at least one within very broad categories and with fairly lax standards. Despite this broad willingness, however, he is unlikely to find anyone.

Thus, many a normal young man will periodically gaze out his window and realize that even in that large city or college campus, there is not a single woman who will have sex with him that night, or even in the foreseeable future. He can go to a bar or party and try to meet a woman and persuade her to sleep with him, but the odds are against him there too. Only if he searches until he finds someone who likes him, and if he makes her his girlfriend, will he have a reliable partner for sex (and even that is not as reliable as most men would like). That takes a lot of time as well as effort and expense. Until that happens, there is no outlet save the sorry compromise of masturbation.

Find a Girlfriend

The following joke circulated in the late 1990s. A wedding party is standing around outside the church shortly before the ceremony. The best man goes up to the groom and asks, "Nervous?" "Not at all," replies the groom, "I couldn't be happier." "Why is that?" asks the best man. "See that woman over there?" says the groom, indicating the bride. "She gives better oral sex than any woman I've ever known. An hour from now, she'll be mine, all mine, for the rest of my life. I can't wait!" A few yards away, the maid of honor goes up to the bride. "Nervous?" she asks. "Not at all," replies the bride, "I couldn't be happier." "Why is that?" asks the maid of honor. "See that man over there?" says the bride, indicating the groom. "An hour from now, we'll be married, and I'll never have to do oral sex on him again for the rest of my life. I can't wait!"

Thus far we have seen the difficulties men face in finding sex partners. Of course, there is one seeming solution for a man: Find a girlfriend. The man's chances of finding someone to have casual sex with him are not good. But surely relationships offer better opportunities.

They do. But they still fall short.

McCabe (1987) conducted a large-scale study of dating couples. Even though the subjects were typically in committed relationships, the men were not getting as much sex as they wanted. Two patterns in particular stand out. First, there were (inevitably) some couples in which one person wanted sex and the other didn't, and so the couple was not having sex. In almost all of these cases, it was the man who wanted sex. Thus, many men in existing relationships find that they cannot have sex at all because their girlfriend does not want to. Part of the reason is that women are slower to reach the point of wanting sex. Cohen and Shotland (1996) found that the average man reported he expected to have sex after about eleven dates, whereas the average woman expected sex only after eighteen dates. Thus, most relationships will go through a phase in which the man wants sex and the woman doesn't. If the woman's wishes prevail, then the couple will have about seven dates on which the man wants sex and the woman does not.

The second pattern to emerge from McCabe's study was even broader. Yes, the man was ready for sex earlier than the woman. But even after they did start having sex, however, the man was likely to want more than the woman. McCabe (1987) summarized her findings in words that must cut like a knife into the sexual hopes of the average young man: "At any particular stage of dating, the desired level of intercourse for men was more than actual experience" (p. 23). In other words, throughout the entire relationship, the man will be sexually disappointed, at least in the sense that he will be having less sex than he wants. But for women, typically, there is little or no gap between desire and reality. The amount of sex the woman desires is on average very close to the amount she has. For men, reality never catches up to desire.

We saw that this remained true even in long-term relationships. Ard (1977) examined desire and reality among couples who had been married for over twenty years. For women, the desired frequency of sex was almost identical to the actual frequency: They were getting exactly as much sex as they wanted. For men, there was a large gap, and most wanted about 50 percent more than they were getting.

Those odds are still far better for men than the odds of convincing a total stranger to have sex with them, as shown in the Clark and Hatfield (1989) study. Men with wives and girlfriends will indeed get more sexual satisfaction than unattached men, but a substantial gap still remains between desire and reality. For men, it is a difference in the degree of sexual frustration, not a difference between deprivation and full satisfaction. Married or single, the average man is not likely to get as much sex as he wants.

Men Talk About Women the Way Women Talk About Food

In our experience, men and women have a fair amount of difficulty understanding each other, and the unsatisfied promiscuous desires of men are often a sore point. Many women object when their boyfriends or husbands read girlie magazines or watch X-rated videos, go to striptease shows, or even look at bikini-clad women on the beach. To many a woman, such acts suggest that the man doesn't like or want her or that he is seeking to replace her. She may be unpersuaded by his protests that such activities are casual pleasures and have no bearing on his feelings about her.

In sex, women's situation is quite different from men's. As we have seen, the issue of wanting something that you cannot have, and indeed of having to conceal your own desires, may be central to male sexuality but is largely absent from the average woman's daily life. Accordingly, to enable women to understand this aspect of men's lives, it may be helpful to search for a different parallel. Specifically, a useful analogy would involve some form of pleasure and temptation that women regard as forbidden.

One of us once had an opportunity to sit quietly in the background and listen to conversations by groups of men and groups of women. This lasted for over a year and included dozens of such conversations. It was interesting to compare the all-male and all-female discussions. Actually in many respects they were fairly similar, but there were pockets of difference.

Two of these areas of difference were food and sex. The women's food conversations were rich with exquisite details, and on some occasions the women would take turns giving a vivid, fond description of some wonderful meal or treat that she had once eaten, as each listened wistfully to the other's pleasure and enjoyed the fantasy of doing it herself. In contrast, the men's conversations about food were duds. At most food was discussed in practical terms, such as how to get some of it very soon.

The men, however, had much livelier and more earnest discussions about sex than the women had. The women didn't discuss sex much (just as the men's conversation rarely turned on food for very long). When the women did talk about sex, the conversations tended to be vague and liberally mixed with light laughter. They did not take turns describing favorite experiences, as they did with food and as the men did with sex, reciting vivid, detailed descriptions, enjoying each other's accounts, and waiting for the chance to relive their own. Nor did the men remain content with delicate euphemisms or evasive language: Clear communication was prized. They often discussed the physical charms of women they knew. Even male professionals at a major conference have been heard to speculate among themselves after hours about what various women they know would look like naked or act like in bed. Women occasionally do this too, but not nearly as often, and more for a laugh than for genuine pleasure.

And so those two topics of conversation were different, although there was a dimension of similarity. If we compare men's and women's food conversations and men's and women's sex conversations, they seem different. But if we compare men's sex conversations with women's food conversations, there was greater similarity: *Men talk about women the way women talk about food.*

Thus, one possible hypothesis about how to translate between the genders is that eating is parallel to sex. If women want to understand men, it is intuitively helpful for women to invoke their own feelings about food. There are perhaps good reasons for this. For men, sex is highly desired but not widely available, especially in terms of their opportunities to have as much (and with as much variety) as they may want. Food has the same position in many women's lives: They desire it highly but feel unable to have all they want, especially in terms of variety (and quantity). The need to curb one's desires, while believing that others are in the enviable position of being able to indulge similar desires, is a central problem with sex for men and with food for women.

In terms of social psychology, the theory of reactance is relevant to both. This theory, articulated first by Brehm (1966), proposes that people dislike being told that they cannot do something. When their freedom is curtailed, they want all the more to do whatever they are told they may not. In particular, the attractiveness of some act is increased by virtue of its being forbidden. This effect of reactance helps explain the parallels between sex for men and food for women. In both cases, what is forbidden becomes all the more desirable.

We are not claiming that the food/sex analogy is an innate aspect of male and female psyches. When men are deprived of food, their conversation changes too. This was shown in a famous study during World War II, in which the researchers wanted to know what would happen to men who did not have enough to eat over a long period of time. Keys, Brozek, Hensdel, Mickelson, and Taylor (1950) subjected conscientious objectors who volunteered for the study in place of military service (or imprisonment for refusing military service) to an enforced period of food deprivation. Compared to the men who went into combat, their task was relatively easy: All they had to do was remain indoors and eat very little. This had its difficult side, however.

How did these hungry men respond? Their conversations among themselves soon drifted to a focus on food. They told jokes about food. They exchanged recipes. The men had library privileges, and they began checking out the cookbooks, just to read them. When the men watched films, the action and sex scenes elicited less response than usual in contrast to the food scenes, which were vividly appreciated. Indeed, in some cases the men would go through the laborious process of rewinding the film by hand in order to replay scenes of eating so they could watch them again. The men had vivid dreams and fantasies about eating all sorts of delicious foods.

Thus, men become obsessed with food when they are forbidden to have what they want. Most men today do not experience this deprivation, however. Young men in particular can eat prodigious quantities of food without worrying that they will gain weight, get sick, lose respect, or any other cost. The food is often readily available to them. Hence it often becomes a fairly minor concern. Young women, in contrast, feel the pressure to lose weight and stay slim, and so food is off-limits to them. With food, men are in the more fortunate position of being able to have what they want, while women must suffer chronic frustration and self-denial. With sex, the roles are reversed: Women can have what they want, but men can't.

Using this translation may help clarify several areas of misunderstanding between the sexes. Thus, for example, the male character in a movie is having an affair but claims to love his wife. The other woman asks, searchingly, "If you love your wife so much, then what are you doing here with me?" The man has no answer. Women viewers nod at the sagacity of the question. Men shake their heads. This may well reflect the difference we have noted in terms of desire for sexual variety and novelty. Sure enough, research on adultery confirms that men are interested in sexual adventures regardless of how they feel about their spouses, but that women tend only to become extramaritally involved if they feel dissatisfied with their husbands in some ways (e.g., Lawson, 1988). To explain the man's mystification with that question in a way that will resonate with women, though, it is helpful translate it into food terms: If you like steak and potatoes, why are you going out for Chinese food? Well, he loves steak and potatoes, but it is nice to have something different once in a while, for the sake of variety. This is not to condone adultry, which carries with it some very serious risks of ruining the marriage, an outcome that may be far more central to the man's (as well as the woman's) happiness than the casual affair was to his happiness. Rather, at least it can explain the desire, even if it cannot justify the action.

Women can perhaps better understand men's dilemma over monogamy if they consider the food analogy. Monogamous marriage is comparable to having your favorite meal every single day for the rest of your life. Of course one wants to have that favorite meal, and often—but now and then it would be nice to eat something different, simply for the sensory enjoyment of variety.

Fine, one might say: If that's how a man feels, he ought not to marry. But that is not really satisfactory either. Even looking at the situation in purely sexual terms, if marriage is like having your favorite meal for dinner every single day, then not marrying the woman may well mean never eating that favorite meal. That would be a significant and painful loss. Moreover, research shows that married men have sex more often than single men, even today (and before the sexual revolution, the difference would have been much bigger). Thus, the man's alternative is between having one's favorite food served constantly and having no variety, versus never having one's favorite food and having to go hungry much of the time. In addition to sex, marriage confers on men a number of other benefits (physical and mental health, love and social support, and so on), thus increasing the attractiveness of the martrimonial bond. Viewed either in its entirety or just in terms of sex, marriage is too attractive to forgo, at least for most men. But it is not perfectly attuned to the man's sexual wishes either.

This is then another facet of the tragedy of the male sex drive: It structures his situation with these choices, none of which is ideal. If only he could be content with one woman, he would be much better off.

Are All Men Promiscuously Inclined?

Thus far we have revealed how the male sex drive differs from the female. It seems to be stronger and to have a greater appetite for variety. On many measures, men show a much greater desire for casual sex and for multiple partners than women show. Evolutionary theorists point out that such a pattern is a very likely result of the difference between men's and women's reproductive systems.

Still, are all men that way? Undoubtedly there are plenty of exceptions in both genders. There are women who eagerly, cheerfully have sex with dozens of men. Meanwhile, there are plenty of men who seem quite content to remain married to the same women for decades without ever being unfaithful to her. Are these men simply making the best of an unsatisfactory solution?

Let us return to the data on desired number of sex partners obtained by Miller and Fishkin (1997). As we indicated, the mean number reported by male college students was 64, which is to say that on average they said that ideally they would like to have sex with 64 women during the rest of their lives. The women's mean was 2.7. This makes it look like men and women are from different planets, as a recent popular book contended. On the other hand, the median number for both men and women was 1.

This discrepancy was considered in Chapter 2, in our discussion of methodological concerns in the social analysis of sexuality. We have to return to it here, because the meaning of the results (as opposed to their capacity to illustrate a methodological point) is highly relevant. The median is a different kind of average from the mean. To get the mean, you add up all the answers and divide by the number of answers. To get the median, you arrange all the answers in order from lowest to highest and then count halfway through the total number. The median is the number that indicates the fiftieth percentile: Half the responses are equal to or less than the median, and half are equal to or greater than the median.

For example, suppose the question about the ideal number of sex partners were put to 16 men. If one man says he wants to have sex with 1,000 women, and the other 15 men say they want 1 each, the median is 1, but the mean is very close to 64. To say 64 is the "average" is correct in one sense but misleading in another. Only one of the men gave an answer higher than 1, which makes 64 an odd "average." And nobody gave an answer that was anywhere close to 64.

Thus, at least half the women AND half the men said that they would ideally like to have sex with just one partner for the rest of their lives. In this respect, men and women appear far more similar than different. Plenty of men seem to want just the same thing that plenty of women want, which is one person to sleep with, period.

You might wonder how the means can be so different if the medians are the same. Means can be affected by a few extreme numbers. Medians can't, which is why researchers prefer medians in many contexts. On the sex partner issue, the mean of 64 was not based on having all the men give answers that were in the 60s. Rather, plenty of men gave answers of 1. Others said they wanted to go to bed with hundreds or even thousands of different women. The big numbers pulled the average up. Since few or no women said they'd like to have such large numbers of sex partners, the women's mean did not move far from their median.

What would the evolutionary theorists say about that? They would point out that monogamous men would certainly be able to pass along their genes, even if they would not be as widely scattered as the promiscuous ones. Moreover, a man who mates with and stays with a single woman can provide more for his children than the man who moves on rapidly to another mate, and so the children of monogamous men would have an advantage in terms of surviving to the age where they would reproduce.

Biologists distinguish between two reproductive strategies, which they call *r*-selected and *K*-selected (Gould & Gould, 1997). The *r*-selected strategies focus on quantity: Produce as many offspring as possible. The *K*-selected ones focus on quality: Produce only a few offspring and take maximum care of them. The patterns were identified in order to describe different species; some kinds of fish will produce thousands or millions of offspring but most will die before reproducing, while most mammals will produce far fewer offspring but invest far more in making certain that most of them survive. Humans are very, very far along on *K*-strategy continuum compared to other species and even compared to other mammals; we have only a few children and invest a lot in helping them to survive. But one may by analogy examine differences between men and women as reflecting the different strategies. Applied to human beings, it is clear that women are of necessity more geared toward the K-strategy than men, because a human female can hardly ever produce more than a dozen or so children. Although the male might lean by nature toward the r-strategy of sowing lots of wild oats and impregnating as many women as possible, the K-strategy will also work for him (especially insofar as most women won't cooperate with his r-oriented hankerings). If a man really wants to pass on his genes, an effective and workable strategy would be to find one good mate, remain faithful (more or less) to her, and provide well for their children. Hence for men both strategies (monogamy and promiscuity) are viable.

There is even a further basis in evolutionary theory for proposing that some men will be inclined toward promiscuity and others will not. If we consider what sort of social organization prevailed in the distant past, before the rise of democracy and monogamy and other principles of modern life, it is probably the one common among species most similar to humans—the alpha male system. The alpha male is the dominant male, which usually means a strong adult at the peak of his powers. Being the chief, he can enforce his preferences on the group, which include considering all the females to be his exclusive sex partners. Other males are allowed to live in the group as long as they submit to his rule and keep away from the women.

At least, that is the system in theory. It is commonly remarked by observers of such groups that other males will occasionally manage to have sex with a female here or there. But they have to make sure the alpha male does not find out.

Thus, the social system in these groups, at least in principle, operates this way. One male gets to have sex with plenty of females. The other males get little or no sex. Our evolutionary past is full of males who had relatively few opportunities for sexual gratification. Maybe they managed to sneak in enough sex to pass on their genes. Still, they weren't able to indulge their promiscuous preferences. Indeed, the better they were able to accept a relatively celibate life, the better they were able to live in the group. If they really insisted on trying to mate with all the women, a conflict with the alpha male would probably arise, and as a result the male (unless he was able to defeat the alpha male and take his place) might be injured, killed, or driven from the group.

Having a weaker, less promiscuous sex drive might therefore be adaptive for some males, especially the less dominant ones. After all, the alpha male could have whatever he wanted, more or less, and certainly some other males would want to replace him. Eventually one would. The alpha male could have many more children than other males.

If one turns away from evolutionary reasoning and looks instead at more proximal causes in social structure, the same result seems likely. A few males can manage to be highly promiscuous, especially ones who are powerful and eminent and can therefore offer more to a woman. But most men would have to be content with far fewer sex partners—indeed, zero or one. Most societies in the history of the world have practiced polygamy (one man with several wives). Obviously, however, only the rich and powerful men could support multiple wives. And unless there was a huge surplus of women—which is fairly rare—polygamy leads to deprivation for some men. The rich man may have a dozen wives, but that means that eleven other men may end up with no wives at all.

Before we regard this question as settled, however, it is important to reflect on a seeming inconsistency between some research findings from different studies. Let us revisit the Clark and Hatfield (1989) study, in which a young woman of about average attractiveness approached attractive men at random and asked them whether they would like to go to bed with her that night. Three-quarters of them said yes.

That result does not square well with Miller and Fishkin's (1997) finding that half the young men in their sample expressed a preference for having only one sex partner for the rest of their lives. If both findings are to be taken literally, and if both can be generalized to the broader population of young men, then one must assume that many of the men who agreed to have sex with Clark and Hatfield's female confederate wanted her to be their only sex partner ever.

This would be especially remarkable given that Clark and Hatfield's confederate did not promise anything else beyond one night of sex. Would these men really have been content to have sex only once, and with this woman, and then never again for the rest of their lives? Were these men going around with the hope of having only one sex partner ever, so that when the woman approached them, they thought, "This is it, this is the one and only"?

One way to reconcile these seemingly incompatible findings is through adaptation level theory and levels of aspiration. Many young men are not having sex. Either they have never had it, or at most they had a little sex with someone who is no longer available to them, so that it has been a long time since they had sex.

It is quite plausible that one lowers one's aspirations to be only one level above what one has. The men who aren't having any sex may well think that what they most want is to have one sex partner. They don't perhaps dream of having dozens of women, because such dreams would make their present circumstances seem all the more deprived and pathetic. To find one woman is a realistic aspiration for the man who has none.

In contrast, men who have had several sex partners may aspire to have several more. Those who have had several recently—a small but important percentage of the population—might well feel comfortable aspiring to have dozens, or hundreds, or perhaps even thousands. A few of these could be enough to pull a mean up to 64, especially in a small sample.

This way of fitting the findings together is plausible. It does, however, return us to the tragic aspect of the male sex drive: One is never satisfied. Adaptation level was labeled the "hedonic treadmill" by some social psychologists (Brickman & Campbell, 1971), because each time one takes a step forward, one soon ends up in the same place. Just as the person who had a $25,000 salary was only briefly overjoyed when he got a raise to $30,000 and soon was dreaming again of another raise, perhaps with each advance in sexual experience, men soon start to want more. Of the men who say they would be happy with only one sex partner in life, perhaps some are correct, but most likely some others would not be. It seems to them as if one would be enough, because one would be such an improvement over none. But if they had one, they would soon want another. And another.

The Zulu Compromise

One of the most interesting questions about male sexuality is whether it can effectively accept halfway measures. If young (unmarried) males can really remain content with an intermediate amount of sexual gratification, then it makes sense to relax the permissiveness toward adolescent sexual activity, although stopping short of intercourse. But if halfway measures simply increase the number illicitly going all the way, then it is preferable to adopt a less permissive attitude toward adolescent sexuality.

This can be illustrated by considering a set of sexual norms that were practiced by the Zulus and other Bantu tribes of South Africa before white people arrived, back around the time of the American Revolution. All the unmarried youngsters of the tribe past the age of puberty were permitted to gather together in one place to neck and pet. They were not supposed to go all the way to full intercourse (Morris, 1965).

In theory at least, this sytem has much to recommend it. The young men and women themselves would benefit from being able to indulge their hormones to some extent, to feel the joys of hugging, kissing, and possibly even stroking of each other. Certainly this would be much nicer for them than having all physical contact with the opposite gender prevented. Meanwhile, the presence of everyone else would constitute a form of surveillance that would in principle be difficult to avoid, and this would presumably help prevent the young couples from crossing the line. Thus it offers something for everyone: The young people get some pleasures that they dearly want, and the society is spared the disruption of unwanted pregnancies, forced marriages, spread of disease, and the other problems that arise from all-out promiscuity.

But does it work? The question is whether the teens would really be content with the partial degrees of physical intimacy as opposed to simply being encouraged to go all the way. Each pleasure may make people want more, and couples who have been necking and petting for years and love each other might be tempted to show their affection by doing something more than what the other kids are doing.

In a way, it is a form of the "commons dilemma," a term that is commonly referred to in circumstances that make the pursuit of individual self-interest detrimental to the group's self-interest. (The concept derives from the word for a communal pasture open to any herd; individual farmers and shepherds tended to overgraze it.) With regard to sex, an individual young person (or couple) may gain by going father than everyone else, but this spoils it for everyone else. If teen pregnancies and other problems arise, the group necking sessions might have to be stopped. This is in a sense tragic for the other young people, because they are then deprived of their pleasures. Everyone would be better off if everyone would respect those limits. But don't bet on it.

Tragic or Merely Pathetic?

One of us recalls discussing the idea of gender differences in sexual desire with a colleague, who thought that men and women in reality desired fairly similar things. In many respects they do, but I held that some differences couldn't be ignored. So I said, imagine a woman who is walking through an airport or train station. Unexpectedly she catches a glimpse of some random man's underpants. He is just a stranger sitting there as she walks by. He is absorbed in reading the newspaper and doesn't realize that passersby can see his underpants.

Can we imagine that, later that evening, the woman would think back on that momentary glimpse with pleasure? That she would deliberately relive it from memory? Can we imagine that that was the high point of her day (assuming, in all fairness, that the day of traveling wasn't that great in general)? Or, going back to when she first sees him, can we picture her reaching her departure gate, turning around to walk past the man again, and then a third time glimpsing him as she found her way back to her gate?

Most people find that difficult to imagine. It seems quite implausible. But reverse the genders, and it does become quite imaginable. Not for all men, and not on all occasions, but often enough. It is certainly quite conceivable that a man would feel and do all those things to see a woman's underpants.

My colleague conceded the point but made a very thought-provoking observation, to which I had no answer. She said, "Men are lucky; they are fortunate to be able to get so much pleasure from so little." I had thought she'd think my anecdote pathetic if not disgusting. Instead, she seemed to be a bit envious that many men could get such a charge out of a stolen glimpse of some random woman's panties. I had never thought about it that way.

What I should have said, though, was that men are not to be envied, because they pay dearly for those small bursts of pleasure. Men enjoy those glimpses so much precisely because they are denied them most of the time. In Victorian times, men would get "hot and bothered" (sexually activated) if they caught a glimpse of a woman's ankle under her long skirt. When ankles are freely displayed to public view, men don't bother wasting a glance on them. Likewise, hardly any regular male beach-goer gets much of a charge out of looking at a woman's swimsuit, even though it might be more revealing than the glimpse of panties up the skirt. When the woman doesn't hide something, it isn't exciting, and above all it isn't satisfying to see it.

And, more to the point, the men are wanting these things but not having them most of the time. The crucial factor is the sum of all the panties he doesn't see. Many a young man spends most of his life in frustration and deprivation, in a vague, never-satisfied state of sexual tension. The stolen glimpse up the skirt or down the neckline is, relatively speaking, a small payoff for all the long hours and days of not being satisfied, for the many times he glances at the knees of all the women seated in the room and cannot see any panties at all.

One of us had a sister who became vice president of the Hanes underwear company. The firm had a lean period and sales were down, and she mentioned to me that they were looking for ways to boost profits. I suggested that she should have the women in the factory each wear a new pair of panties every day and then deposit them in a bin upon leaving work, so the preworn panties could be sold to male fetishists and other mild perverts. I thought the markup would be quite substantial, a way to boost the profit margin without any additional expenses. She thought it was a very funny joke. She repeated it to several colleagues at the firm, and they all had a laugh.

Shortly after that a news item appeared. An American reporter had discovered in Japan a vending machine that sold preworn, unwashed young women's panties, which were considerably more expensive than what a comparable pair would cost if purchased new. Clearly, the cash value of the item was greatly enhanced by the fact that it had been worn recently by a young woman. It is initially hard to fathom why a man (the vending customers were men, obviously) would pay extra money for a piece of clothing that had already been worn and that had certainly little practical value for him. The only apparent explanation is that men found it sexually exciting to possess panties that had recently been worn by a woman they never knew nor even saw.

The excitement of panties is linked to a form of superstitious thinking that may have been common in the premodern era but that also continues to exist in modern life. Experiments on a very different emotional reaction—disgust—have been conducted by Rozin, Millman, and Nemeroff (1986). According to what they call the "law of contagion," much superstitious thinking is based on a belief that things that were once in contact remain in contact. Witches or others who wish to cast a magic spell on someone, for example, may try to gain something that has once been in contact with that person, such as hair or fingernail clippings or clothing. They may then destroy those items on the assumption that the harm will be magically transferred from the things to the person to whom they belonged.

Although such magical thinking may sound primitive and unscientific, Rozin and his colleagues demonstrated that many university students still behave as if it were true. In one study, for example, the researchers offered the students a glass of apple juice. Before the student drank it, the researcher put a sterilized dead cockroach into the glass of juice and then removed it, leaving the juice exactly as it was before. Yet most students were no longer willing to drink the juice, and many even refused to drink a fresh glass of different apple juice poured into a clean glass! Clearly their responses suggested that they felt some continuing link between the cockroach and the glass of apple juice (or indeed to all apple juice).

The fascination with panties invokes the same style of magical thinking, and indeed some fetish behavior may be based on that principle. (Women's panties are, after all, one of the principal foci of fetishes among men.) It seems reasonable to assume that the basic, natural (original) sexual desire of the man is for the woman and her genitals. The panties were in contact with that intimate part of the body, and so some men found it exciting to possess them as if they retained some contact or connection to the woman's genitals.

Are such desires tragic or merely pathetic? It seems degrading and undignified for these men to be reduced to paying for used, unwashed underwear. The lack of dignity points toward the harsher judgment of being pathetic. Tragedy, in the sense described by Arthur Miller (1978), involves showing some positive aspect of human nature and some striving for a fine outcome or ideal, which may be difficult to identify in the purchase of preworn panties. On the other hand, one might see these men as tragic figures trapped by their own inner sexual desires in a world that permits them few means of reaching satisfaction. The humiliation of paying for strangers' unwashed panties is the tragic fall itself.

Whatever value judgment one makes, the power of the drive can scarcely be denied. That men will willingly part with some of their money and some of their dignity for the sake of a minor sexual thrill is revealing. It is reminiscent of the underfed conscientious objectors who were reduced to reading books of recipes and replaying film scenes of banquets in an attempt to satisfy their longings for food. At least for the conscientious objectors, the experiment eventually came to an end, and they were able to eat freely again.

Should the Man Buy the Cow?

We have now seen the dimensions of the problem that faces many men in terms of sexuality. This permits us to assess an interesting basic question about social life in modern Western society: Are marriage and monogamy good for men? Several simple answers can immediately be suggested, but perhaps the correct answer is far from simple.

One simple answer is no, based on the promiscuity of male desire. As we have seen in this and previous chapters, there is a fair amount of evidence that many men's sexual desires include a basic wish to have multiple partners, including periodically finding new ones with whom to enjoy the special thrill of novelty. Settling down with one person is a matter of accepting less than the ideal. The man who promises to remain with his wife "till death do us part" and particularly "to forsake all others" on his wedding day is making a sad compromise, for he believes that his bride is the last woman he will ever have sex with in his entire life. This, after all, was one of the traditional rationales for having a bachelor party on the night before the wedding: Henceforth the man would have no further sex partners, so he has one last fling before settling down.

The assumption has long been that women desire marriage, while men resist it. The stereotypical advice of grandmother to granddaughter is to withhold sex until marriage, because sex is the main incentive by which the woman can convince him to marry her: Why should he buy the cow if he can get the milk for free?

But that is not a full consideration of the matter. Let us look at the question from all angles before we make an assessment.

Darwin's Dilemma

Charles Darwin is justifiably famous for his discovery of the mechanism of evolution via natural selection. It is less known that the same year (1838) in which he made this important discovery, his thoughts were also occupied with a far more common question: whether to marry. He was twenty-nine years old and attracted to his cousin Emma Wedgwood. As luck would have it, his thoughts on the latter question have survived to the present, because he jotted them down on a slip paper that has been preserved in the Cambridge University Library (Macfarlane, 1986).

Darwin was sufficiently troubled by the decision that he used the paper to draw up a list of pros and cons. He titled one column "Marry," and underneath wrote the advantages of marriage as he saw them; he headed the other column "Not Marry," and underneath listed the potential drawbacks. The advantages focused on companionship, especially old age. He did mention the possibility of having children ("If it please God") but spent little time on that alleged advantage. The possible wife was described as a "constant companion" who would be interested in him and would be an "object to be beloved and played with—better than a dog anyhow." Having someone keep house was another advantage, plus the daily pleasures of "Classics of Music and female Chit Chat." The reference to music probably referred to the difficulty of hearing music in the days before recorded or broadcast music. Most girls of the middle classes took piano lessons, and so as adults they were able to play for their husbands. This consideration is less relevant to today's men, because music is freely available without a wife. As for the pleasures of "female Chit Chat," well, those are presumably alive and well.

Under the disadvantages, Darwin listed the loss of freedom to go where and do what he liked. The opportunity to hang out with the guys was seen as possibly lost, and this was a serious consideration in an era when most educated people were men, so that male company offered the main opportunity for intelligent conversation. The possibility that his wife would turn out to be an "idle, indolent fool" was listed, and this risk was increased by the worry that if she did not like living in London, he would have to face relentless boredom living with the empty-headed wife out in the country. Visits with in-laws represented more threats of boredom. Boredom was not the only emotional risk: There might also be anxieties from the added responsibilities, as well as the distress that might result from quarreling. The disadvantages were rounded out with the loss of free time for reading, the need to give in over every trifling issue, and the potentially heavy expenses of raising a family. (Nineteenth-century women did not earn money, so a man's marriage decision carried a substantial financial dimension that is mostly lacking in today's society.)

Sex did not appear on either list. To Darwin's mind, apparently, neither the loss of sexual freedom nor the gain of a regular partner was a significant factor in the decision. Indeed, the paper contains his own resolution: "Marry. Marry. Marry. Q.E.D" (all quotations from Macfarlane, 1986, pp. 3–5). He proposed to Emma, and they were married later that year.

The Broader Context: Culture, Nature, and Monogamy

Marriage occurs in all known human societies, and this apparent universality suggests that it has some natural basis in innate human tendencies. Then again, it is not simply a carryover from our evolutionary past, because other species do not marry as humans do. Smuts (1996) has provided evidence (from papers by Rodspeth and colleagues) that forming long-term, stable pair bonds is a practice that is largely unique to humans, at least among the primates. This discrepancy suggests that something special about human culture produces marriage—although, again, it is something that pretty much every culture handles in the same way.

To be sure, there are some cultures in which multiple simultaneous marriage is possible. Polygamy (one husband, multiple wives) occurs in various places, and although polyandry (one wife, multiple husbands) is rarer, it is not unknown. Even apart from formal marriage, there have often been quasi-multiple-mate systems in which one man will have a primary wife but also a mistress or concubine so high-status hubby can get a little on the side.

Still, the marital pair bond is quite widespread and robust. Even cultures that permit multiple marriage seem to be quite familiar with the two-person marriage. It is probably the most common social bond, along with parent-child, in the world.

Why does monogamous marriage occur with such frequency? Presumably it satisfies something powerful in the human psyche. In particular, it must appeal to men, insofar as men have generally held the political power to make the laws and social practices within which marriage exists. If marriage were disadvantageous to men, it is doubtful that it would have persisted so long in its present form.

Legal and Practical Considerations

The appeal of marriage to men can be debated in rational terms. In today's United States, marriage is a legal contract between two people, and the terms of this contract do not seem to be advantageous to the average man. Financially, the resources of the couple are merged, and if they divorce, they are generally split in a somewhat even fashion. Because men usually earn and have more money (and other resources) than their wives, the man loses out financially by marriage. The essence of the marriage bargain, at least when considered in purely financial terms, is that the man shares his resources with a poorer partner. In addition, some courts still impose alimony and other financial penalties on the man, so if he marries a woman and divorces her, he leaves with much greater financial obligations than he would have if he had not married her.

Many people marry in order to have children, but it is manifestly not necessary to marry in order to have children. Does marriage improve a man's prospects with respect to children? In the current legal situation, a man's options are few. He has little control over whether the woman becomes pregnant, unless he avoids having sex with her; contraception is largely under the woman's control. If she becomes pregnant, the decision of whether to bear the child or have an abortion is almost entirely the woman's, and the man can neither require nor prevent the abortion against the woman's will, whereas she can carry out either decision against his will. She can also decide to leave him, with or without divorce, and given the current legal biases, his chances for retaining custody of the children are small if the woman wants them. His relationship to his children can be reduced to being billed for their financial support. All of these things can happen regardless of whether he is married, but in general his vulnerabilities are greater if he is.

Last, one must reckon with the possibility that he will eventually become disenchanted with the woman and wish to leave her, either to be alone or (more commonly) to form a relationship with someone else. In such a case, it is clear that marriage puts him in a poorer position. If he is not married, he can dissolve the earlier relationship and move on rather easily, but marriage makes it much more difficult and expensive to do so.

These considerations pertain to the present world. They suggest that marriage offers a man little in the way of direct benefits, although it does weaken his legal and financial situation while depriving him of easy options for altering his social and romantic life. The appeal of having sex might offset those sufficiently to encourage men to marry despite those costs, as the grandmotherly advice suggested, but in today's society it is possible for men to obtain sexual partners without marriage, and so sex does not seems a sufficient reason.

Despite all these drawbacks, men do continue to marry. Grandmother was thus at least partly wrong: Men continue to buy the cow. The financial and legal drawbacks of marriage are apparently offset by some other, less tangible benefits.

Some Benefits of Marriage

A very different cost-benefit analysis of marriage was put forward by Bernard in her influential book, *The Future of Marriage* (1982). Writing at the height of the feminist movement, Bernard reviewed an assortment of data and concluded that marriage is actually quite beneficial for men while being harmful and costly for women. Although subsequent research has questioned her conclusions about women—it turns out, not surprisingly, that marriage is good for women too—no one has seriously questioned the considerable benefits that marriage confers on men.

The data about the benefits of marriage are thus beyond dispute. In the first place, there is a difference in simple happiness: Married men are happier than single men. This is a consistent finding across many studies and measures (e.g., Argyle, 1987; Campbell, 1981).

The health and safety benefits are impressive. Married men are healthier than single men in both mind and body. That is, they suffer fewer physical illnesses (and recover faster when they do fall ill) as well as fewer psychological problems. Ultimately, married men live longer. Despite the widely quoted quip that "Married men don't live longer—it just seems longer," the facts are clear that marriage boosts life expectancy.

Married men even benefit in terms of the dangers of accidents and crime. Single men are more likely to be murdered than married men, and probably most other crimes likewise take a heavier toll on single than married men. Single men have more traffic accidents than married men.

Some of these statistics have been questioned on methodological grounds. After all, researchers do not randomly assign people to marry or remain single, and so we cannot be certain that married men were not healthier and saner than single men to begin with. Undoubtedly serious psychological problems make some men less attractive as potential spouses, and so women may simply choose the better men and leave the others behind. Likewise, men who are prone to engaging in criminal activity are themselves more vulnerable to becoming victims of crime, and women may find such men less appealing as potential husbands.

Then again, there are several reasons to believe that marriage confers some direct benefits, even if part of the discrepancy in outcomes is due to the men's own inner properties. For one thing, men show elevated rates of risks and problems when they divorce, and these rates subside when they remarry, so the same men seem to change for the better under the influence of marriage. Likewise, a comparison of Catholic and Protestant clergy (Bernard, 1982) found that the Protestants, who marry, are better off than the Catholics, who do not, and it is difficult to argue that Protestant clergy are inherently different kinds of people than Catholic ones; again, it looks like marriage plays a causal role.

There are even sexual benefits to marriage. We say "even" because sex is supposedly an area in which married men make the large sacrifice of forsaking all other partners and trying to overcome their basic promiscuous desires in order to remain faithful to a single wife. Yet as we have seen, married men do have sex more often than single men (e.g., Laumann et al., 1994). Moreover, judged purely on technical merit, sex with a familiar partner is likely to be superior to sex with a new, first-time partner, simply because the familiar one knows what you like. The new partner may benefit considerably from the excitement of novelty, but she lacks the personalized knowledge of how to give the man the most pleasure.

Marriage or Monogamy?

Then again, most of the data we have discussed show the benefits of marriage, which is not necessarily the same as monogamy. The Chinese emperors married too, but they also maintained a sort of harem containing over a hundred other women, including mistresses and concubines, and they would have sex with all of them regularly (in theory, at least). The benefits of marriage do not necessarily depend on forsaking all other sex partners, especially if the wife can be persuaded to tolerate some infidelity on the man's part.

True, the position of the Chinese emperor is no longer available. Yet Western history and modern society have offered various lucky men the chance to decide their own arrangements, within very broad constraints. In fact, it is easier for a social scientist to determine what men want than what women want, simply by looking at the historical record. This is because women have usually had less political power, whereas individual men have periodically been in a position to set things up to suit themselves.

A review of such findings by Betzig (1986) concluded that there is a fairly consistent pattern to the sex lives of powerful men. They generally choose to marry, but they also arrange to have a steady flow of other women with whom they have sexual affairs ranging from one-night encounters to multiyear affairs. The male kings and emperors of Europe, for example, would almost always have a queen, which is to say a long-term wife. Yet they would also have mistresses and concubines, and many probably also continued to carry on sexual trysts with various women at the royal court.

Even in modern life, the situation is the same. President Clinton was widely admired for the partnership he had with his wife, Hillary. He also achieved notoriety because of his affair with Monica Lewinsky, and various other women accused him of assorted sexual misbehavior. Even if all the allegations are correct, Clinton appears to have led a relatively tame life in comparison with President John Kennedy, who by one account (Hersch, 1997) had daily sessions of nude swimming in the White House pool (at least when his wife, Jackie, was out of town) with female staff and employed several men whose primary function was to bring him new sex partners frequently, a job that included intimidating the women (many of whom were prostitutes) into remaining silent afterward. Kennedy is said to have remarked, "You know, I get a migraine headache if I don't get a strange [i.e., unfamiliar and novel] piece of ass every day" (Hersch, 1997, p.

389). The Secret Service men who were assigned to guard the president's life found that their duties included protecting his privacy for his sexual trysts. Some found the presidential sexual escapades amusing, while others had serious ethical or professional objections and were very disturbed by that aspect of the job (Hersch, 1997). According to other sources (Steyn, 1997), some members of the Secret Service were even instructed to lend a hand: When the president would have sex with a young lady in the White House bathtub, the Secret Service agent was supposed to watch until the president approached orgasm, whereupon he was to push the woman's head under the water. The lack of air caused her vagina to contract, thereby enhancing Kennedy's pleasure.

Kennedy had at least two major advantages over Clinton. First, at the time the media followed a code of respecting the president's privacy, a code that was gone by the time Clinton came along. Second, Kennedy had his brother serving as attorney general, who, as the top law enforcement official in the country, had considerable power to restrict investigations into presidential misconduct. Clinton, in contrast, was publicly humiliated by the investigations chaired by a special investigator who was appointed by his attorney general.

In any case, it is clear that powerful men who can do whatever they want generally prefer to have it both ways: They seek the advantages of marriage but also the pleasures of sexual variety. Nor are the American presidents the only relevant examples of men who can have it their own way. Professional athletes are widely regarded as attractive mates by many women (for reasons that are not entirely clear), and with their vast wealth and fame, these men have the ability to set things up as they want. They too seem to want to have it both ways: Most of them marry, but they also enjoy a continuing assortment of sexual adventures with other women. According to Benedict (1997), a common joke in the National Basketball Association runs like this: "What's the hardest thing about going on the road in the NBA? Trying not to smile when you kiss your wife goodbye before the trip." These men enjoy the benefits of marriage when at home, but their frequent travels give them ample opportunity to sample the charms of the many women who offer themselves to sports stars.

Alternatives to Marriage

Thus, marriage and monogamy can be distinguished to some extent. Still, for the most part, marriage entails monogamy in our society, and so the question of whether this arrangement is good for men is worth considering. Nor should this question be considered in a vacuum but rather in the context of the question "Compared to what?"

In principle, there are three ways in which societies can manage sexuality, and one of them is fairly unusual in reality. One alternative is the alpha male system, which certainly has been the most common in the history of the world, especially if one includes the evolutionary history of other primates. The second is monogamy. The third is widespread promiscuity, with a casual changing of partners (married or unmarried).

The last of these, general promiscuity, has never flourished for long in human history. There have been pockets of it, such as perhaps at the royal courts in medieval Europe (although it is doubtful that the promiscuity was even so "general" there; more likely there were rules, restrictions, and problems). The United States approached it briefly in the 1970s, with great increases in premarital and extramarital sex, including swinging or mate-swapping parties for married couples.

Bailey and Aunger (1995) described some societies in Africa that continue to operate in that fashion. Unfortunately, the costs are high: Venereal disease spreads rapidly, and these infections take a toll on both sexes. Women become sterile at an alarming rate, and so many couples cannot have children. The American phase of swinging appears to have stopped right around the time that a pair of incurable venereal diseases began to spread. The herpes virus epidemic sent a chill through many people who were enjoying casual sex. And then the AIDS epidemic equated sex with death, and that made the herpes scare seem trivial in comparison.

The main alternative to monogamy is therefore the alpha male system in which the top-ranking man enjoys regular sex with an assortment of women, who in theory remain faithful to him, although in practice he may or may not be able to prevent being cuckolded here and there. Apart from these furtive, occasional, surreptitious flings, the other men live in celibacy.

How does that stack up against monogamy? The alpha male himself is seemingly better off with the alpha male system, where he has multiple women, than under monogamy, where he is presumably confined to a single woman. On the other hand, all the rest of the men are better off with monogamy. After all, one sex partner is far more than zero. The alpha male system consigns the majority of men to celibacy with only occasional, intermittent respites, and undoubtedly most men would prefer marriage. Hence, in an important sense, monogamous marriage is genuinely better for the majority of men.

Some may even question how well off the alpha male is. Certainly he seems to have an enviable situation, as long as he is on top. But the alpha male's reign is often tenuous. The younger men are restless under celibacy, and many wish to replace him. Once he loses his alpha status, he is unlikely to regain it, and so he faces celibacy for the rest of his life. So from that point on, even he might have preferred monogamy.

There is one more question, and it is perhaps the most profound and difficult: Is the man really any happier under promiscuity than under monogamy? Is even the alpha male at the peak of his reign happier? The fact that men who lack his options envy him is not, itself, convincing.

It is necessary to consider the adaptation-level effect once more. Men seem doomed to remain on the hedonic treadmill: No matter what they get, they soon wish for more. This may apply in sex too. Men are never satisfied. True, the celibate males may envy the alpha male, but is the alpha really happier than the well married, monogamous American man of today?

The tragedy of the male sex drive is that a man cannot be fully satisfied, sexually, no matter what. Life is a matter of coming to terms with unfulfillment. Whatever sex he gets is not enough. Each step into new territory brings some period of happiness and satisfaction, but in the long run he reverts to discontent and to longing for more.

Thus, the alpha male may have half a dozen women at his disposal, but after a while these may not be enough. Sure, when he first becomes the alpha male, he is likely to have a euphoric phase of sleeping with different women and enjoying all their charms. Once they have lost their novelty, however, and once he grows accustomed to them, he may find himself casting his eyes elsewhere, such as on the harem of another alpha male in a rival tribe. In any case, although he may like having sex with them, it will gradually lose its thrill.

This is, after all, what typically happens in monogamous marriage in our society today, and probably the effect was even more pronounced in previous generations, when premarital sex was fairly rare. The man desires the woman immensely, and when marriage (or at least engagement) finally brings her into his bed, he has a euphoric period of frequent, intensely satisfying sex. And then, as the years go by, the thrill wears off. After having sex with her a hundred or a thousand times, it can no longer produce the passion that it did those first times. Once he thought he would be happy forever if he could only sleep with this woman he loved so much. Years later, he still loves her, but sex with her is no longer the stuff of his dreams.

The implications for society are important. There is simply no arrangement that can provide ongoing satisfaction to men. Whatever level of sexual pleasure they get, they may want more. This is not to say that all possible arrangements are exactly equal. The extremes in particular may be different. When men have almost no sexual opportunities at all, they may be especially malcontent and dissatisfied, and their misbehavior may cause problems. At the other extreme, tolerance of full promiscuity throughout life may be the best way of providing men with satisfaction, especially in a large society where the supply of new sex partners is essentially unlimited. But this sytem does not work in practice. It spreads disease, and women may not like it at all.

For men, then, perhaps the only escape from sexual frustration is the cessation of sexual desire. This may be almost impossible for young men to achieve, although some religious systems have tried. With advancing age, however, some men do seem to reach the point at which the sex drive dwindles toward nothing. That is the fact with which we began this chapter, and we return to it now. It is perhaps understandable why men would not long for a restoration of their sex drive. Lasting peace and satisfaction may only be possible without it.

It's a major trade-off, though. He is free of the long horny hours, weeks, even years—but also loses those precious moments of intense bliss.

A Question of Timing

Our analysis suggests that men should want to get married, given the benefits and advantages. Yet this does not square easily with the popular perception that men are reluctant to commit. How can these two positions be reconciled?

The stereotypical conflict involves a young woman who wants to marry and a man who is reluctant. His foot-dragging suggests that he is reluctant to make a commitment or even that he does not want to get married. Yet perhaps that is an illusion; perhaps he merely wants to remain single for now. He may think that marriage will be fine, even desirable, down the line, but at the moment he is reluctant.

There are good reasons for this. More generally, our analysis has concluded that men should want to marry eventually, but that does not mean that men should be eager to get married as soon as the opportunity arises.

One traditional reason to postpone marriage is financial. We saw this in Darwin's considerations: Marrying was expensive, because the salary that had supported the man during his single years suddenly had to be stretched to support a wife and children. Hence he might want to postpone marriage until he has reached a higher salary and more secure career position.

The financial considerations are perhaps less relevant today, because most wives will bring in some money, which means that the increased strain on the man's income resulting from marriage will be less. But there is another consideration. The longer the man waits, at least up until a point, the better position he will hold in the marriage market. The opposite may be true for the woman, and so man and woman are fated to be in conflict on the optimal timing of marriage.

Let us return to the widely recognized nature of social exchange in marriage. Men are desirable in proportion to their status and resources. Women are desirable in proportion to their youth and beauty. (Other traits such as honesty and intelligence are important too, and to both, but those are not relevant to this analysis.) In an optimal marriage, therefore, a rich and successful man will marry a young and beautiful bride.

The time course of those qualities is quite different, however, and so men's and women's prospects push them in different directions regarding the timing of marital commitment. Youth is by definition fleeting, and the longer a woman waits to marry, the less of it she has. Beauty is correlated with youth, and it is undeniable that women tend to lose their good looks as they get older. A woman will therefore be in the strongest position for attracting the best possible husband early in her adult life.

In contrast, the nature of modern organizational careers involves a slow climb up the pyramid of success. Waiting longer will permit a man to climb higher. The average man has more status and money in his thirties than in his twenties. As such, he will be in a better position for attracting the best possible partner if he waits. True, there are probably limits, and the man who waits until he is sixty years old may find that he has missed his best chances for marriage. But during the marrying decades of young adulthood, each man may find that his prospects improve year by year.

Time thus pushes men and women in different directions, particularly early in adult life, when marriage is possible. It is rational for a woman to seek a good partner fairly early, while she is still in the full bloom of youth and beauty. But it is rational for a man to delay and postpone, so that his prospects become better. We do find it fully rational for men to marry in the long run—but mainly in the long run, rather than right away. It would be foolish for the average man to reject marital commitment altogether, but it is often eminently sensible for him to want to postpone it.

Managing Your Man

Before closing, it is of interest to return explicitly to the female perspective and consider the key implications of this analysis of male sex drive. If it is correct, then a woman can use it as a basis for planning her strategy of how to have a successful marriage. Of course, if it is not correct in some crucial way, you should alter your plan accordingly. But we think it looks like a good fit based on the (admittedly incomplete) information we have.

The first implication has to do with what level of monogamy and fidelity a woman can expect from her husband. Our analysis does *not* mean that a woman should just give up and permit a man to do whatever he wants. There are extensive data showing that men are in general entirely capable of monogamous fidelity.

The crucial distinction is between desire and behavior. It is linked to one of the most basic and powerful distinctions in all of psychology, which is the difference between *automatic* and *controlled* responses (Bargh, 1982, 1989, 1994, 1997; Schneider & Shiffrin, 1977). Automatic things happen immediately, whether you want them or not. Controlled things may or may not happen, depending on your conscious decision. For example, fear of falling is automatic. If you start to fall from a high place, you will feel that inner lurch and panic that is built into human nature. In contrast, an investment decision is something you can control.

Our analysis of male sexuality suggests that desire is automatic, but that behavior is controlled. Men cannot therefore stop themselves from wanting, but they can stop themselves from doing. There is no point in getting angry at your husband for feeling sexual desire toward other women on the beach, because he cannot refrain from feeling that desire. You can, however, expect him to keep his hands to himself and his pants fully zipped. But complaining about his feeling interest or desire toward pictures of nude women, assuming he sees those pictures, is like complaining about the rain or heat: You may not approve of it, but you really can't stop it.

This is not the same, however, as not letting him see the pictures or the women on the beach. We claim only that if he sees them, his desire is probably not preventable. Whether to let him see such stimulating images is another matter. On the whole it is quite plausible, although unproven, that seeing them will increase his desires all the more. He might grow accustomed to them and want more sex, or perhaps his thoughts of sexual things will simply become more frequent and vivid. If sex is utterly absent from a man's surroundings, he can probably reduce the frequency of his sexual urges. After all, the most common path to impulses requires a combination of inner motivation and external stimulus. If we eliminate the external stimuli, he would still have his inner motivation, but it would less often be translated into specific feelings of desire.

To be sure, a motivation can occasionally generate its own stimuli in the form of thoughts, but those are relatively unusual. If a man were to feel sexual arousal only when his own inner imagination furnished him with stimuli, he would have it less often than if he lives in a world with cable television, rented porno movies, Internet porn, women in miniskirts or bathing suits, and strip bars. There is in fact evidence that people who watch more television have more frequent sex (Robinson & Godbey, 1998).

It is an interesting and important question whether this view is correct. If so, then it would really be in women's and society's best interests to restrict male access to any sexual stimulation other than marital intercourse. It might even be easier on the men because they would feel less frustraction, even though they would in effect be living in a state of near sexual starvation compared to the men in the sexually rich surroundings. By rarely thinking about sex, they would minimize the tragedy of the male sex drive. Of course, to follow that logic to the extreme, celibacy would even be easier, but perhaps that is going over the edge. The Catholic priests who are supposed to live in celibacy don't seem to find it easy at all, and one scholar who had devoted most of his career to studying several thousand of them concluded that only about 2 percent really achieve celibacy, with another 8 percent being close to full success. But half of them were utterly hopeless, and most of the rest consistently fell far short of those ideals.

Hence it seems reasonable to allow the man to enjoy looking at others. Indeed, what does it matter if he looks at pornography or goes to strip shows, assuming these are only occasional indulgences and not obsessions that detract from you? Do you really think he will leave you for a stripper? If you do think so, your problems may be far more fundamental than this, and you might want to take additional steps beyond forbidding him to go to the girlie shows. But if his affection for you is sincere and your relationship is good, there is probably no threat in the fact that he occasionally enjoys looking at other women or nude pictures.

The second implication goes to the heart of the tragic dimension of male sexuality: The man won't be fully satisfied no matter what you do. The possibility of continued satisfaction is not built into male sex drive. What it would take to keep a man fully satisfied over a long period of time would be in practical terms impossible: a steady escalation of sexual pleasures, including an increasing variety of partners. (That would require a steady stream of willing and attractive women who would go to bed with him, and most wives are certainly not in a position to arrange any such thing, nor would they want to if they could.)

Thus, male sexual satisfaction is all relative. The only absolute is that the man will sometimes yearn for more, regardless of what he has. He will be making some kind of compromise, some trade-off.

The reality of marriage is therefore the negotiation of the details of that trade-off. He will have to be content with a certain amount of sexual gratification, and regardless of how much he has, he will wish for a bit more. The prudent wife would want to gradually allow him increments in pleasure over a long period, to permit him special favors and pleasures, as it were.

But to do that effectively you should start him off at a low level. You need to negotiate the sexual terms to be quite favorable to you at first. It will be unpleasant for the man to accept a reduction in his sexual diet, so to speak. Hence the best plan is to start him off on a fairly spartan diet and then gradually increase his allowance of pleasures.

Obviously this goes precisely against the course of a woman's own feelings, in an average case. It seems fair to assume that the woman has her strongest sexual desires when the relationship is blossoming, when passionate love is at its height. As we concluded in Chapter 7, that is likely to happen fairly soon after the relationship becomes serious, when intimacy is rising rapidly. To put things more bluntly, the woman will probably be most inclined to offer the man plenty of sex when passionate love is at its maximum, and this will tend to occur early. The newlywed phase (broadly and approximately speaking) is a peak of sexual desire for the woman. Later on, as marriage settles in and especially as children are born, she is not likely to feel like doing it a great deal. Hence just when she ought to be gradually offering him more goodies, she feels like giving him less. These conflicting patterns of desire are difficult to change. The best long-term strategy is therefore to anticipate them and plan around them.

The third implication has to do with how much sex to have in a good marriage. The central problem is likely to be that the man wants more than the woman. If you are the wife, you need to figure out how you are going to deal with his greater appetite.

One solution that some women adopt is to recognize it as a contest or power struggle. He wants to have sex more than you do, so only one of you will win. You can let him win, or you can prevail by preventing sex. Your competitive instinct can click into gear and decide whether you or he should win.

We think the contest approach is destructive. It guarantees that one or the other will be unhappy. If you think of sex as a battle of wills, with him wanting it more and you less, then you may make sure that you win, or you can give in and feel like a sucker. The crucial point is that someone becomes a loser, and so your marriage contains a loser. We think that one excellent sign of a good marriage is one in which both partners feel like winners. If at all possible, avoid having a loser. Hence another solution is to find some way to accommodate the man's greater cravings without having unpleasant experiences yourself or feeling that you have been symbolically defeated. For this, the partial forms of sex may be most effective.

The problem is an unfortunate outgrowth of the women's liberation movement. The goal was to empower women to enjoy their sexuality, and so women were supposed to desire sex and have orgasms at the same rate as men. For a woman to engage in sex just to please her man was seen as an exploitation of her, and in some cases it is. Yet the extreme of full equality is utterly impractical, and therefore to strive for it can be destructive. Insisting that the woman match the man orgasm for orgasm is setting a goal that she cannot reach, unless she keeps sex down to a rate that will leave the man in chronic frustration. Science has not yet established the precise ratio, although we are approaching reasonable estimates. Let us assume that husbands want to have three times as many orgasms as their wives, on average. If your particular situation differs, make the adjustment. (In fact, if you want more than he does, then simply reverse the genders, and apply the same logic.) By that assumption, mutual satisfaction requires some procedure that will enable the husband to have three times as many orgasms as the wife.

In short, some kind of arrangement is needed that will accomplish two things: First, it should give the husband orgasms on the frequent occasions when the wife does not want one. Second, it should keep her exertion and inconvenience down to an acceptable level.

Again, if the solution is for the wife to make herself enter fully into the sexual relations to the point of high arousal and orgasm, and if she has to do this somewhat against her inclinations on a regular basis, then she becomes the loser. She has to make herself get excited and to have an orgasm. Most likely the husband will be waiting during their intercourse for her to have her orgasm, so there is pressure on her as the minutes tick by, and he may get impatient or even sore. This is not likely to increase her desire to repeat the experience tomorrow.

One of our best friends is a bright young investment banker from Ohio who married a Korean woman while he was living in South Korea. When his wife became pregnant, she wanted to do the best possible things for the baby in every respect. Some ancient Korean folk beliefs held that a woman should never have sexual intercourse during pregnancy, and so she confided to her husband that she thought that was necessary. Being a classy guy, he immediately agreed that that was the best plan, and he would respect her wishes.

The next week she spoke with her sister. Sisterly discussions in Korea do not have the same Western reticence about sex, and certain things can be treated in a matter-of-fact fashion. The young wife told her sister that she had taken this traditional plan of no intercourse during pregnancy, because she thought it was best for the baby. Her sister said, carefully, that she respected the woman's decision and that it was very commendable and morally strong. She added, however, that the woman should be sure to masturbate her husband three or four times every week during this period, just to take care of him. The young wife took the advice to heart.

Well, that is just one solution among many, but it does have the virtue of meeting the requirements. Neither the wife nor the husband had to be the loser of a contest. Both could have what they wanted, or pretty close, across many potentially difficult months.

CHAPTER

9

Sex by Force

To a social scientist, a centrally fascinating feature of sex is that one simple act can represent anything from the best to the worst of human nature. At the ideal, sex is "making love": It enables two people to express their deepest positive feelings for each other and cement their commitment to treat each with value and respect, to support and help each other for a lifetime. But at its worst, sex can be a means by which one person seeks his (or, less often, her) own pleasure at another's expense and even expresses his or her contempt and hatred for another by inflicting psychological harm as well as physical dominance.

This chapter is concerned with the dark side of sex. The term *rape* has long been used to refer to sex acts that are forced upon someone against her (or sometimes his) will. Because the word has become encumbered with important legal, emotional, and moral layers of meaning, many researchers now avoid it and prefer to use other terms, such as sexual coercion or forcible sex. (We shall generally use all these terms interchangeably.)

The vagueness of the terms has made it difficult to assess the scope of the problem. Some researchers have been eager to conclude that rape and sexual coercion are widespread, and so they have adopted relatively loose criteria to include such acts as "stealing a kiss" from a woman who has not consented to being kissed. In fact, some studies have concluded that one out of every four American female college students has been raped, leading critics such as Roiphe (1993) to simply refuse to believe them: "If 25 percent of my female friends were really being raped, wouldn't I know it?" (p. 52). Surveys of university women have sometimes yielded such high numbers that schools began opening rape crisis hot lines, and in some cases the administrations were then surprised when these hot lines receive only a handful of calls in an entire year. Roiphe reported, for example, that Princeton University had only two rapes reported to campus security in the ten years prior to her book. At the University of California at Berkeley, which has fourteen thousand female students, only two rapes were reported to the police in one recent year (1990), and only forty to eighty woman had called the campus rape-counseling service (Gilbert, 1992).

Undoubtedly some of the researchers who publicize exaggerated statistics are well intentioned. They hope that by presenting the highest possible numbers of so-called rape victims, they can accomplish two praiseworthy goals. First, they hope to gain the attention of the general public and the lawmakers so that stronger efforts can be made to curtail rape. After all, regardless of the actual prevalence, rape remains a terrible crime, and any rape at all is too much. If a little hype in the form of inflated numbers is necessary to get more action to prevent rape, then it may be worth it. Second, they hope to reassure individual rape victims that they are not alone and should not blame themselves nor refuse to take action. To depict rape as a common crime that most women suffer is, the researchers hope, to replace any shame that an individual victim might feel with a feeling of solidarity across the gender. (Male rape victims are not usually included in this concern, and until recently relatively few studies even sought to ascertain how many men have been subjected to sexual coercion, by men or women.)

Other researchers dispute the strategy as well as the high numbers. They contend that exaggerated claims simply elicit disbelief and ultimately discredit the efforts to improve the situation. To claim that the majority of American women are rape victims is implausible, and so perhaps many people will simply refuse to believe that a serious problem exists. Furthermore, they say, it is ultimately unfair and inappropriate to put a woman who has been beaten and forced at gunpoint to have intercourse, for example, in the same category as a woman whose date kissed her before she was ready to be kissed, or with another woman who had to pull her boyfriend's hands away from the front of her sweater when they were necking. What they went through may have been unpleasant and morally objectionable, but it was not on the same level as being raped.

Like most serious researchers, we have relied on the NHSLS (Laumann et al., 1994) for the most precise estimates of sexual activity. Hence that is the logical place to look for a general estimate about how common rape is. When we turn to that task, however, we find three obstacles prevent us from coming away with a clear and definite answer.

The first obstacle is a technical problem. The researchers goofed, as they themselves admit. Their research included both a written survey and a face-to-face interview. On the written survey, the crucial item was "Have you ever been forced by a man to do something that you did not want to do?" (Laumann et al., 1994, p. 334). They forgot to include the word *sexual*. The literal meaning of the question would therefore refer to any sort of coercion, such as if the man forced the woman to wake up earlier than she wanted to, or to watch a television show that she did not want to see, or to visit his relatives. Twenty percent of women answered yes to this question. The researchers noted that most women probably did understand the question to refer to sex, because most of the questions on the questionnaire referred to sex. People are strongly swayed by context.

In the face-to-face interview, the researchers did explicitly specify the sexual nature of being forced to do something, and 15 percent of women said they had been forced. The researchers decided that for their further analyses they would count all women who answered yes to the force question either on the questionnaire or in the face-to-face interview, and this yielded a total of 22 percent of women. This is the figure usually used from that study, but it may be a little high given the ambiguity of the question. The 15 percent figure (relying on the face-to-face interview only, which asked unambiguously about being forced to do something sexual) would be the lowest estimate. As the researchers also pointed out, the face-to-face interviews yielded lower numbers than the written questionnaire on a variety of issues, probably because some people are reluctant to admit certain things aloud that they may be willing to acknowledge when answering written questions in an anonymous fashion.

Thus, the first obstacle to getting a clear estimate of the prevalence of rape from the NHSLS is the technical problem caused by the mistake in the questionnaire. The number of women surveyed who said they had been forced to do something sexual is apparently between 15 percent and 22 percent. Although this estimate is not nearly as high as some surveys have claimed, it is still shockingly high. Each percentage point refers to about a million American women, and so the survey suggests that somewhere in the neighborhood of twenty million women have been victimized.

The second obstacle to using the NHSLS data involves the extent of victimization. The questionnaire item referred to "something that you did not want to do," and in the face-to-face interview the specification of something sexual was added, but still the extent of sexual contact remained unclear. In general, the NHSLS defined sex as including vaginal or anal intercourse, oral intercourse, and hand-to-genital contact, with or without orgasm. Touching a woman's vagina without her permission would therefore count as forcible sex, whereas touching her breasts without her permission would not. This definition is reasonable, but we should keep in mind that it does not necessarily yield numbers that refer to forcible intercourse. The authors of the study noted that legal definitions of rape do not include hand-to-genital contact, and so the 22 percent figure of sexual victimization does not necessarily mean 22 percent of women were raped in a legal sense. The 22 percent probably also includes some lesser things, depending on how liberally the interviewees interpreted the question about having been forced to do something sexual.

The third obstacle to use of the data is the real stumper, however. The NHSLS researchers asked men whether they had ever forced a woman to do something sexual. Less than 3 percent of men said yes (2.8 percent, to be precise). At first glance, this number is far out of synchrony with the female responses. The problem is reminiscent of the discrepancy in number of sex partners, which we discussed in Chapter 2. How can 22 percent of women have been forced sexually, if only 3 percent of men forced women?

The obvious answer would be that a handful of men perpetrate all these acts. If each rapist raped seven different women, on average, and there was no overlap, then 3 percent of men could accomplish the rape of 21 percent of women. But the "obvious" answer does not appear to be correct. The seven-to-one ratio might apply in principle if these men were going around raping strangers. As we shall see, however, most of these acts of forcible sex involved partners in close, long-term relationships. In plain terms, the women were forced by men they loved or married. Because people do not usually have such long-term sexual relationships with so many different people, these numbers would not be able to add up properly to account for the seven-to-one discrepancy.

Again, we are inclined to conclude that the huge discrepancy between men and women in reports of forcible sex arise because men and women are processing information differently. They may differ in how they label, how they count, or how they remember events. In Chapter 2, we suggested that different rules for counting sex helped explain why men claim to have had more sex partners than women: Men count as sex certain acts that women do not.

Unfortunately that difference works against us here (at least for purposes of understanding the discrepancy in rape reports). If men count more acts as sex than women, then one would expect more men to claim to have forced a woman to perform sex acts than women would claim to have been forced—exactly the opposite of what has been found. This makes the problem worse. Some other discrepancy in how information is processed must be at work here. The next section will provide one plausible basis.

Victims and Perpetrators Think Differently

One of the earliest ideas in social psychology was that people's perceptions are shaped by their biases and expectations. In an influential early study (Hastorf & Cantril, 1954), students from two universities viewed identical footage of a controversial, dirty football game between their schools and counted the numbers of rule violations each team made. Students from Dartmouth counted about equal numbers of violations by both teams, whereas Princeton students counted almost twice as many violations by Dartmouth. Students also tended to rate their own team's violations as minor and the other team's violations as flagrant. The implication was that students identified with their own university and were therefore predisposed to see their own side as relatively benevolent and their opponents as malicious and dangerous. In other words, their identification with their school biased their perceptions.

Recent work has explored how some other roles likewise can bias how people process information and draw conclusions. In particular, victims and perpetrators appear to think and understand events in different ways. To victims, transgressions are severe, have lasting consequences, are unquestionably immoral, and often occur in repeated patterns. To perpetrators, the same kinds of events seem less severe, have temporary consequences, fall into morally gray areas, and tend to be isolated and one-time events. Perpetrators seem unable or unwilling to understand the suffering of victims. Victims seem unable or unwilling to understand the motives and concerns of perpetrators (see Baumeister, Stillwell, & Wotman, 1990; Gordon & Miller, in press; Mikula, Athenstaedt, Heschgl, & Heimgartner, in press). Each group seems to see its own feelings and reactions in clear, vivid ways, while the experience of the other role is hazy and vague. It seems likely that these differences reflect differences in both how the events are processed while they are happening and how biased memory can reconstruct them.

There are several other aspects of sex that contain victim-perpetrator discrepancies. With regard to infidelity, for example, victims and perpetrators see things quite differently. Hansen (1987) found that people rated their own infidelities as doing less damage to the relationship than their partner's infidelities. The maximum response of saying that the unfaithful act "hurt a great deal" was endorsed by only 9 percent of men and 14 percent of women, when they were talking about how their own acts hurt their partner. When talking about how their partner's acts had hurt them, however, 45 percent of men and 30 percent of women endorsed that response of maximum hurt. Spanier and Margolis (1983) found that people said their own extramarital activity was a result, not a cause, of problems in the relationship, but that their spouse's extramarital activity was a direct cause of relationship problems. Gordon (1999) also found that people assigned to identify with the victim of a partner infidelity had more negative judgments of the perpetrator than people who had been assigned to identify with the perpetrator.

These discrepancies may well contribute to the gender gap in perceptions of sexual coercion. Sexual coercion, especially as studied in the NHSLS, is something that men do to women. Women are thus the victims, while men are the perpetrators. Perpetrators tend to downplay the events and see them as morally ambiguous, whereas victims may see clear moral lines. That would be a major reason that women perceive rape where men do not: As victims, women are more aware of what is being done to them (particularly in terms of their lack of consent) and of stark moral lines being crossed, whereas such things are much hazier in the men's view. Likewise, if the man does not intend to force the woman and simply applies a little extra pressure to go farther when they are already engaged in heavy petting, he might conceivably fail to count this as an act of force, while to the woman the man's intentions may seem less clear than her own sense of being violated.

Who is correct? This question is quite difficult to answer in any victim-perpetrator discrepancy, because one needs an objective standard against which to measure victims and perpetrators. The fact that victims and perpetrators differ from each other merely guarantees that one or the other is distorting the effects, but it is difficult to establish which one. The usual assumption is that the victim tells the truth, because the perpetrator might be lying to escape his guilt. But if we are dealing with biased information processing, rather than outright lying, then either or both could be distorting the facts.

A laboratory test of distortions was conducted by Stillwell and Baumeister (1997). They furnished people with an objective account of a transgression, and people were supposed to identify with either the victim or the perpetrator (randomly assigned by the experimenter) and then tell the story in their own words as if it had happened to them. The stories people furnished were consistent with the victim-perpetrator differences found in other studies, and so these experiments were consistent with the general patterns. What was important, though, was that the researchers could then compare these stories against the original text to count errors. They could thus tell who was making errors.

The results were somewhat surprising: Victims and perpetrators made almost exactly the same number of errors. Both victims and perpetrators made more errors than the control group (who was simply assigned to tell the story in its original form, as if it had happened to someone else), so the results do not reflect ordinary difficulties of learning and remembering. Bias was clearly at work. Both victims and perpetrators were biasing the story, and to about the same degree.

But of course victims and perpetrators made systematically different *kinds* of errors. Victims tended to exaggerate the severity of the consequences and to downplay extenuating circumstances that reduced the perpetrators' guilt, whereas perpetrators tended to do the opposite.

These results suggest that both victims and perpetrators are biased. Applied to the rape statistics, these results suggest that the true incidence of rape may lie somewhere between the men's figure of 3 percent and the women's of 22 percent. There is, however, one qualification: Stillwell and Baumeister found that most of the errors made by both victims and perpetrators involved deleting things that had happened, rather than fabricating things that had not happened. It is easier to forget than to invent, apparently (or at least it is more common). This line of reasoning would point toward the women being more accurate in regard to whether rape occurred.* Hence we shall assume that the "true" incidence of sexual coercion is closer to the figures derived from women's reports than from men's reports.

Before we apply the findings of victim-perpetrator bias to the gender difference in perception of rape, however, we should consider other explanations based in gender differences. As we have seen, we can rule out one area of difference, because men perceive more events as sex than women: This event would push in the opposite direction. Still, some might argue that men are simply more insensitive than women to their partner's wants and needs (Byers & O'Sullivan, 1988), and so male insensitivity is mainly responsible for the difference in consent. Another possibility, to which we shall return later, is the belief that women say no when they mean yes, and that men thus sometimes disregard women's protests or refusals and push ahead to force sex on women who do not want it (e.g., Muehlenhard & Hallabaugh, 1988).

These questions can be resolved by seeing whether the same victim-perpetrator difference is found when women are the perpetrators and men are the victims. If so, then there is nothing special about gender in this regard, and the victim and perpetrator roles are the culprits. In contrast, if there is only a difference when men force women and not when women force men, then we should invoke gender alone to explain the discrepancy.

Relevant data were furnished by O'Sullivan, Byers, and Finkelman (1998; see also Byers & O'Sullivan, 1988). They surveyed male and female college students about sexual coercion, including questions about both victim and perpetrator experiences. The gap was almost identical for men and women. Episodes in which men coerced women into sexual activity were reported by about twice as many women (43.5 percent) as men (20.0 percent). Likewise, episodes in which women coerced men into sexual activity were reported by about twice as many men (18.5 percent) as women (8.8 percent).[†] To be sure, those numbers suggest that men coerce women more than women coerce men, and both genders agree on that. But female coercion of males does reveal the same role bias in that far more men say they are victimized than women admit to coercing men. The victim-perpetrator gap appears to be independent of gender.

The Typical Rape

The word *rape* conjures up a familiar stereotype. A woman is out walking alone at night, especially in a deserted place such as a dark street or parking lot. A strange man attacks and overpowers her, with either physical strength or a weapon. He forces her to submit to his wishes and then disappears, never to be seen again. In another scenario, a man

---

*Then again, if the definition of rape is sex without consent, it is logically possible that some women had forgotten some expression of consent, even just a membled "Okay" or "Maybe later," which she may not even have meant but which might have helped convince the man that it was acceptable to continue.

[†]These numbers for men coercing women are of course higher than those from the NHSLS. The difference is probably due to methodological differences, including sampling and wording of questions.

breaks into a woman's apartment, finds her there alone, and forces her to have sex, again using either physical force or a weapon.

In the previous section, we mentioned the finding from the NHSLS that most rapes follow a very different scenario. Although the stereotype does correspond to some real events (and moreover ones that may be especially traumatic for the victims), the rapist as the violent stranger is in the distinct minority. In fact, Laumann et al. (1994) concluded that only about 4 percent of incidents of sexual coercion (of men forcing women) involve strangers.

Instead of strangers, it appears to be lovers and boyfriends who are mainly responsible for sexual coercion. When women were asked to indicate who had forced them into sexual activity against their will, almost half said that the man was someone with whom they had once been in love. Another 9 percent identified the spouse as the culprit. Combining those categories, therefore, we can conclude that over half the incidents of sexual coercion involve lovers and husbands. (The remainder of cases were about equally divided between well-known and casual acquaintances, plus the 4 percent by strangers.)

These data change the way we must think about sexual coercion (and rape prevention too). Women are at far greater risk from their husbands and lovers than from strangers. It is necessary to understand sexual coercion as typically occurring in the context of a developing or ongoing romantic relationship. This picture is confirmed by the study by O'Sullivan et al. (1998), which found that almost three out of every five (58.7 percent) victimized women said they had engaged in consensual sex with the same person on a previous occasion. Two out of five (38 percent) had in fact been coerced by the same man on a previous occasion, suggesting that (1) the sexual coercion was to some extent a repeating pattern in the relationship, and (2) women do not necessarily stop interacting with men who rape or coerce them. The latter conclusion is confirmed by other data showing that 42 percent of rape victims later engage in consensual sex with men who had raped them (Koss, 1988), and that only about a quarter of women refuse to have any further contact with the man after an incident of sexual coercion (Murnen, Perot, & Byrne, 1989). Many women (25–30 percent) said they were friends with men who had on a previous occasion sexually attacked and raped them, and some (11 percent) said that the man who had attacked and raped them was still their current boyfriend (Murnen et al., 1989).

An important study by the respected sex researcher Eugene Kanin (1985) compiled results from seventy-one men who admitted having committed date rape. Naturally there is no way to tell how typical these men are of rapists in general. The simple fact that they admitted engaging in date rape is enough to set them apart from the many men who deny their actions (although some of the men in the study had initially denied their rape but had come forward after hearing Kanin lecture about date rape). Moreover, Kanin reported that only a few of the incidents had been reported to the police, and in every case the charges had been dropped later, so the men did not show up in any official statistics about rape. Still, their accounts are relevant and fascinating.

Kanin found that most of the date rapes occurred between a man and a woman who had had two to five previous dates with each other. Most of the men had had some degree of consensual sexual contact with the victim on the earlier dates. More importantly, most had had some amount of consenting sexual contact on the date that involved the rape. The most common pattern, apparently, was that the couple was involved in heavy petting and oral sex. The woman wanted to stop at that point, but the man forced her to engage in vaginal intercourse.

Such episodes raise substantial practical problems. A woman (or a man) has every right to refuse to have intercourse even after consenting to oral sex, but juries are often suspicious of women who claim to have been raped when they admit to consenting to oral sex. These rapists admitted, at least by the time of the study, that they knew the woman did not want to have genital intercourse and thus were consenting to only the oral sex, but under those circumstances a woman is both physically and legally vulnerable. Oral sex requires partially removing someone's clothes as well as finding a relatively secluded setting. (Very few couples have their first oral sex in a restaurant, for example.) In such a compromising situation, it is not difficult for a man to force a reluctant woman to have intercourse.

We shall return to Kanin's findings at several points in this chapter, because his study provided a rich glimpse into the minds of men who admit to perpetrating date rape. For now, however, the key point is to incorporate the scenes it describes into our image of rape. The violent stranger in the dark alley may well commit one kind of especially dangerous and traumatic rape. A far more common kind occurs, however, when the woman has consented to engage in highly arousing sexual activity with the man but wants to stop short of full intercourse.

This is not to say that women can never refuse to go all the way once they have begun. Ample evidence indicates that most men stop at whatever point the woman refuses (e.g., Byers, 1988), as of course they should. But limited sexual contact does make some men want to continue no matter what, and so it puts the woman at risk for being raped if he forces the issue.

This view of sexual coercion also fits well with the social exchange analysis of sexuality that we have featured at various points in this book. Sex is something that men get from women, according to this view. Rape is thus a violation of the rules of exchange. The man takes more than the woman wants to give. Rape is to normal (consenting) sex like stealing is to purchasing. Metaphors of theft or looting may be apt to depict what happens in rape: A man uses force or threat to get something that he wants but cannot legally or properly obtain. (Cases in which women force men to have sex complicate this analysis, however.)

Before we continue with this discussion, however, we must face up to another view of rape that is undoubtedly familiar to many readers. The scenario that emerges from the NHSLS and the work by Kanin and others depicts rape in the context of sexual activity. The social exchange theory represents rape as an illicit approach to getting sex. Yet is rape really about sex at all? Isn't it basically a matter of power, aggression, and dominance?

The Radical Feminist Theory of Rape

Rape has long been classed as a sex crime, and all definitions (including legal) featured sexual activity as a key part of it. This does not necessarily mean that sex is the main goal or point of rape, but for a long time that was the basic assumption. Indeed, early thinking about rape depicted it as something done by men who cannot obtain sex any other way, perhaps because they were unattractive to women or lacked the social skills to persuade women to consent to sex.

These early theories about rape ran into problems and contradictions, however. For one thing, as we shall see, rapists typically have had more sex than other men, or at least they claim to have more. That is, rapists have had more partners and more frequent sexual activity than other men (Kanin, 1965). Moreover, although single men figure prominently in the ranks of rapists, there is no denying that many rapists are married, and moreover that other rapists have girlfriends with whom they engage in consensual sex. Their deficits in social skills were also difficult to prove, and many studies concluded that rapists did indeed have suitable social skills (e.g., Koralewski & Conger, 1992). Certainly at least the rapists who had wives and girlfriends had proven that they had sufficient social skills and other assets to persuade someone to have sex with them.

Around 1970, feminist theorists began to put forward a radically different theory of rape. The best known of these works was Brownmiller's (1975) book *Against Our Will.* Although other writers had anticipated her views to some extent (e.g., Millet, 1971; Griffin, 1971; Greer, 1970, 1973), Brownmiller's work became a widely known best-seller and featured a forceful, persuasive statement of the new theory. Several key features deserve to be noted.

First and foremost, Brownmiller proposed that rape is not really about sex at all. In her view, rape is an act of power and violence. It is something men do to dominate women and keep them in a fearful, inferior position in society. (Clearly, Brownmiller was dismissing cases in which women rape or coerce men.) In an important sense rape is thus a political act rather than a sexual one, because the goal is to enforce men's power over women.

Second, Browmiller argued that rape is rooted in culture, especially the patriarchal (male-dominated) culture of North America and Western Europe. According to this view, rape is something men learn from socialization in a culture that was created and run by men for their own benefit. Rape is a means to sustain the political status quo, and the awareness of it as a tool has been passed along from father to son. She used the term *rape culture* to describe how society teaches its young men to rape.

Brownmiller's third point addressed a seeming problem in the first two, since fathers do not actually teach their sons to rape, and most men never come close to raping a woman. In fact, most men claim that they would not rape and that such force or violence would be a sexual turn-off. To remedy this problem, Brownmiller (1975) said that rape is essentially a conspiracy that "is nothing more or less than a conscious process of intimidation by which all men keep all women in a state of fear" (p. 5). Only some men actually commit rape, but all men benefit by their acts, because the actual incidents of rape are common enough to intimidate all women into remaining politically subservient to men. All men who have not actually raped thus share the guilt for rape and are in fact supporters of a "rape culture." Moreover, Brownmiller insisted that all men consciously and deliberately support rapists.

The theory that rape was not about sex but rather power and domination was rapidly embraced by many writers, and it is fair to say it had become the leading position on the issue by about 1980. Although a few dissenting voices were heard, Brownmiller's theory dominated the field among experts and laypersons alike. This probably reflected the ascendancy of radical feminist thinking at the time rather than any firm basis in the data, which were not actually very strong. Tedeschi and Felson (1994) summarized the dominance of Brownmiller's view thus: "We can think of no other assertion in the social sciences that has achieved such wide acceptance on the basis of so little evidence" (p. 313).

To be sure, some facts were taken as support for the radical feminist view. For example, as noted, many rapists already had sex partners, so the feminists thought it was obvious that for these men, rape was a means of asserting power over women rather than a way of obtaining more sex.

An influential work by Groth (1979) followed the radical feminist line in analzying rape as driven by concerns of power and sadistic pleasure rather than sexual satisfaction. Groth reported that a fair number of rapists experienced sexual dysfunctions during the rape, particularly an inability to get or sustain an erection. Although such cases were a minority of rapes, they were far more common than the typical incidence of sexual dysfunctions among the average man of comparable age and background. This was taken to indicate that rape was not really about sex, because some rapists showed failures of sexual arousal.

Central to Brownmiller's argument was the assumption that rape reflects an implicit conspiracy by all men. Toward this end, it was necessary to find some evidence that the majority of nonrapist men might rape under some circumstances. Considerable excitement therefore accompanied the publication of works by Malamuth and his colleagues (1980, 1983), who used a procedure that asked young men whether they would they engage in rape if they could be assured of not getting caught or punished. In various studies between one-third and two-thirds of the young men said yes. Actually, although it was reported that way, they did not really say yes. The procedure was to have the man rate the likelihood that he might ever rape on a 5-point scale, and any response except the lowest extreme was taken as a yes. "Probably not," for example, was defined as a yes, because the man did not absolutely and permanently rule it out.

The high willingness of young men—in some cases a majority of them—to say they might rape a woman under ideal circumstances was taken as evidence in support of the male conspiracy theory that Brownmiller supported. It converged with her accounts of rape during wartime: In some cases, victorious armies follow the military conquest of a city with widespread raping of its women. Because the soldiers are presumably ordinary young men rather than seasoned rapists, the military rapes support the view that any man could become a rapist (or at least many men; it is not clear what percent of soldiers actually take part in military rapes, and some soldiers object strenuously to the practice.)

The meaning of these findings about willingness to rape was questioned by Martin and Kerwin (1991). They noted that many of the studies yielding the highest rates of such willingness relied on getting the men sexually aroused. Malamuth and Check (1980), for example, exposed men to sexual stimulation until they reached a full erection, whereupon their willingness to rape was measured. This yielded one of the highest rates of favorable answers (69 percent). In another study, men read sexually arousing passages from a sex-oriented magazine before responding to the rape question. Martin and

Kerwin noted that if sexual arousal yielded high rates of willingness to rape, then perhaps rape was about sex after all.

On the basis of their reading of the literature, Martin and Kerwin concluded that men in such studies tend to take a sexual attitude in answering the question about whether they might ever rape someone. This of course violated the central assumption of Brownmiller's theory, which is that rape is not about sex but rather violent dominance. This theory relies on the well-established concept of priming, which holds that once a thought is activated in someone's mind, it tends to influence the person's subsequent thinking (Bargh, 1989, 1994; Bower, 1986; Higgins, Rholes, & Jones, 1977; Wyer & Srull, 1980). Priming, which is a process of "mental leftovers," is a surprisingly powerful and common effect.

Martin and Kerwin then went on to conduct their own experiment on willingness to rape. They asked each man the crucial question of whether he might be willing to rape someone if he were sure he could get away with it. Before the question was asked, however, the men received one or another set of questions. For half the men, these questions focused on sex, such as whether the man enjoyed casual sex and how much foreplay he liked to have before intercourse. These questions were designed to prime the men with sexual thoughts so that the rape question would have a sexual context. The other men were asked questions about violent behavior, such as whether they would use force to get what they want or whether they would hit a woman. These questions were intended to prime thoughts of violence rather than sex.

The context of the rape question had a dramatic effect. When it was presented after the questions about various sexual activities, 29 percent of the men expressed at least a minimal willingness to rape. In contrast, when it was presented after the questions about violence, only 12 percent expressed any such willingness. (The man's response was counted as indicating some willingness if he gave any answer other than the extreme and absolute no, which undoubtedly helped to boost the percentage of positive responses.) The rape item was rated by a 5-point scale with end points marked "not at all likely" and "extremely likely," and so any response except 1—"not at all likely"—was counted as indicating some willingness to rape.

Thus, the statistics on willingness to rape probably reflect context: Men are thinking about rape as a sexual fantasy, not as a violent act. The favorable responses by men are thus parallel to the fantasy of being raped expressed relatively frequently by women. Although a fair number of women enjoy that as an occasional sexual fantasy, few or none of them really want to be raped. In fact, there are more women who claim to enjoy the fantasy of being forced or raped than there are men who report being willing to consider ever doing it, although both are large minorities. Probably the two patterns are similar in their psychological meaning, and neither has any known relation to actual participation in rape. Greendlinger and Byrne (1987) specifically found that men's reported willingness to commit rape (as measured with such a scale) had no correlation with actually engaging in any coercive sexual behavior.

Are women any different in their willingness to rape? Clements-Schreiber, Rempel, and Desmerais (1998) found that a majority of women said they would use overt pressure to get sex from a reluctant man under some conditions, suggesting again that women are quite similar to men in many respects. Both will say, at least hypothetically, that they might use force to get what they want.

A more general study of this issue was conducted by Ellis and Beattie (1983), and indeed their article was entitled "The Feminist Explanation for Rape: An Empirical Test." If rape results from male domination, they argued, then rape should be most common when men are most dominant. By the same token, increasing gender equality should reduce rape. Across twenty-six U.S. cities, Ellis and Beattie looked for correlations between rape rates and fourteen different indexes of gender equality. The results were disappointing for the feminist theory. Of the fourteen possible correlations with rape rates, ten failed to reach significance, indicating that most measure of gender equality show no relation to rape. Of the remaining four that were significantly related to rape, three were in the direction opposite to the feminist theory—in other words, more gender equality was associated with more rape, not less. When more sophisticated statistical analyses that employed corrections for the various effects were used, only one of the fourteen correlations remained significant, and that one was opposite to the feminist view that male domination leads to rape.

Thus, there was never a strong basis in the research findings for the view that rape is not about sex. Still, Brownmiller's work and the supporting voices of many radical feminist authors were widely influential. In particular, the forces of political correctness supported the feminist position, and researchers had to tread very carefully if they wanted to disagree. Nonetheless, research findings began to accumulate that raised serious doubts about the theory that rape is not about sex. For example, the study by Kanin (1985) is difficult to reconcile with this view. The incidents in his sample occurred in the midst of heavy petting or oral sex. The men were involved in sexual activity at the time, and the main thing they wanted was to have intercourse; when the women refused, the men forced them. To depict those acts as part of a deliberate conspiracy to intimidate women, and to deny that sex was uppermost in the men's minds at the time, seems scarcely plausible. They wanted sex right then, and they weren't above using a little extra muscle to get their date to comply.

In 1988, Palmer published an influential paper that carefully examined and rejected the radical feminist view that rape was not sexually motivated. He was clear in acknowledging that feminism had made many important and meaningful contributions to society, including improvements in the way rape victims are treated by the legal system. He was not an antifeminist by any means, but he could not accept the theory that rape is not about sex.

Palmer first laid out twelve key arguments that had been used to buttress the claim that rape was not sexually motivated and then rejected each one as either illogical or inconsistent with the evidence. For example, one argument was that rape cannot be about sex because many rapists have other, consenting sex partners. But the fact of having one sex partner does not guarantee that a man has no desire for other women. Palmer pointed out that many men who use pornography or go to prostitutes are married, but that no one claims that pornography and prostitution are not about sex. Obviously, marital infidelity is committed by people who have regular sex partners (by definition), but it is generally assumed to be centrally motivated by sex.

Another argument was that rape is often premeditated, to which Palmer replied, "So what?" It is true that some sexual behavior is spontaneous, but other sex (including much consensual sex) is premeditated. People arrange to meet with their lovers at motels, or they plan to try to seduce a desired partner, and so forth.

Another argument was that rapists are relatively young, with few men past the age of fifty committing rape. This view assumed that men continue to desire sex into old age, whereas their aggressive tendencies diminish. As Palmer contended, however, there is plenty of evidence that the sex drive diminishes too as men get older.

We noted that the relatively high rate of sexual dysfunction experienced by men during rape had been used to argue that rape does not arise from sexual desire. In Palmer's view, such evidence is ambiguous. If a man were only interested in having sex and therefore tried to rape someone, he might well have difficulty sustaining an erection because of fear of getting caught, guilt, anxiety, or other emotions. Rapes also tend to occur when a man is intoxicated or on drugs, and such substances interfere with sexual response.

A final argument was the one Brownmiller (1975) printed in capital letters on the cover of her book: "Rape victims are not only the 'lovely young blondes' of newspaper headlines—rapists strike children, the aged, the homely—all women." Yet Brownmiller was wrong. Obviously, not "all women" are raped. Furthermore, multiple studies show that rape victims are disproportionately selected from attractive young women in their teens and early twenties. True, there are some older and younger victims, but Palmer said that it seems reasonable to propose that rapists choose their targets based on a combination of attractiveness and vulnerability as opposed to attractiveness alone. Old and very young victims may be less desirable sexually to the average person (although some men do exhibit sexual preferences for these categories of women), but their physical vulnerability may make up for that: A child or old woman presumably cannot fight off a would-be attacker as well as a young adult woman in her prime could. Even so, Palmer cited several studies that concluded that less than 5 percent of rape victims are past the age of fifty.

Another review published several years later by Tedeschi and Felson (1994) came to similar conclusions: In countries where convicted rapists are castrated, they are afterward less likely to commit rape or other crimes against women. Since castration has its primary impact on a man's sexuality, this finding points to a strong sexual component of rape.

Also, rapists have high sex drives as well as peer groups that put pressure on them to have sex (Kanin, 1985; Lisak & Roth, 1988). Rapists typically report that sex was their goal. They also report that they would have preferred not to use force and wished the victim had simply acquiesced to sex, which runs precisely counter to the view that rapists mainly want to commit acts of violence and regard the sex part as secondary. Such facts led Tedeschi and Felson to conclude that rape is precisely what it appears to be: a man's attempt to obtain sex by any means necessary, including force.

A similar conclusion was reached by Ghiglieri (1999), who quoted some remarks from a serial rapist that he claimed are typical of the sentiments of such men. When asked the difference between sex with a woman who consented and one who refused consent, the rapist said, "There was no difference at all." He said all he wanted was sex. Some women had to be forced, "but I didn't enjoy doing it. It wasn't a turn-on." He "wanted things as easy as I could get them." If she consented, that was perfect. If she didn't consent, "I would threaten . . . or exert any kind of violence." To do so, however, "was nothing for me then, but I didn't like it" (p. 98). The rapist's position was thus quite clear: Using force was a hassle, it held no attraction for him, and he would only resort to it if it were required to obtain sex.

The role of the rapist's peer group is relevant. As we said, rapists and other sexually coercive men have peer groups who put a great deal of pressure on them to have sex (Kanin, 1985; Lisak & Roth, 1988). Supporters of Brownmiller's (1975) view might see this as a sign of the rape culture—men encourage other men to rape. Yet the peer groups draw the line at coercion. Heilbrun and Loftus (1986) found that peer pressure reduced rather than increased sexual aggression by male college students. Apparently, peer groups encourage men to seek consensual sex but discourage them from obtaining it by force.

Small events point toward the same conclusion. After South Africa ended its apartheid and black Africans took over the government, the official tolerance for sexual activities was greatly liberalized. Homosexuality was tolerated, brothels and massage parlors were permitted, and so forth. One enterprising farmer came up with a scheme that seems straight out of Brownmiller: Male tourists and locals would pay for a "hooker hunt" out in the *bushveld* ("From Calvinism to Cruising," 1999). The gist of this activity was that a naked woman (in fact a prostitute) would hide out in the wild as the men would track and "shoot" her with the sort of gun that is used in the popular North American sport of paintball, whose "bullets" leave a splotch of paint (and often a bruise) that furnish proof that the victim has indeed been shot.

Thus, the scheme had just the mix of sex and violence that the radical feminist theory warned about. The woman's nudity indicated her vulnerability rather than any explicit intention of love-making. Groups of men pursued her and shot her, and their conquest of her was established as victory in the competition. This, supposedly, was precisely what rape was all about: violence with a thin veneer of sexual titillation.

But the business failed. Not enough customers were attracted by this prospect. The failure constrasted sharply with the flourishing success of other parts of the South African sex industry. Apparently, plenty of men are willing to pay to have sex with a woman, but hardly any will pay to shoot her. Once again, it appears that sex, not violence, is what men want from women.

Before we completely discard the radical feminist view that rape is not sex, however, we think it is useful to refer once more to the discrepant perspectives of victims and perpetrators. Feminist theories were explicitly based on women's experiences, and most women know rape mainly from the victim's perspective if at all. The view that rape is not about sex may be inaccurate as an account of men's motives for raping, but then it seems unfair to expect that a theory based in women's experiences would furnish a valid account of why men commit acts against women. Even if Brownmiller's theory is completely wrong about why men commit rape, it may still be correct about how victims experience rape. Whatever it may be to its perpetrators, rape is certainly not sex to its victims.

Indeed, even the seemingly most outlandish aspect of Brownmiller's theory makes some sense as an account of the victim's view. She proposed that rape was part of a conscious conspiracy by which all men intimidate all women and keep them in a state of fear and submission. This view is indefensible on many counts, as can be seen by the facts that most men do not rape, that most men do not find rape appealing, that many men prosecute and punish rapists, and so forth. If Brownmiller were correct, even nonraping men would be happy to hear about acts of rape, because these supposedly advance the male cause of keeping women in their place. Whenever the television news reported a rape, the men in the room would give each other high fives. Taken literally, Brownmiller's thesis says that men are deliberately complicit in getting their own daughters or girlfriends raped, whereas in fact most men are extremely upset when a woman they love is victimized. As a theory about all men, this is plainly wrong.

Such conspiracy theories do not fit the facts about perpetrators. They do, however, correspond somewhat to what some victims experience. The basis for this may be what Baumeister (1997) called the *magnitude gap* as a general principle of evil and violent behavior: The transgression is much more important to the victim than to the perpetrator. For the victim to understand the perpetrator, therefore, it is necessary to face up to the heartbreaking realization of how little the act meant to the person who committed it. Many victims refuse to accept this and prefer to believe that what they suffered was part of some evil conspiracy or other grand pattern. The victim, in other words, prefers to think that the perpetrator was as heavily involved and deeply affected as the victim was.

That sort of conspiracy thinking is not limited to rape. As Baumeister and Catanese (in press) discuss, similar patterns of bogus conspiracies have been postulated by other groups of victims. Many African Americans, for example, believe that AIDS, crack cocaine, poverty, and gang violence are part of a conspiracy by the white American majority and the federal government to destroy the black population. This may be easier for them to accept than the idea that mere indifference is responsible. Likewise, many Jewish writers on the Holocaust have insisted that killing Jews was the overriding goal of Hitler and the Nazis, and that fighting the war and establishing their own vision of an ideal society were secondary. This sort of conspiracy thinking is an understandable response to the immense suffering of many victims and their expectation that only something immensely evil and deliberate could be responsible for it.

In other words, rape is not a conspiracy by all men to instill fear in all women, but some victims may feel as if it were. A victim of rape may well start to fear all men, or at least a large number of them. As we have seen, many men who commit rape do not even seem to remember doing so, and probably this reflects on the relatively trivial importance that their use of force had for them. It cannot, however, be trivial to the victim, and so to her it seems more plausible that there is a male master plan.

Understanding the Rapist

The preceding section rejected one of the main theories about why men commit rape, namely as a broad public strategy for subjugating women. If that view is wrong, what can replace it? Unfortunately the present state of knowledge does not include an established consensus on a single correct theory about the causes of sexual coercion, although there have been various suggestions.

Not surprisingly, evolutionary psychologists have come forward to propose that rape may have evolved as a way by which some men can pass along their genes, especially men who are not likely to enjoy the privileges of the alpha male. These theories are, however, difficult to evaluate rigorously, and they leave plenty of questions about exactly which men will commit rape. We think that sociocultural and situational factors seem more promising than biological ones for explaining rape.

In this section, we shall draw on some influential theories in social and personality psychology to offer a novel theory about rape (based on Baumeister, Catanese, & Wallace, 1999). This theory is firmly based in what is known about general principles of human behavior and about rape in particular, but of course as a new theory it has not been directly tested, and so it must be regarded as just a plausible idea. Still, for the field of rape, no established and proven theory is available, and so a speculative possible theory is all we are likely to be able to get at this point.

Reactance Theory

The first idea we shall borrow is the concept of reactance. This theory, and even the word itself, were introduced in 1966 by Brehm, who proposed that people have a basic drive to maintain their freedom to do what they want. When someone tells them they may not do something, they react negatively and sometimes angrily against that person. The concept of reactance is thus somewhat similar to the lay concept of "reverse psychology," by which supposedly you can make your child want to wash the dishes and clean his room by telling him not to do so.

Brehm proposed that people have any or all of three responses when they see their freedoms being taken away. First, they feel an increased desire for whatever is forbidden to them. Second, they tend to initiate behaviors to try to reassert their freedom by doing what they have been told they cannot do. Third, they may attack or otherwise behave aggressively toward the person who told them not to do whatever it was.

Hence, if a teacher tells a child that she may not play with a certain toy, the child can exhibit any of three responses. First, she may find the toy more interesting and appealing than she did previously. Second, she may try to play with the forbidden toy after all. Third, she may hit or yell at the teacher.

Reactance and Rape

Now let us apply Brehm's theory to rape. The context is one in which a man wants to have sex with a woman but the woman refuses. (To be sure, in some cases women coerce or rape men. Because these cases are rarer, we shall focus on male rape of females. It is possible that similar processes apply when the genders are reversed, but that is a complex question.) She thus takes away his opportunity to do something that he wants, namely to have sex.

This context of men wanting sex from women is certainly a plausible and common one. We have reviewed ample evidence that men want sex more often than women, and that particular women often refuse men's offers of sex, particularly when this is outside of a current, ongoing, good sexual relationship.

The scenario that emerged from Kanin's (1985) study of admitted rapists is particularly relevant. In the most common case, the man and the woman had already had several dates and were engaging in some sexual activity at the time of the rape. Oral sex may well lead a man to think that the woman will consent to full intercourse. When she refuses, he may feel as if something he wanted and even expected is taken away from him. He may react negatively.

All three of the reactance responses may be involved in rape. First, the man may feel increased desire to have sex with her when she refuses. There is some evidence to support the idea that women who are not available for sex are desired more strongly than others. Many men report, for example, that they experience strong sexual desires for their wives just when they are going through a divorce: The woman who has become unavailable to him is suddenly more appealing.

One study documented the increased desire for women who become unavailable. The context is totally different, but the principle is the same. Pennebaker et al. (1979) got the idea from a country music song that claimed the "girls get prettier at closing time," referring to the alleged enhancement of attractiveness of women in a bar when the bar was about to close (because the women are about to go home and become unavailable). He had male bar patrons rate the attractiveness of female patrons at various times during the evening, and sure enough the women received higher marks just as the bar was about to close. (He did not, however, control for any possibility that the men themselves might have been more intoxicated at closing time, which conceivably could have an independent effect on how appealing they found the women to be.)

The second consequence of reactance was that the person should try to do what is forbidden. This of course is the essence of rape: The man tries to force the woman to have sex after she refuses to do so willingly. Several studies have documented that the risk of rape is especially high among ex-spouses and former dating partners. These fit the reactance pattern especially well, because the man formerly did enjoy the opportunity to have sex with the woman, but now that opportunity is denied to him, and so he tries to reassert it by force. In the study by O'Sullivan, Byers, and Finkelman (1998), for example, over half the rape victims had formerly had consensual sex with the perpetrator. The pattern of stalking is also related here: Many stalkers are former husbands or boyfriends who try to remain present in the lives of women who have rejected them (Nicastro, Cousins, & Spitzberg, 1999).

This view also puts a slightly different slant on the rapist's goal. To be sure, in a broad sense his goal is sexual. In the reactance view, the rapist's goal is to possess the woman sexually, and this conquest is perhaps primarily symbolized by penetration rather than orgasm. She says no, and he stakes his claim to her by entering her. His pleasure and orgasm may be of secondary importance, although naturally he would prefer to have them.

Putting the emphasis on penetration rather than orgasm helps explain several surprising facts about rape. For one thing, as several studies show, a fair number of rapes do not culminate in orgasm for the man (e.g., Groth, 1979). Groth's studies with convicted rapists found that one out of every three rapists experienced some form of sexual dysfunction during the rape, with the largest category including erectile dysfunction (impotence) and retarded ejaculation (inability to reach orgasm). These rates are much higher than young men of a comparable age report in consensual sexual intercourse.

Even more surprisingly, studies have found that rapists do not report that they received a great deal of sexual pleasure from the rape. In a series of interviews with convicted rapists in prison, Scully (1990) asked them to rate their degree of sexual pleasure on a 10-point scale. The average response was about 3, indicating fairly low pleasure. (This finding has also been seen as fitting the view that rape is not about sex, although the low yield of sexual pleasure does not prove that the men were not looking for pleasure. In many cases, they expected the rape to be more sexually satisfying than it turned out to be.) To be sure, convicted rapists may differ in important ways from the more common date rapist, and it is plausible that rape occurring in the dating and oral sex scenario described by Kanin (1985) would yield more pleasure. Still, the point is that the pleasure from forcible sex is not nearly as high as the pleasure from consenting sex. The reactance theory can explain that the man's immediate goal is to demonstrate sexual possession of the woman by entering her.

The third consequence of reactance is to act aggressively toward the person who has restricted your freedom. In rape, the woman would be the target, because she is the one who refused the man's advances. He may well become angry at her for denying him the sex he wanted or expected, and he may use more than the minimum amount of force necessary to make her comply with his wishes. There is in fact some evidence that sexually coercive men believe more strongly than other men that it is all right to use force if a woman leads a man on and then refuses sex (Berkowitz, Burkhart, & Bourg, 1994).

The aggressive consequence of reactance helps explain findings that women who resist rape are often injured more severely than other victims. In fact, one of the consequences of Brownmiller's (1975) book was a change in policy. Brownmiller claimed that rape occurred in part because girls and women were taught to be passive and to submit to men, and she encouraged women to take self-defense lessons and to defend themselves against rape by fighting back. When these suggestions were broadly implemented, however, the net result was not so much a reduction in rape but an alarming increase in the cases in which women were not only raped but also severely beaten and injured. Rape prevention advice for girls and women has therefore shifted away from advocating the use of physical force to resist rape.

A further clarification is necessary. Part of the reactance theory says that the rape occurs in part because the woman refuses the man's sexual advances. This view is not intended to shift blame off the rapist and on to the woman. In our view, both men and women have every right to refuse any sexual activity, including saying no to intercourse after consenting to other sexual acts. Some men (especially sexually coercive men) do in fact think that the use of force is justified when a woman refuses sex after getting a man aroused, but in our view they are completely wrong. The use of force to obtain sex is never justified.

Thus there is at least some broad plausibility to the idea that reactance theory can help explain rape. In order for the theory to be satisfactory, however, it would have to be modified to address several clear and obvious problems.

For one thing, sexual refusal is common but rape is rare. If women's sexual refusals engendered reactance that caused men to rape them, then many dates and other interactions would end in rape. Clearly, however, most men accept a woman's right to refuse, and in fact most men say they would stop all efforts to initiate sex as soon as a woman makes a clear refusal (Byers, 1988).

Another question is whether men do in fact see women's refusals as a threat to their freedom. Men may want or hope for sex, but they do not necessarily expect it. In many cases, they probably do not. Under such circumstances, a woman's refusal would not lead to reactance. This could in principle solve the first problem we mentioned (that refusal is common but rape is rare), but only if it could be shown that rapes occur when men do in fact expect sex and hence see women's refusals as threats to their freedom.

The broader issue, however, is how any man could believe he has a right to have sex with a woman when she refuses. Nearly all moral theories hold that one person's rights end where another person's body begins. How could any man feel that one of his freedoms is being taken away when a woman tells him that she does not want to have sex with him?

Reactance alone thus cannot provide a full explanation of sexual coercion, at least not without substantial clarification. Hence we turn now to a second line of work that may help solve these problems.

Narcissism, the Dark Side of High Self-Esteem

The crux of the problems with the reactance theory is that rape grows out of a fairly common situation but that only a few men resort to force. The theoretical challenge is therefore to identify what sort of men will do this. What type of personality traits set sexually coercive men apart from others?

In our view, a leading candidate is the trait of narcissism, which has emerged as an object of study in recent years as researchers have begun to search for the "dark side" of high self-esteem. It is named for a man in Greek mythology who fell in love with his own image as reflected in a pond; he became indifferent to the love of other people and cared only about himself. The term *narcissism* is also linguistically related to the word *narcotic*, implying perhaps that people sometimes become addicted to loving themselves.

Clinical psychologists began using the term *narcissism* in Freud's day to refer to self-love and in particular to a personality disorder that is defined in the American Psychiatric Association's *Diagnostic and Statistical Manual of Mental Disorders* (1994) as characterized by at least five of the following patterns: a grandiose sense of self-importance; frequent fantasies of enjoying great power, success, wealth, beauty, or brilliance; belief that oneself is special and unique and hence can only be understood by other elite individuals; arrogance or haughtiness; excessive quest for admiration; envy, either as a tendency to envy others or to believe that oneself is the target of others' envy; exaggerated or unrealistic sense of entitlement; willingness to exploit others; and lack of empathy toward others. In more recent editions of the *Manual*, the last criterion (empathy) shifted from regarding these people as unable to empathize with others to being simply unwilling to empathize. Thus, the narcissist is capable of seeing and appreciating others' views, but he or she does not always make the effort.

Although these criteria were devised for the sake of diagnosing clinical patients, probably most readers can think of people who fit them. Sure enough, research psychologists picked up on the ideas of narcissism and began to think in terms of a personality pattern that is spread through the so-called normal population. A measure was devised to assess people from all walks of life in terms of their degree of narcissism (Raskin & Terry, 1988).

This application of the trait of narcissism quickly proved useful. In one relevant context, it helped resolve a long-standing debate about the link between self-esteem and aggression. For decades, psychologists had believed that low self-esteem caused aggression, but a review of studies on violent individuals showed that they tended to have quite favorable opinions of themselves, contrary to the low self-esteem theory (Baumeister, Smart, & Boden, 1996). Yet the opposite view, that high self-esteem causes aggression, was not tenable either, because plenty of people with high self-esteem are not aggressive. Laboratory research confirmed that pure measures of self-esteem have little or no relation to aggression, but that narcissists are prone to lash out at others, especially when the others have criticized or disrespected them (Bushman & Baumeister, 1998). Violent offenders who have been convicted of murder, rape, robbery, assault, and similar crimes score above average in narcissism, as compared to other men of their same age (Bushman, Baumeister, Phillips, & Gilligan, 1999).

Applied to rape, the concept of narcissism therefore seems quite promising as a way of sorting the men who will respect a woman's refusal from those who press ahead and use force on her. Narcissists do in fact exhibit higher rates of reactance than other people (Catanese & Yost, 1999). Meanwhile, rapists also show various patterns that suggest narcissism. For one thing, many of them tend to be quite conceited. When interviewing convicted rapists in prison, Scully (1990) was surprised to find that they described themselves as "multitalented superachievers" and boasted about their many wonderful traits, including their love-making skills.

Narcissists want to think well of themselves and want others to think well of them. Rapists likewise show such patterns. In the prison study, many rapists told Scully that they believed their victims regarded them favorably, which is absurd in the face of actual statistics—especially because the victim had to press charges and testify in order to put the man in prison!

Along the same lines, several studies have found that sexually coercive men tend to have male peer groups that put pressure on them to have sex (Kanin, 1985; Lisak & Roth, 1988). The rapists feel they must have sexual conquests to boast about in order to maintain their status in the group. These men tend to use plenty of legal and marginal methods to convince women to have sex, such as claiming to be in love with them or trying to get them drunk. The use of force is often one of the last resorts when lesser methods fail to seduce the woman.

The victim-perpetrator discrepancy in reporting of rape makes sense when viewed in the context of narcissism. As we concluded earlier, the discrepancy is mainly caused by men's failure to remember or acknowledge that they used force to pressure a woman into sex. If rape were primarily about force rather than sex, it is unlikely that men would forget using force, but if rapists are narcissists seeking sex, then they would be highly inclined to forget their use of force. After all, a man who has to force women to have sex with him does not sound like an admirable or skilled lover but more like a desperate person. The narcissist wants to regard his sexual escapades as tributes to his sex appeal and charm, and he wants to boast about them to his friends. Therefore he wants to erase any fact that he had to force the woman. The way he'd prefer to tell it, the woman thought he was so wonderful that she was happy to give him sex.

A key part of narcissism is the inflated sense of entitlement. Narcissists believe that they are special and therefore deserve to have others treat them preferentially. Consistent with this emphasis, Bushman and his colleagues (1999) found that the entitlement section of the narcissism scale was the one that produced the biggest and most reliable differences between violent prisoners and college students. This helps resolve another of the problems we noted in applying reactance theory to rape, namely the question of whether the rapists might really feel that the woman owed them sex or that they had a right to pursue their pleasure even by coercive means.

The exaggerated sense of entitlement is related to several types of sexual coercion. In one category, a couple has been dating for a period of time and are already in love. (Remember, the NHSLS found that the largest single category of rapes was committed by someone the woman was in love with at the time.) In these cases, the woman is not ready to have intercourse. Most men will wait more or less patiently until their partner is ready (McCabe, 1987), but a narcissist may feel that the woman owes him sex after a certain amount of time, effort, and money have been expended. The narcissist may also feel that if he fails to obtain sex from his girlfriend after a certain number of dates, he will lose face in front of his pals, and so he uses force to give him the conquest he thinks he deserves.

In other cases, the narcissistic man may have just begun dating a woman but believes he is entitled to have sex with her anyway. Possibly he thinks he is charming, or perhaps other women have permitted him to have sex early in the relationship, and so he thinks each new partner owes it to him.

In recent years, there have been increasing reports that successful athletes perpetrate acts of sexual violence against women (Benedict, 1997). These do not seem to emerge from any general pattern of violence or hatred of women on the part of the men. But athletes are celebrities in our society, which can well increase their narcissism. Moreover, there are many women who do have sex with athletes on a relatively casual basis, without asking for much in return. If an athlete succumbs to the temptation to start regarding himself as a special being who is entitled to such treatment, he may grow angry at a woman who fails to give him what he expects and may therefore force her. The highly publicized rape conviction of boxing champion Mike Tyson was an example of this pattern. He did not prowl a dark alley and leap upon an innocent victim. Rather, he believed he was dating her, and she agreed to come to his hotel room, where he raped her. We are not offering any justification for his action, and we reiterate that a woman (or a man) has a right to refuse sex at any point. But to a narcissistic male accustomed to getting what he wants, a woman's refusal may provoke anger and the use of force.

The inflated sense of entitlement helps explain one other surprising pattern among rapists: In her prison interviews with rapists, Scully (1990) reported that many of the men told her their victim was known to be sexually loose in the sense that she had had sex with many men. These claims are plausible, because having a higher than usual number of lifetime sex partners is a risk factor for rape (Laumann et al., 1994). But it is surprising that the men would describe their victims in those terms. Morally, of course, her prior acts are irrelevant, and legally it would seem to put the man in a worse position. After all, if she has consented to have sex with many previous men, she certainly knows what consent is, and so her accusation of rape should gain in credibility. It seems self-defeating for rapists to claim that their accusers were known to have consented to sex with other men.

Yet to a narcissist, there may be a certain twisted logic to claiming that the victim was promiscuous. The narcissist believes he is better than other men, and so he cannot easily accept the fact that a woman might say yes to other men but no to him. If the woman is known to be a sexual being, then the narcissist feels entitled to have sex with her if he wants. Her refusal seems unreasonable to him.

The other features of narcissism are likewise reflected in sexual coercion. Narcissists tend to have an exploitative attitude toward others, and of course sexual coercion exploits a woman for the man's pleasure. As we noted, sexually coercive men tend to use a broad range of illicit techniques for obtaining sex, such as trying to get the woman drunk or making false promises of love.

The narcissist's lack of empathy is particularly helpful in understanding rapists. Several researchers have asked rapists what they thought their victim was experiencing during the rape. One category of answers is that they thought the woman was enjoying it, which already indicates low empathy, because approximately 0 percent of rape victims report any pleasure at all. (In fact, Scully [1990] reported that some convicted rapists continued to believe that the woman had really wanted to have sex with them, even though the men had had to use a knife or gun to coerce them!)

Another, even more common answer was that the rapists had simply not thought about what the victim was experiencing and did not know what she felt at all. This seems astonishing: How can someone engage in such an intimate contact as sex without even having some idea of what one's partner is feeling? But narcissists can turn off their empathy and be indifferent to what their victims feel.

The empathy point is also relevant to another interesting line of work. Researchers had begun fairly early to measure the reactions of rapists versus noncoercive men to violent pornography. Not surprisingly, the rapists were more aroused by such films, and this was taken as supporting various theories (including the radical feminist view that rape is about violence). When critics objected that it might simply reflect a high sex drive, researchers responded by comparing how the two groups reacted to nonviolent erotica. Typically there was no difference between the groups: Both rapists and nonrapists found nonviolent sex films arousing. There, said the researchers, sexual violence clearly has a special appeal to rapists.

But that conclusion is misleading too. If violent sex had a special appeal to rapists, then they should exhibit higher arousal to violent sex films than to nonviolent sex films, but that is not what generally happened. Instead, rapists showed high arousal to both kinds of films. To normal men, however, any hint of force or violence was a severe turn-off. The implication was that rapists simply liked to look at all sex films and did not care very much whether the woman was depicted as consenting or objecting, which is consistent with the theory that these men have low empathy.

Let us sum up the findings. It is quite true that the current state of knowledge does not yield a single clear explanation for why men commit rape. Over the past three decades, theories about rape have been dominated by the radical feminist view that it is not sexual, which no longer fits the data, and to a lesser degree by evolutionary arguments that are somewhat plausible but that do not offer a very thorough explanation. We have proposed a theory that seems to fit the current facts, although it must be regarded as far from a proven truth. Borrowing from social and personality psychology, we propose that many acts of rape conform to a pattern of narcissistic reactance. Certain highly conceited, exploitative men respond aggressively when a woman refuses to have sex with them and force her to submit to their wishes.

The Victim's Dilemmas

The previous section was devoted to trying to understand the motives and inner processes that enable men to engage in sexual coercion. Yet even if the rapist were fully understood, that might not be of much practical help for rape victims (although a thorough understanding of its causes might help efforts to reduce or prevent rape). Helping victims must continue to be our society's primary concern with regard to sexual coercion, and so in this section we refocus on the victim.

Contrary to stereotypes, there is no single pattern that defines all victims of sexual coercion. The research literature contains vastly different portraits. Some evidence that rape has lasting harmful effects is available from various sources. For example, a well-known study of women who were sexually coerced during childhood found that many of them were still groping painfully for an explanation and continued to suffer even two or three decades after the fact (Silver, Boon, & Stones, 1983). And Rynd (1988) found that rape victims reported loss of enjoyment of sex after the rape: Apparently the victimization led to a lasting decrease in their capacity to find sexual satisfaction. The victims also reported various somatic (physical health) complaints that increased after the rape.

On the other hand, a study by Murnen et al. (1989) found that most victims "communicated varying degrees of acceptance of the unwanted sex" (p. 101), and that "some seemed eager to label this person [the rapist] a friend" (p. 104). The authors also concluded that the low rate of reporting of these incidents of sexual coercion, along with the woman's subsequent continued friendship with the man who had coerced her, reflected the victim's belief that the event was not important. Similar variability emerged from the NHSLS and follow-up analyses (Laumann et al., 1994, 1999), which found that although many victims of sexual coercion suffered long-term impairments of health, well-being, and sexuality, plenty of others showed no signs of lasting harm.

The wide variability in responses can be ascribed to at least two factors. First, incidents of sexual coercion span a wide continuum, and some are clearly much more traumatic than others. Second, women (and men) differ substantially in their ability to cope with sexual victimization, as with any kind of trauma or misfortune, and so even identical episodes may cause lasting distress to some women while having relatively brief and minimal effects on others.

The variation in the effects of the incidents is easy to see. We noted that estimates of the incidence of victimization vary widely from one study to another, because some count only severe traumas involving forced intercourse, whereas others count even a quick unwanted kiss as sexual coercion. Even with forced intercourse, there may be wide variation depending on the circumstances. In some incidents, women are attacked and brutally beaten by strangers, leaving them fearing for their lives. In other cases, the woman was in love with the man and consented to undress and engage in foreplay or oral sex, and thus the coercion involved him pushing her beyond a limit she had set. In both of these situations, the man is morally in the wrong and the coercion is unjustifiable, but it is hard to doubt that the average woman would suffer more in the former than in the latter case.

The variation in the impaact of rape on women was the focus of an investigation by Meyer and Taylor (1986), who began by reviewing existing evidence about how women adjust to rape: Many victims suffer lasting fear and anxiety, sexual dissatisfaction, depression, and other problems, whereas others are virtually free of any symptoms past the first month or two after the incident. Meyer and Taylor wanted to understand how victims' own inner coping processes could help mediate these different outcomes. They surveyed victims contacted through a rape crisis center, a method that probably screened out both the mildest reactions (by people who would never even call the crisis center) and the most severe (by those whom counselors and therapists might shield from participation in such a study). Indeed, 83 percent of their sample had been raped by strangers, which is far out of line with the NHSLS conclusion that only 4 percent of incidents of sexual coercion involve strangers.

Self-blame was one focus of Meyer and Taylor's investigation. An earlier, influential study of people who were paralyzed in traffic accidents and other mishaps had found that people who blamed themselves adjusted *better* than those who did not (Bulman & Wortman, 1977). This finding created a stir, because the general assumption had been that victims are better off when they do not blame themselves. The new interpretation, however, argued that blaming yourself restores some sense of control: If I brought this on myself, such as by taking a foolish chance, then I can prevent future misfortunes by changing my behavior. In contrast, if I could have done nothing to prevent this misfortune, then I cannot prevent further disasters.

Subsequent work failed to find that self-blame was consistently associated with better adjustment among various groups of victims. Janoff-Bulman (1979, 1992) concluded that there are two types of self-blame, which have very different effects. *Behavioral self-blame*, which means attributing your misfortune to your own actions, may be beneficial because it restores a sense of control. In contrast, *characterological self-blame*, which means attributing your misfortune to the type of person you are (for example, "This happened because I'm a bad person who deserves to suffer"), is not constructive and may even impair recovery. You cannot change the type of person you are, and so seeing your troubles as rooted in your unchanging essential nature implies that more disasters are likely to come your way and that there is nothing you can do about them.

Both kinds of self-blame were found among Meyer and Taylor's (1986) sample. Indeed, they concluded that about half the victims blamed themselves for the rape incident, at least in part. (Janoff-Bulman's [1979] study had yielded an even higher figure: She concluded that three out of four rape victims engage in self-blame.) Yet the distinction between behavioral and characterological self-blame failed to differentiate the women who coped well from those who did not. On the contrary, Meyer and Taylor found that both types of self-blame were associated with poor adjustment.

Other aspects of how the victims coped with rape were correlated with good versus bad adjustment, although it is impossible to tell from such data what is the cause and what is the effect. Women who engaged in stress reduction practices, such as thinking positive thoughts and seeking calm through meditation, adjusted better than other victims. Meanwhile, women who withdrew from others and stayed home much of the time tended to fare worse than others. The victims themselves often mentioned receiving counseling and talking to friends and family (as well as taking more precautions to prevent further victimization) as the most helpful strategies for coping with the rape.

Thus, it appears that self-blame does not contribute to coping with rape by strangers. Yet as we have seen, most forcible sex does not occur between strangers. Even if stranger rape could be completely eliminated, it would make only a small dent in the total amount of sexual coercion in the United States (although it would have a bigger effect on official rape statistics, which tend to emphasize stranger rapes because coercion within romantic couples generally goes unreported to police).

Victims of coercion by romantic partners and acquaintances may face a different set of adjustment challenges. In general, these episodes may be less traumatic than stranger rapes, particularly because they are less likely to include physical violence. For them, repairing the relationship may be a significant aspect of the adjustment process. A man who forces sex on a woman has clearly violated her trust to some degree, and so the future of the relationship may be jeopardized. Murnen et al. (1989) found that the man's attitude made a substantial difference: Women were far more willing to forgive him if he apologized for the incident.

The Dilemma of Reporting

Until recently, our society treated rape victims rather harshly. Police and other investigators were suspicious of many rape charges. If a rape case went to trial, the lawyer for the defense would often question the victim's motives and behavior as a way of creating a doubt in the jury's minds as to whether she had in fact consented. The common suggestion that the victim had "asked for it," such as by wearing sexy clothing, often ended up making the victim feel like she was responsible for the incident and led some to discuss the legal investigation as a "second victimization" of the woman.

Why have people been inclined to blame the victim? One reason undoubtedly has to do with the belief in a just world (Lerner, 1980). The essence of this belief is that people get what they deserve in life, and so by implication they must deserve whatever they get. The ideal of a fair and just society was one of the main foundations of the American nation, and people want to believe that it has been realized (by and large). Certainly from the start America was far fairer to more people than other countries were at the time the Constitution was written, and it continues to be among the world leaders in fairness and justice by most measures.

The theory about belief in a just world extends beyond societal ideals, however, to include important personal motives. As we saw in Chapter 2, most people believe themselves to be good, respectable, deserving individuals, and so it is comforting to them to believe that the world is largely just and fair, because if it is, then their own goodness will be rewarded.

These idealistic and personally comforting beliefs work to the disadvantage of rape victims (and other crime victims), however. If the world is fair and people get what they deserve, then rape victims must have somehow deserved to be raped, possibly because their own actions caused the rape to happen. Although such sentiments are generally wrong and quite unfair to the victim, they may appeal to the public and in particular to the jury, who will think that if the woman was raped because of her own actions or character, then other people have nothing to fear. In contrast, if they conclude that her behavior was perfectly normal and proper but that she was raped anyway, this implies that rape can happen to anyone, including to them or their families. In such cases, the truth is quite distressing, and people may prefer to believe that the event was in some way the victim's fault.

These patterns create a serious dilemma for the victim. On the one hand, she may want to report the crime and have the rapist prosecuted. Even apart from her own feelings, she may feel that it is her civic duty to report the crime to prevent the rapist from victimizing other women in the future. The laws cannot be enforced unless victims press charges, and society cannot afford to let rape laws go unenforced.

Yet for her to report the crime is to expose herself to the questions and even attacks that a rape victim must often face. To dwell on the crime is undoubtedly to prolong her own suffering. As Meyer and Taylor (1986) showed, many victims tend to blame themselves for rape anyway, and facing a jury who tends to blame them would reinforce and intensify those beliefs and the accompanying distress.

To some extent, the patterns of blaming the rape victim have subsided. The feminist movement of the 1970s deserves substantial credit for altering society's attitudes about rape and for creating the need for a more sensitive, supportive understanding of the rape victim. The legal process has undoubtedly gotten better for victims, although it is still far from easy.

Ultimately, recovery from any sort of trauma requires putting the episode behind oneself and facing the future. Roxanne Silver, who has spent her life studying many forms of trauma and victimization, has summarized one general conclusion this way: People who are oriented toward the future tend to do well and recover effectively, whereas those who remain focused on the past (particularly the episode) tend to adjust poorly (e.g., Holman & Silver, 1998). Thus, if a rape victim presses charges, she remains focused on the trauma (possibly for several years, depending on the legal process), which may impair her ability to recover and get on with her life.

The Dilemma of Consent

Unfortunately the legal system still contains a serious flaw that works to the disadvantage of rape victims: In many trials, the jury's verdict depends on evaluating the conflicting accounts of the rapist and the victim—and the biggest conflict concerns whether the victim consented to sex. Because the American legal system is set up to protect the innocent, any reasonable doubt is officially enough to produce a not guilty verdict. In rape trials, the accused rapist is the defendant, and so he benefits from those reasonable doubts. In other words, the burden of proof is often on the woman: She must prove that she did not consent to sex. Such proof is difficult under any circumstances, but it is especially difficult given the conditions under which much sexual coercion occurs.

Take a typical case of the sort that Kanin (1985) found common among the men who admitted to engaging in date rape. The man and the woman go out on several dates. On one date, the woman invites him up to her apartment (or accompanies him willingly to his). They kiss and stroke each other. She takes off some or all of her clothes, and they have oral sex. He wants to have vaginal intercourse. She says no. He forces her.

Kanin reported that none of the cases in his sample went to trial, and it is understandable why: What chance would the woman have had? If she told the exact truth, while the man insisted that she had consented to the vaginal intercourse, how could she prove him wrong? The defense lawyer would ask why she had taken off her clothes if she did not want to have sex with him? The jury would almost certainly entertain some reasonable doubt.

It is difficult to design a social system that is free of that problem. The goal would be to shift the burden of proof off the victim and onto the perpetrator, without ultimately sending innocent men to prison. Social psychology has, however, found solutions to problems of consent in its own practices. In the wake of revelations that medical researchers had occasionally performed experiments without their subjects' consent, psychologists have adopted guidelines to protect both the participants and researchers from the problems that might ensue if someone felt harmed by research procedures. Central to these guidelines is the practice of informed consent: The research participant typically signs some statement indicating that he or she has been informed of what will take place and willingly agrees to complete the procedure.

Could such a practice work with sex? States would pass laws requiring men to obtain a signed consent form from the woman before intercourse. (A gender-neutral form of this law would require both parties to give each other a signed form.) Presumably a one-sentence statement would be enough. Copies of this form could be distributed in condom packages and made available in other ways.

Obviously the exchange of legal documents, even brief ones, would complicate certain aspects of sex. Seduction would become more difficult, because instead of gradually persuading someone to go each step farther, it would be necessary to stop and sign forms, which means that the target of the seduction could stop and consider whether the encounter was really a good idea.

Another obstacle would be that many people would not want to know that other people possessed documents that they had signed to consent to sexual intercourse. This may be particularly true for women (and even more so for famous women). After all, imagine owning a form signed by Marilyn Monroe, or Madonna, or Hillary Clinton. Decades later, these could prove to be an embarrassment to the woman, and they might fetch high prices at public auctions even years after her death. Probably some law to protect the confidentiality of signees would be necessary (as it is with research participants now).

Adultery would also be affected. For a woman to have sex outside of marriage is always a risk, because if her infidelity is discovered by her husband, she might suffer personal and legal penalties. This does not necessarily speak against the idea, though: A procedure that reduced marital infidelity, which a consent form for sex would surely do, would be considered by many to be a good thing, because most people regard extramarital sex as immoral.

But although requiring a signed consent form for sex would probably create some problems for various women (and possibly men), it would at least offer strong protection to rape victims. The signed consent form would make life easier for the victim and harder for the adulterer, but they are not on the same footing, and our society's first obligation would seemingly be to protect the rape victim rather than the adulterer.

Naturally any couple could go ahead and have sex without signing the consent forms. Those cases might continue much as they do now. The difference would be that the man would be taking the risk. The legal rule would be as follows: If the woman came back and accused him of rape, and if sexual intercourse between them were established, then he would be presumed guilty unless he had a signed consent form. He might prove his innocence in some other way, but still the burden of proof would be on him, not on her, as it generally has been throughout world history. If there is no other proof, and it comes down to his word against hers, the rule could be that he must produce the signed form or lose.

The sexual experience itself might be changed by requiring a consent form. For one thing, as a general principle an explicit act of consent tends to make people enjoy what they are doing somewhat more. Research on cognitive dissonance, for example, has shown that people hold more positive attitudes toward various actions if their own consent to them is made salient beforehand (Linder, Cooper, & Jones, 1967).

Sex might also change even among couples who decide to skip the consent form. Because the man would be the one taking the risk, he would have an extra incentive for making sure that the experience was a good one for the woman. He would probably feel some need to treat her more positively, lest she accuse him of rape afterward—a charge from which he could then not well defend himself, because he had failed to get her signature.

Putting the man at risk in that way would certainly alter some of the balance of power and other interaction contingencies between men and women. But probably those shifts would be generally to the good. Men, after all, are larger and stronger than women, and so giving men an extra incentive to be nice to women is probably a good idea by and large.

One could in fact question whether the informed consent law would actually affect the majority of cases of sex (even between unmarried people). Probably men would still be willing to take their chances if a woman refused. The lack of a consent form would really only become a problem for a man who found himself on trial for rape. And such rape trials are extremely rare in proportion to the number of incidents of sexual intercourse that take place throughout society every day.

Is it plausible that our society will begin requiring proof of consent to sex? It would certainly be consistent with the shift toward greater legal regulation of everyday life as well as with trends regarding proof of consent. Once upon a time, business deals were sealed with little more than a handshake, and research participants were simply run through procedures without any legal documents. Now the laws are increasingly present. Still, requiring legal documents to be signed prior to sexual intercourse seems like a big step, and getting people to actually use them on a regular basis is an even bigger one.

Without some such procedure, however, the burden of proof remains on the rape victim, and it is generally a very difficult burden to handle. Throughout history, most sexual activities have taken place in private. That very privacy ensures that different accounts come down to his word against hers. The way the system is set up now, the reasonable doubt requirement means that his word is likely to prevail. If our society is to make rape trials more sympathetic to the victim, something must be changed to let the woman sometimes get the benefit of the doubt.

10 Sex and Prejudice

The Marriage Bed as a Bastion of Racism and Sexism

Is the United States a deeply prejudiced society? The answer can only be, "Compared to what?" Compared to American ideals of equal opportunity and freedom for all, the current society falls far short, and there can be no denying that racism and sexism continue to exist and cause problems for many individuals. On the other hand, compared to most other countries in the history of the world, the United States is a paragon of freedom and opportunity. Women and minorities are far better off in today's United States than they have been in most other societies, including America's own past, when legal restrictions kept people on narrow life paths that offered them almost no chance to taste the best rewards society had to offer.

We concur with the assessment of Orlando Patterson, an eminent scholar and Harvard professor, as well as an African American: "The sociological truths are that America, while still flawed in its race relations is now the least racist white-majority society in the world; has a better record of legal protection of minorities than any other society, white or black; offers more opportunities to a greater number of black persons than any other society, including all those of Africa" (quoted in Krauthammer, 1997). Again, the degree of racism you identify in the United States depends on what you compare it to: It is far short of ideal, but better than most.

The progress that the United States has made toward offering freedom and opportunity to all its citizens owes much to affirmative action programs that sought to redress historical injustices by preferential treatment. The society's main schools, universities, government agencies, and corporations had been founded and developed by white males, and for a long time only white males were allowed to participate in them. During the feminist and civil rights movements, however, these were thrown open aggressively, so that they were pressured to make themselves more diverse.

The courts led the way in integrating schools, neighborhoods, corporations, and other institutions. They began to interpret the laws aggressively, and judges punished organizations that excluded women and minorities until they changed. The courts, which is to say a great many idealistic white male judges, fined companies that failed to hire black people, prosecuted organizations that refused to promote women, mandated the busing of schoolchildren across town so that the schools would be racially integrated, and so forth. In short, they helped the American ideal of integration come closer to reality.

Despite their good works and noble intentions, however, the courts could be accused of major hypocrisy: They insisted that everyone else integrate, but they did not take many steps to promote integration in their own sphere. Marriage, in particular, is largely under the control of the legal system, but the courts did not inconvenience themselves by insisting that marriage should show progress in integration. The courts imposed their ideal vision on everyone else, but they did not implement it in their own back yard.

In this chapter, we will explore the idea that marriage is America's strongest remaining bastion of racism and sexism. The argument is that the American patterns of marriage perpetuate inequality between the races and between the sexes, and that this inequality will serve to perpetuate prejudice and other bad consequences.

If this argument is correct, it suggests that further progress in eliminating racism and sexism may require some important changes in the way Americans marry. Our society has come far in its efforts to end prejudice and discrimination, but perhaps it will be unable to approach its ideals of full equality as long as inequality is entrenched in the patterns of marriage. Possibly some changes in those patterns should be contemplated.

Of course, some might object: You can't tell people whom to marry, because marriage is a private choice and as such an essential exercise of individual freedom. Yet such objections are quite similar to those raised several decades ago when the government wanted to end discrimination in restaurant service or housing. You can't tell people whom to sell their house to, because the home is private property, and choice of a buyer is a vital exercise of individual freedom. A restaurant is a private business, and you can't tell an owner what members of the public should or should not be served there, because that infringes on his freedoms.

Perhaps we cannot force people to marry, sell to, or serve people they dislike. But we can punish them for making choices in a way that is harmful to society at large—or we can at least reward other people who make choices that do help society achieve its goals. Ultimately the government can't really force people to do very many things. Mainly it can manipulate some of the penalties and, better, can make symbolic gestures that express and shape the society's values. If the government were to decide that interracial marriage were a good thing, for example, it might encourage the practice by enacting some positive sign of approval.

We shall consider the racism and sexism issues separately, because the relevant aspects of marriage are quite different. Hence let us leave sexism for a moment and focus on racism.

Because issues of prejudice are politically sensitive and because it is common for most participants in such debates to accuse each other of bias, we shall acknowledge our own political views up front. We favor equality and integration. As Martin Luther King, Jr., stated, integration is the most democratic and morally commendable idea in the entire history of racial politics, and it is probably the key to equality of opportunity. We recognize that many American citizens are currently leaning toward the support of racial separation, but we are skeptical (although willing to be convinced) that such a philosophy will work out well. Integration seems the best policy to us, and partial or limited integration is less likely to bring success than full integration. And full integration would include integrating families, rather than just neighborhoods or schools. For moral reasons, therefore, we support interracial romance as a positively desirable social trend, comparable to racial integration of sports teams, law firms, and apartment buildings. Still, our primary commitment is to finding the truth, and so we would willingly change our views if the data should point toward a different pattern as being better for society as a whole and fairer to all individuals involved.

Racism in Marriage

Shakespeare's famous play *Romeo and Juliet* depicts two young people in love with each other despite strong pressures from both families against the relationship. The families have been rivals and hold long-standing grudges, but the young couple want only to be together. The moral issue seems straightforward to modern audiences: Of course the families should bury their antagonisms and allow the couple to be happy together.

Yet audiences in Shakespeare's day may not have seen the play with the same values, and it may have had much greater and more controversial moral implications. In those days, family loyalty was considered much more important than personal feelings, and some considered passionate love to be a kind of mental derangement that caused irrational behavior (e.g., Stone, 1977). For the young couple to go against their families' wishes to pursue their own selfish happiness and passion-crazed goals was thus morally questionable.

Modern audiences might be able to appreciate *Romeo and Juliet* more along the lines Shakespeare had in mind if the staging were changed to make the opposition to the couple's romance more plausible. One of several possible ways of doing this would be to cast Juliet as a young black woman, while keeping Romeo white (or, conversely, to have Romeo black and Juliet white). (The musical *West Side Story* took a step in this direction by recasting the tale as an interethnic romance.) Many people today are ambivalent or even hostile toward interracial romance, and the families' opposition to the romance would be something that modern audiences could understand.

America's failure to racially integrate families can be appreciated statistically. Imagine, for a moment, that skin color were no more important than hair color or eye color or blood type. Imagine, in other words, that the United States were a fully integrated society, with black, white, Asian, and other ethnicities mixing freely and intermarrying without paying any heed to such differences.

Marriage across racial lines would therefore occur at the same rates one would predict by drawing names randomly from a hat. Today's society breaks down roughly as 12 percent black, 9 percent Latino, 5 percent Asian, 2 percent Native American, and 72 percent white of European descent. Those would reflect the odds of what any given person's spouse would be. For the minorities, marrying someone from the same minority group would be extremely unlikely. For example, 95 percent of Asians would marry someone who was not Asian, and 88 percent of black people would marry someone who was not black.

The actual distribution of marriage today is radically different from that hypothetical picture of total integration. For example, if there were no discrimination involved, 88 percent of married black women would have nonblack husbands. In reality, according to the 1990 census, only 2 percent of married black women have nonblack husbands (Stevens & Tyler, in press). The dramatic difference between 2 percent and 88 percent shows the magnitude of racial bias in mate selection. Racial segregation is the norm in marriage.

Is this peculiar to marriage, or does it apply to all sexual relations? Evidence suggests that there is almost as much race-based selection in sex partners in general as in marriage. People overwhelmingly go to bed with members of their own race. The NHSLS found that the same-race bias was alive and well even in nonmarital, noncohabitational partnerships: Across black and white Americans, 90 percent of their sex partners were from their own same race. Latinos were somewhat more willing to take non-Latino partners, but they still displayed a pronounced favoritism for members of their own group (Laumann et al., 1994).

The sex partner data are relevant because, as one begins to look for the causes of the same-race bias in mate selection, one might suspect that "the system" forces people to avoid members of other races. To be sure, for a long time the legal system did prohibit marriage across racial lines. It was not until the 1960s that the last laws against interracial marriage (miscegenation) were ended in the United States. Those laws were enacted under the aegis of racial bias, and indeed it seems difficult to understand how someone could be opposed to interracial marriage without being motivated by racial prejudice. In other words, what reason other than racism is there for opposing interracial marriage?

Today, it is not so much the system as the individual people themselves who exercise racial discrimination. In choosing their sex partners, and later in choosing their spouses, the majority of individual Americans show a strong preference for members of their own race.

To be sure, the bias may not be specific to sex. As Laumann et al. (1994) have pointed out, people get their sex partners from their social networks, and informal social networks may be racially segregated. If a young Asian American man, for example, grows up in a neighborhood where nearly all the families are Asian American and attends schools that are likewise full of his own kind, it would be surprising if his sex partners and spouse were any different. Marriages between Asian Americans and African Americans are statistically rather rare, but this may reflect the fact that the two groups do not socialize together a great deal and hence have little opportunity to form the romantic attachments that can lead to marriage.

Is the Low Rate of Intermarriage a Problem?

Let us first consider whether the relative lack of interracial marriage is a problem. After all, many societies have regarded intermarriages as bad. Mixed marriages, whether mixed by religion, race, ethnicity, or other categories, have often been subjected to social and legal pressures. The United States has recently changed its laws to tolerate interracial marriage, but many Americans remain opposed to it.

Still, the fact that some societies have upheld racial discrimination as being good and have put the force of law behind it does not mean that it is desirable. Many societies have enforced racial separation in housing, occupation, education, and other spheres, but others have argued convincingly that such separation is often harmful. It is important to consider the social consequences and implications of marital segregation.

Money is always important in a society, and the implications of marital segregation on money are clear. If one group has more money than another, intermarriage will distribute the wealth more equitably, whereas segregated marriage patterns will tend to preserve economic inequality. In the United States, black and Latino people are often poorer than the white majority. If people only marry within their racial group, these economic inequalities will be preserved. Blacks and Latinos people will continue to be poorer, generation by generation, because they start off that way. But if they intermarried with the relatively prosperous whites, the economic difference would quickly dwindle.

On the other hand, any special cultural resources that a particular group has will be jeopardized by intermarriage. It is possible (although not proven) that some cultural resources might require a certain kind of environment in order to be preserved. Certainly people have long felt that their group identity could be jeopardized by intermarriage. Immigrants often preserve loyalty to their country of origin, and they fear that if their children marry people from another group, the link to the homeland would be lost. Hence they teach and pressure their children to avoid dating anyone outside their own group.

The implications for racial prejudice itself must be acknowledged. The more that two groups remain separate, the more easily they can be categorized. Stereotypes often have their roots in a mentality that sorts "us" from "them." But if "our" children marry "their" children, the groups cease to have clearly drawn lines. Categorizing becomes increasingly difficult. Recent studies of social perception have confirmed the link between prejudice and distinctions: Highly prejudiced people are more careful and thorough about deciding borderline cases (such as in ascertaining whether someone is black or white) than are less prejudiced individuals (Blascovich et al., 1997). Interracial mixing makes it more difficult for bigots to map out their social world and divide "us" from "them."

Research has confirmed that intimate interactions can help reduce prejudice. Several studies by McLaughlin-Volpe, Aron, Wright, and Reis (1999) involved having people keep a brief diary that recorded all their interactions for several weeks. Prejudice (as measured by a questionnaire) was not related to the total number of interracial interactions, nor to the variety of interaction—but it was significantly related to the number and frequency of *close or intimate* interactions with people from other races. The more close and intimate interactions with members from other races, the less prejudice. In plain terms, having an interracial neighbor may not do much to reduce prejudice, whereas having interracial relatives will.

Moreover, by tracking these trends over time, the researchers were able to ascertain that the causal arrow works both ways. That is, prejudice makes people avoid interracial interactions, but a lack of intimate interactions with members of other races also contributes to maintaining and increasing prejudice. When people start having more intimate interactions with people of other races, their prejudices diminish. The effect of good quality interactions on reducing prejudice was the strongest effect they found (McLaughlin-Volpe et al., 1999). By extension, it seems likely that if people began dating, sleeping with, and marrying people of other races, their prejudices would dwindle drastically.

In fact, interracial marriage may diminish prejudice even among people other than the spouses themselves. Wright, Aron, McLaughlin-Volpe, and Ropp (1997) showed that prejudice and negative attitudes toward members of other racial and ethnic groups are reduced simply by knowing someone who has a friend in the outgroup. Simply observing friendships that cross group boundaries seems to have a valuable effect toward reducing prejudice in the observer. If your best friend married someone from a different race, your own negative attitudes or stereotypes about that race would be likely to grow weaker.

Although the modern United States is especially troubled over issues of racial prejudice, it is important to realize that other prejudices have been powerful at various times in history. The waves of immigration from Europe, for example, often fostered strong prejudices. Eastern Europeans such as Poles and Romanians were regarded as being of inferior intelligence. Irish were supposedly drunkards prone to violence. Italians were regarded as a scheming, greedy clan that all too readily tended to become corrupt and criminal.

These stereotypes gradually diminished, however, and intermarriage must be given a substantial amount of the credit. The immigrants often lived in small communities composed largely of their own nationality (e.g., "Little Italy"), but their children moved out and married people from other ethnic groups. After several generations of intermarriage, the ethnic distinctions could not be made in any meaningful way, and the stereotypes became impossible to sustain (except, perhaps, toward new immigrants from the same source).

Recent data confirm the changes. Stevens and Tyler (in press) noted that in 1910, 98 percent of Italian American women had husbands of Italian descent. In 1990, the vast majority married non-Italians. Thus, what once appeared as ironclad, immutable gulfs between ethnic groups have now all but disappeared. This has not occurred with race, though: The odds of a black woman having a black husband are 9,000 times greater than the odds of a nonblack woman having a black husband.

Perhaps a major reason that racial prejudices have not followed European nationality prejudices into oblivion is that people did not marry across racial lines. Skin color provided a stronger cue for group difference than anything available to distinguish members of some other groups. A fourth-generation descendant of a German immigrant does not look much different from a fourth-generation descendant of an Italian, Polish, or British immigrant. But skin color and other physical markings keep the races visibly distinct for many generations.

Can we look to history to teach us about the effects of promoting versus opposing intermarriage? There is a relevant historical precedent. The Roman Empire suppressed rebellions by Jews and eventually decided that it could not allow the Jewish state to continue to exist. Jews were scattered throughout the known world, and before long their homeland in Israel was conquered by Muslim Arabs. Yet the Jews living in de facto exile struggled to maintain their separate identity, religion, and traditions. Opposing intermarriage was regarded as vital to the Jews' survival as a people. For many centuries of European history, Jews and Christians avoided intermarriage yet lived side by side.

Was this costly? Undoubtedly it was. Strong prejudices survived among both Jewish and Christian Europeans. Many careers were barred to Jews, although their access to certain prosperous professions (including banking and medicine) allowed some of them to accumulate wealth.

The prejudices survived with separateness, and they often took an ugly turn. When the pope organized a Crusade to reclaim the Holy Land for Christianity, many embarking Christians celebrated their religious commitment by attacking and killing their longtime Jewish neighbors (e.g., Runciman, 1951–54). The Spanish Inquisition emerged when attempts to persecute Jews backfired in unexpected ways, and anti-Semitism fueled many of its worst excesses (Roth, 1964). Even in the twentieth century, after Christians and Jews had been living together for far more than a thousand years, there was still mass murder of Jews by Christians. And although the Nazi Holocaust was exceptional in its degree of systematic horror, it was far from the only violent outburst of anti-Semitism in the twentieth century.

None of these facts offers much hope for the prospect that Americans can live together comfortably, without prejudice, while maintaining separate communities who refuse to intermarry. On the other hand, the survival of the Jewish people depended on the refusal to intermarry. As Carmichael (1992) has pointed out, when the Jews lost their homeland and were dispersed through the Roman Empire, they were simply experiencing what many other peoples had already endured. The fate of these peoples was generally to disappear as a distinct group. With no government and no country, they spread through other lands and mingled with the peoples who lived there, and as they intermarried they lost any distinctive identity. The Jews survived as a people precisely because they refused to intermarry.

Such, then, is the dilemma faced by many minority groups. To refuse to intermarry is very likely to perpetuate their status as a minority and as the target of prejudice, but to intermarry is to sacrifice their unique identity. Individuals survive better if intermarriage is the norm. The collective group survives better if intermarriage is avoided. The well-being of the individual is thus in opposition to the well-being of the group.

Which is preferable overall? American values have traditionally favored individual rights over collective, and the support for integration was in part an outgrowth of this deeply American value. On the other hand, there has been a recent trend to reject the American "melting pot" scenario in favor of the enduring coexistence of separate groups. Two visions of the United States are thus in conflict.

In a sense, then, integration and diversity are two opposing values. The question of interracial marriage is one clear example of this. Intermarriage is simply one further step toward racial integration, and people who believe in racial integration must eventually regard the marriage bed as needing integration just as much as the workplace. On the other hand, people who want to preserve the separate identity of their own race will likely oppose integration—in marriage above all.

Inequality in Prejudice?

Prejudice and discrimination are usually ascribed to the dominant members of a culture. In the United States, that means white males. Still, it is not entirely clear that they are the ones most opposed to interracial romance. One scholar discussed the issue in 1966 and noted that many members of minority groups resist intermarriage too. "Of all the discriminations practiced against Negroes, Orientals, Indians, and other ethnic minorities, the prohibition against intermarriage is the one which the minority groups are least interested in abolishing," he observed (Weinberger, 1966, p. 160).

To be sure, not all groups show the same degree of same-race preference in sex and marriage. Some intermarry far more readily than others. It is challenging to consider what these differences might mean.

Blacks and whites are undoubtedly the most distinctive racial groups in today's United States, and far more attention is paid to race relations between blacks and whites than to relations among other groups. That difference is therefore one place to look. The 1990 census results show a clear asymmetry: Black men marry white women far more often than white men marry black women. Similar patterns are found in choice of sex partners regardless of marriage (Laumann et al., 1994).

White men and black women thus are in jeopardy of being accused of greater prejudice than their counterparts (black men and white women). It is not immediately clear, however, which one rejects the other. One approach would be to look at their openness to other races, such as Asians and Latinos. White men appear to be willing to mate with women from those groups, but black women do not mate with men from those groups. Thus, black women stand out as having the strongest same-race preference of any group in the United States in terms of sex and marriage partners.

Let us start considering the possible explanations for this. The most obvious must be considered first, which has to do with the availability of mates. If we assume that most people have some degree of same-race bias, then people who have plenty of available partners from their own racial group might be less likely to seek out mates from other groups.

This explanation fails to explain the same-race loyalty of black women, however. In fact, it increases the puzzle. There is a shortage of black men relative to black women. Various factors contribute to this imbalance, including a higher childhood mortality that affects males disproportionately, a relatively high death rate among young adult black men, and a heavy toll taken by the prison system. By some estimates, one out of every three black Americans in their twenties is either in prison or on probation ("A Social Profile," 1998). This reduces the number of eligible black men available to marry black women, because many women regard men with such legal problems as poor prospects for marriage, and of course the ones in prison do not even meet new women.

If black women were the most open of all groups to dating and marrying people from other races, this effect would easily be dismissed as being a result of the gender imbalance. One would conclude that, of course, black women have to marry men from other races because of the shortage of black men. But they do not. Instead, they retain their relatively exclusive preference for black men and do not marry others. As a result, many black women spend most of their lives without a husband or male partner. Given the economic and psychological benefits of marriage, the lack of black husbands is a significant hardship for these women. One is tempted to feel sorry for them. On the other hand, if these women remain unmarried simply as victims of their own racism, one would feel less sympathy. Why don't black women find nonblack mates? At present there is no clear answer to this question, but several possible explanations await clear data. Let us consider them each in turn.

One possible explanation is based on a general pattern based on differences in group size. Among political scientists, it is generally agreed that when a large and a small group exist in close proximity, the smaller group tends to have the greater prejudice. This is probably a natural and adaptive response in general, because small groups are generally more vulnerable to losing group competition than large groups. Obervations based on different groups in Europe show that small groups tend to have negative and even hostile attitudes toward the large group, while the large group has only vaguely negative attitudes toward the small group. After all, the large group can threaten the small group's very existence, but the small group is not usually a serious threat to the large group, and at most the small group serves as an occasional scapegoat for the large group. For example, patterns of sport support reflect these one-way feelings. Germany is larger than Holland, whereas Belgium is smaller. The Dutch report that when the Dutch national team is eliminated from the world soccer competition, they would support the Belgian national team as a friendly neighbor, but the Belgians would never root for the Dutch. In contrast, the Dutch fans would never support the German team no matter what else happened, whereas the Germans often support the Dutch after the German team is out. In both cases, the smaller country holds stronger and more negative attitudes toward the larger country.

Is it plausible that black people have more prejudice than white people, as the different group size pattern would predict? Judd, Park, Ryan, Brauer, and Kraus (1995) conducted a series of studies to examine same-race preferences in several samples of black and white people. They considered two forms of prejudice. One was "outgroup homogeneity," which is the belief that people of the other group are all the same. They called the other "ethnocentrism," by which they meant simply the view that one's own group consists of better people than the other group. Both patterns were found in both blacks and whites, but they were stronger among blacks.

This explanation does not quite fit the evidence, because it suggests that both black men and women would show a greater same-race preference than whites (but perhaps less than Latinos, Asians, and other smaller groups). As we have seen, black women seem to have a much greater bias than black men in this regard. Then again, it is difficult to compare men against women in terms of openness to a variety of sex partners, because men desire variety more than women. A man's attitude toward sleeping with someone from a different race might become more positive because of factors of sexual novelty and the like, whereas women might be less open because of fear of exploitation or other possible concerns. The history of exploitation of black women by white society and others could well help sustain these fears. Still, sexual novelty is hardly an explanation for marriage. Most men and most women want to marry, and you can only marry one person at a time.

The history of exploitation brings up another possible explanation, however. Let us assume that most people start off with a high tendency toward prejudice. This fits well with what is known about in-group bias. Many social-psychological studies have shown that people favor members of their own group in various ways, even if the group is created without any substantial basis or has just formed. An influential article by Brewer (1979) referred to how people will treat members of their group preferentially even when there is little or no practical reason to do so. Simply put, people just tend to support their own group mindlessly.

There is in fact an interesting story behind this line of research. It was discovered in the 1960s that people would give members of their own group preferential treatment, even in a group of strangers who were put together in a one-time laboratory study. Henri Tajfel and his colleagues designed a research program to ascertain the basis for this preference: Was it because one is similar to members of one's own group, or shares their fate, or knows them, or has emotional bonds with them, or sees them as extensions of oneself? Tajfel's approach was to start off with a group that would be so arbitrary and meaningless that no in-group bias would be found and then gradually to it add other factors, one at a time, to see which one factor (or combination of factors) proved decisive in creating in-group bias.

The program failed—but in a very interesting way (see Billig & Tajfel, 1973; Tajfel, 1970; Tajfel & Billig, 1974; Tajfel, Flament, Billig, & Bundy, 1971; Turner, 1985). It failed because the researchers were unable to create any group that was arbitrary and meaningless enough to prevent in-group bias. People showed favorability to their own group no matter how seemingly random or inconsequential it was. In simpler terms, you can bring people into the laboratory, and by a flip of the coin assign some to wear red hats and the others to wear blue hats. Within an hour, the ones wearing blue hats will be saying what idiots or scoundrels the red hats are, and vice versa. People become loyal to their in-group quite readily.

If this view is correct, then prejudice is the natural condition of the human being, and it is only overcome by considerable effort and education. This indeed is the core of an influential work by Devine (1989), who showed that prejudiced and nonprejudiced people both know stereotypes and think of them when they meet someone from the target group. The difference between prejudiced and nonprejudiced people is that the nonprejudiced ones override those prejudicial reactions and instead make themselves adopt egalitarian attitudes. Prejudice is like an ingrained bad habit that requires exertion to overcome.

And why do some people overcome it? The main reasons in modern society is that groups have learned that their prejudices oppress and harm others, and so out of their own moral idealism (supported by social pressures) they strive to rid themselves of those attitudes. In American society, a campaign of public education against racial prejudice is now in its fourth decade, but it has been mainly aimed at white people, whose prejudices contributed to the poverty, illiteracy, and other disadvantages of black citizens. This could help explain the findings by Judd et al. (1995) that we described earlier. It is in a way reassuring to learn that white antiblack prejudice is less than black antiwhite prejudice, because it suggests that these decades of public education aimed at reducing antiblack prejudice have accomplished some genuine reduction in that prejudice. It would be discouraging to think that prejudices remain as strong as ever despite all society's efforts to counteract and reduce them.

That brings us back to African American women. They have hardly ever oppressed anybody—indeed, even if they had wanted to oppress people, they were not often in a position to do so, given their lack of political and economic power. Hence there was never any major, concerted effort to persuade black women to overcome their prejudices. It is possible that black women have the same negative attitudes toward out-groups that most people start off with, simply because there was never any social pressure for black women to change those attitudes. That could help explain their pronounced preference for same-race mates.

Thus far we have focused on explanations based on the notion that black women have relatively high rates of same-race preference. It is, however, also necessary to consider the possibility that all other groups are prejudiced against them. In other words, it is conceivable that white men, Asian men, Latino men, Native American men, and others all hold negative attitudes toward African American women and often refuse to have sex with them or to marry them. Although the usual pattern of prejudice is to show favoritism toward one's own group over all other groups, it is certainly conceivable that other groups might all selectively hold prejudices only toward black women.

Two patterns of research findings offer two variations on the view that everyone is prejudiced against black women. One pattern has more to do with personality style than race per se. An assumption of this view is that most couples marry in such a way that the man can be the dominant partner in the marriage. (The next section will elaborate on this in relation to how marriage perpetuates sexism.) For a marriage to function smoothly, therefore, it is typically helpful if the woman is more submissive than the man.

Black women, however, are not all that submissive. In fact, on several measures, they show up as highly assertive, even more assertive than other groups. Adams (1980) found that white men and black women were more assertive than black men or white women. This was not an isolated finding. Adams noted, for example, that assertiveness training and other empowerment movements of 1970s feminism were largely rejected by black women as irrelevant to their needs. White women had been brought up to be self-denying and so could benefit from assertiveness training, but black women did not have any such problem.

Hence either white or black men can mate comfortably with a white woman, who may well emerge as relatively submissive. (We speak here only of broad averages; there are plenty of exceptions, just as there are plenty of interracial marriages of all permutations.) Black women, however, are too strong-willed to submit to most men, and this makes them less attractive as potential mates to a broad variety of men. This view would likewise predict certain marriage patterns between whites and Asians, insofar as Asians are generally less assertive and more submissive than whites. White women would therefore be problematic or unappealing as mates for Asian men. White men, on the other hand, could fit well with submissive Asian women.

The assertiveness view suggests that black women end up being victims of both racial and gender stereotypes. Men may want submissive women to marry, by and large, and black women are too strong to put up with such male domination. Hence many black women end up alone rather than stifling themselves to fit into oppressive gender roles.

A potential problem with this view is that assertiveness alone would make white men more suitable than black men as potential spouses for black women. If black women are more assertive than black men, as Adams (1980) found, then an all-black marriage would often have a wife who was more assertive than a husband. Clearly, assertiveness alone cannot offer an explanation for the marriage patterns, but it could be one factor that contributes to a general reluctance among many groups of men to marry black women.

The final possibility that must be considered is that many men regard black women as not being physically attractive, which makes them less appealing both as marriage partners and even as sex partners. In American society, stereotypes of beauty are based on the white majority, and the white ideals include various facial features and physical slimness that are relatively unsuited to the African American woman. Some black women do of course manage to conform to the prevailing standards of beauty, but for many black women that is difficult to do.

What are the ideals of beauty? Research has recently confirmed a suggestion first made by the philosopher Immanuel Kant (1924 [1790]), who proposed that the mind aggregates all instances it sees into a kind of composite picture that is thus the most typical or average, and that then becomes the prototype of beauty. Langlois and Roggman (1990) used computer-generated and computer-altered faces to show that the most symmetrical faces, with the most typical features and fewest deviations from the statistical average, were judged to be the most beautiful.

If this is correct, then any minority group is at a disadvantage. Black women are only a small proportion of women in the United States, so they would be deviate more from the statistical average and hence be judged as less attractive. By the same token, white women in Africa or Asia would be judged to be relatively ugly, as long as they were in the minority. Their facial features would be statistically deviant, which is generally associated with being unattractiveness.

A refinement of this theory has been proposed by evolutionary psychologists. Symons (1995) has proposed that light coloring is itself a feature associated with beauty. The reason, he argued, was that men seek young women who have not yet produced any children, because men do not want to invest their resources in raising other men's children. As women grow older and have children, their skin typically becomes darker, as does their hair. Lightness of skin and hair is therefore a universal signal that a woman is young and has not had children yet. For example, the idea that blonde women are especially attractive seems to recur all over the world; in no known culture do blonde women dye their hair dark in numbers that approach the frequency with which dark-haired women try to turn blonde. Symons reports evidence that within any given race (including African Americans), women with lighter skin color are generally regarded as more attractive than darker women. By extension, it could be that differences between races follow the same rule that lighter equals more beautiful, which puts black women in an unfortunate position. Symons claims that when Japan was opened to world commerce in the 1800s after centuries of isolation, the Japanese held generally negative attitudes toward all foreigners and their practices. They did, however, think that white women were quite beautiful, but they had the opposite reaction to black women.

What can be concluded? There is a remarkably low rate of interracial marriage and even of interracial sex, and black women form the statistical extreme in that they are least likely to have a sex partner or marriage partner from another race. Given the present state of knowledge, this anomaly is open to a variety of possible explanations: Possibly black women hold prejudices against others and favor their own group, or possibly all other groups are prejudiced against them. The answers are of both theoretical and practical interest, and are likely to emerge from research findings in the coming decade or two.

Sexism in Marriage

Let us turn now to marriage. The contribution of marriage to sexism is quite different from its role in racism, if only because people overwhelmingly marry someone from the same race as themselves—but of the opposite gender.

In principle, marriage unites a man and a woman in a relationship marked by mutual respect, support, love, and appreciation. This very mutuality could well promote equality. If it did, this might go a long way toward producing equality of the sexes throughout society. Men and women could recognize each other as equal partners in the social enterprise, whether this refers to electing the government or raising a child.

In practice, however, people marry in ways that preserve inequality between the sexes. The key to understanding this is something that is called the *marriage gradient* (see Bernard, 1982): The man is usually slightly above the woman in various measures of social status. Typically, the husband is about four years older than his wife (apart from teen marriages; see Atkinson & Glass, 1985; also Spanier & Glick, 1980). Husbands tend to have a higher salary and be slightly more educated. Of course, they are also taller, heavier, and stronger.

Who do you think will end up being the boss?

Imagine forming a close friendship or business partnership with someone of your own gender. Imagine that this person is four years older than you and also has a couple more years of education. Imagine that this person has more money for putting in joint enterprises and activities. And, for good measure, imagine that this person is physically larger (taller and stronger). Most of the time the two of you might well operate as equals, but if there were a question or disagreement, the odds are that you'd be inclined to defer to your friend's judgment.

Then imagine the reverse: Your friend is four years younger than you are, is less well educated, has less money, and is physically smaller. If there were a question or disagreement, probably you'd be more willing to insist that your view should prevail. As a general rule, it would seem reasonable to assume that you would know better than your friend about most things.

One of us used to cover these patterns in a lecture course, and on the examinations the students would summarize them in ways that reflected actor-observer and self-serving biases. The actor-observer bias is the tendency for people to attribute their own actions to the situation and other people's actions to their inner traits and dispositions (Jones & Nisbett, 1971). The self-serving bias is the tendency to take credit for good things but to deny blame for failure, and in particular to shift the responsibility for bad things to others. Students often tended to attribute the marriage gradient to faults in the other gender. Men would describe the gradient as indicating that women were basically social climbers if not outright gold diggers who marry men for their money and status. Women would describe the same gradient as reflecting the pathetic insecurity of men: A man can't accept a woman as an equal, so he hunts for someone young and foolish (relative to him) who will defer to him and look up to him.

In reality, though, neither men nor women bear primary responsibility for the marriage gradient. As far as we can tell, both cooperate to sustain it. Men will marry their secretaries but rarely their bosses; women show the opposite pattern in their marital preferences. Comforting as it may be to blame the opposite gender for these patterns, there is nothing to suggest that either gender is opposed to the patterns or is reluctant about going along with them.

The social exchange theory offers one possible explanation for these patterns. If women give sex to men, then men must offer something in return. Therefore the sexual interaction will only seem fair if the man offers more than the woman in terms of nonsexual resources and attributes. Because sex is something that she contributes to the exchange, a woman is better able than a man to attract a partner with money, education, and other social advantages.

Usually the marriage gradient is discussed in terms of the people who get left out. If each tier of women mates with men who rank one tier higher, then the highest ranking women and the lowest ranking men will have a hard time finding mates. This is indeed a well-established problem. Rich, older, highly educated women regard only a very small, elite group of men as suitable mates. Poor, young, uneducated men often have trouble attracting women.

A version of this problem occurs in dating and is familiar on most college campuses. Women date men their own age or older, while men date women their own age and younger. Freshman year, therefore, is often a fairly exciting time for the young woman, because the campus is full of eligible men. For the young man, however, freshman year tends to be a lonely and frustrating time, with plenty of dull weekends, envy of upperclassmen, or efforts to sustain the long-distance relationship with last year's girlfriend (who is still in high school).

By senior year, however, the positions are reversed. The senior man can date any woman on campus and often maintains a busy social life. In contrast, for a woman, senior year is often anticlimactic, with relatively few prospects for new romantic relationships. She may be the one hanging on to the long-distance relationship with last year's boyfriend, who has gone on to law school or graduate school in another state.

For present purposes, however, we are less interested in the people who are left out by the marriage gradient system than in the effect it has on the people who do marry in that way. If men and women pair up constantly in ways that put the man in the superior position, how can we expect the society as a whole to come to see women as equal to men?

To be sure, men and women interact in many settings and contexts, and they have ample opportunity to see each other in multiple roles. Yet the importance of the spouse should not be underestimated. People often perceive groups based on one or more prototypes, which is to say based on one or more very familiar and salient members of that group. Undoubtedly most people know their spouses better than any other member of the opposite sex, and so the spouse operates as a very important prototype. When people generalize about the opposite gender, they probably start by considering their spouse.

One might hope that the differences in education, age, and status would become less and less important as marriage continues. There is a smattering of evidence to suggest that relationship partners become more similar over time in various ways. On the other hand, certain major events tend to make the differences bigger and even more meaningful.

Some years ago the two authors of this book traveled to Italy. One attraction was the spectacular island of Capri, most of which lies high above the water due to sheer rock faces that rise straight up from the sea. To reach the top part of the island, it is necessary to take a chairlift from one of the lower areas. The lift is somewhat scary, especially as one sees it from the bottom: You simply sit in a chair that hangs from a cable, and you are whisked away up a fairly steep slope, off into the unknown.

We watched young couples come to this chairlift. In Italy, as in most of the Western world, the norm in "one-at-a-time" places is "ladies first." Yet somehow each couple seemed to come to the opposite decision on this chairlift. We counted thirty-four couples on the lift during the brief time we watched (see, social scientists don't lose their curiosity about people on vacation!), and in thirty-three of them the man went first.

What was striking was that each couple approached the chairlift as a novel issue and somehow made the same deliberate, conscious decision over and over (indeed one that went against the general norm that ladies go first). Probably it was just that the situation seemed a bit frightening and unknown, and so somehow it was appropriate that the older and stronger one go first. In most couples, that is the man.

In a similar fashion, many couples face the prospect of parenthood with a genuine effort to think about what would be the best procedure for all concerned, but they repeatedly come to the same conclusion. Many couples hold to the principle that both careers are important and that equality should be the norm. Still, one partner has to accept some career sacrifices in order to care for children. Someone has to take time off from education or shift to part-time work for a few years. Someone has to get off the fast track for promotion.

Even if the couple faces those decisions with fully open minds and an earnest commitment to equality, they will usually decide that the woman's career is the one to sacrifice. If nothing else, the reason may be financial. The man makes more money than the woman (usually), so the *total family* would lose more money if he were to cut back to part-time than if she were to cut back. In other words, if his salary is higher than hers, then half of his salary is more than half of hers, and so it would be foolish for both of them to give up half of his salary rather than half of hers. In other words, it always turns out to be the rational decision that the wife's career should be the one to sacrifice.

Similar decisions may be made at other points, such as when one career can be advanced if the couple moves to a different city, thus setting the other career back. The couple has more riding on the man's career, and changes to it will make a bigger difference to the family, and so his career will tend to get preference.

Having children can contribute to inequality in a variety of ways that go beyond career and money issues. Research findings suggest that many young couples maintain a good approximation of equality prior to parenthood, but once children appear the sex roles become more traditional, which means that the woman's position tends to be inferior (Belsky, Lang, & Huston, 1986). Fathers of young children tend to spend an increased amount of time pursuing their careers, while young mothers tend to spend more time in child care.

Although many couples agree in principle that the responsibility for raising the children will be divided equally among them, the usual outcome is for the woman to do much more than the man. In many cases this comes as a deep disappointment to the woman, and in fact research findings show that the decline in marital happiness that is commonly found among young mothers is often mediated by disillusionment and disappointment over the father's involvement (Ruble, Fleming, Hackel, & Stangor, 1988). Women who expect more from their husbands tend to be more disappointed and hence unhappier as mothers than women who expected less.

In any case, there are multiple reasons to think that American sexism will persist as long as people mate in these unequal ways. Whether people can actually change is another question. Evolutionary psychologists contend that women's desire to marry higher status men is innate, as is men's interest in younger women (e.g., Buss & Schmitt, 1993). There is some evidence suggesting that as women become more equal to men in societal roles, the age gap in marriage tends to diminish (Eagly & Wood, 1999).

Chapter 6, on erotic plasticity, suggested that women may be better able than men to adjust their sexual desires toward socially appropriate targets. Women might therefore be able to change in order to find lower status men desirable. Still, it takes two people to make a marriage, and unless men could also alter their selection criteria, it could be difficult to change this pattern of marrying—along with its consequences for sustaining sexism and gender stereotypes.

What Can Be Done?

People's preferences for mates and sex partners may well be deeply rooted, and it remains to be seen how much society could do to change them. But where prejudice and discrimination are concerned, resistance that has been deeply rooted in many spheres has yielded (somewhat) to influence to change.

How would a society go about increasing interracial marriage? If the courts were to regulate themselves the same way they regulate others, they might begin by setting numerical targets. To enforce these, they would have to insist that a certain proportion of marriages be interracial. As long as there are not enough interracial couples to fill the quota, same-race couples would not be permitted to marry. The result might be a long waiting list: Same-race couples would register to marry but could only hold the ceremony whenever enough interracial couples had come along.

The waiting list procedure would create some serious problems, of course. Couples who were already pregnant and wanting to marry to legitimize their babies might be unable to do so, and so more babies would be born out of wedlock. (Whether the lack of official marriage would alter the relationship among the couple, with or without childbirth, is an important question to which we do not know the answer.) On the positive side, the waiting list might generate considerable social support for interracial marriages. Every couple wishing to marry would be inclined to cheer each time an interracial union takes place, because each one would move them closer to the day when they themselves could marry.

Apart from imposing quotas by fiat, another approach would be to enact legislation that would express symbolic support for interracial romance and perhaps aid these couples in getting started. One standard form of governmental incentives is tax benefits, and these might be used. For example, the government might pass a law saying that interracial spouses would get a significant reduction in income tax on the lesser salary of the pair. Given the current socioeconomic situation, this procedure would most directly benefit black women, which seems, on an a priori basis, to be a desirable outcome. More to the point, it would make black women more desirable as potential spouses to nonblack men, thus helping to solve the problem of black women remaining single throughout most of their lives. It would also help express societal support for interracial romance.

One might worry that some people would contract marriage as a business arrangement simply for the sake of the tax advantages. Some of this might happen, but probably not too much. After all, you can only marry one person at a time, and so marrying for money would preclude marrying someone else for love later. Moreover, such marriages would enable the disadvantaged minority members to gain access and claims to the wealth of their partners, so even if such purely financial marriages were occasionally made, they would have the effect of redistributing a fair amount of wealth.

We doubt that many people would choose marriage partners simply based on tax considerations. A successful intervention has to work at a much earlier point in the process: It has to make initial interracial meetings and dates more likely. Once people are dating people from other races, the marriages are likely to follow.

Imagine, for example, a white man approaching a table where three white and one black women are having lunch. He has a chance to meet and speak briefly with them, and perhaps this might lead him to ask one woman for a date. By today's norms, he would probably regard the black woman as the least likely prospect, and so he will focus any flirtatious efforts on one of the white women. But if the government were to express support for interracial romance by offering tax advantages or other incentives, he might be moved to give the black woman more attention.

With the marriage gradient in gender, it is again necessary to consider how to change the norms. There is less legal or policy precedent for equalizing the status of marriage partners than there is for seeking racial integration, so we are skeptical that passing laws would help. Perhaps feminism could take up spousal equality as an issue, however. Feminism has already experimented with attempting to influence choices of sex partners, such as by the briefly influential view that lesbianism is the only sexual pattern that is politically correct for a liberated woman. Changing from heterosexuality to lesbianism is perhaps asking too much, but feminist rhetoric might encourage women to marry their educational and social inferiors, contrary to the traditional pattern. If feminist speakers sought to eliminate the marriage gradient, perhaps some female bosses would marry their male secretaries, or female physicians might marry male nurses, and more marriages would end up with women in the superior status position.

CHAPTER

11   Concluding Remarks

The main thrust of this book has been to treat sex as a social phenomenon. By saying that, we are not denying that physical, physiological, biological, and evolutionary factors play important roles—nor even have we excluded those factors from our analyses. All we mean is that we have treated sex as a meaningful human activity that shapes and is shaped by human relationships and interactions. Sex is a way that people relate to each other, and even the most private of sexual thoughts and acts are often affected by social concern such as norms, values, guilt, and love.

In dealing with sex as a social phenomenon, we have sought to apply many of the ideas and principles of social psychology to sexuality. Again, we do not intend to dismiss the potential contributions of clinical psychology or physiology to sexual science. But for most people, sex is neither a clinical matter nor a physiological process, but rather a human and social activity. As such, it can best be illuminated by using social psychology's stock in trade: attitudes, norms, relationship processes, prejudice, aggression, self-esteem, and the rest.

One theme that ran through the book was the application of the social exchange theory to sex. We proposed that sex is something that women give to men, and hence that much sexual activity can be analyzed in the context of ongoing exchange relationships and processes. This turned out to be a helpful way of looking at things, and where we could pit it against competing theories (such as those that relate to the suppression of female sexuality), it fared rather well.

Still, we should not overstate the value of our approach. There are many sexual phenomena that do not easily fit into our simple social exchange analysis. For example, recent work has shown that sexual coercion works both ways, and there are many reports of instances in which women pressure or force men into sexual activity against the men's will (Anderson & Struckman-Johnson, 1998). The view that women give sex to men has difficulty explaining why women would take sex. (Then again, perhaps the late recognition of that phenomenon is a positive sign: Maybe people were slow to notice that females coerce males because it does violate the general exchange pattern.)

We have noted many questions that remain open for research. Although these have been mentioned throughout the book, let us summarize some of the main unresolved issues here.

First, the bases for female erotic plasticity are not known. The gender difference in plasticity seems hard to dispute, given the wide assortment of evidence for it. But why are women more malleable with regard to sex? Any or all of the suggested explanations could be true, and there may be others as well.

Likewise, there is no doubt that interracial sex and interracial marriage are relatively rare, but the reasons for this rarity are not know. We sketched several possible explanations, and again any or all of them may be correct, but the present state of knowledge doesn't let us draw any firm conclusions. As we pointed out, research on African American women may be especially useful in shedding light on resistance to interracial romance, because those individuals show the highest rates of same-race bias among any groups.

One of the most fascinating questions concerns the effects of partial sexual permissiveness. Some cultures have kept people in a state of almost complete sexual deprivation except for marital intercourse, whereas others have permitted all sorts of premarital and extramarital activity. Neither extreme seems ideal. Yet what happens if people are permitted halfway measures? Undoubtedly people derive some satisfaction from these partial activities, and probably some of them stimulate people to want to go farther. The question of whether the satisfaction can outweigh the stimulation is crucial to forming an enlightened public policy. For example, if pornography constitutes merely a "safe sex" form of promiscuity, then many people might be able to use it to satisfy their desires for sexual novelty without causing harm, in which case pornography would serve a very valuable social function. On the other hand, if watching pornography mainly makes people more likely to desire and engage in other activities, especially extramarital sex, promiscuity, or sexual harassment or coercion, then pornography would have to be deemed socially undesirable. In the context of the tragic aspect of male sexuality, these questions take on particular urgency: Can men learn to be content with partial satisfaction, or is severe deprivation the best way to prevent men from all manner of sexual misbehavior?

We noted that many of the theoretical debates in sexuality research have focused on the nature versus nurture question, pitting evolutionary theories against social constructionism. Both theories could stand some improvement and refinement. Social constructionism has to move beyond the simple, vague formulation that everything can be explained based on the happenstance of ill-defined cultural values or patriarchy. The views that modern America is a rape culture, for example, in which all men consciously conspire to rape to subjugate women, provide a very poor fit to the known facts. We do not doubt that culture affects sexuality, but we think the area needs new and more precise theories about the nature of culture and the means of influence. Moreover, some recognition of the rather severe limits on what culture can accomplish would be very appropriate. It does not seem likely that people (and especially not men, given their low plasticity) will simply and easily change all their patterns of sexual desire and activity based on arbitrary cultural prescriptions.

Although in many instances evolutionary theory is more specific about precisely what patterns of desire and activity will be biologically based, it too has some weak links. We suggested, in particular, that the paternity uncertainty aspect is not strongly supported by the facts. This view holds that men's attitudes are mainly geared toward preventing them from having to raise other men's children. Yet many men cheerfully and willingly raise other men's children, in adoption or stepfamilies, and meanwhile male sexual possessiveness and jealousy have not been eliminated by the birth control pill. At a deeper level, the fact that human beings share so much of their genetic makeup with all other human beings makes the selfish gene arguments harder to reconcile with a strong urge toward paternity certainty.

We reviewed plenty of evidence that women have less sexual desire than men. Most of the findings come from the modern United States, however (although we doubt that data from other parts of the world are likely to reverse the pattern). It is not easy to rule out social and cultural explanations for this discrepancy. There are, moreover, wide variations among individuals, and it is almost certain that some women have far more sexual desire than some men. Further research might make valuable contributions by finding any exceptions to the broad pattern of stronger male sex drive. We proposed one already: During the relationship phase in which intimacy is rising most rapidly, men and women may approach equality in sexual desire. That theory too requires more precise data.

We have noted that many people make bad choices in sex. Women often seem attracted to dangerous, trouble-prone men, and some women seem to fall repeatedly into destructive relationships. Men, meanwhile, often act as if they are unable to say no to a sexual opportunity, even if they can recognize in advance that they will end up regretting having had sex with that person. Both men and women take foolish risks of disease and pregnancy. Although research has yielded some insight into the processes that lead to bad sexual decisions, there is undoubtedly much more yet to be learned.

Much yet to be learned: that is the humbling and possibly discouraging state of current knowledge about sex. It is also the hallmark of great intellectual opportunity. The time is ripe for rapid progress in the area of sexuality, because research methods are improving and ideas are emerging. Over the next few decades, many men and women will have fine careers by collecting data about sexuality. Some of their work will answer the questions we have outlined here. Our social sciences have only begun to develop a fact-based, scientific understanding of sexuality. Sex is too important, and too fascinating, to continue to be neglected.

REFERENCES

Abbey, A. (1982). Sex differences in attributions for friendly behavior: Do males misperceive females' friendliness? *Journal of Personality and Social Psychology, 42,* 830–838.

Abbey, A., Ross, L. T., McDuffie, D., & McAuslan, P. (1996). Alcohol and dating risk factors for sexual assault among college women. *Psychology of Women Quarterly, 11,* 173–194.

Abel, E. (1998). Sexual risk behaviors among ship- and shore-based Navy women. *Military Medicine, 163,* 250–256.

Abramson, P. R. (1973). The relationship of the frequency of masturbation to several aspects of personality and social behavior. *Journal of Sex Research, 9,* 132–142.

Abramson, P. R. (1990). Sexual science: Emerging discipline or oxymoron? *Journal of Sex Research, 27,* 147–165.

Abramson, P. R., & Pinkerton, S. D. (1995). *With pleasure: Thoughts on the nature of human sexuality.* New York: Oxford University Press.

Acker, M., & Davis, M. H. (1992). Intimacy, passion, and commitment in adult romantic relationships: A test of the triangular theory of love. *Journal of Social and Personal Relationships, 9,* 21–50.

Acton, W. (1857). *The functions and disorders of the reproductive organs.* Philadelphia.

Adams, C. G., & Turner, B. F. (1985). Reported change in sexuality from young adulthood to old age. *Journal of Sex Research, 21,* 126–141.

Adams, K. A. (1980). Who has the final word? Sex, race, and dominance behavior. *Journal of Personality and Social Psychology, 38,* 1–8.

Ajzen, I., & Fishbein, M. (1977). Attitude-behavior relations: A theoretical analysis and review of empirical research. *Psychological Bulletin, 84,* 888–918.

Alexander, M. (1982). Passion play. In SAMOIS (Ed.), *Coming to power* (pp. 228–242). Boston: Alyson.

Altman, I., & Ginat, J. (1996). *Polygamous families in contemporary society.* New York: Cambridge University Press.

Amabile, T. M., DeJong, W., & Lepper, M. R. (1976). Effects of externally imposed deadlines on subsequent intrinsic motivation. *Journal of Personality and Social Psychology, 34,* 92–98.

American Psychiatric Association. (1994). *Diagnostic and statistical manual of mental disorders* (4th ed.). Washington, DC: Author.

Amsterdam Sex Museum. (1999). Unpublished exhibition notes, Amsterdam.

Anderson, P. B., & Struckman-Johnson, C. (Eds.). (1998). *Sexually aggressive women: Current perspectives and controversies.* New York: Guilford.

Antonovsky, H. F., Shoham, I., Kavenocki, S., Modan, B., & Lancet, M. (1978). Sexual attitude-behavior discrepancy among Israeli adolescent girls. *Journal of Sex Research, 14,* 260–272.

Arafat, I. S., & Cotton, W. L. (1974). Masturbation practices of males and females. *Journal of Sex Research, 10,* 293–307.

Arafat, I. S., & Yorburg, B. (1973). On living together without marriage. *Journal of Sex Research, 9,* 97–106.

Ard, B. N. (1977). Sex in lasting marriages: A longitudinal study. *Journal of Sex Research, 13,* 274–285.

Argyle, M. (1987). *The psychology of happiness.* London: Methuen.

Arias, I., Samios, M., & O'Leary, K. D. (1987). Prevalence and correlates of physical aggression during courtship. *Journal of Interpersonal Violence, 2,* 82–90.

Aries, E. (1996). *Men and women in interaction: Reconsidering the differences.* New York: Oxford University Press.

Arndt, W. B., Foehl, J. C., & Good, F. E. (1985). Specific sexual fantasy themes: A multidimensional study. *Journal of Personality and Social Psychology, 48,* 472–480.

Aronson, E., & Linder, D. (1965). Gain and loss of esteem as determinants of interpersonal attractiveness. *Journal of Experimental Social Psychology, 1,* 156–171.

Asayama, S. (1975). Adolescent sex development and adult sex behavior in Japan. *Journal of Sex Research, 11,* 91–112.

Atkinson, M. P., & Glass, B. L. (1985). Marital age heterogamy and homogamy, 1900 to 1980. *Journal of Marriage and the Family, 47,* 685–691.

Bailey, J. M., & Martin, N. G. (1993, September). *A twin registry study of sexual orientation.* Paper presented at the annual meeting of the International Academy of Sex Research, Provincetown, MA.

Bailey, J. M., & Pillard, R. C. (1991). A genetic study of male sexual orientation. *Archives of General Psychiatry, 48,* 1089–1096.

Bailey, J. M., & Pillard, R. C. (1995). Genetics of human sexual orientation. *Annual Review of Sex Research, 6,* 126–150.

Bailey, J. M., Pillard, R. C., Neale, M. C., & Agyei, Y. (1993). Heritable factors influence sexual orientation in women. *Archives of General Psychiatry, 50,* 217–223.

Bailey, J. M., & Zucker, K. J. (1995). Childhood sex-typed behavior and sexual orientation: A conceptual analysis and quantitative review. *Developmental Psychology, 31,* 43–55.

Bailey, R. C., & Aunger, R. V. (1995). Sexuality, infertility, and sexually transmitted disease among farmers and foragers in central Africa. In P. Abramson & S. Pinkerton (Eds.), *Sexual nature sexual culture* (pp. 195–222). Chicago: University of Chicago Press.

Banaji, M. R., & Steele, C. M. (1989). Alcohol and self-evaluation: Is a social cognition approach beneficial? *Social Cognition, 7,* 137–151.

Barber, R. N. (1969). Prostitution and the increasing number of convictions for rape in Queensland. *Australian and New Zealand Journal of Criminology, 2,* 169–174.

Bargh, J. A. (1982). Attention and automaticity in the processing of self-relevant information. *Journal of Personality and Social Psychology, 43,* 425–436.

Bargh, J. A. (1989). Conditional automaticity: Varieties of automatic influence in social perception and cognition. In J. S. Uleman & J. A. Bargh (Eds.), *Unintended thought: Causes and consequences for judgment, emotion, and behavior* (pp. 3–5) New York: Guilford.

Bargh, J. A. (1994). The four horsemen of automaticity: Awareness, attention, efficiency, and control in social cognition. In R. S. Wyer & T. K. Srull (Eds.), *Handbook of social cognition* (2nd ed., Vol. 1, pp. 1–40). Hillsdale, NJ: Erlbaum.

Bargh, J. A. (1997). The automaticity of everyday life. In R. S. Wyer (Ed.), *The automaticity of everyday life: Advances in social cognition* (Vol. 10, pp. 1–61). Mahwah, NJ: Erlbaum.

Barker, V. (1982). Dangerous shoes, or what's a nice dyke like me doing in a get-up like this? In SAMOIS (Ed.), *Coming to power* (pp. 101–104). Boston: Alyson.

Barry, H., & Schlegel, A. (1984). Measurements of adolescent sexual behavior in the standard sample of societies. *Ethnology, 23,* 315–329.

Bart, P. B. (1993). Protean women: The liquidity of female sexuality and the tenaciousness of lesbian identity. In S. Wilkinson & C. Kitzinger (Eds.), *Heterosexuality: Feminism and psychology reader.* London: Sage.

Bartell, G. D. (1970). Group sex among the mid-Americans. *Journal of Sex Research, 6,* 113–130.

Bateman, A. J. (1948). Intrasexual selection in Drosophila. *Heredity, 2,* 349–368.

Bauman, K. E., & Wilson, R. R. (1974). Sexual behavior of unmarried university students in 1968 and 1972. *Journal of Sex Research, 10,* 327–333.

Baumeister, R. F. (1984). Choking under pressure: Self-consciousness and paradoxical effects of incentives on skillful performance. *Journal of Personality and Social Psychology, 46,* 610–620.

Baumeister, R. F. (1986). *Identity: Cultural change and the struggle for self.* New York: Oxford University Press.

Baumeister, R. F. (1987). How the self became a problem: A psychological review of historical research. *Journal of Personality and Social Psychology, 52,* 163–176.

Baumeister, R. F. (1988a). Gender differences in masochistic scripts. *Journal of Sex Research, 25,* 478–499.

Baumeister, R. F. (1988b). Masochism as escape from self. *Journal of Sex Research, 25,* 28–59.

Baumeister, R. F. (1988c). Should we stop studying sex differences altogether? *American Psychologist, 43,* 1092–1095.

Baumeister, R. F. (1989). *Masochism and the self.* Hillsdale, NJ: Erlbaum.

Baumeister, R. F. (1991a). *Escaping the self: Alcoholism, spirituality, masochism, and other flights from the burden of selfhood.* New York: Basic Books.

Baumeister, R. F. (1991b). *Meanings of life.* New York: Guilford.

Baumeister, R. F. (1993). Understanding the inner nature of low self-esteem: Uncertain, fragile, protective, and conflicted. In R. Baumeister (Ed.), *Self-esteem: The puzzle of low self-regard* (pp. 201–218). New York: Plenum.

Baumeister, R. F. (1997). *Evil: Inside human violence and cruelty.* New York: W. H. Freeman.

Baumeister, R. F. (in press). Gender differences in erotic plasticity: The female sex drive as socially flexible and responsive. *Psychological Bulletin.*

Baumeister, R. F., & Bratslavsky, E. (1999). Passion, intimacy, and time: Passionate love as a function of change in intimacy. *Personality and Social Psychology Review, 3,* 49–67.

Baumeister, R. F., & Catanese, K. (in press). Victims and perpetrators provide discrepant accounts: Motivated cognitive distortions about interpersonal transgressions. In J. Forgas, K. Williams, & L. Wheeler (Eds.), *The social mind.* New York: Cambridge University Press.

Baumeister, R. F., Catanese, K., & Wallace, H. M. (1999). *Rape and sexual coercion as narcissistic reactance.* Manuscript submitted for publication.

Baumeister, R. F., & Leary, M. R. (1995). The need to belong: Desire for interpersonal attachments as a fundamental human motivation. *Psychological Bulletin, 117,* 497–529.

Baumeister, R. F., Smart, L., & Boden, J. M. (1996). Relation of threatened egotism to violence and aggression: The dark side of high self-esteem. *Psychological Review, 103,* 5–33.

Baumeister, R. F., Stillwell, A., & Wotman, S. R. (1990). Victim and perpetrator accounts of interpersonal conflict: Autobiographical narratives about anger. *Journal of Personality and Social Psychology, 59,* 994–1005.

Baumeister, R. F., Tice, D. M., & Hutton, D. G. (1989). Self-presentational motivations and personality differences in self-esteem. *Journal of Personality, 57,* 547–579.

Baumeister, R. F., & Twenge, J. M. (1999). *Two conspiracy theories regarding the suppression of female sexuality.* Manuscript in preparation, Case Western Reserve University, Ohio.

Baumeister, R. F., & Wotman, S. R. (1992). *Breaking hearts: The two sides of unrequited love.* New York: Guilford Press.

Baumeister, R. F., Wotman, S. R., & Stillwell, A. M. (1993). Unrequited love: On heartbreak, anger, guilt, scriptlessness, and humiliation. *Journal of Personality and Social Psychology, 64,* 377–394.

Beck, J. G., Bozman, A. W., & Qualtrough, T. (1991). The experience of sexual desire: Psychological correlates in a college sample. *Journal of Sex Research, 28,* 443–456.

Belenky, M. F., Clinchy, B. M., Goldbergher, N. R., & Tarule, J. M. (1986). *Women's ways of knowing.* New York: Basic Books.

Bell, A. P., & Weinberg, M. S. (1978). *Homosexualities: A study of diversity among men and women.* New York: Simon & Schuster.

Bell, A. P., Weinberg, M. S., & Hammersmith, S. K. (1981). *Sexual preference: Its development in men and women.* Bloomington: Indiana University Press.

Belsky, J., Lang, M. E., & Huston, T. L. (1986). Sex typing and division of labor as determinants of marital change across the tradition to parenthood. *Journal of Personality and Social Psychology, 50,* 517–522.

Belsky, J., Lang, M. E., & Rovine, M. (1985). Stability and change in marriage across the transition to parenthood: A second study. *Journal of Marriage and the Family, 47,* 855–865.

Bem, D. J. (1996). Exotic becomes erotic: A developmental theory of sexual orientation. *Psychological Review, 103,* 320–335.

Bem, D. J. (1998). Is EBE theory supported by evidence? Is it androcentric? A reply to Peplau et al. (1998). *Psychological Review, 105,* 395–398.

Benedict, J. (1997). *Public heroes, private felons: Athletes and crimes against women.* Boston: Northeastern University Press.

Bergström-Walan, M.-B., & Nielsen, H. H. (1990). Sexual expression among 60–80-year-old men and women: A sample from Stockholm, Sweden. *Journal of Sex Research, 27,* 289–295.

Berkowitz, A. (1992). College men as perpetrators of acquaintance rape and sexual assault: A review of recent research. *College Health, 40,* 175–181.

Berkowitz, A. D., Burkhart, B. R., & Bourg, S. E. (1994). Research on college men and rape. In A. D. Berkowitz (Ed.), *Men and rape: Theory, research, and prevention programs in higher education* (pp. 3–19). San Francisco: Jossey-Bass.

Bernard, J. (1982). *The future of marriage.* New Haven: Yale University Press.

Bernat, J. A., Calhoun, K. S., & Stolp, S. (1998). Sexually aggressive men's responses to a date rape analogue: Alcohol as a disinhibiting cue. *Journal of Sex Research, 35,* 341–348.

Berscheid, E. (1983). Emotion. In H. H. Kelley, E. Berscheid, A. Christensen, J. Harvey, T. Huston, G. Levinger, E. McClintock, L. Peplau, & D. Peterson (Eds.), *Close relationships* (pp. 110–168). New York: Freeman.

Betzig, L. (1986). *Despotism and differential reproduction: A Darwinian view of history.* New York: Aldine.

Billig, M., & Tajfel, H. (1973). Social categorization and similarity in intergroup behavior. *European Journal of Social Psychology, 3,* 27–51.

Billy, J. O. G., & Udry, J. R. (1985). Patterns of adolescent friendship and effects on sexual behavior. *Social Psychology Quarterly, 48,* 27–41.

Birenbaum, A. (1970). Revolution without the revolution: Sex in contemporary America. *Journal of Sex Research, 6,* 257–267.

Blascovich, J., Wyer, N. A., Swart, L. A., & Kibler, J. Z. (1997). Racism and racial categorization. *Journal of Personality and Social Psychology, 72*, 1364–1372.

Blau, P. N. (1964). *Exchange and power in social life*. New York: Wiley.

Blumstein, P. W., & Schwartz, P. (1977). Bisexuality: Some social psychological issues. *Journal of Social Issues, 33*(2), 30–45.

Blumstein, P. W., & Schwartz, P. (1983). *American couples*. New York: Simon & Schuster (Pocket).

Boddy, J. (1989). *Wombs and alien spirits: Women, men, and the Zar cult in northern Sudan*. Madison: University of Wisconsin Press.

Boddy, J. (1998). Violence embodied? Circumcision, gender, politics, and cultural aesthetics. In R. Emerson Dobash & Russell P. Dobash (Eds.), *Rethinking violence against women* (pp. 77–110). Thousand Oaks, CA: Sage.

Boston Women's Health Book Collective. (1976). *Our bodies, ourselves: A book by and for women*. New York: Simon & Schuster.

Bower, G. H. (1986). Prime time in cognitive psychology. In P. Elen (Ed.), *Cognitive research and behavior therapy: Beyond the conditioning paradigm*. Amsterdam: North Holland.

Branden, N. (1994). *The six pillars of self-esteem*. New York: Bantam.

Brehm, J. W. (1966). *A theory of psychological reactance*. New York: Academic Press.

Breslin, F. C., Riggs, D. S., O'Leary, K. D., & Arias, I. (1990). *Journal of Interpersonal Violence, 5*, 247–258.

Brewer, M. B. (1979). Ingroup bias in the minimal intergroup situation: A cognitive-motivational analysis. *Psychological Bulletin, 86*, 307–324.

Brickman, P., & Campbell, D. T. (1971). Hedonic relativism and planning the good society. In M. H. Appley (Ed.), *Adaptation level theory: A symposium* (pp. 287–302). New York: Academic Press.

Brockner, J. (1984). Low self-esteem and behavioral plasticity: Some implications for personality and social psychology. In L. Wheeler (Ed.), *Review of personality and social psychology* (Vol. 4, pp. 237–271). Beverly Hills, CA: Sage.

Broude, G. J., & Greene, S. J. (1976). Cross-cultural codes on twenty sexual attitudes and practices. *Ethnology, 15*, 409–429.

Brown, J. D. (1986). Evaluations of self and others: Self-enhancement biases in social judgments. *Social Cognition, 4*, 353–376.

Brown, N. R., & Sinclair, R. C. (1999). Estimating number of lifetime sexual partners: Men and women do it differently. *Journal of Sex Research, 36*, 292–297.

Brownmiller, S. (1975). *Against our will: Men, women, and rape*. New York: Simon & Schuster.

Bullough, V. L., & Brundage, J. (1982). *Sexual practices and the medieval church*. Buffalo: Prometheus.

Bulman, R., & Wortman, C. (1977). Attributions of blame and coing in the "real world": Severe accident victims react to their lot. *Journal of Personality and Social Psychology, 35*, 351–383.

Burger, J. M., & Burns, L. (1988). The illusion of unique invulnerability and the use of effective contraception. *Personality and Social Psychology Bulletin, 14*, 264–270.

Bushman, B. J., & Baumeister, R. F. (1998). Threatened egotism, narcissism, self-esteem, and direct and displaced aggression: Does self-love or self-hate lead to violence? *Journal of Personality and Social Psychology, 75*, 219–229.

Bushman, B. J., Baumeister, R. F., Phillips, C. M., & Gilligan, J. (1999). *Narcissism and self-esteem among violent offenders in a prison sample*. Manuscript submitted for publication.

Buss, D. M. (1985). Human mate selection. *American Scientist, 73*, 47–51.

Buss, D. M. (1988). The evolution of human intrasexual competition. *Journal of Personality and Social Psychology, 54*, 616–628.

Buss, D. M. (1989). Sex differences in human mate preferences: Evolutionary hypotheses tested in thirty-seven cultures. *Behavioral and Brain Sciences, 12*, 1–49.

Buss, D. M. (1994). *The evolution of desire*. New York: Basic Books.

Buss, D. M., Larsen, R. S., Westen, D., & Semmelroth, J. (1992). Sex differences in jealousy: Evolution, physiology, and psychology. *Psychological Science, 3*, 251–255.

Buss, D. M., & Schmitt, D. P. (1993). Sexual strategies theory: An evolutionary perspective on human mating. *Psychological Review, 100*, 204–232.

Buzwell, S., & Rosenthal, D. (1996). Constructing a sexual self: Adolescents' sexual self-perceptions and sexual risk-taking. *Journal of Research on Adolescence, 6*, 489–513.

Byers, E. S. (1988). Effects of sexual arousal on men's and women's behavior in sexual disagreement situations. *Journal of Sex Research, 25*, 235–254.

Byers, E. S., & Heinlein, L. (1989). Predicting initiations and refusals of sexual activities in married and cohabiting heterosexual couples. *Journal of Sex Research*, *26*, 210–231.

Byers, E. S., & O'Sullivan, L. F. (1988). Similar but different: Men's and women's experiences of sexual coercion. In P. Anderson & C. Struckman-Johnson (Eds.), *Sexually aggressive women* (pp. 144–168). New York: Guilford.

Byrne, D. (1977). Social psychology and the study of sexual behavior. *Personality and Social Psychology Bulletin*, *3*, 3–30.

Califia, P. (1983). A secret side of lesbian sexuality. In T. Weinberg & G. Kamel (Eds.), *S and M: Studies in sadomasochism* (pp. 129–136). Buffalo: Prometheus.

California Task Force to Promote Self-Esteem and Personal and Social Responsibility. (1990). *Toward a state of self-esteem*. Sacramento: California State Department of Education.

Call, V., Sprecher, S., & Schwartz, P. (1995). The incidence and frequency of marital sex in a national sample. *Journal of Marriage and the Family*, *57*, 639–652.

Campbell, A. (1981). *The sense of well-being in America*. New York: McGraw-Hill.

Caplan, P. (1984). The myth of women's masochism. *American Psychologist*, *39*, 130–139.

Carmichael, J. (1992). *The Satanizing of the Jews: Origin and development of mystical anti-Semitism*. New York: Fromm International.

Carns, D. E. (1973). Talking about sex: Notes on first coitus and the double sexual standard. *Journal of Marriage and the Family*, *35*, 677–688.

Carver, C. S., & Scheier, M. F. (1981). *Attention and self-regulation: A control-theory approach to human behavior*. New York: Springer-Verlag.

Carver, C. S., & Scheier, M. F. (1990). Origins and functions of positive and negative affect. *Psychological Review*, *97*, 19–35.

Catanese, K., & Yost, J. (1999). Reactance and narcissism. Unpublished laboratory data, John Carroll University, Cleveland.

Chapkis, W. (1997). *Live sex acts: Women performing erotic labor*. New York: Routledge.

Charbonneau, C., & Lander, P. S. (1991). Redefining sexuality: Women becoming lesbian in midlife. In B. Sang, J. Warshow, & A. J. Smith (Eds.), *Lesbians at midlife: The creative transition* (pp. 35–43). San Francisco: Spinsters Books.

Christensen, H. T., & Carpenter, G. R. (1962). Value-behavior discrepancies regarding premarital coitus in three Western cultures. *American Sociological Review*, *27*, 66–74.

Christiansen, K. O. (1977). A preliminary study of criminality among twins. In S. Mednick & K. Christiansen (Eds.), *Biosocial bases of criminal behavior* (pp. 89–108). New York: Gardner Press.

Christopher, F. S. (1988). An initial investigation into a continuum of premarital sexual pressure. *Journal of Sex Research*, *25*, 255–266.

Clark, M. S., & Reis, H. T. (1988). Interpersonal processes in close relationships. *Annual Review of Psychology*, *39*, 609–672.

Clark, R. D., & Hatfield, E. (1989). Gender differences in receptivity to sexual offers. *Journal of Psychology and Human Sexuality*, *2*, 39–55.

Clausen, J. (1990). My interesting condition. *Journal of Sex Research*, *27*, 445–459.

Clements-Schreiber, M. E., Rempel, J. K., & Desmerais, S. (1998). Women's sexual pressure tactics and adherence to related attitudes: A step toward prediction. *Journal of Sex Research*, *35*, 197–205.

Clore, G. L., Wiggins, N. H., & Itkin, G. (1975). Gain and loss in attraction: Attributions from nonverbal behavior. *Journal of Personality and Social Psychology*, *31*, 706–712.

Cohen, L. L., & Shotland, R. L. (1996). Timing of first sexual intercourse in a relationship: Expectations, experiences, and perceptions of others. *Journal of Sex Research*, *33*, 291–299.

College Board. (1976–77). *Student descriptive questionnaire*. Princeton: Educational Testing Service.

Collias, N. E., & Collias, E. C. (1970). The behavior of the West African village weaverbird. *Ibis*, *112*, 457–480.

Cott, N. F. (1977). *The bonds of womanhood*. New Haven: Yale University Press.

Cott, N. F. (1979). Passionlessness: An interpretation of Victorian sexual ideology, 1790–1850. In N. Cott & E. Pleck (Eds.), *A heritage of her own* (pp. 162–181). New York: Simon & Schuster.

Cotton, W. L. (1975). Social and sexual relationships of lesbians. *Journal of Sex Research*, *11*, 139–148.

Cowan, L. (1982). *Masochism: A Jungian view*. Dallas: Spring Publications.

Cowan, G., & Dunn, K. F. (1994). What themes in pornography lead to perceptions of the degradation of women? *Journal of Sex Research*, *31*, 11–21.

Craig, M. E., Kalichnan, S. C., & Follingstad, D. R. (1989). Verbal coercive sexual behavior among college students. *Archives of Sexual Behavior*, *18*, 421–434.

Cramer, D. (1993). Personality and marital dissolution. *Personality and Individual Differences, 14*, 605–617.

Crary, W. G. (1966). Reactions to incongruent self-experiences. *Journal of Consulting Psychology, 30*, 246–252.

Croake, J. W., & James, B. (1973). A four-year comparison of premarital sexual attitudes. *Journal of Sex Research, 9*, 91–96.

Crocker, J., & Schwartz, I. (1985). Prejudice and ingroup favoritism in a minimal intergroup situation: Effects of self-esteem. *Personality and Social Psychology Bulletin, 11*, 379–386.

Crooks, R., & Baur, K. (1999). *Our sexuality.* Pacific Grove, CA: Brooks/Cole.

Csikszentmihalyi, M. (1990). *Flow: The psychology of optimal experience.* New York: Harper & Row.

Daly, M., & Wilson, M. (1988). *Homicide.* Hawthorne, NY: Adline de Gruyter.

Darlington, R. B. (1975). *Radicals and squares: Statistical methods for the behavioral sciences.* Ithaca, NY: Logan Hill Press.

Davis, C. M., Blank, J., Lin, H.-Y., & Bonillas, C. (1996). Characteristics of vibrator use among women. *Journal of Sex Research, 33*, 313–320.

Deci, E. L. (1971). Effects of externally mediated rewards on intrinsic motivation. *Journal of Personality and Social Psychology, 18*, 105–115.

DeLamater, J. (1981). The social control of sexuality. In R. Turner & J. Short (Eds.), *Annual review of sociology,* (Vol. 7, pp. 263–290). Palo Alto, CA: Annual Reviews.

DeLamater, J. (1989). The social control of human sexuality. In K. McKinney & S. Sprecher (Eds.), *Human sexuality: The societal and interpersonal context* (pp. 30–62). Norwood, NJ: Ablex.

DeLamater, J. D., & Hyde, J. S. (1998). Essentialism vs. social constructionism in the study of human sexuality. *Journal of Sex Research, 35*, 10–18.

DeLamater, J. D., & MacCorquodale, P. (1979). *Premarital sexuality: Attitudes, relationships, behavior.* Madison: University of Wisconsin Press.

DeMaris, A. (1997). Elevated sexual activity in violent marriages: Hypersexuality or sexual extortion? *Journal of Sex Research, 34*, 367–373.

Derber, C. (1979). *The pursuit of attention: Power and individualism in everyday life.* New York: Oxford University Press.

Des Barres, P. (1987). *I'm with the band: Confessions of a groupie.* New York: Jove.

Devine, P. G. (1989). Stereotypes and prejudice: Their automatic and controlled components. *Journal of Personality and Social Psychology, 56*, 5–18.

Diamond, J. (1997). *Why is sex fun? The evolution of human sexuality.* New York: Basic Books.

The disappearing Czech intellectual. (1999, August 21). *The Economist,* p. 41.

Dixon, J. K. (1984). The commencement of bisexual activity in swinging married women over age thirty. *Journal of Sex Research, 20*, 71–90.

Downey, L., Ryan, R., Roffman, R., & Kulich, M. (1995). How could I forget? Inaccurate memories of sexually intimate moments. *Journal of Sex Research, 32*, 177–191.

Driscoll, R. H., & Davis, K. E. (1971). Sexual restraints: A comparison of perceived and self-reported reasons for college students. *Journal of Sex Research, 7*, 253–262.

du Bois-Reymond, M., & Ravesloot, J. (1996). The roles of parents and peers in the sexual and relational socialization of adolescents. In K. Hurrelmann & S. Hamilton (Eds.), *Social problems and social contexts in adolescence* (pp. 175–197). New York: Aldine de Gruyter.

Dunne, M. P., Martin, N. G., Statham, D. J., Slutske, W. S., Dinwiddie, S. H., Bucholz, K. K., Madden, P. A. F., & Heath, A. C. (1997). Genetic and environmental contributions to variance in age at first sexual intercourse. *Psychological Science, 8*, 211–216.

Dunning, D. (1999). A newer look: Motivated social cognition and the schematic representation of social concepts. *Psychological Inquiry, 10*, 1–11.

Duval, S., & Wicklund, R. A. (1972). *A theory of objective self-awareness.* New York: Academic Press.

Eagly, A. H. (1987). *Sex differences in social behavior: A social-role interpretation.* Hillsdale, NJ: Erlbaum.

Eagly, A. H., & Wood, W. (1999). The origins of sex differences in human behavior: Evolved dispositions versus social roles. *American Psychologist, 54*, 408–423.

Earle, J. R., & Perricone, P. J. (1986). Premarital sexuality: A ten-year study of attitudes and behavior on a small university campus. *Journal of Sex Research, 22*, 304–310.

Eccles, J. (1982). *Sex differences in achievement patterns.* Paper presented at a meeting of the American Psychological Association, Washington, DC.

Echols, A. (1984). The taming of the id: Feminist sexual politics, 1968–83. In C. Vance (Ed.), *Pleasure and danger: Exploring female sexuality* (pp. 60–72). Boston: Routledge and Kegan Paul.

Ehrenreich, B., Hess, E., & Jacobs, G. (1986). *Remaking love: The feminization of sex.* Garden City, NY: Doubleday Anchor.

Einon, D. (1994) Are men more promiscuous than women? *Ethology and Sociobiology, 15,* 131–143.

Eley, T. C., Lichtenstein, P., & Stevenson, J. (1999). Sex differences in the etiology of aggressive and nonaggressive antisocial behavior: Results from two twin studies. *Child Development, 70,* 155–168.

Elliott, L., & Brantley, C. (1997). *Sex on campus.* New York: Random House.

Ellis, B. J., & Symons, D. (1990). Sex differences in sexual fantasy: An evolutionary psychological approach. *Journal of Sex Research, 27,* 527–555.

Ellis, L., & Beattie, C. (1983). The feminist explanation for rape: An empirical test. *Journal of Sex Research, 19,* 74–93.

Erikson, E. H. (1959). *Identity and the life cycle.* New York: Norton.

Eysenck, H. J. (1971). Masculinity-femininity, personality and sexual attitudes. *Journal of Sex Research, 7,* 83–88.

Eysenck, H. J. (1972). Personality and sexual behavior. *Journal of Psychosomatic Research, 16,* 141–152.

Eysenck, H. J. (1973). Personality and attitudes to sex in criminals. *Journal of Sex Research, 9,* 295–306.

Eysenck, H. J. (1974). Personality, premarital sexual permissiveness, and assortative mating. *Journal of Sex Research, 10,* 47–51.

Eysenck, H. J. (1976). *Sex and personality.* London: Temple Smith.

Eysenck, H. J. (1980). Personality, marital satisfaction, and divorce. *Psychological Reports, 47,* 1235–1238.

Fallon, A. E., & Rozin, P. (1985). Sex differences in perceptions of desirable body shape. *Journal of Abnormal Psychology, 94,* 102–105.

Faludi, S. (1993, September 13). What's troubling troubled boys: Who's keeping score? *Newsweek.*

Fang, B. (1976). Swinging: In retrospect. *Journal of Sex Research, 12,* 220–237.

Faunce, P. S., & Phillips-Yonas, S. (1978). Women's liberation and human sexual relations. *International Journal of Women's Studies, 1,* 83–95.

Fazio, R. H., Powell, M. C., & Herr, P. M. (1983). Toward a process model of the attitude-behavior relation: Accessing one's attitude upon mere observation of the attitude object. *Journal of Personality and Social Psychology, 44,* 723–735.

Festinger, L. (1954). A theory of social comparison processes. *Human Relations, 7,* 117–140.

Finger, F. W. (1975). Changes in sex practices and beliefs of male college students: Over thirty years. *Journal of Sex Research, 11,* 304–317.

Fisher, W. A., & Byrne, D. (1978). Sex differences in response to erotica: Love versus lust. *Journal of Personality and Social Psychology, 36,* 117–125.

Ford, K., & Norris, A. E. (1993). Urban Hispanic adolescents and young adults: Relationship of acculturation to sexual behavior. *Journal of Sex Research, 30,* 316–323.

Forni, E. (1980). Women's role in the economic, social, and political development of Somalia. *Afrika Spectrum, 15,* 19–28.

Franklin, D. (1987). The politics of masochism. *Psychology Today, 21*(1), 52–57.

Freud, S. (1938). Sadism and masochism. In T. Weinberg & G. Kamel (Eds.), *S and M: Studies in Sadomasochism* (pp. 30–32). Buffalo: Prometheus. (Reprinted from A. A. Brill [Trans.], *Basic writings of Sigmund Freud.* New York: Modern Library)

Freud, S. (1961). The economic problem of masochism. In J. Strachey (Ed. and Trans.), *The standard edition of the complete works of Sigmund Freud* (Vol. 19, pp. 159–170). London: Hogarth Press. (Original work published 1924)

Freund, M., Leonard, T. L., & Lee, N. (1989). Sexual behavior of resident street prostitutes with their clients in Camden, New Jersey. *Journal of Sex Research, 26,* 460–478.

Friday, N. (1980). *Men in love.* New York: Dell.

From Calvinism to cruising. (1999, September 25). *The Economist,* p. 55.

Gagnon, J. H., & Simon, W. (1968). The social meaning of prison homosexuality. *Federal Probation, 32,* 28–29.

Garner, D. M., Garfinkel, P. E., Schwartz, D., & Thompson, M. (1980). Cultural expectations of thinness in women. *Psychological Reports, 47,* 483–491.

Gay, P. (1984). *The bourgeois experience: Education of the senses.* New York: Oxford University Press.

Gelles, R. J., & Straus, M. A. (1988). *Intimate violence: The causes and consequences of abuse in the American family.* New York: Simon & Schuster/Touchstone.

Ghiglieri, M. P. (1999). *The dark side of man: Tracing the origins of male violence.* Reading, MA: Perseus.

Giallombardo, R. (1966). *Society of women: A study of a women's prison.* New York: Wiley & Sons, Inc.

Gilbert, N. (1992). Realities and mythologies of rape. *Society, 29*, 4–10.

Gilligan, C. (1982). *In a different voice: Psychological theory and women's development.* Cambridge: Harvard University Press.

Gilovich, T. (1991). *How we know what isn't so.* New York: Free Press.

Glass, D. C., Singer, J. E., & Friedman, L. N. (1969). Psychic cost of adaptation to an environmental stressor. *Journal of Personality and Social Psychology, 12*, 200–210.

Golden, C. (1987). Diversity and variability in women's sexual identities. In Boston Lesbian Psychologies Collective (Ed.), *Lesbian psychologies: Explorations and challenges* (pp. 19–34). Urbana: University of Illinois Press.

Goode, E., & Haber, L. (1977). Sexual correlates of homosexual experience: An exploratory study of college women. *Journal of Sex Research, 13*, 12–21.

Gordon, A. K. (1999). *Perceptions of betrayal: The effects of type of infidelity, gender, perspective, and means of discovery.* Manuscript submitted for publication.

Gordon, A. K., & Miller, A. G. (in press). Perspective differences in the construal of lies: Is deception in the eye of the beholder? *Personality and Social Psychology Bulletin.*

Gould, J. L., & Gould, C. G. (1997). *Sexual selection: Mate choice and courtship in nature.* New York: Freeman/Scientific American.

Gray, J. (1993). *Men are from Mars, women are from Venus.* New York: HarperCollins.

Greenblat, C. S. (1983). The salience of sexuality in the early years of marriage. *Journal of Marriage and the Family, 45*, 289–299.

Greendlinger, V., & Byrne, D. (1987). Coercive sexual fantasies of college men as predictors of self-reported likelihood to rape and overt sexual aggression. *Journal of Sex Research, 23*, 1–11.

Greene, G., & Greene, C. (1974). *S-M: The last taboo.* New York: Grove Press.

Greer, G. (1970). *The female eunuch.* New York: Bantam.

Greer, G. (1973). Seduction is a four-letter word. *Playboy, 20*, 80–82, 164, 178, 224–228.

Greer, G. (1999). *The whole woman.* New York: Knopf.

Griffin, S. (1971). Rape: The all-American crime. *Ramparts, 10*, 26–36.

Griffit, W. (1981). Sexual intimacy in aging marital partners. In J. Marsh & S. Kiesler (Eds.), *Aging: Stability and change in the family* (pp. 301–315). New York: Academic.

Groth, A. N. (1979). *Men who rape: The psychology of the offender.* New York: Plenum.

Guttentag, M., & Secord, P. F. (1983). *Too many women? The sex ratio question.* Beverly Hills, CA: Sage.

Haller, J. S., & Haller, R. M. (1974). *The physician and sexuality in Victorian America.* New York: Norton.

Handy, B. (1998, August 31). How we really feel about fidelity. *Time*, pp. 52–53.

Hansen, G. L. (1987). Extradyadic relations during courtship. *Journal of Sex Research, 23*, 382–390.

Hansen, W. B., Hahn, G. L., & Wolkenstein, B. H. (1990). Perceived personal immunity: Beliefs about susceptibility to AIDS. *Journal of Sex Research, 27*, 622–628.

Hariton, E. B., & Singer, J. L. (1974). Women's fantasies during sexual intercourse. *Journal of Consulting and Clinical Psychology, 42*, 313–322.

Harris, R., Yulis, S., & Lacoste, D. (1980). Relationships among sexual arousability, imagery ability, and introversion-extraversion. *Journal of Sex Research, 16*, 72–86.

Harrison, D. A., Bennett, W. H., Globetti, G., & Alsikafi, M. (1974). Premarital sexual standards of rural youth. *Journal of Sex Research, 10*, 266–277.

Harter, S. (1993). Causes and consequences of low self-esteem in children and adolescents. In R. Baumeister (Ed.), *Self-esteem: The puzzle of low self-regard* (pp. 87–116). New York: Plenum.

Hastorf, A., & Cantril, H. (1954). They saw a game: A case study. *Journal of Abnormal and Social Psychology, 49*, 129–134.

Hatfield, E. (1984). The dangers of intimacy. In V. Derlega (Ed.), *Communication, intimacy, and close relationships* (pp. 207–220). New York: Academic.

Hatfield, E. (1988). Passionate and companionate love. In R. J. Sternberg & M. L. Barnes (Eds.), *The psychology of love* (pp. 191–217). New Haven: Yale University Press.

Hatfield, E., & Walster, G. W. (1978). *A new look at love.* Lantham, MA: University Press of America.

Hazan, C., & Shaver, P. R. (1994). Attachment as an organizational framework for research on close relationships. *Psychological Inquiry, 5*, 1–22.

Heilbrun, A. B., & Loftus, M. P. (1986). The role of sadism and peer pressure in the sexual aggression of male college students. *Journal of Sex Research, 22*, 320–332.

Heise, D. R. (1967). Cultural patterning of sexual socialization. *American Sociological Review, 32*, 726–739.

Helson, H. (1964). *Adaptation-level theory: An experimental and systematic approach to behavior.* New York: Harper.

Hendrick, C., & Hendrick, S. (1983). *Liking, loving, and relating.* Monterey, CA: Brooks/Cole.

Herdt, G. H. (1981). *Guardians of the flutes: Idioms of masculinity.* New York: McGraw-Hill.

Herek, G. M. (1988). Heterosexuals' attitudes toward lesbians and gay men: Correlates and gender differences. *Journal of Sex Research, 25,* 451–477.

Herek, G. M., & Capitanio, J. P. (1999). Sex differences in how heterosexuals think about lesbians and gay men: Evidence from survey context effects. *Journal of Sex Research, 36,* 348–360.

Herer, E., & Holzapfel, S. (1993). The medical causes of infertility and their effects on sexuality. *Canadian Journal of Human Sexuality, 2,* 113–120.

Herold, E. S., Corbesi, B., & Collins, J. (1994). Psychosocial aspects of female topless behavior on Australian beaches. *Journal of Sex Research, 31,* 122–142.

Herold, E. S., & Mewhinney, D.-M. K. (1993). Gender differences in casual sex and AIDS prevention: A survey of dating bars. *Journal of Sex Research, 30,* 36–42.

Herold, E. S., & Way, L. (1983). Oral-genital sexual behavior in a sample of university females. *Journal of Sex Research, 19,* 327–338.

Herrenkohl, E. C., Herrenkohl, R. C., Egolf, B. P., & Russo, M. J. (1998). The relationship between early maltreatment and teenage parenthood. *Journal of Adolescence, 21,* 291–303.

Hersh, S. M. (1997). *The dark side of Camelot.* Boston: Little, Brown.

Hershberger, S. L. (1997). A twin registry study of male and female sexual orientation. *Journal of Sex Research, 34,* 212–222.

Hicks, E. K. (1996). *Infibulation: Female mutilation in Islamic northeastern Africa.* New Brunswick: Transaction.

Higgins, E. T., Rholes, W. S., & Jones, C. R. (1977). Category accessibility and impression formation. *Journal of Experimental Social Psychology, 13,* 141–154.

Hill, C. T., Rubin, Z., & Peplau, L. A. (1976). Breakups before marriage: The end of 103 affairs. *Journal of Social Issues, 32,* 147–168.

Hill, M. S. (1988). Marital stability and spouses' shared time: A multidisciplinary hypothesis. *Journal of Family Issues, 9,* 427–451.

Hite, S. (1976). *The Hite report: A nationwide study of female sexuality.* New York: Dell.

Hite, S. (1979). *The Hite report on female sexuality.* New York: Knopf.

Hobart, C. W. (1958). The incidence of romanticism during courtship. *Social Forces, 36,* 362–367.

Hollar, D. S., & Snizek, W. E. (1996). The influences of knowledge of HIV/AIDS and self-esteem on the sexual practices of college students. *Social Behavior and Personality, 24,* 75–86.

Holman, E. A., & Silver, R. C. (1998). Getting "stuck" in the past: Temporal orientation and coping with trauma. *Journal of Personality and Social Psychology, 74,* 1146–1163.

Homans, G. C. (1950). *The human group.* New York: Harcourt, Brace, & World.

Homans, G. C. (1961). *Social behavior: Its elementary forms.* New York: Harcourt, Brace, & World.

Hood, R. W., Spilka, B., Hunsberger, B., & Gorsuch, R. (1996). *The psychology of religion: An empirical approach.* New York: Guilford.

Hsee, C. K., & Abelson, R. P. (1991). The velocity relation: Satisfaction as a function of the first derivative of outcome over time. *Journal of Personality and Social Psychology, 60,* 341–347.

Hsee, C. K., Abelson, R. P., & Salovey, P. (1991). The relative weighting of position and velocity in satisfaction. *Psychological Science, 2,* 263–266.

Hsee, C. K., Salovey, P., & Abelson, R. P. (1994). The quasi-acceleration relation: Satisfaction as a function of the change in velocity of outcome over time. *Journal of Experimental Social Psychology, 30,* 96–111.

Hu, S., Pattatucci, A., Patterson, C., Li, L., Folker, D., Cherny, S., Kruglyak, L., & Hamer, D. (1995). Linkage between sexual orientation and chromosome Xq28 in males but not in females. *Nature Genetics, 11,* 248–256.

Hull, J. G. (1981). A self-awareness model of the causes and effects of alcohol consumption. *Journal of Abnormal Psychology, 90,* 586–600.

Hull, J. G., & Young, R. D. (1983). Self-consciousness, self-esteem, and success-failure as determinants of alcohol consumption in male social drinkers. *Journal of Personality and Social Psychology, 44,* 1097–1109.

Hunt, M. (1974). *Sexual behavior in the 1970s.* Chicago: Playboy.

Hurlbert, D. F., & Whittaker, K. E. (1991). The role of masturbation in marital and sexual satisfaction: A comparative study of female masturbators and nonmasturbators. *Journal of Sex Education and Therapy, 17,* 272–282.

Huston, T. L., Surra, C. A., Fitzgerald, N. M., & Cate, R. M. (1981). From courtship to marriage: Mate selection as an interpersonal process. In S. Duck & R. Gilmour (Eds.), *Personal Relationships* (Vol. 2: *Developing personal relationships*, pp. 53–88). New York: Academic Press.

Hyde, J. S., & DeLamater, J. (1997). *Understanding human sexuality* (6th ed.). Boston: McGraw-Hill.

James, W. H. (1981). The honeymoon effect on marital coitus. *Journal of Sex Research, 17*, 114–123.

Jankowiak, W. R. (1995). *Romantic passion: A universal experience?* New York: Columbia University Press.

Janoff-Bulman, R. (1979). Characterological versus behavioral self-blame: Inquiries into depression and rape. *Journal of Personality and Social Psychology, 37*, 1798–1809.

Janoff-Bullman, R. (1992). *Shattered assumptions: Towards a new psychology of trauma*. New York: Free Press.

Janus, S. S., Bess, B., & Saltus, C. (1977). *A sexual profile of men in power*. Englewood Cliffs, NJ: Prentice-Hall.

Janus, S. S., & Janus, C. L. (1993). *The Janus report on sexual behavior*. New York: Wiley.

Jensen, A. R. (1998). *The g factor*. Westwood, CT: Praeger.

Jesser, C. J. (1978). Male responses to direct verbal sexual initiatives of females. *Journal of Sex Research, 14*, 118–128.

Johnson, W. S. (1979). *Living in sin: The Victorian sexual revolution*. Chicago: Nelson-Hall.

Johnston, J. (1973). *Lesbian nation: The feminist solution*. New York: Simon & Schuster.

Jones, E. E., & Nisbett, R. E. (1971). *The actor and the observer: Divergent perceptions of the causes of behavior*. Morristown, NJ: General Learning Press.

Judd, C. M., Park, B., Ryan, C. S., Brauer, M., & Kraus, S. (1995). Stereotypes and ethnocentrism: Diverging interethnic perceptions of African American and White American youth. *Journal of Personality and Social Psychology, 69*, 460–481.

Julien, D., Bouchard, C., Gagnon, M., & Pomerleau, A. (1992). Insiders' views of marital sex: A dyadic analysis. *Journal of Sex Research, 29*, 343–360.

Kacelnik, A. (1999, March). *Sex, mind, behaviour, and evolution*. Paper presented at the annual meeting of Eastern Psychological Association; Providence, RI.

Kahn, J., Smith, K., & Roberts, E. (1984). *Familial communication and adolescent sexual behavior* (Final report to the Office of Adolescent Pregnancy Programs). Cambridge, MA: American Institute for Research.

Kamel, G. W. L. (1983). The leather career: On becoming a sadomasochist. In T. Weinberg & G. Kamel (Eds.), *S and M: Studies in sadomasochism* (pp. 73–79). Buffalo, NY: Prometheus.

Kanin, E. J. (1965). Male sex aggression and three psychiatric hypotheses. *Journal of Sex Research, 1*, 221–231.

Kanin, E. J. (1985). Date rapists: Differential sexual socialization and relative deprivation. *Archives of Sexual Behavior, 14*, 219–231.

Kanin, E. J., Davidson, K. D., & Scheck, S. R. (1970). A research note on male-female differentials in the experience of heterosexual love. *Journal of Sex Research, 6*, 64–72.

Kant, I. (1924). *Kritik der Urteilskraft* [Critique of judgment]. Hamburg, Germany: Felix Meiner Verlag. (Original work published 1790)

Kant, I. (1929). *Kritik der praktischen Vernunft* [Critique of practical reason]. Hamburg, Germany: Felix Meiner Verlag. (Original work published 1787)

Keegan, J. (1976). *The face of battle*. New York: Military Heritage Press.

Kellerman, J., Lewis, J., & Laird, J. D. (1989). Looking and loving: The effects of mutual gaze on feelings of romantic love. *Journal of Research in Personality, 23*, 145–161.

Kelley, J. (1978). Sexual permissiveness: Evidence for a theory. *Journal of Marriage and the Family, 40*, 455–468.

Kendrick, K. M., Hinton, M. R., Atkins, K., Haupt, M. A., & Skinner, J. D. (1998). Mothers determine sexual preferences. *Nature, 395*, 229–230.

Kenrick, D. T., Sadalla, E. K., Groth, G., & Trost, M. R. (1990). Evolution, traits, and the stages of human courtship: Qualifying the parental investment model. *Journal of Personality, 58*, 97–116.

Keys, A., Brozek, J., Henschel, A., Mickelson, O., & Taylor, H. L. (1950). *The biology of human starvation* (Vol. 1). Minneapolis: University of Minnesota Press.

King, K., Balswick, J. O., & Robinson, I. E. (1977). The continuing premarital sexual revolution among college females. *Journal of Marriage and the Family, 39*, 455–459.

Kinsey, A. C., Pomeroy, W. B., & Martin, C. E. (1948). *Sexual behavior in the human male*. Philadelphia: Saunders.

Kinsey, A. C., Pomeroy, W. B., Martin, C. E., & Gebhard, P. H. (1953). *Sexual behavior in the human female*. Philadelphia: Saunders.

Kitzinger, C. (1987). *The social construction of lesbianism*. London: Sage.

Kitzinger, C., & Wilkinson, S. (1995). Transitions from heterosexuality to lesbianism: The discursive production of lesbian identities. *Developmental Psychology, 31,* 95–104.

Klassen, A. D., Williams, C. J., & Levitt, E. E. (1989). *Sex and morality in the U.S.: An empirical enquiry under the auspices of the Kinsey Institute.* Middletown, CT: Wesleyan University Press.

Kling, K. C., Hyde, J. S., Showers, C. J., & Buswell, B. N. (1999). Gender differences in self-esteem: A meta-analysis. *Psychological Bulletin, 125,* 470–500.

Knafo, D., & Jaffe, Y. (1984). Sexual fantasizing in males and females. *Journal of Research in Personality, 18,* 451–467.

Knoth, R., Boyd, K., & Singer, B. (1988). Empirical tests of sexual selection theory: Predictions of sex differences in onset, intensity, and time course of sexual arousal. *Journal of Sex Research, 24,* 73–89.

Kohlberg, L. (1984). *The psychology of moral development: The nature and validity of moral stages.* New York: Harper & Row.

Kohlberg, L. (1981). *The philosophy of moral development: Moral stages and the idea of justice.* San Francisco: Harper & Row.

Koralewski, M., & Conger, J. C. (1992). The assessment of social skills among sexually coercive college males. *Journal of Sex Research, 29,* 169–188.

Koss, M. P. (1988). Hidden rape: Sexual aggression and victimization in a national sample of students in higher education. In A. W. Burgess (Ed.), *Rape and sexual assault* (Vol. 2, pp. 3–25). New York: Garland.

Krauthammer, C. (1997, June 29). Apology is not ours to give. *Cleveland Plain Dealer,* p. 2-E.

Langhorn, M. C., & Secord, P. F. (1955). Variations in marital needs with age, sex, marital status, and regional composition. *Journal of Social Psychology, 41,* 19–37.

Langlois, J. H., & Roggman, L. A. (1990). Attractive faces are only average. *Psychological Science, 1,* 115–121.

LaPlante, M. N., McCormick, N., & Brannigan, G. G. (1980). Living the sexual script: College students' views of influence in sexual encounters. *Journal of Sex Research, 16,* 338–355.

Laumann, E. O., Gagnon, J. H., Michael, R. T., & Michaels, S. (1994). *The social organization of sexuality: Sexual practices in the United States.* Chicago: University of Chicago Press.

Laumann, E. O., Paik, A., & Rosen, R. C. (1999). Sexual dysfunction in the United States: Prevalence and predictors. *Journal of the American Medical Association, 281,* 537–544.

Lawson, A. (1988). *Adultery: An analysis of love and betrayal.* New York: Basic Books.

Leary, M. R., & Kowalski, R. (1995). *Social anxiety.* New York: Guilford.

Leary, M. R., Tambor, E. S., Terdal, S. K., & Downs, D. L. (1995). Self-esteem as an interpersonal monitor: The sociometer hypothesis. *Journal of Personality and Social Psychology, 68,* 518–530.

Le Boeuf, B. J. (1974). Male-male competition and reproductive success in elephant seals. *American Zoology, 14,* 163–176.

Lee, J. A. (1983). The social organization of sexual risk. In T. Weinberg & G. Kamel (Eds.), *S and M: Studies in sadomasochism* (pp. 175–193). Buffalo, NY: Prometheus.

Lehrke, R. (1997). *Sex linkage of intelligence: The X-factor.* Westport, CT: Praeger.

Leigh, B. C. (1989). Reasons for having and avoiding sex: Gender, sexual orientation, and relationship to sexual behavior. *Journal of Sex Research, 26,* 199–209.

Leigh, B. C. (1990). The relationship of substance use during sex to high-risk sexual behavior. *Journal of Sex Research, 27,* 199–213.

Leitenberg, H., & Henning, K. (1995). Sexual fantasy. *Psychological Bulletin, 117,* 469–496.

Leith, K. P., & Baumeister, R. F. (1996). Why do bad moods increase self-defeating behavior? Emotion, risk taking, and self-regulation. *Journal of Personality and Social Psychology, 71,* 1250–1267.

Lepper, M. R., & Greene, D. (1979). *The hidden costs of reward.* Hillsdale, NJ: Erlbaum.

Lepper, M. R., Greene, D., & Nisbett, R. E. (1973). Undermining children's intrinsic interest with extrinsic reward: A test of the "overjustification" hypothesis. *Journal of Personality and Social Psychology, 28,* 129–137.

Lerner, M. J. (1980). *The belief in a just world: A fundamental delusion.* New York: Plenum.

Lewis, R. A. (1973). Parents and peers: Socialization agents in the coital behavior of young adults. *Journal of Sex Research, 9,* 156–170.

Libby, R. W., Gray, L., & White, M. (1978). A test and reformulation of reference group and role correlates of premarital sexual permissiveness theory. *Journal of Marriage and the Family, 40,* 79–92.

Libby, R. W., & Nass, G. D. (1971). Parental views on teenage sexual behavior. *Journal of Sex Research, 7,* 226–236.

Licht, H. (1934). *Sexual life in ancient Greece.* New York: Dutton.

Lightfoot-Klein, H. (1989). *Prisoners of ritual: An odyssey into female genital circumcision in Africa.* New York: Haworth Press.

Linder, D. E., Cooper, J., & Jones, E. E. (1967). Decision freedom as a determinant of the role of incentive magnitude in attitude change. *Journal of Personality and Social Psychology, 6,* 245–254.

Lisak, D., & Roth, S. (1988). Motivational factors in nonincarcerated sexually aggressive men. *Journal of Personality and Social Psychology, 55,* 795–802.

Luschen, M. E., & Pierce, D. M. (1972). Effect of the menstrual cycle on mood and sexual arousability. *Journal of Sex Research, 8,* 41–47.

Macfarlane, A. (1986). *Marriage and love in England: Modes of Reproduction, 1300–1840.* Oxford: Basil Blackwell.

Malamuth, N. M., & Check, J. V. (1980). Penile tumescence and perceptual responses to rape as a function of victim's perceived reactions. *Journal of Applied Social Psychology, 10,* 528–547.

Malamuth, N. M., & Check, J. V. (1983). Sexual arousal to rape depictions: Individual differences. *Journal of Abnormal Psychology, 92,* 55–67.

Mandler, G. (1975). *Mind and emotion.* New York: Wiley.

Mann, J., Berkowitz, L., Sidman, J., Starr, S., & West, S. (1974). Satiation of the transient stimulation effect of erotic films. *Journal of Personality and Social Psychology, 30,* 729–735.

Margolis, M. L. (1984). *Mothers and such: Views of American women and why they changed.* Berkeley: University of California Press.

Markus, H. R., & Kitayama, S. (1991). Culture and the self: Implications for cognition, emotion, and motivation. *Psychological Review, 98,* 224–253.

Martin, L., & Kerwin, J. (1991). *Self-reported rape proclivity is influenced by question context.* Paper presented at the convention of the American Psychological Society, Washington, DC.

Masters, W. H., & Johnson, V. E. (1966). *Human sexual response.* Boston: Little, Brown.

Masters, W. H., & Johnson, V. E. (1970). *Human sexual inadequacy.* Boston: Little, Brown.

Maticka-Tyndale, E., Herold, E. S., & Mewhinney, D. (1998). Casual sex on spring break: Intentions and behaviors of Canadian students. *Journal of Sex Research, 35,* 254–264.

McCabe, P. (1987). Desired and experienced levels of premarital affection and sexual intercourse during dating. *Journal of Sex Research, 23,* 23–33.

McCauley, E. A., & Ehrhardt, A. A. (1980). Sexual behavior in female transsexual and lesbians. *Journal of Sex Research, 16,* 202–211.

McLaughlin-Volpe, T., Aron, A., Wright, S., & Reis, H. T. (1999). *Intergroup social interactions and intergroup prejudice.* Manuscript submitted for publication.

McNamara, J. A. (1985). *A new song: Celibate women in the first three Christian centuries.* New York: Harrington Park Press.

Mead, M. (1935). *Sex and temperament in three primitive societies.* New York: Morrow.

Mecca, A. M., Smelser, N. J., & Vasconcellos, J. (Eds.). (1990). *The social importance of self-esteem.* Berkeley: University of California Press.

Mercer, G. W., & Kohn, P. M. (1979). Gender difference in the integration of conservatism, sex urge, and sexual behaviors among college students. *Journal of Sex Research, 15,* 129–142.

Mettee, D. R., & Aronson, E. (1974). Affective reactions to appraisal from others. In T. Huston (Ed.), *Foundations of interpersonal attraction* (pp. 236–284). New York: Academic Press.

Meyer, C. B., & Taylor, S. E. (1986). Adjustment to rape. *Journal of Personality and Social Psychology, 50,* 1226–1234.

Meyers, S. A., & Berscheid, D. (1997). The language of love: The difference a preposition makes. *Personality and Social Psychology Bulletin, 23,* 347–362.

Michael, R. P., & Zumpe, D. (1971). Patterns of reproductive behavior. In E. Havez (Ed.), *Comparative reproduction of nonhuman primates* (pp. 205–242). Springfield, IL: Thomas.

Michael, R. T., Gagnon, J. H., Laumann, E. O., & Kolata, G. (1994). *Sex in America: A definitive survey.* New York: Warner Books.

Mikula, G., Athenstaedt, U., Heschgl, S., & Heimgartner, A. (in press). Does it only depend on the point of view? Perspective-related differences in justice evaluations of negative incidents in personal relationships. *European Journal of Social Psychology.*

Miller, A. (1978). Tragedy and the common man; also, The nature of tragedy. In R. Martin (Ed.), *The theater essays of Arthur Miller* (pp. 3–11). New York: Viking. (Original work published 1949)

Miller, B. C., & Moore, K. A. (1990). Adolescent sexual behavior, pregnancy, and parenting: Research through the 1980s. *Journal of Marriage and the Family, 52,* 1025–1044.

Miller, C. T., & Downey, K. T. (1999). A meta-analysis of heavyweight and self-esteem. *Personality and Social Psychology Review, 3,* 68–84.

Miller, L. C., & Fishkin, S. A. (1997). On the dynamics of human bonding and reproductive success: Seeking windows on the adapted-for human-environmental interface. In J. Simpson & D. Kenrick (Eds.), *Evolutionary social psychology* (pp. 197–235). Mahwah, NJ: Erlbaum.

Millet, K. (1971). *The prostitution papers: A candid dialogue.* New York: Basic Books.

Mirande, A. M. (1968). Reference group theory and adolescent sexual behavior. *Journal of Marriage and the Family, 30,* 572–577.

Mischel, W., Ebbesen, E. B., & Zeiss, A. R. (1976). Determinants of selective memory about the self. *Journal of Consulting and Clinical Psychology, 44,* 92–103.

Money, J. (1990). *Vandalized lovemaps.* Buffalo, NY: Prometheus.

Morokoff, P. J. (1986). Volunteer bias in the psychophysiological study of female sexuality. *Journal of Sex Research, 22,* 35–51.

Morokoff, P. J., & Gilliland, R. (1993). Stress, sexual functioning, and marital satisfaction. *Journal of Sex Research, 30,* 43–53.

Morris, D. R. (1965). *The washing of the spears: The rise and fall of the Zulu nation.* New York: Simon & Schuster.

Moser, C., & Levitt, E. E. (1987). An exploratory-descriptive study of a sadomasochistically oriented sample. *The Journal of Sex Research, 23(3),* 322–337.

Mosher, C. D. (1980). *The Mosher survey: Sexual attitudes of forty-five Victorian women* (J. MaHood & K. Wenburg, Eds.). New York: Arno Press.

Muehlenhard, C. L., & Hallabaugh, L. C. (1988). Do women sometimes say no when they mean yes? The prevalence and correlates of women's token resistance to sex. *Journal of Personality and Social Psychology, 54,* 872–879.

Murnen, S. K., Perot, A., & Byrne, D. (1989). Coping with unwanted sexual activity: Normative responses, situational determinants, and individual differences. *Journal of Sex Research, 26,* 85–106.

Murphy, S. (1992). *A delicate dance: Sexuality, celibacy, and relationships among Catholic clergy and religious.* New York: Crossroad.

Myers, D. (1992). *The pursuit of happiness.* New York: Morrow.

Napheys, G. H. (1871). *The transmission of life: Counsels on the nature and hygiene of the masculine function.* Philadelphia.

National Research Council. (1993). *Understanding and preventing violence.* Washington, DC: National Academy Press.

Newcomb, M. D. (1985). Sexual experience among men and women: Associations within three independent samples. *Psychological Reports, 56,* 603–614.

Newcomb, M. D. (1986). Notches on the bedpost: Generational effects of sexual experience. *Psychology: A Quarterly Journal of Human Behavior, 23,* 37–46.

Newcomer, S., & Udry, J. R. (1987). Parental marital status effects on adolescent sexual behavior. *Journal of Marriage and the Family, 49,* 235–240.

Newman, K. S. (1988). *Falling from grace: The experience of downward mobility in the American middle class.* New York: Free Press.

Nicastro, A. M., Cousins, A. V., & Spitzberg, B. H. (1999, June). *The tactical face of stalking.* Paper presented to the convention of the International Network on Personal Relationships, Louisville, KY.

Nolin, M. J., & Petersen, K. K. (1992). Gender differences in parent-child communication about sexuality. *Journal of Adolescent Research, 7,* 59–79.

Norman, C., & Aron, A. (1995, June). *The effect of exciting activities on relationship satisfaction: A laboratory experiment.* Paper presented at the International Network on Personal Relationships, Williamsburg, VA.

Oates, G. L. (1997). Self-esteem enhancement through fertility? Socioeconomic prospects, gender, and mutual influence. *American Sociological Review, 62,* 965–973.

Offir, J. T., Fisher, J. D., Williams, S. S., & Fisher, W. A. (1993). Reasons for inconsistent AIDS-preventive behaviors among gay men. *Journal of Sex Research, 30,* 62–69.

O'Kane, M. (1997, December 13). The Taliban's annihilation of woman. *The Age* (Melbourne, Australia), p. 19.

O'Leary, K. D., Barling, J., Arias, I., Rosenbaum, A., Malone, J., & Tyree, A. (1989). *Journal of Consulting and Clincial Psychology, 57,* 263–268.

Oliver, M. B., & Hyde, J. S. (1993). Gender differences in sexuality: A meta-analysis. *Psychological Bulletin, 114,* 29–51.

O'Neill, G. C., & O'Neill, N. (1970). Patterns in group sexual activity. *Journal of Sex Research, 6,* 101–112.

O'Sullivan, L. F., & Allgeier, E. R. (1998). Feigning sexual desire: Consenting to unwanted sexual activity in heterosexual dating relationships. *Journal of Sex Research, 35,* 234–243.

O'Sullivan, L. F., & Byers, E. S. (1992). College students' incorporation of intiator and restrictor roles in sexual dating interactions. *Journal of Sex Research, 29,* 435–446.

O'Sullivan, L. F., Byers, E. S., & Finkelman, L. (1998). A comparison of male and female college students' experiences of sexual coercion. *Psychology of Women Quarterly, 22,* 177–195.

Palmer, C. T. (1988). Twelve reasons why rape is not sexually motivated: A skeptical examination. *Journal of Sex Research, 25,* 512–530.

Palmer, J. D., Udry, J. R., & Morris, N. M. (1982). Diurnal and weekly, but no lunar rhythms in human copulation. *Human Biology, 54,* 111–121.

Patton, D., & Waring, E. M. (1985). Sex and marital intimacy. *Journal of Sex and Marital Therapy, 11,* 176–184.

Pearlman, S. F. (1987). The sage of continuing clash in lesbian community, or will an army of ex-lovers fail? In Boston Lesbian Psychologies Collective (Ed.), *Lesbian psychologies: Explorations and challenges* (pp. 313–326). Urbana: University of Illinois Press.

Pelletier, L. A., & Herold, E. S. (1988). The relationship of age, sex guilt, and sexual experience with female sexual fantasies. *Journal of Sex Research, 24,* 250–256.

Pennebaker, J. W., Dwyer, M. A., Caulkins, R. S., Litowicz, D. L., Ackerman, P. L., & Anderson, D. B. (1979). Don't the girls get prettier at closing time: A country and western application to psychology. *Personality and Social Psychology Bulletin, 5,* 122–125.

Perlman, D., & Fehr, B. (1987). The development of intimate relationships. In D. Perlman & S. Duck (Eds.), *Intimate relationships: Development, dynamics, and deterioration* (pp. 1–29). Beverly Hills, CA: Sage.

Perloff, L. S., & Fetzer, B. K. (1986). Self-other judgments and perceived vulnerability to victimization. *Journal of Personality and Social Psychology, 50,* 502–510.

Perspectives. (1996, October 14). *Newsweek,* p. 27.

Petty, R. E., & Wegener, D. T. (1998). Attitude change: Multiple roles for persuasion variables. In D. Gilbert, S. Fiske, & G. Lindzey (Eds.), *Handbook of social psychology* (4th ed., Vol. 1, pp. 323–390). Boston: McGraw-Hill.

Phillis, D. E., & Gromko, M. H. (1985). Sex differences in sexual activity: Reality or illusion? *Journal of Sex Research, 21,* 437–443.

Plotnick, R. D. (1992). The effects of attitudes on teenage premarital pregnancy and its resolution. *American Sociological Review, 57,* 800–811.

Porter, J. F., Critelli, J. W., & Tang, C. S. K. (1992). Sexual and aggressive motives in sexually aggressive college males. *Archives of Sexual Behavior, 21,* 457–468.

Price, S. J., & McKenry, P. C. (1988). *Divorce.* Newbury Park, CA: Sage.

Propper, A. M. (1981). *Prison homosexuality: Myth and reality.* Lexington, KY: Heath & Company.

Proulx, J., Aubut, J., McKibben, A., & Cote, M. (1994). Penile responses of rapists and nonrapists to rape stimuli involving physical violence or humiliation. *Archives of Sexual Behavior, 23,* 295–310.

Raskin, R., & Terry, H. (1988). A principal-components analysis of the Narcissistic Personality Inventory and further evidence of its construct validation. *Journal of Personality and Social Psychology, 54,* 890–902.

Reed, J. P., & Reed, R. S. (1972). Pornography research using direct erotic stimuli. *Journal of Sex Research, 8,* 237–246.

Regan, P. C., & Berscheid, E. (1995). Gender differences in beliefs about the causes of male and female sexual desire. *Personal Relationships, 2,* 345–358.

Reik, T. (1957). *Masochism in modern man* (M. H. Beigel & G. M. Kurth, Trans.). New York: Grove Press. (Original work published 1941)

Reinholtz, R. K., & Muehlenhard, C. L. (1995). Genital perceptions and sexual activity in a college population. *Journal of Sex Research, 32,* 155–165.

Reinisch, J. M. (1990). *The Kinsey Institute new report on sex.* New York: St. Martin's.

Reis, H. T., & Patrick, B. C. (1996). Attachment and intimacy: Component processes. In E. Higgins & A. Kruglanski (Eds.), *Social psychology: Handbook of basic principles* (pp. 523–563). New York: Guilford.

Reis, H. T., & Shaver, P. (1988). Intimacy as an interpersonal process. In S. Duck (Ed.), *Handbook of personal relationships* (pp. 367–389). Chichester, England: Wiley.

Reiss, I. L. (1967). *The social context of premarital sexual permissiveness.* New York: Holt, Rinehart, & Winston.

Reiss, I. L., Anderson, R. E., & Sponaugle, G. C. (1980). A multivariate model of the determinants of extramarital sexual permissiveness, *Journal of Marriage and the Family, 42,* 395–411.

Reiss, I. L. (1986a). *Journey into sexuality: An exploratory voyage.* New York: Prentice-Hall.

Reiss, I. L. (1986b). A sociological journey into sexuality. *Journal of Marriage and the Family, 48,* 233–242.

Reissman, C., Aron, A., & Bergen, M. R. (1993). Shared activities and marital satisfaction: Causal direction and self-expansion versus boredom. *Journal of Social and Personal Relationships, 10,* 243–254.

Renaud, C., Byers, E. S., & Pau, S. (1997). Sexual and relationship satisfaction in mainland China. *Journal of Sex Research, 34,* 399–410.

Reuben, D. (1969). *Everything you always wanted to know about sex.* New York: Bantam Books.

Ridley, M. (1993). *The red queen: Sex and evolution in human nature.* New York: Penguin.

Riskind, J. H., & Maddux, J. E. (1993). Loomingness, helplessness, and fearfulness: An integration of harm-looming and self-efficacy models of fear. *Journal of Social and Clinical Psychology, 12,* 73–89.

Riskind, J. H., & Maddux, J. E. (1994). Loomingness and the fear of AIDS: Perception of motion and menace. *Journal of Applied Social Psychology, 24,* 432–442.

Riskind, J. H., & Wahl, O. (1992). Moving makes it worse: The role of rapid movement in fear of psychiatric patients. *Journal of Social and Clinical Psychology, 11,* 349–364.

Riskind, J. H., Moore, R., & Bowley, L. (1995). The looming of spiders: The fearful perceptual distortion of movement and menace. *Behaviour Research and Therapy, 33,* 171–178.

Roberts, J. A. F. (1945). On the difference between the sexes in dispersion of intelligence. *British Medical Journal, 1,* 727–730.

Roberts, T., & Pennebaker, J. W. (1995). Gender differences in perceiving internal state: Toward a his-and-hers model of perceptual cue use. In M. Zanna (Ed.), *Advances in experimental social psychology* (Vol. 27, pp. 143–175). San Diego: Academic Press.

Robinson, I. E., & Jedlicka, D. (1982). Change in sexual attitudes and behavior of college students from 1965 to 1980: A research note. *Journal of Marriage and the Family, 44,* 237–240.

Robinson, J., & Godbey, G. (1998, February). No sex, please . . . we're college graduates. *American Demographics,* pp. 18–23.

Robinson, R., Ziss, K., Ganza, B., Katz, S., & Robinson, E. (1991). Twenty years of the sexual revolution, 1965–1985: An update. *Journal of Marriage and the Family, 53,* 216–220.

Rodgers, V. L., & Rowe, D. C. (1990). Adolescent sexual activity and mildly deviant behavior: Sibling and friendship effects. *Journal of Family Issues, 11,* 274–293.

Roebuck, J., & McGee, M. G. (1977). Attitudes toward premarital sex and sexual behavior among black high school girls. *Journal of Sex Research, 13,* 104–114.

Roiphe, K. A. (1993). *The morning after: Sex, fear, and feminism on campus.* Boston: Little, Brown.

Rosario, M., Meyer-Bahlburg, H. F. L., Hunter, J., Exner, T. M., Gwadz, M., & Keller, A. M. (1996). The psychosexual development of urban lesbian, gay, and bisexual youths. *Journal of Sex Research, 33,* 113–126.

Rosenbluth, S. (1997). Is sexual orientation a matter of choice? *Psychology of Women Quarterly, 21,* 595–610.

Roth, C. (1964). *The Spanish Inquisition.* New York: Norton.

Rozin, P., Millman, L., & Nemeroff, C. (1986). Operation of the laws of sympathetic magic in disgust and other domains. *Journal of Personality and Social Psychology, 50,* 703–712.

Rubin, L. (1990). *Erotic wars: What happened to the sexual revolution?* New York: Farrar Straus & Giroux.

Ruble, D. N., Fleming, A. S., Hackel, L. S., & Stangor, C. (1988). Changes in the marital relationship during the transition to first-time motherhood: Effects of violated expectations concerning division of household labor. *Journal of Personality and Social Psychology, 55,* 78–87.

Runciman, S. (1951–54). *A history of the Crusades* (3 Vols.) New York: Cambridge University Press.

Rust, P. C. (1992). The politics of sexual identity: Sexual attraction and behavior among lesbian and bisexual women. *Social Problems, 39,* 366–386.

Rust, P. C. (1993). Neutralizing the political threat of the marginal woman: Lesbians' beliefs about bisexual women. *Journal of Sex Research, 30,* 214–228.

Rynd, N. (1988). Incidence of psychometric symptoms in rape victims. *Journal of Sex Research, 24,* 155–161.

Sack, A. R., Keller, J. F., & Hinkle, D. E. (1984). Premarital sexual intercourse: A test of the effects of peer group, religiosity, and sexual guilt. *Journal of Sex Research, 20,* 168–185.

Salovey, P., Hsee, C. K., & Mayer, J. D. (1993). Emotional intelligence and the self-regulation of affect. In D. M. Wegner & J. W. Pennebaker (Eds.), *Handbook of mental control* (pp. 258–277). Englewood Cliffs, NJ: Prentice Hall.

Sanders, S. A., & Reinisch, J. M. (1999). Would you say you "had sex" if. . . ? *Journal of the American Medical Association, 281,* 275–277.

Savin-Williams, R. C. (1989). Parental influences on the self-esteem of gay and lesbian youths: A reflected appraisals model. *Journal of Homosexuality, 17,* 93–109.

Savin-Williams, R. C. (1990). *Gay and lesbian youth: Expressions of identity.* New York: Hemisphere.

Scacco, A. M. (1975). *Rape in prison.* Springfield, IL: Charles Thomas.

Scarry, E. (1985). *The body in pain: The making and unmaking of the world.* New York: Oxford University Press.

Schachter, S., & Singer, J. E. (1962). Cognitive, social, and physiological determinants of emotional state. *Psychological Review, 69,* 379–399.

Schaefer, M. T., & Olson, D. H. (1981). Assessing intimacy: The PAIR inventory. *Journal of Marital and Family Therapy, 7,* 47–60.

Schäfer, S. (1976). Sexual and social problems of lesbians. *Journal of Sex Research, 12,* 50–69.

Schaffer, M. D. (1990, August 15). Sex: A special challenge for many clergy members. *Denver Post,* p. 6B.

Schenk, J., & Pfrang, H. (1986). Extroversion, neuroticism, and sexual behavior: Interrelations in a sample of young men. *Archives of Sexual Behavior, 15,* 449–455.

Scherzer, T. (1998). Domestic violence in lesbian relationships: Findings of the Lesbian Relationship Research Project. *Journal of Lesbian Studies, 2,* 29–47.

Schmidt, G., & Sigusch, V. (1970). Sex differences in response to psychosexual stimulation by films and slides. *Journal of Sex Research, 6,* 268–283.

Schmidt, G., & Sigusch, V. (1972). Changes in sexual behavior among young males and females between 1960–1970. *Archives of Sexual Behavior, 2,* 27–45.

Schneider, W., & Shiffrin, R. M. (1977). Controlled and automatic human information processing: Detection, search, and attention. *Psychological Review, 84,* 1–66.

Schofield, M. (1968). *The sexual behavior of young people.* Harmondsworth, England: Penguin.

Schwartz, M. F., & Masters, W. H. (1983). Conceptual factors in the treatment of paraphilias: A preliminary report. *Journal of Sex and Marital Therapy, 9,* 3–18.

Scott, G. G. (1983). *Erotic power: An exploration of dominance and submission.* Secaucus, NJ: Citadel Press.

Scully, D. (1990). *Understanding sexual violence.* Hammersmith, London, England: HarperCollins Academic.

Scully, D., & Marolla, J. (1984). Convicted rapists' vocabulary of motive: Excuses and justifications. *Social Problems, 31,* 530–544.

Seal, D. W. (1997). Interpartner concordance of self-reported sexual behavior among college dating couples. *Journal of Sex Research, 34,* 39–55.

Sedikides, C., Oliver, M. B., & Campbell, W. K. (1994). Perceived benefits and costs of romantic relationships for women and men: Implications for exchange theory. *Personal Relationships, 1,* 5–21.

Seligman, M. E. P. (1994). *What you can change and what you can't: The ultimate guide to self-improvement.* New York: Knopf.

Shandall, A. A. (1967). Circumcision and infibulation of females. *Sudan Medical Journal, 5,* 178–212.

Shandall, A. A. (1979). *Circumcision and infibulation of females.* Switzerland: Terre des Hommes.

Sherfey, M. J. (1966). The evolution and nature of female sexuality in relation to psychoanalytic theory. *Journal of the American Psychoanalytic Asssociation, 14,* 28–128.

Sherwin, R., & Corbett, S. (1985). Campus sexual norms and dating relationships: A trend analysis. *Journal of Sex Research, 21,* 258–274.

Shilts, R. (1987). *And the band played on: Politics, people, and the AIDS epidemic.* New York: Viking Penguin.

Shock, N. W., Greulich, R. C., Andres, R., Arenberg, D., Costa, P. T., Lakatta, E. G., & Tobin, J. D. (1984). *Normal human aging: The Baltimore longitudinal study of aging.* Baltimore: NIH Publications.

Shorter, E. (1975). *The making of the modern family.* New York: Basic Books.

Shorter, E. (1982). *A history of women's bodies.* New York: Basic Books.

Sigusch, V., & Schmidt, G. (1973). Teenage boys and girls in West Germany. *Journal of Sex Research, 9,* 107–123.

Sigusch, V., Schmidt, G., Reinfeld, A., & Wiedemann-Sutor, I. (1970). Psychosexual stimulation: Sex differences. *Journal of Sex Research, 6,* 10–24.

Silver, R. L., Boon, C., & Stones, M. H. (1983). Searching for meaning in misfortune: Making sense of incest. *Journal of Social Issues, 39,* 81–102.

Sinclair, R. C., & Brown, N. R. (1999, April–May). *Discrepant partner reports: Do women encode sexual experiences more deeply than men do?* Paper presented at the annual convention of the Midwestern Psychological Association, Chicago.

Sipe, A. W. R. (1995). *Sex, priests, and power: Anatomy of a crisis.* New York: Brunner/Mazel.

Smith, G. E., Gerrard, M., & Gibbons, F. X. (1997). Self-esteem and the relation between risk behavior and perceptions of vulnerability to unplanned pregnancy in college women. *Health Psychology, 16,* 137–146.

Smith, J. R., & Smith, L. G. (1970). Co-marital sex and the sexual freedom movement. *Journal of Sex Research, 6,* 131–142.

Smith, T. (1994). Attitudes toward sexual permissiveness: Trends, correlates, and behavioral connections. In A. S. Rossi (Ed.), *Sexuality across the life course* (pp. 63–97). Chicago: University of Chicago Press.

Smuts, B. (1996). Male aggression against women: An evolutionary perspective. In D. Buss & N. Malamuth (Eds.), *Sex, power, conflict* (pp. 231–268). New York: Oxford University Press.

A social profile: drug abuse. (1998, March 29). *The Economist,* p. 27.

Solomon, R. L., & Corbit, J. D. (1974). An opponent-process theory of motivation: I. Temporal dynamics of affect. *Psychological Review, 81,* 119–145.

Sommers, C. H. (1994). *Who stole feminism? How women have betrayed women.* New York: Simon & Schuster/Touchstone.

Spanier, G. B., & Casto, R. F. (1979). Adjustment to separation and divorce: A qualitative analysis. In G. Levinger & O. C. Moles (Eds.), *Divorce and separation: Context, causes, and consequences.* (pp. 211–227). New York: Basic Books.

Spanier, G. B., & Glick, P. (1980). The life cycle of American families: An expanded analysis. *Journal of Family History, 5,* 97–111.

Spanier, G. P., & Margolis, R. L. (1983). Marital separation and extramarital sexual behavior. *Journal of Sex Research, 19,* 23–48.

Spengler, A. (1977). Manifest sadomasochism of males: Results of an empirical study. *Archives of Sexual Behavior, 6,* 441–456.

Spitzer, B. L., Henderson, K. A., & Zivian, M. T. (1999). Gender differences in population versus media body sizes: A comparison over four decades. *Sex Roles, 40,* 545–565.

Sprecher, S. (1989). Premarital sexual standards for different categories of individuals. *Journal of Sex Research, 26,* 232–248.

Sprecher, S., Barbee, A., & Schwartz, P. (1995). "Was it good for you, too?": Gender differences in first sexual experiences. *Journal of Sex Research, 32,* 3–15.

Sprecher, S., & Hatfield, E. (1996). Premarital sexual standards among U. S. college students: Comparison with Russian and Japanese students. *Archives of Sexual Behavior, 25,* 261–288.

Sprecher, S., McKinney, K., & Orbuch, T. L. (1991). The effect of current sexual behavior on friendship, dating, and marriage desirability. *Journal of Sex Research, 28,* 387–408.

Sprecher, S., & Regan, P. C. (1996). College virgins: How men and women perceive their sexual status. *Journal of Sex Research, 33,* 3–15.

Sprecher, S., Regan, P. C., McKinney, K., Maxwell, K., & Wazienski, R. (1997). Preferred level of sexual experience in a date or mate: The merger of two methodologies. *Journal of Sex Research, 34,* 327–337.

Stanislaw, H., & Rice, F. J. (1988). Correlation between sexual desire and menstrual cycle characteristics. *Archives of Sexual Behavior, 17,* 499–508.

Staples, R. (1973). Male-female sexual variations: Functions of biology or culture. *Journal of Sex Research, 9,* 11–20.

Stark, R. (1996). *The rise of Christianity.* Princeton: Princeton University Press.

Steele, C. M., & Southwick, L. (1985). Alcohol and social behavior: I. The psychology of drunken excess. *Journal of Personality and Social Psychology, 48,* 18–34.

Sternberg, R. J. (1986). A triangular theory of love. *Psychological Review, 93,* 119–135.

Stevens, G., & Tyler, M. K. (in press). Ethnic and racial intermarriage in the United States: Old and new regimes. In N. Denton & S. South (Eds.), *American diversity: A demographic challenge for the twenty-first century.* Albany: SUNY–Albany Press.

Steyn, M. (1997, December 13). Don't mention the dark side. *The Age* (Melbourne, Australia), *News Extra,* p. 7.

Stillwell, A. M., & Baumeister, R. F. (1997). The construction of victim and perpetrator memories: Accuracy and distortion in role-based accounts. *Personality and Social Psychology Bulletin, 23,* 1157–1172.

Stodghill, R. (1998, June 15). Where'd you learn that? *Time,* pp. 52–59.

Stokes, J. P., Damon, W., & McKirnan, D. J. (1997). Predictors of movement toward homosexuality: A longitudinal study of bisexual men. *Journal of Sex Research, 34,* 304–312.

Stone, L. (1977) *The family, sex, and marriage in England, 1500–1800.* New York: Harper & Row.

Straus, M. (1980). Victims and aggressors in marital violence. *American Behavioral Scientist, 23,* 681–704.

Strouse, J. S., & Buerkel-Rothfuss, N. L. (1987). Media exposure and the sexual attitudes and behaviors of college students. *Journal of Sex Education and Therapy, 13,* 43–51.

Sue, D. (1979). Erotic fantasies of college students during coitus. *Journal of Sex Research, 15,* 299–305.

Svenson, O. (1981). Are we all less risky and more skillful than our fellow drivers? *Acta Psychologica, 47,* 143–148.

Swim, J. K. (1994). Perceived versus meta-analytic effect sizes: An assessment of the accuracy of gender stereotypes. *Journal of Personality and Social Psychology, 66,* 21–36.

Symons, D. (1995). Beauty is in the adaptations of the beholder: The evolutionary psychology of human female sexual attractiveness. In P. Abramson & S. Pinkerton (Eds.), *Sexual nature, sexual culture* (pp. 80–118). Chicago: University of Chicago Press.

Tajfel, H. (1970). Experiments in intergroup discrimination. *Scientific American, 223,* 96–102.

Tajfel, H., & Billig, M. G. (1974). Familiarity and categorization in intergroup behavior. *Journal of Experimental Social Psychology, 10,* 159–170.

Tajfel, H., Flament, C., Billig, M. G., & Bundy, R. F. (1971). Social categorization and intergroup behaviour. *European Journal of Social Psychology, 1,* 149–177.

Tannahill, R. (1980). *Sex in history.* New York: Stein and Day/Scarborough.

Tavris, C., & Sadd, S. (1978). *The Redbook report on female sexuality.* New York: Dell.

Taylor, S. E., & Brown, J. D. (1988). Illusion and well-being: A social psychological perspective on mental health. *Psychological Bulletin, 103,* 193–210.

Tedeschi, J. T., & Felson, R. B. (1994). *Violence, aggression, and coercive actions.* Washington, DC: American Psychological Association.

Thibaut, J. W., & Kelley, H. H. (1959). *The social psychology of groups.* New York: Wiley.

Thiessen, D. (1994). Environmental tracking by females. *Human Nature, 5,* 167–202.

Thompson, A. P. (1983). Extramarital sex: A review of the research literature. *Journal of Sex Research, 19,* 1–22.

Thornton, A. D., & Camburn, D. (1987). The influence of the family on premarital attitudes and behavior. *Demography, 24,* 323–340.

Thornton, A. D., & Camburn, D. (1989). Religious participation and adolescent sexual behavior. *Journal of Marriage and the Family, 51,* 641–653.

Triandis, H. C. (1989). The self and social behavior in differing cultural contexts. *Psychological Review, 96,* 506–520.

Trivers, R. (1972). Parental investment and sexual selection. In B. Campbell (Ed.), *Sexual selection and the descent of man* (pp. 136–179). New York: Aldine de Gruyter.

Trivers, R. (1985). *Social Evolution.* Menlo Park, CA: Benjamin/Cummings.

Turner, J. C. (1985). Social categorization and the self-concept: A social cognitive theory of group behavior. In E. J. Lawler (Ed.), *Advances in group processes: Theory and Research* (Vol. 2, pp. 77–121). Greenwich, CT: JAI Press.

Udry, J. R. (1980). Changes in the frequency of marital intercourse from panel data. *Archives of Sexual Behavior, 9,* 319–325.

Ulrich, L. T. (1979). Vertuous women found: New England ministerial literature, 1668–1735. In N. Cott & E. Pleck (Eds.), *A heritage of her own* (pp. 58–80). New York: Simon & Schuster.

Vanwesenbeeck, I., Bekker, M., & van Lenning, A. (1998). Gender attitudes, sexual meanings, and interactional patterns in heterosexual encounters among college students in the Netherlands. *Journal of Sex Research, 35,* 317–327.

Vendenberg, S., McKusick, V., & McKusick, A. (1962). Twin data in support of the Lyon hypothesis. *Nature, 194,* 505–506.

Waldo, C. R., Hesson-McInnis, M. S., & D'Augelli, A. R. (1998). Antecedents and consequences of victimization of lesbian, gay, and bisexual young people: A structural model comparing rural university and urban samples. *American Journal of Community Psychology, 26,* 307–334.

Walkowitz, J. R. (1980). *Prostitution and Victorian society: Women, class, and the state.* Cambridge: Cambridge University Press.

Wallen, K. (1995). The evolution of female sexual desire. In P. Abramson & S. Pinkerton (Eds.), *Sexual nature, sexual culture* (pp. 57–79). Chicago: University of Chicago Press.

Waller, W., & Hill, R. (1951). *The family: A dynamic interpretation.* New York: Dryden. (Original work published 1938)

Walsh, A. (1991). Self-esteem and sexual behavior: Exploring gender differences. *Sex Roles, 25,* 441–450.

Walster, E., Walster, G. W., Piliavin, J., & Schmidt, L. (1973). "Playing hard to get": Understanding an elusive phenomenon. *Journal of Personality and Social Psychology, 26,* 113–121.

Ward, D. A., & Kassebaum, G. G. (1965). *Women's prison: Sex and social structure.* Chicago: Aldine.

Watt, J. D., & Ewing, J. E. (1996). Toward the development and validation of a measure of sexual boredom. *Journal of Sex Research, 33*, 57–66.

Weinberger, A. D. (1966). Interracial marriage—Its statutory prohibition, genetic import, and incidence. *Journal of Sex Research, 2*, 157–168.

Weis, D. L. (1998). The use of theory in sexuality research. *Journal of Sex Research, 35*, 1–9.

Weis, D. L., Rabinowitz, B., & Ruckstuhl, M. F. (1992). Individual changes in sexual attitudes and behavior within college-level human sexuality courses. *Journal of Sex Research, 29*, 43–59.

Weiss, R. S. (1979). The emotional impact of marital separation. In G. Levinger & O. C. Moles (Eds.), *Divorce and separation: Context, causes, and consequences* (pp. 201–210). New York: Basic Books.

Werner-Wilson, R. J. (1998). Gender differences in adolescent sexual attitudes: The influence of individual and family factors. *Adolescence, 33*, 519–531.

Whisman, V. (1996). *Queer by choice*. New York: Routledge.

Whitley, B. E. (1988). Sex differences in heterosexuals' attitudes toward homosexuals. *Journal of Sex Research, 24*, 287–291.

Wicker, A. W. (1969). Attitudes versus actions: The relationship of verbal and overt behavioral responses to attitude objects. *Journal of Social Issues, 25*, 41–78.

Wiederman, M. W. (1993). Demographic and sexual characteristics of nonresponders to sexual experience items in a national survey. *Journal of Sex Research, 30*, 27–35.

Wiederman, M. W. (1997). The truth must be in here somewhere: Examining the gender discrepancy in self-reported lifetime number of sex partners. *Journal of Sex Research, 34*, 375–386.

Williams, L., & Sobieszczyk, T. (1997). Attitudes surrounding the continuation of female circumcision in the Sudan: Passing the tradition to the next generation. *Journal of Marriage and the Family, 59*, 966–981.

Wilson, E. O. (1975). *Sociobiology: The new synthesis*. Cambridge: Harvard University Press.

Wilson, W. C., & Durrenberger, R. (1982). Comparison of rape and attempted rape victims. *Psychological Reports, 50*, 198.

Wilson, W. C. (1975). The distribution of selected sexual attitudes and behaviors among the adult population of the United States. *Journal of Sex Research, 11*, 46–64.

Winegar, K. (1990, November 27). Self-esteem is healthy for society. *Minnesota Star Tribune*, pp. 1E–2E.

Wiseman, C. V., Gray, J. J., Mosimann, J. E., & Ahrens, A. H. (1992). Cultural expectations of thinness in women: An update. *International Journal of Eating Disorders, 11*, 85–89.

Wright, R. (1994a). *The moral animal: Evolutionary psychology and everyday life*. New York: Pantheon.

Wright, R. (1994b, August 15). Our cheating hearts: Devotion and betrayal, marriage and divorce: How evolution shaped human love. *Time*, p. 144.

Wright, S. C., Aron, A., McLaughlin-Volpe, T., & Ropp, S. A. (1997). The extended contact effect: Knowledge of cross-group friendships and prejudice. *Journal of Personality and Social Psychology, 73*, 73–90.

Wyer, R. W., & Srull, T. K. (1980). Category accessibility and social perception: Some implications for the study of person memory and interpersonal judgments. *Journal of Personality and Social Psychology, 28*, 841–856.

AUTHOR INDEX

SUBJECT INDEX